WITHDRAWN

S0-BLV-292

DATE DUE

A FRAMEWORK
FOR IMMIGRATION

A FRAMEWORK FOR IMMIGRATION

Asians in the United States

Uma A. Segal

Columbia University Press

New York

Columbia University Press
Publishers Since 1893
New York   Chichester, West Sussex

Copyright © 2002 Uma Anand Segal

Library of Congress Cataloging-in-Publication Data
Segal, Uma Anand.
    A framework for immigration
        p. cm.
    ISBN 0-231-12082-6 (cloth : alk. paper)—ISBN 0-231-12083-4 (pbk. :
alk. paper)
    1. Asian Americans—Social conditions. 2. Asian Americans—Government
policy. 3. Asian Americans—Services for. 4. United States—Emigration and
immigration—Government policy. I. Title.

E184.O6 S44 2002
305.895073—dc21

                                                            200206786

Columbia University Press books are printed on permanent and
durable acid-free paper.
Printed in the United States of America
c 10 9 8 7 6 5 4 3 2 1
p 10 9 8 7 6 5 4 3 2 1

CONTENTS

PREFACE

Asian Americans constitute the fastest-growing minority in the United States, by both birth and immigration. Stereotypic portrayals of Asians as academic and economic achievers have reflected the accomplishments of only one segment of this group. Collectively, Asian Americans live in poverty, are underserved or poorly served by human services, and are undercompensated in the workforce. Many newly arriving immigrants, as well as U.S.-born Asians, are in need of the resources in the country, yet few who use those resources are from Asian groups. In addition, a tendency to perceive Asian Americans as a single homogeneous group obscures the reality that while all Asian Americans share some similarities in culture, the various groups do exhibit significant differences. Historical experiences in their countries of origin and in the United States also differ, as do the resources they bring to this country, the response of this country to their entry, and the ease with which they adapt, or are allowed to adapt, to life in the United States.

Chapter 1 provides the foundation of the book, presenting a framework for understanding the emigration/immigration experience, regardless of the country of origin or of immigration.

Chapters 2 and 3 focus on the history of the homelands of Asian immigrants, with particular attention to the periods during which waves of immigration to the United States occurred. The social, cultural, and economic aspects of the country of origin provide what are known as the "push" factors in immigration theory. Chapter 2 deals with those countries that had a substantial wave of emigration to the United States before 1965 and the liberalization of American immigration policies. Chapter 3 explores the more recent history of the countries accounting for post-1965 immigration.

Chapter 4 surveys the nation's response to Asian immigration beginning with the arrival of the first group, the Chinese, in the nineteenth century through the present, including changes in immigration policy and their implications. Chapter 5 brings the reader into the present and discusses the current adjustment of Asian Americans, some of the issues they face, and their position in contemporary U.S. society.

Chapters 6 and 7 focus on public policies that are particularly pertinent to Asian Americans and their implications for services to this population, while chapter 8 examines the experience of U.S.-born Asian Americans, their definition of self, and their perceptions of their heritage. Finally, chapter 9 brings together the effect of the historical experience of Asian Americans in the United States, current perceptions of them and among them, implications for human services, and guidelines for working with them.

The aim of the book is to provide to the reader an understanding of the Asian American experience and a recognition that the profile of the Asian American is shaped not only by the immigrants and their descendants themselves but by the nation's response to their presence. This response begins with U.S. immigration policy and continues with the level of inclusion that immigrants are permitted in the functioning of U.S. society.

ACKNOWLEDGMENTS

This book was long in the planning stage and even longer in the writing. I am extremely fortunate to have a family that has remained a steadfast source of ideas, support, and encouragement throughout this lengthy process, from the conceptualization of the idea and the search for a publisher to the completion of the last chapter and the editing process, and all the while allowing me the time and space to write. Madhav not only patiently and consistently encouraged me but helped me chart the direction of the book, often providing general suggestions, specific insights, alternative approaches, pertinent journal and news articles, or the development of ideas for the cover; he was particularly motivating whenever the project appeared too daunting and I felt the urge to renege on it. Zubin and Sahil, who have taught me a great deal (although they may not feel it has been sufficient) about the bicultural experience, pushed me with humor and appreciation. Consistent with Asian traditions of family and community support, Nazneen Mayadas has maintained unwavering confidence in my ability, Vivodh Anand mailed me timely literature, and my sisters-in-law and brothers-in-law, as well as our friends, propelled me with their enthusiastic interest regarding the project's progress. I am also grateful to both Holly Neumann and Jan McInroy who painstakingly edited the manuscript at different stages. Finally, I thank John Michel, Columbia University Press, and the reviewers for believing that the idea for this book was worthwhile and, by agreeing to publication, helping me increase my knowledge about several Asian American groups.

A FRAMEWORK
FOR IMMIGRATION

PROLOGUE

RACISM

Andrea Clark

It's in the Way

It's in the way you patronise
The way that you avert your eyes
The way that you cannot disguise
Your looks of horror and surprise

It's the assumptions that you make
On my behalf and for my sake
And in the way you do not hear
The things we tell you loud and clear

It's in the way you touch my hair
The way you think, The way you stare
It's right there in your history
Just like slavery for me

It's in the language that you use
The way that you express your views
The way you always get to choose
The way we lose

It's when you say "No offence to you"
And then offend me, as you do
It's in your paper policy
Designed by you, for you, not me

It's in the power you abuse
It's on TV, it's in the news
It's in employment, in your school
The way you take me for a fool

It's in the way you change my name
The way that you deny my pain
It's in the way that you collude
To tell me it's my attitude

It's in your false democracy
It's in the chains you cannot see
It's how you talk equality
And then you put it back on me

It's in the way you get annoyed
And say I must be paranoid
It's in the way we have to fight
For basic fundamental human rights

It's in the invasion of my space
It's how you keep me in my place
It's the oppression of my race
IT'S IN MY FACE.[1]

Written by an African American, this poem nevertheless captures the feelings of many people of color, including Asian Americans, as they experience discrimination, lack of understanding, stereotyping, and patronization. Xenophobia is apparent in many instances; for example, efforts at awareness about Asians in the United States have been fraught with stereotyping:

> There is no infallible way of telling [Chinese and Japanese people] apart. Even an anthropologist, with calipers and plenty of time to measure heads, noses, shoulders, hips, is sometimes stumped. A few rules of thumb—not always reliable. . . . Japanese—except for wrestlers—are seldom fat; they often dry up and grow lean as they age. The Chinese often put on weight. The Chinese expression is likely to be more placid, kindly, open; the Japanese more positive, dogmatic, arrogant. Japanese walk stiffly erect, hard-heeled. Chinese, more relaxed, have an easy gait, sometimes shuffle.[2]

1

Introduction:
A Framework for the
Immigration Experience

Deep in its heart, the world thinks America is the bravest, sweetest, toughest, funniest place on earth, and for once the world is right. . . . Which is why the world comes here. And when immigrants arrive, some kind of magic happens: they do extraordinary things, things they couldn't do at home.

—Noonan 1994:178

Immigrants, refugees, and asylum seekers: they flock to the shores, the airports, and the borders of the United States of America annually, in increasing numbers. As diverse as the groups that arrive, the immigrant experience is colored by the reasons they leave their countries of origin, their attraction to the United States, their resources, and their reception in the United States. The nation is young and composed almost entirely of immigrants. Other than Native Americans, all other ethnic American groups arrived to begin new lives. Even Native Americans were uprooted through policies that displaced them to reservations from their original lands. Thus, Americans are all immigrants "whose origins were various but whose destinies become American" (Pedraza 1996:1).

The phenomenon of immigration is neither novel nor recent but has been part of the human experience since time immemorial, resulting from economics, politics, and religion, as well as simply from a yen for exploration and adventure. While migration may occur as a response to crisis, it can at the same time be a search for opportunity. Hence the experience of immigration to the United States begins not when immigrants arrive at its borders but long before, while they are still in their home countries. It is there that the impetus for emigrating arises, and

Figure 1.1 A Framework for Immigration

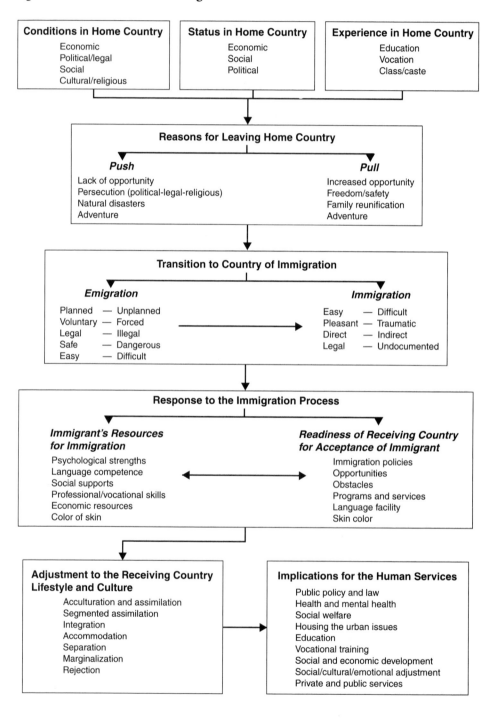

it is from there that immigrants draw the resources—economic, social, and emotional—to undertake the greatest challenge of their lives. The process, starting with emigration from the home country and progressing through adjustment to life in the United States, is lengthy and complex, and the success of the immigrant depends on the interplay of personal and environmental factors.

Figure 1.1 identifies the salient factors in the immigration process, regardless of country of origin or country of destination, and provides a framework for the variety of dimensions involved.

Not all people in other countries of the world have both the desire and the wherewithal to immigrate to the United States. Even if they do wish to emigrate from the country of origin and have the resources to do so, the opportunity must present itself. This chapter delineates the framework for the immigration experience (fig. 1.1), and subsequent chapters discuss the disparate experiences of Asian immigrants to the United States in light of this model.

THE IMMIGRANT IN THE COUNTRY OF ORIGIN

The personal situations of potential immigrants and the societal circumstances in their home countries interact to provide the incentive to set in motion the mechanisms for emigrating. National conditions of consequence may be the political or legal atmosphere, economic opportunities, the social climate, and cultural and religious freedoms. Personal status and resources are also significant players in decisions to leave, and they work in tandem with other factors to enable, or require, individuals to depart from their homelands. Frequently the wealthy and elite or the more highly educated and skilled are the ones who have the opportunity to leave. These resources enable them to purchase transport, and once they are in the new country, they can transfer their skills to employment in that nation. On the other hand, those of low status, with few transferable skills, may not have the visible means to migrate but may have the personal fortitude and desire to leave for more promising opportunities. For example, some highly educated computer analysts who are already doing well in their homelands may wish to further improve their quality of life and to experience new opportunities, and so they may emigrate. Others who are just as well placed but do not have the same yen for adventure and may in fact be wary of change are less likely to leave their homes. At the other end of the spectrum, those who have little in their own lands may also have the drive to better their opportunities and may be willing to risk traveling into the unknown in the hope that their lives will improve. Although sometimes refugees are forced to leave their homelands, not all individuals who are exploited there have the personal fortitude or the willingness to seek alternatives to what they already know for fear that the unknown may be worse.

Conditions in Home Country

When conditions in a home country are satisfactory and meet physical, social, and emotional needs, the likelihood of its citizens leaving is minimal. Economic, political, and religious turbulence, however, often increases dissatisfaction and causes mass migrations.

Poor economic conditions, low income, and overcrowding in the home country may force individuals to seek opportunities elsewhere. Since 1996 and well into 2002, Indonesia has experienced a long economic crisis that continues to deepen, and news reports indicate that political corruption precludes any possibility of rapid recovery. With foreign business and investors scared away by political instability and with the devaluation of the currency, employment options for many Indonesians are limited. International migration is driven by imbalances in supply and demand for labor, which promote low wages in countries where labor is plentiful and higher wages where labor is scarce. Dire economic conditions may affect basic subsistence or at least make it impossible for individuals to fulfill their aspirations, causing them to voluntarily explore alternatives. Poor economic conditions may be exacerbated by weather conditions. The winter of 2000, for example, was the most severe one in fifty years in North Korea, resulting in predictions of serious food shortages in the upcoming year.

Political upheavals can be instrumental in increasing dissatisfaction in home countries. When those who hold political power in nations change, when power structures change, or when individuals disagree with political ideologies, the climate becomes ripe for emigration. War and political and religious persecution have fueled several movements, such as the migration of Southeast Asians during the Vietnam War and that of the Bosnians during the conflicts in Bosnia-Herzegovina, as individuals flee unbearably oppressive forces and seek political or religious asylum in other countries. Present-day wars, particularly, target civilians—not soldiers—with torture and abuse. Some high-profile political campaigns, such as the Chinese crackdown on the Falun Gong spiritual movement, are fraught with torture and maltreatment, yet authorities fail to investigate them. International, civil, cultural, and religious strife often results in the violation of human rights. Amnesty International, an international organization committed to the preservation of human rights, consistently identifies ongoing human rights violations across the globe.[1] In a survey of 195 countries between 1997 and mid-2000, Amnesty International (2000) found reports of torture or ill-treatment by state officials in more than 150 nations. These included the rape and torture of women, the execution of prisoners, the torture of those who contradicted the government, and the victimization of anyone who disagreed with the ruling elite. Precipitating circumstances that increase the probability of persecution result in involuntary migration or the forced migration of groups and, frequently, in refugee status in the countries to which these individuals turn. Refugee movements are reported daily by the United Nations High Commissioner for Refugees.[2] In the first two weeks of April 2001, more than 10,000 Somali refugees arrived in Kenya, stating that they were fleeing interfactional fighting in Bula Hawa on the Somali border.

Finally, gender plays a significant role in immigration opportunities and outcomes. Especially for women, restrictive traditions and social conditions have encouraged adventure and migration with anticipation of freedom from total dependence and confining customs and expectations (Espiritu 1997; Pedraza 1996). Recently, female victims of domestic violence have been offered asylum because their own governments have been unwilling or unable to protect them. Women are less likely to migrate than men because the opportunities abroad for them are fewer and the constraints at home are greater, but when possibilities do arise, either in the form of asylum from gender-related violence[3] or in the opportunity to study or work in highly skilled occupations such as nursing or the computer software industry, they may leave their countries of origin in greater numbers than might be expected from familial and societal norms. The tremendous changes produced by the process of immigration allow women to break out of traditional roles and patterns of dependence and assert freedoms unenvisioned in their homelands.

Status in Home Country

The socioeconomic backgrounds of those who immigrate vary widely. Contrary to popular belief, it is not always the poorest or the most oppressed who leave their countries. Unless one is a refugee, one must have the resources—physical, economic, educational, social, and emotional—

to make the transition. Unlike escapees, voluntary emigrants tend to be governed from the start by socioeconomic variables (Portes and Rumbaut 1990). In general, both legal and undocumented immigrants are self-selecting and possess the necessary ambition, energy, fortitude, and adaptability (Fukuyama 1994). Economic status in the home country is a primary component of voluntary immigration, yet not all immigrants are seeking to escape unemployment and destitution. The primary reason for voluntary migration is "the gap between life aspirations and expectations and the means to fulfill them in the sending countries" (Portes and Rumbaut 1990:12). Portes and Rumbaut identify three types of voluntary immigrants: laborers, entrepreneurs, and professionals.

Labor migrants are those who are able to scrape together the financial resources to emigrate from their countries of origin in hopes of finding better-paying jobs. With low levels of education and few skills that are applicable in the industrialized world, these workers, such as many Mexicans who come to the United States, move in search of menial and low-paying jobs in fruit picking, domestic situations, and service in the food industry. Though the wages they earn are low by U.S. standard, they nevertheless increase the earning capacity of these workers. In their home countries, their economic standing may be weak, their status in the country's social order may be low, and their political voice may be unheard. Usually these labor migrants are not isolated individuals seeking to improve their lot but family representatives sent to support those who remain behind. Although families must invest income and suffer the absence of some of their members, such representative migration is perceived as insurance against sudden declines in economic opportunities. By sending earning members to other countries, families can diversify their economic risks. The longer migration exists between specific countries, the greater the likelihood that poorer individuals, a larger proportion of women and children, and a smaller percentage of undocumented immigrants will move between those countries (Massey 1990).

Entrepreneurial immigrants are those with considerable business acumen and expertise who recognize the opportunity for growth and development through emigration. With their skills and access to sources of capital and labor in their own countries, they already possess the makings of success. In carving an avenue for economic mobility for themselves, they enable others, often from the extended family or from the same region in the country of origin, to follow. Their sociopolitical standing in their home country is significantly higher than that of migrant workers, and they generally have access to networks through which they can explore resources and opportunities in other countries.

Professional immigrants, considered those that create the "brain drain" from their homelands when they leave, are highly educated individuals with strong professional skills, often in areas such as engineering, medicine, and technology. These workers emigrate to enhance their careers, not to escape poverty. Although they rarely accept menial jobs, they usually do enter at the bottom of their respective occupational ladders and progress based on merit, regardless of the extent of their training, experience, and expertise. In addition to high academic and professional achievement, these individuals usually have financial, familial, and social support for emigration. Their reasons for emigrating are more likely to be to further their own opportunities than to improve the family's economic condition. Furthermore, they are often people who could have had a strong political voice in their homelands had they chosen to remain.

Refugees or displaced persons who must immigrate have a very different home-country status from that of voluntary immigrants. While the latter plan their move as opportunely as possible given their resources and the networks they have established, refugees' emigration experience is often sudden and traumatic. Flight from the home country precludes thorough planning or the mobilization of resources. Armed conflict is more often occurring not between nations but within them, in the form of guerrilla warfare or full-fledged civil war, and internal abuse of a country's nationals is becoming more commonplace. Most frequently identified are political or religious refugees who belong to minority groups and find themselves targeted for persecution and oppression. Bosnian Muslims, marked for elimination, were forced to flee their homes in record numbers; Tutsis were brutally attacked, and many who were not killed during the 1994 genocide in Rwanda left the country if they could. Increasingly, women are fleeing domestic violence and being accorded asylum in other nations (Seith 1997). In 2000 Amnesty International included in its reports for the first time a recognition of domestic violence as a form of human rights violation, stating that "many of the most violent forms of gender-based abuse occur within the family" (60). In fact, a number of nations have laws that grant the right to discriminate against and abuse women and restrict their freedom of movement, expression, and association. Women who challenge these restrictions are subject to cruel, inhuman, or degrading punishments (Amnesty International 2000).

While a higher socioeconomic status does not necessarily affect refugees' ability to escape persecution if they remain in their homelands, it does provide them greater opportunities to avoid potential terrorism. They are more cognizant of environmental factors and the personal dangers lurking in the political shadows, and hence they often flee before the full-fledged eruption of hazards. Highly educated, affluent, and well-connected citizens who can rapidly adjust to other societies usually constitute the first wave of refugees from a country torn by international or civil war. Successive groups of refugees from such traumatized countries are usually farmers, peasants, and laborers, who leave only after experiencing the perils and degradations of persecution.

Experience in the Home Country

Closely linked with one's status in the home country is experience that may be transferable. Education and vocation are the two primary factors that affect transition. Literacy provides individuals with knowledge that opens a world of opportunity by equipping them with the tools to be lifelong learners. With the skills of literacy, they are able to read and better comprehend situations that are initially alien. While knowledge of the language of the country to which they are immigrating greatly enhances the process of adjustment, being literate in their native language reinforces self-efficacy and strengthens prospects of pursuing learning in other environments. In general, the higher the level of education, the greater is one's ability to adjust outside the home country.

A second important element in the adjustment process is profession. The extent to which professions are transportable depends on whether they are useful to the economy of the country of destination. Individuals who have spent their lives in agrarian communities, developing competence in farming, and then attempt a transition to a fast-paced computerized and industrialized society will most likely find that their farming skills are obsolete. On the other hand, practice in computer software enhances the likelihood of finding a niche in a technological environment.

While the importance of education and vocation cannot be overemphasized, competence in these two areas does not always ensure the same level of success outside one's home country. Another factor that must be taken into account is language competence, which may be not only a mediating variable but the principal initial barrier confronting all immigrants, from the least-educated peasants to the most-educated professionals. For example, it is not unusual for a practicing physician—an individual with a high level of education and a profession that is valued in most environments—to lack the language skills needed to pass licensing examinations. Those who have only conversational knowledge of a language may find highly sophisticated, scientific medical jargon difficult to understand and consequently may be forced into fields that are not commensurate with their knowledge and skills.

Across the world, class and caste determine the hierarchy of societies. In many nations, one's position is bestowed by birth, and while movement from one class to another is possible—though difficult—changing caste is impossible.[4] Bound by the threads of tradition, regardless of skill, values, or hopes, those of the lower classes and castes simply do not have access to certain opportunities (Tinker 1995). Caste, always, and class, often, dictate the professions to which people may aspire, the style of life they can lead, and where they must reside, and interaction across levels of class and caste may be precluded. Expectations of behavior and relationships may hinder growth and development for people of the lower strata and put in the path of the higher strata opportunities and experiences that they may neither merit nor have the capability to utilize fully.

Thus assessment of the immigration experience requires an evaluation of the economic, political, social, cultural, and religious conditions in the home country. In order to discern the reasons that a member of a subgroup chooses to leave, the group's status must be viewed in context and the individual's experience in the country of origin must be explored.

REASONS FOR LEAVING THE HOME COUNTRY

An overarching question in immigration literature is why people choose to leave one country for another. Moving to another country is an arduous undertaking even under optimum circumstances. Emigration requires elaborate preparation, great financial cost, loss of social and family ties, acquisition of a new language, and learning an alien culture. Despite the sizable number of immigrants around the world, those who actually do migrate compose only a minuscule proportion of the earth's population (Parfit 1998; Portes and Rumbaut 1990). The National Geographic Society (1998) estimated that in 1990 only 2 percent of the human race—about 120 million people—lived outside the country of birth. Nevertheless, with increasing globalization and ease of transportation and transnational relocation, migration will continue to rise. While the configuration of events leading to migration may differ among individuals, immigration scholars have identified two phenomena that interact to provide the catalyst for migration: a "push" from the country of origin and a "pull" to the country of immigration. Most of the literature suggests two types of immigrants: those who plan to leave their countries indefinitely and those who intend to return after achieving specific goals. In reality, some who expect to leave permanently do return, while others who plan to migrate only temporarily end by making their residence in the host country permanent.

The Push

The push out of the country of origin often emerges from the internal conditions there and increases with the personal circumstances of individuals. Most notable among these are the lack of economic opportunity, persecution by the majority or a powerful minority, and the difficulties caused by natural disasters.

A primary reason for both legal and illegal emigration is the lack of economic opportunity in the region of one's birth. This appears to cut across all socioeconomic levels of immigrants, from the poor, who may live at a relatively low subsistence level or who leave to escape unemployment, to the highly educated and wealthy, who cannot attain their aspirations at home. Thus both those who have little in their own countries, such as migrant workers from Mexico, and those with more education and assets, such as computer software experts from China and India, may migrate to improve their options. This push may be internal, causing individuals to seek emigration opportunities for themselves. On the other hand, it may be a strategy for survival of the family that sends a member to a land where employment options are greater and income earned abroad can be filtered back to support remaining family members. In fact, transfer of funds from migrants to their family members in the home country constitutes one of the largest types of movement of money worldwide (Parfit 1998).

Over the course of history it has become apparent that political and religious motivations often force people to flee their homelands, especially when human rights have been violated in the name of religion (Mayadas, Elliott, and Ramanathan 1998) or because of political chauvinism. War-torn countries, such as Vietnam, Bosnia-Herzegovina,

Afghanistan, and Rwanda, have seen the mass exodus of groups who are targeted for persecution. Whether such strife is caused by foreign invaders or by internal factions, its victims suffer torture, destruction, loss of jobs and sources of subsistence, and the forced breakup of communities and families.[5] If they are not killed outright, they may be subjected to incarceration, rape, and numerous other horrific and degrading experiences. For example, the ethnic Karen minority in Myanmar fled to Thailand in 1997 after Burmese security forces destroyed their homes and relocated members of their community. To escape such situations, individuals and families may be forced to leave their homes, regardless of how hazardous the circumstances or how low the probability of succeeding. Sometimes the land of asylum does not provide the safety they seek, as the Karen community learned in Thailand. The Thai authorities ordered them to return to Myanmar, and they were dragged from their shelters by Thai soldiers. Even in the absence of political or religious persecution, living in environments where political and religious changes result in ideological conflicts and dissatisfaction can be hazardous enough to make emigration appear most attractive.

Another important cause of human migration is the occurrence of natural disasters, such as earthquakes, famines, and floods. Some natural disasters, such as volcanic eruptions, may cause such destruction that many driven from their homes are never able to return. The wealthy and the poor, the educated and the uneducated, professional and peasant, employed and unemployed all may be forced to leave their homes, and sometimes their countries, in search of more physically stable environments.

In addition to environmental and national conditions that push people out of their countries of origin, personal dissatisfaction, sparse individual resources, and unique constraints that prevent individuals from attaining their goals in their own homelands may result in migration. Most immigration literature has tended to be gendered, focusing on the experience of males as though they were the only immigrants (Chow 1996; Espiritu 1997; Glenn and Parreñas 1996; Okihiro 1996). The push for women to leave their homes has traditionally been different from that for men. Women are usually the family nurturers, rarely the primary bread-winners, and hence they must remain in the homeland to maintain familial norms until they are called to be reunited with their spouses who emigrated earlier. However, this is not the case for all immigrant women. Now studies are finally beginning to focus on the role of gender in immigration, and results reveal that larger numbers of women than would have been expected left their homes to avoid constraining tradition and social customs that prevented them from exercising freedom in decision making.

Though the negative push factors discussed above may account for a good deal of emigration, a more proactive reason is the need for adventure. Many movements did not reflect difficulties that forced people from their homes, but rather individuals and groups that migrated in order to explore other lands (Cohen 1995). Kleiner et al. (1986) decry the pervasive tendency of the social sciences to view migration in negative terms. In biographies, novels, and films, the humanities are more likely to present migration as a desirable phenomenon, reflecting the spirit of adventure and discovery among people who elect to leave the known and go in search of alternative life experiences. Interest in exploration is a powerful force that both pushes people from their homelands and pulls them to foreign ones.

The Pull

The pull of another country or region works in tandem with the push from the home country. In the absence of dissatisfaction in the country of origin, it is not likely that individuals will move, but moving from the familiar to the unfamiliar may occur because something elsewhere is more attractive (even if it is the search for adventure) than whatever an individual or group currently possesses, and the prospect of acquiring or achieving that "something" is impossible or difficult without the move.

Neoclassical economic approaches suggest that potential migrants are rational income maximizers who will move to new environments whenever the anticipated gains of moving are sufficiently high (Espenshade 1995; Massey et al. 1993). Economic incentives, however, may not be the sole motivators in this cost-benefit analysis. The benefit-and-cost comparison is weighed not only as economic achievement but also in terms of social and emotional gains and in view of economic investment and social losses. While economic opportunity is often an underlying or even primary reason for emigrating, it is certainly not the only one.

Portes and Rumbaut (1990) present a much simpler and broader rationale for immigration: people immigrate because they can. Many immigrate to attain the dream of a lifestyle that they are unable to achieve in their home countries. Enhanced educational and social opportunities may also increase the "pull" of other countries. Entry into a country may be made possible by the relaxation of immigration laws and policies. Postcolonial access and the presence of international connections, coupled with the desire for exploration, may spur immigration. The attraction may be freedom from religious and political persecution, as well as freedom from restrictive societal and traditional expectations. Significant among these may be the desire and opportunity for reunification with family members who emigrated earlier. Finally, people may immigrate simply because they are attracted to the natural beauty of a country (Reed, Kraft, and Rudulph 1985).

Awareness that there are economic opportunities in other countries is itself a draw for individuals who are interested in improving their personal situations. However, it is also not unusual for employers in host countries—countries to which people immigrate—to actively recruit workers for fields in which there are labor shortages. This proactive search for foreigners to fill positions in a particular country may reflect either a lack of qualified native personnel in a specific field or a lack of local interest in filling these positions.

The attractiveness of social opportunities was mentioned in the early writings of Park (1928), who suggested that the many difficulties experienced by the immigrant were offset by "liberation . . . from the shackles of tradition," which allowed individuals to take the initiative and develop without the constraints of social structure and custom found in their own lands. The idea of immigration to other countries is especially enticing to women caught in strictly patriarchal, patrilineal traditions of dependency on men. In these cases, leaving firmly entrenched perceptions of the role of women for countries that exhibit different, less restrictive expectations is the lure.

Many immigrants, especially in recent years, have left their countries in search of better or higher education. When educational opportunities are greater in other countries, either because there are more institutions or because the quality of education is superior, young adults may immigrate and work for a few years in the host country in order to gain experience and to solidify their knowledge. As their familiarity with the new country increases and they begin to integrate into its society, the probability that they will remain increases. Educational opportunities blend into professional and vocational opportunities, and as the draw that attracted some immigrants to a particular country changes, so do their goals and aspirations, and they remain in the country to which they migrated.

Human rights violations are of particular concern in many nations, and freedom from political, cultural, and religious persecution is greater in some countries than it is in others. As people flee from persecution in their own countries, they are drawn to countries that offer them freedom. Hence the promise of safety may be the enticement. When people move by choice, they avoid high-risk destinations (Altman 1995).

Once an immigrant group establishes itself in a country, it forms a network that links its members with each other and also with family members and other kin in the home country, thus providing a channel through which friends and family can be recruited from the home country for employment. Although traditional societies voluntarily send few emigrants, the disruption of traditional lifestyles (i.e., changes from agrarian to industrial economies) sometimes forces emigration, and offers of employment draw individuals away from their homes. Ethnic networks, particularly formal ones such as Chinatown in San Francisco or New York and "Little India" in New York or New Jersey, can promote and support individuals, making the process of emigration less fearsome and more attractive.

Finally, people may immigrate simply because they become attached to a country. With increasing globalization and with transcontinental travel being so commonplace, people are more able to journey to other countries and may become enamored of one that they visit (Reed, Kraft, and Rudulph 1985). If it pleases their sense of aesthetics or if they feel a bond with the natives, they may choose to settle there.

The reasons that lead people to emigrate from a particular country and the reasons that lead them to immigrate to another are myriad, yet the two factors occur in tandem. There must be both a push out of one country and a pull to another. While the strength of each may vary, the two work in concert to provide the immigrant with the incentive to make the move from one place to the next. Therefore, the home country pushes people out, and the host country pulls them in by providing opportunities, perhaps directly inviting immigrants to fulfill labor markets, opening immigration policies, or furnishing other attractive incentives (Portes and Rumbaut 1990).

TRANSITION TO COUNTRY OF IMMIGRATION

Movement between countries requires emigration from the one and immigration into the other. Emigration is the exodus from one country, while immigration is the process of moving in from a foreign country.

Emigration

The process of emigration itself may or may not be planned, voluntary, legally sanctioned, safe, or easy. Much depends upon conditions in the home country, the immigrant's life there, and the reasons for leaving. The more voluntary, planned, and legally sanctioned the move, the more likely it is to be safe and easy—which in turn will affect the quality of the immigration experience. Even if the process is relatively simple, however, the social and emotional costs to the emigrant can be very high. Regardless of the reasons, leaving a country of one's birth requires relinquishing all that is familiar. Emigration involves separating oneself from most family members and friends, long-established and well-understood traditions, language and culture, familiar styles of living, known environments and climates to which one is adjusted, and other external factors that help define individuals' identities and support their existence and persistence. At the best of times, emigration is a complex and arduous process, but other conditions can exacerbate the situation.

Planned emigration usually occurs when political and social conditions in the country of origin are relatively stable and when individuals have the material and intrapersonal resources to improve or change their opportunities and experience. This often occurs in conjunction with voluntary migration. However, planned and voluntary migrations may or may not be legally sanctioned. Large numbers of undocumented immigrants to several countries move out of their countries of origin without the appropriate papers to live and work where the opportunities for them and their families are greater than in their homelands. These individuals, nevertheless, must choose to emigrate and must carefully plan their travel route, because discovery can be hazardous if not fatal. Emigration that is planned, voluntary, and legal is more likely to be safe. On the other hand, acquiring the appropriate legal permission and documents may be rather difficult, involving complex negotiations with rigid bureaucracies.

Sometimes planned and legally sanctioned moves may not be voluntary. Slavery and indentureship result in forced emigration as individuals are uprooted and transported to other lands against their wishes to work for invaders or stronger groups (Ishemo 1995). Expulsions and political exile also constitute forced emigration, as individuals must leave because of their political views or behavior. Other instances of forced emigration occur when those who are undesirable to the state are transported elsewhere. State-sponsored emigration that promotes the settlement of individuals abroad lies somewhere between voluntary and forced emigration. It is often difficult to determine if the choice is personal or if the state-sponsored promotion pressures individuals to such a degree that remaining in the home country is likely to result in persecution (Heffernan 1995).

Gender has always played an important part in whether or not an individual emigrates. Only in recent years have single women emigrated in significant numbers. In earlier times, single women rarely emigrated unless they were going to marry a man in the receiving country, and they frequently found themselves exploited by men, usually for prostitution. If single women did move, they went to prearranged destinations where they were received by males or they traveled with male relatives. It was more likely for women who were married to move with their spouses and families or to move to join their families. Whether single or married, women traditionally traveled on a planned and legal basis, though perhaps not entirely voluntarily. It is now more probable that both single and married women will emigrate by choice and respond to the push and pull factors that have traditionally encouraged male emigration.

While many individuals plan their exodus, others leave suddenly, without planning. Many emigrants depart, often against their will, to avoid persecution, or the fear of persecution, because of the destruction inflicted on their homes through war, during revolutions, or in the aftermath of natural disasters. The fear of persecution results in sudden refugee movements as people flee in the hope of finding both safety and freedom elsewhere. Often the educated and elite of a nation have the political knowledge and foresight to identify potential difficulties, and they form the first wave of refugee movements before conditions in their countries deteriorate to intolerable levels. Their political and social resources, both within their home countries and in the countries to which they immigrate, allow them to plan a safe and relatively easy departure.

Subsequent waves of refugees tend to have fewer resources and, unlike other emigrants, leave their countries under duress. Without a well-established plan of escape, and without material resources, they find themselves in dangerous situations. Overcrowding in unsafe vehicles such as boats and vans can result in accidents, heat exhaustion, illness, hunger, thirst, and even death, as was illustrated by the Vietnamese boat people (those who fled by boat for neighboring countries and for the United States) and is still evidenced by those who cross borders illegally, packed in vans with little air or light. Not only are means of transportation unhealthy and unsafe, but when refugees arrive at their destinations, the facilities there are overcrowded and insufficient, as in Macedonia in April 1999, when 1,800 people arrived on one train at Blace and where overcrowding in refugee camps was a serious problem. Persons in these circumstances are also subject to extreme stress, and their inability to cope with the ordeals can be manifested in anger and violence. Moreover, discovery of their flight by those in power can result in torture or death.

Some natural disasters, such as famines, are gradual and chronic and allow those with resources time to formulate their plans for emigration. Others, such as floods, volcanic eruptions, or earthquakes—the 2000 earthquake in Gujrat, India, and the 1994 earthquake in Kobe, Japan, for example, are sudden, occurring in an instant, with no respect for the "haves" and the "have-nots." Conditions resulting from such disasters may make emigration both complex and risky, and even if it is legally approved and the nation provides resources to support the movement, it is usually involuntary. Although natural disasters do not discriminate between those with resources and those without, the process of emigrating is eased for those with family and friends elsewhere and those with the financial resources to move once they can emerge from the location of the disaster.

As in many other experiences in life, the process of emigration is greatly facilitated by status, resources, and experience. Unless others forcibly uproot individuals from their homes, emigration is easier and safer for individuals of means, regardless of circumstances in the home country. Even under ideal conditions, when emigrants are prepared and have a voluntary, planned, legal, safe, and easy move, the costs to them are high as they leave the familiar for the alien. The reaction to emigration is often ambivalent.

Immigration

Like emigration, immigration to another country occurs for a variety of reasons. If immigration to the new country is direct, or if the host country is the country of choice, the experience can be less traumatic than otherwise. Much depends on the receiving country's immigration policies and the perception of immigrants by the receiving agents at the first port of call. When these are unequivocally welcoming, the experience is less likely to further traumatize those who have left their homelands. Immigration itself is an issue about which many people in host countries are ambivalent and often contentious (Lee 1998; National Research Council 1998). Some segments of society perceive immigrants as assets to the receiving country, while others view them as threats that deplete it of resources and endanger the opportunities of the natives. These perceptions are reflected in the treatment of immigrants as they are met by border authorities.

For legal immigrants, ease of entry into a country involves a number of processes, including the acquisition of an immigrant visa. Depending upon existing immigration policies, visa acquisition can be completed rapidly or it can require that the applicant wait interminably with little hope of being granted permission to enter. Countries prefer to grant visas to those who have the potential to contribute to their well-being. Virtually every industrialized nation, and many developing ones as well, now house populations of immigrants who are undocumented and who cross borders without official authorization. While for them there is no question of seeking an entry visa, the likelihood of being apprehended and imprisoned or returned to their country of origin increases exponentially. On the other hand, they may well be able to rapidly find employment in marginal jobs that the natives regard as undesirable.

The trauma of entry may be exacerbated by the travel necessary to reach the destination—the modes of transportation, the safety and comfort of that transportation, and the route followed. Depending on their resources, whether immigrants are legally admitted into a receiving country and whether they are transported by airplane (for example) directly to their destination will affect how satisfactory the process is for them. It will also set the tone for the initial days in the host country. Legality does not ensure ease of entry, however. Refugees may be legally admitted into a host or asylum country (Mayadas and Segal 2000), yet be transported in overcrowded boats, trucks, or trains from their countries of origin to the asylum country. This experience may endanger their health, increase the possibility of transportation breakdown and accidents, increase the stress and interpersonal conflict among passengers, and limit access to food and water. Such events will make immigration difficult and will increase the possibility of trauma and long-term psychological distress.

Finally, in order to immigrate to the country of choice, individuals may have to go through two or three intermediate nations. If they are unable to get legal (or even undocumented) direct entry into a specific country, they may still leave their homes for alternative destinations. This is especially true for refugees who stay for long periods in asylum countries, anticipating eventual acceptance into a country for permanent residence. Voluntary emigrants may also leave their homes for an intermediate country to await the opportunity to enter the preferred nation.

What becomes apparent is that legal emigration is often, although not always, based on personal decisions. Immigration, on the other hand, is highly contingent on whether the host country is willing to allow entry. Refugee movement out of a country and undocumented immigration into a country are unendorsed by authorities. Movements that are not legally sanctioned exponentially multiply the difficulties, dangers, and trauma of people in passage, while those that are approved allow people greater access to comfort and ease of transit.

RESPONSE TO THE IMMIGRATION PROCESS

The complexity of reactions to immigration must be viewed from two perspectives, that of the immigrant and that of the receiving country. Immigration frequently poses a dilemma, with the associated benefits and costs, for both parties. It would be simplistic to suggest that when the benefits outweigh the costs, the response is positive and vice versa. Much depends on current political, economic, and social conditions in the receiving country, factors that influence the country's response and the experience of immigrants. The resources that they bring with them also affect their reactions to the situation. These two sets of factors—the immigrants' resources for immigration and the receptiveness of the country to which they emigrate—are highly interactive, each affecting the other.

Immigrant's Resources for Immigration

"Give me your tired, your poor, your huddled masses yearning to breathe free," reads the Emma Lazarus poem inscribed on the Statue of Liberty in New York Harbor. While a laudable sentiment, it hardly reflects the face of all immigrants, to the United States or elsewhere. Regardless of the circumstances in their home countries, their reasons and experience of leaving there, or the process of entering the host country, most immigrants arrive at their destinations with a number of assets. Those who leave their homelands, even under the most deplorable circumstances, are not the most needy, weak, and oppressed.

Those who are able to reach and enter the host country have, at the very least, physical, emotional, and psychological fortitude. People with no education, no resources, and few personal strengths are less likely to leave their homelands, and if they do leave, they are less likely to survive. Hence, to understand immigrants' response to the process of emigrating, it is essential to identify their resources.

A large proportion of immigrants, both legal and undocumented, leave their homes in search of improved economic opportunities. The literature suggests that the distribution of these economic migrants is bimodal: one group consists of the educated and skilled, who have substantial financial resources in their home countries; the other consists of those with minimal education, skills, and material resources. The former group seeks to enhance career opportunities and lifestyles, while the latter migrates to accept relatively menial jobs that nevertheless will provide economic improvement. Thus, even in the absence of transferable skills, they often possess personality characteristics that can ease the transition.

The availability of economic resources enhances rapid independence and adjustment in new countries. Immigrants with sufficient financing will find housing and meet their other needs more readily than those who have little or who have had to leave their material wealth in their homelands. However, financial assistance may be available from other sources. The presence of family or other members of the immigrant community in the host country who are willing to pool funds can ease adjustment.

New immigrants sometimes arrive with little facility in the language of the host country. The absence of language skills can be their primary obstacle. Without language ability, seeking housing or employment, accessing health care and other services, and learning a vocation become impossible. Those immigrants who are competent in the language are much better prepared and are able to negotiate their needs through a nation's bureaucracies more readily than are those who have no functional knowledge of the language. Literacy, or the ability to read and write, as well as speak, the primary language of the host country, further improves job opportunities.

The stresses of immigrants and refugees in translocation are enormous and well documented.[6] Many are associated with the trauma of dramatic emigration-immigration processes. Others result from the culture shock of being in an alien environment where language, social structures, norms, expectations, and values differ radically from those that have been fundamental to the immigrants' understanding of themselves. Well-understood role relationships change, and established patterns of interaction are questioned. When immigrants have the psychological strength to cope with these stresses, they are more likely to adjust and be able to control the direction of their lives. On the other hand, they may experience posttraumatic stress disorder. Without sufficient and appropriate social and emotional support, and perhaps therapy, they may find the immigration experience unsatisfactory and remain unhappy, resenting their lives in the new land and pining for their homeland and all that is familiar.

Finally, a characteristic that immigrants cannot change is the color of their skin. Nor can they alter the global hierarchy of races (Espiritu 1996). If the host country appreciates the skin color and race of the immigrant, these features of the person may prove to be assets. Conversely, if they are not valued, or if the natives are threatened or prejudiced against them, the process of adjustment can be arduous. To balance the negative effects of being of the "wrong" race and skin color, immigrants may need to have a number of other assets. Particularly useful are professional skills, language competence, and psychosocial strength. When immigrants fill a need in the society and can contribute to its well-being, skin color may not constitute as major an obstacle as when they have little perceived value to the host country. Furthermore, although indications are that skin color universally defines "foreignness," regardless of specific culture, identity, behaviors, or network affiliation (Reitz and Sklar 1997), the "appropriate" skin color may not preclude prejudice and racism (Hickman and Walter 1995).

Thus, the immigrants' ability to find their niche in the new country depends greatly on the resources they bring. Economic, professional, and educational resources, along with language capability, are the most obvious assets that can help an individual ease into a new society. A number of other personal strengths also appear to be instrumental in making the transition less formidable. Social supports through some kind of network, both in the receiving country and among those who accompany immigrants, such as family members, ensure some familiarity in the new environment. More important, perhaps, is the psychological efficacy of individuals, including ability to weather stressful and dangerous experiences, flexibility in adjusting to unknown circumstances, faith in their own capabilities, and strength and hope for the future. Certainly physical health is important in enhancing adjustment as well, as illness prevents individuals from exercising their strengths. And finally, as mentioned above, skin color may serve as a resource or a barrier for the immigrant. Such strengths help immigrants conquer the numerous hurdles in the transition from the familiar to the alien.

Readiness of the Host Country to Receive Immigrants

A receiving country's readiness to accept immigrants in general or a single immigrant group in particular is itself a complex matter. When immigration is viewed as inextricably bound to a nation's political, economic, and social well-being, as well as to its future security interests, it is more likely to be welcomed than if it is not. Once again, a number of conditions act jointly to enhance acceptance of immigration. Nevertheless, many countries have in place only a temporal immigration policy, reflecting what is believed to benefit the country at a particular moment. Nations also fulfill international agreements in resettlement of or granting asylum to large numbers of people, both to facilitate government action and to act for humanitarian reasons. Existing alongside the policies that allow immigration are others that permit the expulsion or deportation of foreign nationals.

In general, public immigration policy is closely bound to economic and national needs. Opportunities may be available to immigrants yet fraught with obstacles, mirroring the nation's ambivalence toward a particular immigrant group. The country's receptiveness is also reflected in the available programs for the immigrants, including basic health, education, and welfare services, as well as programs that can provide psychosocial and emotional support. The acceptance of a group is highly influenced by the country's openness to diversity and to ethnically specific variables, such as language facility, skin color, and other characteristics associated with race. The identities of immigrants are shaped not only by the social location of their group within the host society but also by the position of their country of origin within the global racial order (Espiritu 1996). In nations across the globe, even in countries with people of color, fairer skin and Occidental features are highly valued characteristics.

Refugee migration, which is usually chaotic, requires substantial adjustments by receiving countries. Many must renegotiate their policies regarding short- and long-term asylum and must struggle to bear the burden of the pressures associated with such movements. Unlike the flight of refugees, economic movement, which is planned and voluntary, forms a chain that links the world and is a significant part of the trend toward a global system of economics and communications that pushes the international community toward change (Parfit 1998). National public policy and public perception may differ with regard to receptivity to immigrant flow, depending on the economic needs of particular indigenous groups. Foreigners who specialize in skills that are not readily available in the host country may fill the needs of the business community, yet immigration policy may limit the number of newcomers, much to the dismay of executives experiencing shortages in staff (Bruner 1997). Quantitative immigration policy restrictions may heighten illegal immigration, or groups may enter under nonimmigrant programs, such as trainee or exchange agreements. On the other hand, immigration policy may be relatively open and natives may perceive a threat of lost employment opportunities.

The extant literature is variable regarding the effect of immigration on employment opportunities for indigenous people. Some studies suggest that immigrants displace few native residents but secure those positions that are unfilled or that the natives are unwilling to accept. Employers often turn to foreign labor to meet the less stable portions of economic demands that remain unfilled by local workers. Some studies contend that the effects of immigrants on the wages and earnings of natives are nonexistent or small, and can in fact be positive (Bean, Lowell, and Taylor 1988). Other studies indicate that increases in immigration can significantly hurt employment levels of some groups (Cobb-Clark and Kossoudji 1994; Kposowa 1995). The impact of immigrants on natives' economic options depends on the current business needs in the country and whether the natives have the skills and interest to meet those needs. It is also true that for other reasons employers may consider some immigrant groups who have particular skills to be more attractive as employees than indigenous people. Perhaps the immigrants are willing to work for lower wages, or they exhibit desirable cultural and social characteristics, such as a strong work ethic, or they have fewer social and familial ties in the host country and thus are more available for work.

The classic economic approach to understanding the incorporation of immigrants has been to measure individual-level data on human capital indicators such as education and language ability and then correlate the returns of wages and earnings with those characteristics (Waters and Eschbach 1995). Thus, even when opportunities are available, immigrants' access to them varies according to educational level, professional skills, and language facility. Their qualifications do not ensure access; it is more often determined by social acceptance and the employers' areas of discrimination.

In addition to obstacles associated with discrimination, immigrants entering a new society often encounter other barriers to full inclusion in economic activities. The absence of the network ties necessary to gain access to or succeed in certain occupations or professional or internal labor markets may exclude those with foreign credentials. The skills of immigrants, especially refugees, are often concentrated in specific occupations and may not be directly transferable.

As discussed above, the readiness of a country to receive immigrants can be gauged by its immigration policies and the availability of economic opportunities. Another important indicator of its willingness to accept foreigners lies in the programs and services that it makes available to the immigrant community. These may be newly established programs intended to increase the efficiency and safety of the immigration process itself and to ease the transition, or they may be existing programs that immigrants may access. Institutions that facilitate international movement also help perpetuate the flow of immigrants and may include legitimate human service organizations or black market and smuggling organizations that help undocumented immigrants to cross borders clandestinely (Espenshade 1995).

Once individuals have entered the host country, they may have access to programs and services developed to ease their adjustment, among them housing and employment opportunities; vocational, professional, and language training institutes; social, family, and psychological support services; and networking opportunities. When immigrants encounter such a well-prepared welcome, they are more likely to respond positively and adjust rapidly. In addition to the extra programs that may be necessary to facilitate immigration, the country can indicate its willingness to accommodate the new residents by allowing them access to existing health, education, and welfare services. Permitting immigrants access requires a proactive effort to connect them to a system with which they are unfamiliar. As in the area of policy and economy, public policy and public perception may be divided as the debate continues about the extent to which immigrants who utilize the health, education, and social services deplete those resources for the local nationals (Espenshade 1995; Simon and Alexander 1993). This discussion continues despite evidence showing that immigrants often contribute more to the public coffers than they receive in public services (Simon 1996) and that they rapidly become self-sufficient and contributing members of the society. Even undocumented immigrants, who initially experience downward economic mobility when they enter a country and perhaps use more of the receiving country's services at that time, usually reverse this trend (Espenshade 1995).

Immigration policies are adjusted to reflect a balance between economic self-interest and humanitarianism and international agreement. Primary international concerns have to do with admission of refugees and those seeking asylum. A country's policies reflect its attitude toward multiculturalism and ethnic diversity. Throughout history immigration was not regulated, and some nations, particularly in their early years, welcomed immigrants for economic and political reasons, allowing an equal flow of most immigrant groups to their shores (Churgin 1996). However, racism and the fear of unacceptable or undesirable cultural traits have always served to limit or prevent the immigration of particular groups. Honest acceptance of immigrants must include acknowledgment of the value of difference and multiculturalism, including tolerance of immigrants' difficulty in mastering the native language, acceptance of differing cultural values and activities, and recognition that skin color does not reflect an individual's worth. Thus the receiving country's readiness for immigrants in general, or specific immigrant groups in particular, can be evidenced at several levels—governmental, societal, and individual. Governmental policies may or may not reflect the need of business for foreign workers, societal programs may or may not meet the needs of immigrant communities, and individuals may or may not feel threatened by the introduction of immigrant populations. For the successful inclusion of immigrants, international migration, social integration, and human rights must all be addressed (European Centre 1999). Specific legal mechanisms to prevent discrimination may help the development of programs and services to ensure immigrant adjustment.

Even if the receiving country is relatively ready to embrace immigrants, and the appropriate policies, economic opportunities, programs and services, and approval of cultural differences are in place, the passage for these newcomers is influenced by their individual resources and their ability to cope with the transition. To understand the process of transition, both sets of variables—the strengths of the immigrants and the readiness of the receiving country—must be explored, as must their interaction.

ADJUSTMENT TO RECEIVING COUNTRY

The range of material on the adjustment of immigrants to a new country is immense. At issue is economic, psychosocial, and cultural adjustment, and many theories have developed surrounding involvement of foreigners in the cultures of indigenous people. Individuals adjust to new circumstances in a variety of ways and to various degrees depending on their resources, their desire, and the receiving country's acceptance. The literature suggests that there may be a continuum along which individuals adjust to the host country and that their position on the continuum may change over time.

The extent to which immigrants become a part of another society, its lifestyle, and its culture is portrayed by the continuum presented in figure 1.2. At one end lies total assimilation, while at the other end lies total rejection.

Early assimilation theorists believed that total assimilation into a "melting pot" was the ideal and that becoming similar to the dominant group in the destination country should be the goal of all immigrants. This perspective, based on the assumption that in order to gain equal access to the resources in a receiving country, diverse groups gradually shed their own traditions (Zhou 1997), is still maintained by some strong supporters of classical assimilationist theories (Alba and Nee 1997). The assimilationists postulated that migration resulted in the emergence of the "marginal man," who was at the same time attempting to assimilate into the host culture and being drawn back into the traditional culture (Parks 1928). Warner and Srole (1945), however, suggested that the external factors of the society, such as the natives' response to immigrants' skin color, language of origin, and religion, also played a significant part in the assimilation of particular groups. Gordon (1964), on the other hand, argued that the assimilation process began with cultural assimilation, and then progressed through structural, marital, identificational, attitudinal, behavioral, and civic assimilation, but it did not necessarily result in total assimilation, since that depends on acceptance by the dominant group. The classical assimilation theorists viewed distinctive ethnic traits as disadvantageous to

Figure 1.2 The Continuum of Adjustment

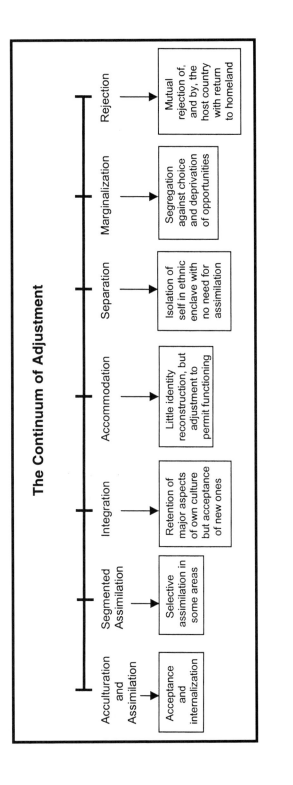

The Continuum of Adjustment

| Acculturation and Assimilation | Segmented Assimilation | Integration | Accommodation | Separation | Marginalization | Rejection |

Acceptance and internalization

Selective assimilation in some areas

Retention of major aspects of own culture but acceptance of new ones

Little identity reconstruction, but adjustment to permit functioning

Isolation of self in ethnic enclave with no need for assimilation

Segregation against choice and deprivation of opportunities

Mutual rejection of, and by, the host country with return to homeland immigrants (Zhou 1997) and held that until and unless they relinquished their traditions they would remain "marginal." Undergirding these classical theories is the belief that the goal of immigrants is, and should be, complete internalization of the receiving country's values, attitudes, and behaviors.

In fact, indications are that such internalization is not necessarily preferred by immigrants, allowed by indigenous peoples, or even possible, given personal and environmental circumstances. The acculturation of individuals assumes that they acclimate themselves to a new culture and society, often converting their ways of thinking and their behavior. The effects of acculturation on the life satisfaction of immigrants appear to be mixed. Three aspects of acculturation—perception of acceptance by natives, change in cultural orientation, and language use—have been found to be associated with better mental health in individuals (Mehta 1998). Complete acculturation can result in assimilation or in such conformity that one blends in with another group. The original culture is determined to be inconsequential, whereas contact with the majority is considered very important (Van Oudenhoven, Prins, and Buunk 1998). The more the immigrant group affirms the values of the receiving country by assimilating, the greater the likelihood of acceptance by the natives. Consistent with this, the more positive the reactions of the indigenous people to the immigrants, the greater the life satisfaction of the latter and the higher their feelings of competence (Vanselm, Sam, and Van Oudenhoven 1997).

While the traditional pattern of acculturation presented in much of the literature suggests assimilation into the dominant society, a second direction leads to permanent poverty and assimilation into the underclass (Portes and Zhou 1993). Moreover, though generally positively associated with life in a new country, assimilation appears also to adversely affect family life and organization (Faragallah, Schumm, and Webb 1997). Increased assimilation contradicts traditional expectations of members of an immigrant group, may expose underlying ethnocentrism, and may result in discontent (Rumbaut 1997).

Hence, rather than assimilating in all areas of their lives, immigrants are more likely to become partially assimilated. Although frequently associated with second-generation immigrants, segmented assimilation is applicable also to the immigrant group (Bankston and Zhou 1997; Zhou 1997). This form of assimilation associates rapid economic progress with the conscious preservation of the immigrant community's values, culture, and social relationships (Portes and Zhou 1993). The interaction of individual factors (those identified in this framework as the immigrants' resources) and the contextual factors of the society (such as racial stratification, economic opportunities, and spatial segregation) determines the areas in which individuals assimilate with the dominant society (Zhou 1997). With the appropriate personal resources, many immigrant groups are able to assimilate economically, filling professional positions that allow them to succeed in middle-class society. Economic assimilation allows them to purchase homes and other material goods, and they become assimilated in the professional environment. Nevertheless, they may separate their professional and personal lives, maintaining strong attachments to their language of origin, social relationships with members of their own immigrant group, and traditional values, culture, and familial roles. Such segmented assimilation and the ability to function effectively in different cultural environments tends to lead to positive self-perceptions of global self-worth (Birman 1998).

Similar to segmented assimilation is the phenomenon of integration. The tradition of "uniqueness" remains strong (Shuval 1998) as individuals retain major elements of their own heritage yet accept new behavior and values that do not conflict with their old ones, adding to their total repertoire. While they do accept new ideas, integrationists do not relinquish any of their own traditions, as both the original culture and contact with the majority are considered important (Van Oudenhoven, Prins, and Buunk 1998). Integration, accommodation, and separation are sparsely represented in immigration literature, but these mechanisms also provide ways to help immigrants cope in the receiving country. Although these coping strategies may reflect the responses of the indigenous people, the focus is on the choice of the immigrating individuals. Personal perception and ethnic consciousness anchor individuals to their ethnic group through a sense of belonging as well as a commitment to the group's values, beliefs, behaviors, conventions, and customs (Dasgupta 1998). The conscious attempt to preserve tradition reflects the immigrants' efforts to control the course of their own acculturation (Dasgupta 1998).

Unlike assimilation in its various forms, integration, accommodation, and separation—three methods of acclimating oneself to a new or alien situation—require little identity reconstruction. In integration, immigrants identify qualities that are of value to them in the dominant society and incorporate them into their existing Weltanschauung. On the other hand, immigrants who accommodate the lifestyle of the dominant group merely adjust to it and learn to function within it, without internalizing or accepting it as being valuable for their own survival or progress. Finally, the separatists isolate themselves from the members of the host community. The original culture is considered to be important, and contact with the dominant group is not (Van Oudenhoven, Prins, and Buunk 1998). Many immigrants live and work in ethnic enclaves and have little or no association with the majority society, and though they are affected by governmental policy and programs, the impact is not so great that it requires them to modify their values and lifestyles or to question their identity.

Although some groups may choose to remain aloof from the native population, immigration literature abounds with historical themes of exclusion and marginalization, often based on the personal and cultural characteristics of the immigrant population. Dominant societies reflect their xenophobia by social and economic marginalization of groups, usually arising from racial status (Daly 1996; Hjerm 1998). Migrants are segregated against their will by being confined to menial jobs and relegated to deplorable housing conditions in the least desirable sectors of large metropolitan areas (Daly 1996). Marginalization, in which both the original culture and contact with the majority are seen as unimportant (Van Oudenhoven, Prins, and Buunk 1998), creates a class of immigrants working on the fringes of society, without full rights and having access to few resources. Movements in several nations continue to formally curtail the rights of those who do not conform to the national standards of language, culture, and ethnicity (Daly 1996). Unlike the "marginal man" of classical assimilation theory, which views the immigrant as struggling forward in the process of becoming acculturated and assimilating into the majority culture, "marginalized" groups are deprived of the options and the resources even to begin to assimilate.

The phenomenon of rejection once again requires the interplay of immigrants' personal characteristics and resources, the contextual circumstances and opportunities available to or denied them, and their perceptions of the dominant culture's values and traditions. On occasion, immigrants may not accept, or feel accepted by, the receiving country to such a degree that they decide to leave it. While this may be caused by antagonistic relationships between the two groups, living in an alien culture may result in enough discomfort and dissatisfaction that immigrants elect to return to their countries of origin or to move to another nation in which they may feel more at ease. Those who have the resources to assimilate or integrate into a society can evidence such a reaction to the host country; immigrants who have been deprived and marginalized can also demonstrate it. While rejection can mirror a society's discrimination against a group, it can also be an indication of the immigrants' prejudice against the nation's values and lifestyle. Hence, rejection may be mutual or it may be unidirectional.

It is clear that there is no simple formula that can dictate how immigrants will adjust to the host country or will allow the inhabitants of the receiving country to accept them. Much depends on the resources the immigrants bring, the readiness of the country to welcome their presence, and the value of the host country, its opportunities, and traditions for the immigrants. Immigrants' abilities to adjust will differ. Some will wish to assimilate into the dominant society. Others will prefer, or will be forced, to remain separate, and yet others will choose or be forced to leave the host country to return either to their own lands or to others that may be more hospitable.

IMPLICATIONS FOR HUMAN SERVICES

Across the globe, people are immigrating. They immigrate across continents and across nations. With the ease of transportation and changes in immigration and refugee policies, increasing numbers of people are migrating from their places of birth to escape conditions at home or to explore opportunities in foreign lands. Receiving countries have felt their impact and must modify, expand, or develop policies, programs, and services for them. When immigrants arrive with enough resources that they are able to contribute to the host country, it may not find it as necessary to enact changes as it does when the immigrants do not have sufficient resources. Nevertheless, the influx of people of differing traditions, values, expectations, and skills bears implications for human services, ranging from public policy and law to individual psychosocial adjustment.

The nation's policies and laws must be reviewed to ensure that the formal structures of the society are in place for the diversifying population. These policies and laws might revolve around the nation's foreign policies and international relationships with sending countries as well as with immigration itself and the extent to which the immigration laws will be inclusive or restrictive. The receiving country must also address economic, health care, social welfare, and education policies and must ensure that immigrants have the protection of the nation's legal system. Economic policy that deals with business functions and practices, including hiring, wages, and equal access must ensure that immigrants are familiar with relevant economic policy, are able to exercise their rights, and are protected from exploitation. Health care policy may revolve around the diverse issues of public health and community needs, including primary care. Health promotion and protection issues may focus on education and prevention for immigrants, especially new arrivals. Issues surrounding health expenditures and health coverage for the immigrant must be resolved, as must those having to do with the actual delivery of services, access and utilization opportunities, and mechanisms to assess the satisfaction of immigrants with the quality of health care. Policies should ensure that opportunities are available for immigrants and the nature of any barriers to adequate health care is addressed.

Japan's Ministry of Education, the Monbusho, states that education constitutes the foundation of all social systems (1997). Immigrants may or may not have had an adequate education. The educational system and education policy in the host country must allow access to levels and types of education and institutions that are appropriate to the needs of immigrants, and the adequacy of existing educational programs for immigrants must be evaluated. Adult education programs to improve literacy will ensure that these individuals are better equipped to adjust to the new environment. Furthermore, appropriate education for the children of immigrants must take into account difficulties that can occur as children enter a school system without a working knowledge of the language medium of instruction. Schools ought to accommodate variations in cultural patterns and behavior, and recognize that the experience of emigrating, even in the best of circumstances, is traumatic for both adults and children.

Vocational education and training rather than traditional education may be an alternative that provides immigrants with the tools necessary to develop a trade. It must be responsive to social change and industry trends (Monbusho 1997) and must take into account the values, personality, capabilities, and interests of the immigrants. Concurrent with this should be an aim to ensure that immigrants' knowledge of the local language is enhanced to improve competence in communication. Vocational education and training, though subsidized by the government, can be administered through either the public or the private sector, so that training is, in fact, consistent with societal needs. Such training should ensure the quality of teachers, such that they are both well versed in the trade and sensitive to the particular issues and obstacles faced by immigrant communities.

Welfare policies must guarantee that all immigrants have admittance to appropriate public welfare services and subsidies and are connected to private welfare programs as necessary. Hence, public policy and law must be reviewed frequently to assess their adequacy for all the nation's residents and should be modified to remove barriers to the administration and utilization of the services they govern.

In addition to ensuring that health and mental health services are available, receiving countries may need to encourage immigrants to use them both for prevention and remediation. Immigrants and refugees may be unlikely to utilize preventive health care, such as vaccination against disease or annual medical checkups; they may, in fact, not seek medical attention until an illness has progressed to dangerous levels. The literature also suggests that many refugees are subject to psychosomatic ailments, though mental illness is not acceptable in many parts of the world; many suffer from posttraumatic stress disorder but receive little intervention. Not only must health and mental health services be sensitive to the unique needs of immigrants, but they must also develop educational programs to emphasize the importance of health care. To be appropriate for different populations, the health care system should also be familiar with unique characteristics of immigrant groups that make them especially susceptible to particular forms of disease. Furthermore, the system must be culturally sensitive if unfamiliar forms of health care intervention are difficult for particular immigrant groups to accept or if other interpersonal barriers prevent immigrants from seeking, utilizing, or following through on services.

Emerging from a belief in the value of mutual aid, social welfare programs and services provide assistance, financial or otherwise, to people in need through governmental resources. Thus social welfare programs are supported by the government and directly affect well-being by providing the services or funds to improve the quality of individuals' lives. They address a number of concerns and should be made available and accessible to immigrant groups. Program policy-makers and administrators should be aware of the implications of immigration for social security and pension benefits as well as for public aid, aid for people with disabilities, and aid to families. Services to families may include child and elder welfare programs and be sensitive to immigrant concerns. Social welfare programs should also address the unique needs of women and recognize that in many parts of the world, women are second-class citizens without equal access to services, including health and education programs, nor do they receive adequate nutrition. Consistent with the thrust of social welfare, programs and services must be constantly vigilant about the ever-changing states of dependency and their social contexts.

As important as the need for income for most individuals is the need for adequate and safe housing. Most immigrants gravitate toward large urban areas, where housing is difficult to find and unsatisfactory unless one has sufficient fiscal resources. Housing and urban development programs of receiving nations may need to promote accessibility for immigrants by providing subsidized housing, at least until they are financially able to manage on their own incomes. Subsidies can prevent overcrowding, which can create health and fire hazards. The literature suggests that receiving countries are often not sensitive to the housing needs of immigrants and, in fact, erect barriers that force immigrants into the streets (Daly 1996). Affordable community housing may meet the needs of immigrants with limited finances.

While the delivery of services is paramount, many services may establish sustainable development as a goal. Immigrants must be given the social and economic tools to succeed in their new countries. In addition to providing them with economic subsidies, housing, and health care, traditional, community, and vocational education programs ought to provide the components for them to move out of dependency on society's human service programs. Hence, knowledge about prevention of disease, ability to function through society's institutional structures, and acquisition of the skills to earn an income within the legitimate economy of the country will increase the likelihood that they will be able to attain self-sufficiency. At the same time, social and mental health services need to recognize the difficulties associated with the immigration experience and assist in the immigrants' adjustment to the receiving country. This may include helping immigrants understand the norms and expectations of the country as well as the implications for their own traditions and family and community relationships, and the interplay among them.

Certainly all the types of human services discussed, and others not identified here, can be administered by the public sector, the private sector, or charitable and nongovernmental organizations. The United Nations is often instrumental in furthering cooperation between the private and the public sectors, an especially significant collaboration when governmental resources are inadequate to meet burgeoning needs.

It is safe to say that the flow of immigrants strains the receiving country's human services systems. It behooves policymakers and service providers to be cognizant of the experience of immigrants so that they can appropriately meet the needs and the demands of this group. In admitting immigrants, a nation makes a commitment to them. Unless it is willing to help them through the transitional period of adjustment, their unmet economic, social, health, and mental health needs can in both the short and the long term drain resources from the nation. On the other hand, attention to these very same immigrants may accelerate their becoming contributing members of the society.

Much in the immigrant experience is shared—from emigration to immigration, including reactions to and from the receiving country. However, many experiences are unique to a particular immigrant group and to a specific individual. Receiving countries need to recognize that migration across their borders will persist as improvements in transportation and reasons for moving continue to emerge. They must educate themselves about the causes and effects of the immigration of particular groups. The framework presented in this chapter can help leaders develop an understanding of the immigration experience and may provide a foundation for the interpretation of the experience of particular immigrant groups within the context of the receiving country's readiness to accept them. As immigration continues to increase, it will be imperative for policymakers and service providers to become more sensitive to the unique needs of these new arrivals and to assess the degree to which programs and services are inclusive and supportive or xenophobic and discriminatory. Such evaluations can help to ensure that programs are modified to achieve a mutually satisfactory adjustment for both the immigrant group and the host country.

2

Pre-1965 Emigration: Leaving the Homeland for the United States

What was . . . striking about most of the migrants was how they were stirred by a common discontent, and how they came search-ing for a new start. . . . "Poverty hurt," but hunger and want were not what essentially defined the migrants. . . . The migrants were unique in a felicitous way: they were the dreamers . . . and their dreams inspired them to take risks.

—TAKAKI 1989:66

Motivations for emigration are myriad, and personal choices are rarely clear. No single cause serves as a sufficient impetus for so dramatic a change as leaving one's homeland, one's roots, and all that is familiar. Whether the move is voluntary or not, whether it is the result of careful planning, the effect of war, the aftermath of a natural disaster, or enforced political exile, it still requires personal choice. Not all who are discontented with their lives in their homelands, afflicted by the ravages of war, forced from their homes because of natural disasters, or have their lives threatened by those in political power choose to leave—or truly have the option of leaving. Only rarely are those in the most extreme distress able to leave. Such a drastic step requires that one must have, at the very least, the personal and internal resources, including self-confidence and hope, to risk losing all that is known. Some people leave in order to further enhance their already comfortable lives or to achieve educational, professional, and other personal objec-tives that cannot be met in their homeland. What binds all emigrants is the awareness that certain needs can be better filled outside their coun-tries of origin.

Immigration theorists write of the *push* and *pull* in the emigration-immigration process. The "push" comprises the factors, which may be environmental or intrapersonal, that fuel an individual's discontent. The "pull" from another nation may exacerbate that discontent. While personal stories humanize Asian immigration to the United States, it is clear that there have been waves of exodus to the United States from different Asian nations since the 1850s, and the emigration of these people has been the result of a combination of historical social-political-economic conditions in their home countries. These have been balanced by the then contemporary social-political-economic climate in the United States and perceptions of Asians among U.S. nationals.

During specific periods in the history of the United States, groups of immigrants from various Asian nations have entered the country. While U.S. immigration policy and economic needs have greatly defined immigration patterns, the primary impetus for emigration has usually been conditions in the home country and the individual's discernment of options within them. Thus, to place Asian immigration to the United States in context, it may be useful to review the events and the climate in the country of emigration during particular immigration waves. As historians underscore, a significant connection often exists between the past and the present (Nehru 1946).

CHINESE EMIGRATION: 1848–1882

An Overview of the Nation's History

Chinese history dates back to the twenty-first century B.C. Through the centuries, a distinctly Chinese civilization emerged with a unique philosophy, language, writing, and art, and it has persisted to the present. China long viewed itself as the center of the universe, calling itself Zhongguo, or the Middle Kingdom, and it saw little threat from surrounding societies that it perceived as being barbaric. Of particular concern about Chinese history is that often Chinese scholars have experienced pressure to interpret the past in conformity with the political imperatives of the present (Roberts 1998), and historians and social scientists have raised probing questions about the state of historiography in China (Shinn and Worden 1994). Since the 1980s, however, there has been a move toward correcting the presentation of historical events.

The modern China, believed to have begun in 1644 with the Manchu conquest and the establishment of the Qing Dynasty (1644–1912), saw two governments—one for the conquerors and one for the vanquished. Emperor Qianlong (1736–1796) redistributed lands held by the gentry and imposed higher taxes on the wealthy in an attempt to equalize power in the nation. However, corruption and fraud in the government were rampant, and European traders began pressing for trading rights, gradually opening up the country to Western influences. In 1800 China was drawn into a number of relationships with the West, and since then it has experienced periodic rebellion and revolution (Roberts 1998). The perceptions of both Westerners and the Chinese are that by the end of the eighteenth century imperial China had reached an irreversible state of decline. The destruction of the empire was believed to result from internal decay rather than from external aggression. The decay resulted not only from bureaucratic corruption but also from the inability of the country to achieve technological progress and from the effects of the rapid growth of the Chinese population, which increased from 143 million in 1741 to 432 million in 1851.

The dramatic growth of the Chinese population occurred before Western contact, foreign trade, or industrialization had reached significant levels. Factors contributing to it may have been the internal peace maintained under Manchu rule during the eighteenth century, the control of disease, and, most important, the abundant grain supply, which increased sixfold between 1400 and 1800 and rose 50 percent more during the next 150 years. Animals and other farm products also increased substantially. Despite enormous growth in population and food supply, the labor-intensive farming system soon led to overuse of all arable land and reached a point of diminishing returns, leading to a gradual decrease in the person-to-land ratio.

Farmers' wives turned to making silk and weaving cotton, yet these attempts to supplement the farm family's household income meant that women and children had to spin and weave all day to eke out the pittance that would prevent starvation (Fairbank 1992). This, coupled with the triage of China's nineteenth-century experience—domestic rebellion, foreign invasions, and efforts of the ruling elite to control and preserve their empire—provides the backdrop for the emigration process. Furthermore, because of a lack of interest in European goods, Britain was running a trade deficit with China. To reverse the trend, the East India Company, a British firm, began exporting opium to China from India. The drug, used for medicinal purposes, soon entered China as a recreational drug, and China began aggressively enforcing laws against opium use and distribution to control the resulting trade deficit, resulting in the first of two Opium Wars between Britain and China.

After 1850, the Qing Dynasty experienced widespread rebellions. Inflation, rising taxes, and increased foreign intervention heightened discontent. Between 1846 and 1848, flood and famine were epidemic, increasing poverty and hunger. Disease, an onslaught of bandits, and declining markets for native handicrafts led to greater tensions. A deep-seated anger against the landed gentry finally flared under the leadership of Hong Xiuquan, a mystic who promoted his own brand of Christianity, claiming that God had instructed him to overthrow the Manchus and establish a popular government. Blaming conditions on Chinese values, the Taiping (Great Peace) Rebellion was born under the guidance of Hong. The Taipings attempted to adopt Western thinking, abolishing concubines, arranged marriages, footbinding, and opium smoking. This rebellion was initially victorious, but soon the Taipings lost sight of their objectives and confounded their allegiance and began supporting landlords rather than tenants, and the Qing government finally crushed the rebellion. Subsequently, the Miao Rebellion (1850–1872), the Nian Rebellion (1853–1868), and the two Muslim Rebellions (1856–1873 and 1862–1873) challenged the Qing leadership, but went the way of most peasant rebellions: uprising, rebellion, defeat, and restoration (Fairbank 1992; Roberts 1998). These rebellions exacted an enormous toll from the population, dropping the census numbers by approximately 100 million between 1850 and 1875. The gentry reestablished itself, the power of local governments was increased, and the government moved toward *ziqiang*, or "self-strengthening." The slogan of *ziqiang* was "Chinese learning as the base, Western studies for use" (Roberts 1999:185).

In the eighteenth century, China was extremely prosperous, but by the middle of the twentieth century the country appeared to be poor and underdeveloped. Some believe that Western imperialism had damaged the economy, denied economic development, and discredited the government. Others argued that the West shocked China into economic reform, and still others believed that Western influence was marginal at best (Roberts 1998). Nevertheless, many believe that the Chinese economy during the latter part of the nineteenth century suffered from three main disadvantages: (a) the impact of foreign trade on the handicraft textile industry, (b) the siphoning off of wealth to pay for opium and meet unfair trade terms, and (c) Western industrial oppression that prevented China from positioning itself to obtain a share of the market (Roberts 1998). Other changes were evident in the

nineteenth century. Christian missions had been present since the Tang
Dynasty, had survived the Manchu conquest, and formally benefited
from the emperor's tolerance in 1692. Their primary focus, however,
was on religious conversion. Beginning in the 1840s, they contributed
to the society by establishing schools for children, and by the turn of the
century, medical missionaries pioneered the training of Chinese doctors
in Western medicine and issues of public health. Following the Taiping
era of reconstruction, the gentry-elite became active in the revival of
Confucian academic education and invested itself in urban and community welfare. Subsequently, beginning in the late 1890s, the rise of
nationalism occurred along with the rise of a reformist urban elite that
proposed local self-government, constitutionalism, and modernization.

Chinese Emigration to the United States

The Boxer Uprising in 1900 and the Chinese Revolution followed,
establishing the Republic of China in 1912. But emigration to the
United States from China began in the 1840s, soon after the Opium
Wars (1839–1842 and 1856–1860) and continued through the several
rebellions. Ecological factors as well as the rebellions and their suppression had severe demographic and economic consequences for the nation
and for vast numbers of its peasant population. For centuries, Chinese
subjects had been prohibited from leaving their country, and few emigrated from areas surrounding Peking. However, in Southern China,
large numbers had moved to other Asian countries in search of adventure and better opportunity. With the need for cheap labor for large
projects in other countries, however, contract labor became popular, as
did the export of hapless Chinese peasants.

Large numbers of Chinese peasants were taken in bondage as
"coolies," or slave laborers, to Peru, the West Indies, and other nations
in the West, where they were bullied, oppressed, and abused. In contrast, a significant number emigrated to the United States and Australia
of their own volition, tempted by the relatively high wages they would
earn in these countries; contrary to popular stereotypes and myths,
these emigrants were not "coolies." Many paid their own way, hoping
to find gold in the United States, and often borrowed the necessary
monies under the credit-ticket system, which provided them with passage and expenses but obligated them to repay twofold the amount
borrowed. Although there were only 43 Chinese documented in the
United States before 1850, the discovery of gold in California in 1848

resulted in an influx of Chinese immigrants, and in the next three decades, more than 225,000 Chinese males arrived in the United States (Wong 1995b). Opportunities abroad, coupled with the poor economic, political, and social conditions in China, encouraged emigration.

Not all Chinese immigrants to the United States during this period were peasants, nor did all come to work as laborers. A number of the Chinese immigrants were merchants. Between 1870 and 1900, 40 percent of the Chinese in San Francisco and Sacramento were shopkeepers and merchants who had come seeking new opportunities for enterprise. Many maintained their business operations in China. From 5 to 12 percent were professionals and artisans, while the rest were wage earners. In the rural areas, however, more than 80 percent were service workers and farm laborers (Takaki 1989).

Regardless of their occupations, these Chinese immigrant men who came to the United States brought with them a staunch desire to work, were willing to commit energy and time to their endeavors, were reliable and responsible, and produced high-quality output. Their hope for the future, their belief in their investment, and their confidence in their abilities were evident as many scraped together their meager savings in order to purchase transpacific travel tickets. In the spirit of enterprise, they demonstrated their fortitude in withstanding the difficulties of travel and adjustment to a foreign land, where they were unfamiliar with the language, customs, and lifestyle. Their flexibility was evident as they moved from one form of enterprise to another when opportunities in one area came to an end and were replaced by possibilities in other fields.

The Immigration of Chinese Women

Notably absent from the emigrant population to the United States were Chinese women. Single women did not travel alone to distant places, and married women had to remain at home to care for the children and the husband's parents. As second-class dependents, they were tied to family and home and had to stay within the confines of their villages (Yung 1986). Most Chinese immigrants to the United States were of a group called Punti, which practiced footbinding on its women, making it difficult for them to travel and work abroad. In addition to preventing the extra financial burden of travel, keeping women in China assured the husbands' families that the sons would return after making their fortunes. Men who worked abroad perceived themselves as sojourners, staying only long enough to pay off their debts and save enough money to increase their family status when they returned to their homeland (Lyman 1968). In practice, however, this rarely occurred, as the men were hardly ever able to accumulate enough to return home or even to pay for the transportation of their wives to the United States.

During the very early Chinese immigration to the United States, in the 1950s, although U.S. laws allowed women to enter as freely as men, Chinese cultural constraints prevented their emigration, and therefore their numbers were very small. The few married women who did enter were usually the wives of Chinese merchants. Women who attempted to join their husbands were entreated by the family in China not to break custom and not to expose themselves to the perils they would encounter at sea. The majority of Chinese women and young girls in the United States in the latter part of the century identified themselves as "prostitutes," as most were kidnapped or sold into prostitution. Unlike Chinese men, these women immigrants were not free individuals. Many lived lives of slavery, often becoming opium addicts, seeking the drug as an escape from the degradation and abuse they encountered daily. Yet they provided an important source of comfort to the Chinese males who were separated from their wives and who, because of U.S. antimiscegenation laws, were forbidden from developing relationships with non-Chinese women.

The second immigration flow of Chinese occurred between 1945 and 1953 and reflected the profile of most Asian immigration during the postwar period of 1945–1965 in that it was overwhelmingly female. This was the result of the partial liberalization of immigration policies that allowed Asian women to enter the United States to be reunited with their husbands. Between 1945 and 1953, 12,000 Chinese migrated to the United States, and 89 percent of them were female (Lee 1956); this trend continued through the 1950s. Women during the fifties accounted for 50 to 90 percent of the entrants. A large proportion of these women were older and had been separated from their husbands for fifteen or more years, some for as long as twenty-five years. Several thousand Chinese women were also admitted under the War Brides Act when approximately 6,000 Chinese American men married women in China and brought them back to the United States before the act expired on December 30, 1949. The large numbers of women who entered the country during these years not only substantially equalized the Chinese gender ratio in the United States but also allowed the Chinese population to grow, both by immigration and by birth.

Reasons for Immigration

A popular interpretation of immigration was that people were uprooted from their ancestral homes and were desperate and in dire straits. Especially if they were peasants, poor, or uneducated, they were forced to relocate to strange lands. Push-pull theory suggests that desperation may not have been a primary reason for emigration. Peasants may have already experienced several migrations within their homelands in response to economic change and the existing market economy and may have already been so preconditioned to migration that they chose to immigrate to maintain their status and economic lifestyles (Barton 1975; Ng 1995). Immigration involves major investment of time, money, and hope. In anticipation of some future gain, immigrants sacrifice much of the emotional and social comfort associated with home and community. It is not only the educated, elite, and merchant classes who are adventurers, it is also the peasants, laborers, or any people with visions of something better who emigrate voluntarily. The combination of poor economic and social conditions in China, including overcrowding, drought, and war, pushed many out of their homeland. Discovery of gold in California, tales of streets being lined with this precious metal, and the availability of jobs drew large numbers of Chinese to the United States to seek their fortunes. Improvements in, and lowered costs for, transoceanic travel also made migration more realistic for many during the early years of Chinese immigration to the United States.

Although Chinese immigration to the U.S. truly began in 1850, because of social and personal barriers, the flow began to decrease after the first three decades and was effectively formally terminated in 1882 with the Chinese Exclusion Act. Immigration resumed after World War II with the arrival of several thousand women, most of them wives and children of Chinese men who were already in the United States.

JAPANESE EMIGRATION: 1882–1923

An Overview of the Nation's History

Archaeological findings indicate that human beings inhabited the Japanese islands as long ago as 30,000 B.C. The Japanese as a distinct group, however, are believed to have been living there on a Stone Age level in the third century B.C. and as hunters and gatherers until the Yayoi Period (300 B.C.–300 A.D.), when they were introduced to agriculture and metalwork by groups of Koreans who settled in Japan (Meyer 1993). Although the actual time of the origination of the Japanese culture is not clear, the language, social structure, and religion cannot be dated before this period. Furthermore, in the Yayoi Period, the Japanese were suddenly and dramatically moved into the agricultural age. Japan appeared in Chinese history as early as 57 A.D. as a land of more than a hundred tribal communities, with no writing or political cohesion; the Japanese did not begin writing their history until 600 A.D., about two hundred years after Chinese script was introduced via Korea and fifty years after Buddhism arrived in the country.

While there is disagreement about the origins of Japanese culture and the extent of Korean and Chinese influence, historians agree that modern Japan had its roots in the Tokugawa Period (1600–1868), a late-feudal period and the formative age for institutions that contributed to the nation's social stability as well as to its oppression of others in later years (Beasley 1995). National traditions of culture and ideas took form as a commercial economy germinated, and despite some beliefs that this was a "vegetative" period for the Japanese nation, the political structure was dynamic and vital (Ravina 1999). Nevertheless, throughout the era peasant revolts grew more frequent, and by the mid-nineteenth century there was internal discontent and a growing desire for modernization as well as an external threat of expansion from the West. The Tokugawa rulers were forced out of power in 1867, and a new political era, the Meiji Period (1868–1912), began, in which "self-strengthening," using foreign ideas and Japanese foundations, became important as the country moved toward modernization.

Throughout the early years of the Meiji Period, Japan would have been categorized as a "Third World" or "developing" nation. The young central government had little control over the population or the resources of the Japanese islands. The economy was overwhelmingly agrarian, and the country's foreign trade consisted of exports of primary products from the land and imports of manufactured goods from the industrialized Western nations. During the four and a half decades of the Meiji Period, however, Japan modernized its political, economic, and social institutions and became a world power. Its wealth increased as the agricultural and industrial sectors of its economy moved forward.

The stability that ensued was reinforced by a political structure in which all citizens of the nation, including the leaders and the general population, held common national goals (Meyer 1993).

During the first two decades of the Meiji Period, between 1868 and 1890, Japan's leaders focused on internal changes and immediate practical concerns, laying the foundation for modernizing the country. Stability was a primary goal, and the importance of functional governmental organs was recognized. Since the economy was precarious, dramatic steps were taken. Modern industries were instituted, and attempts were made to modernize thinking. Japan quickly embraced Western customs and ideas, using the West's educational philosophy to socialize its citizens. During the second half of the Meiji Period, Japan, now with strong internal structures, became active in the world economy and politics. The nation became economically solvent, heavily industrialized, and proactive in foreign trade. After an initial enchantment with Western culture and education, Japan's leaders became concerned about possibly replicating some of the deleterious effects of rapid change seen in Western society and reverted to tradition and a national system of education. Education continued to embody both literacy and skills in mathematics, but these basics were supplemented by teachings about Japanese values and the promotion of a national identity. Schooling was compulsory for both boys and girls in 1879, and by 1910 the elimination of tuition fees resulted in a school attendance rate that neared 100 percent.

The population of Japan grew from about 35 million in 1872 to 55 million in 1920. While a few hundred thousand emigrated to the United States and Brazil, and a further two million to other Asian countries, the majority remained in the homeland. A significant proportion of the nation's citizens moved to urban areas, indicating the push and pull phenomena evidenced in most migration movements. The advantage of internal migration over immigration, however, is the general familiarity of the migrants with the culture, language, and tradition of the area where they settle (Waswo 1996). Family ties remained with the villages, since only the eldest male son migrated and most members of the family continued to farm the land for several successive generations. In 1920 more than half of the 27 million workforce in Japan was engaged in agriculture and forestry. Farm incomes failed to keep pace with the rest of the economy, however, and by 1910 they had dropped by 50 percent. Meanwhile, employment opportunities in nonagricultural areas, particularly in government, grew steadily. Government officials, police officers, teachers, military personnel, and workers in government arsenals and factories were more numerous than people employed by private enterprises. Women were also employed in the modern sector, particularly in the textile industry, and were active participants in shaping the economy. In fact, the first strike in modern Japan was staged by female silk-reelers in 1886.

While incomes, opportunities, and quality of life improved for many, those in the poorest sector found themselves condemned to living in industrial slums or in the narrow and dark dwellings of old commercial areas. Such poverty also extended beyond the urban areas of Japan to rural locations, where the land was not very fertile and farmers could not diversify their crops; many were plunged into poverty and hard labor. Furthermore, with modernization, the Japanese no longer believed that they were destined for a particular quality of existence, but many found that better alternatives were well beyond their reach. The result was palpable discontent. Tenant associations emerged that represented collective interests against landlords and prompted a number of violent tenancy disputes, beginning in 1917. Industrial towns and cities also experienced turbulence over wages that were low for men and even lower for the women and children, who worked twelve-hour shifts before 1900.

Japan's military ascension during the Meiji Period was also noteworthy. By the 1890s, the nation was able to assert itself through efforts at expansion and wars with China (1894–1895) and Russia (1904–1905). The victories led to a worldwide recognition of Japan as a rival and a vital player in world politics and the world economy. In a reversal of the pattern that began in 607 A.D. and continued for 1,300 years, after 1898 Chinese youth entered Japan to study (Reynolds 1993), and Russia's developmental patterns in economics, politics, education, and lifestyles, at the same time, began mimicking those of Japan (Black et al. 1975).

Following Emperor Meiji's death in 1912, his third son, Taisho, ascended to the throne. Unlike his father, Taisho did not play an active role in Japanese politics, because of both physical and mental health problems. However, his reign, called the Taisho Period (1912–1926), was known by some as the Taisho democracy because of its relative liberalism. With the population burgeoning, the nation had to focus on the important issues of employment and associated benefits, military security, increasing imports and exports, and the wide-ranging ramifications of modernization. The new perception of the emperor as a mortal and head of the state, rather than as the absolute authority, was a monumental change, and the Diet, as a decision-making body, gained substantially more power. At the same time, by 1913 overexuberance about industrial investment and a top-heavy governmental structure caused the Japanese economy to flounder. Economic recovery began with World War I. As the attention of European industry moved toward the production of arms, Japan, whose military participation was relatively limited, continued its industrialization and found ready markets in Asia, Europe, and Africa. Although Japan entered World War I, it was primarily to expand its Asian interests and to honor its 1911 commitment to Great Britain, in which each country agreed to support the other in the event of an attack by a third party.

Clearly the Meiji and Taisho Periods in Japanese history were times of rapid and dramatic change that moved Japan from an agrarian to an industrial economy. With this move came a complex of socio-political-economic developments that affected the environment both within and outside its boundaries, most of which benefited a large segment of the population. Other segments were further oppressed by the changes in tradition and in options. But it was during this period that Japan moved from relative isolation to a position as an important player in the world economy.

Japanese Emigration to the United States

The Japanese, like the Chinese, were prohibited from leaving Japan for more than two centuries, with the era of isolation beginning in 1639 and ending in 1853 when Commodore Matthew C. Perry intruded into the country. Although the government continued to ban emigration, it ceased to have the level of control it had once exerted. The first group emigrations occurred in 1868 and 1869, when the Hawaiian consul general in Japan secretly recruited 148 contract laborers to Hawaii, and a German merchant took 40 Japanese to California to work on a silk farm. A small group of political refugees escaped to California in the 1870s. In 1884, when the Japanese government permitted the recruitment of contract laborers by Hawaiian plantation owners, emigration exploded in response to internal pressures for international migration that had been building for at least a decade (Takaki 1989).

While some segments of the Japanese population benefited greatly during the Meiji era, most farmers across Japan suffered great economic hardships. The urban poor also found themselves in dreadful economic conditions. With no alternatives or hopes for a change in their positions, these groups viewed emigration as their only opportunity for a less bleak future. Those who were able to migrate, however, were not the urban poor who lived in abject poverty but those from farming families. Although some emigrated to the United States hoping to make it their permanent home, most Japanese emigrants, like their Chinese counterparts, hoped one day to return to their homeland after having earned enough to buy back land that they had lost through immense debts. Most were young male representatives, often the second sons, selected to make their fortunes and send money home so that the families could discharge their debts. Under the Japanese inheritance system, to keep family ownership of the land intact, one son, usually the eldest, inherited all property. Therefore the eldest could not leave Japan. The second son, who was obligated to care for the parents as they aged, was also responsible for making the fortune needed to support them. So great was the belief in success in the West that many farmers mortgaged their property to pay the fare for a son to travel abroad. In one year a laborer could save the equivalent of one thousand yen, an amount equal to a Japanese governor's income (Ito 1973). These sons took their responsibility seriously, and most sent money home, knowing that if they did not, their families would lose their land (Modell 1971).

Usually those who emigrate, particularly if they emigrate voluntarily, are not the poorest of the poor or the most desperate. At the very least, they have the ability to withstand risks and venture into the unknown. Unlike the Chinese emigrants, or any other Asian immigrant group to the United States during the late nineteenth and early twentieth centuries, most Japanese emigrants were literate, thanks to the system of compulsory education in Japan, and brought with them an average of eight years of schooling. Furthermore, the average immigrant to the United States from Japan arrived with more money than did individuals from Europe (Takaki 1989). With the unification of the country during the Meiji era, once it began allowing emigration the government was able to control the process. Emigrants were no longer perceived as representatives of their families. They were emissaries of the homeland and had to meet certain qualifications to present a positive Japanese image to the West. Lower-class Japanese, those who were not literate, and those who were not healthy were denied emigration because they would reflect poorly on Japan's national honor.

Aware that itinerant bachelor societies often fell prey to prostitution, gambling, and substance abuse, the Japanese government, contrary to Eastern tradition and preference, encouraged the emigration of women to prevent a repetition of the Chinese experience in the United States. Although the first decade of Japanese migration to the United States was composed of young men, and they, too, began engaging in socially undesirable activities, by 1900 Japanese women began entering the country with support from the United States, which also feared the formation of another large bachelor community. In 1908, however, in response to anti-Japanese sentiment and fears that the Japanese were taking jobs from U.S. nationals, the United States and Japan signed the Gentlemen's Agreement, in which Japan agreed to limit the emigration of laborers, though the parents, wives, and children of Japanese men who were already in the United States would continue to be permitted to immigrate. Thus the split family system so commonly found among the Chinese emigrants was uncommon among the Japanese.

The Emigration of Japanese Women

When Japanese women left their native land for the United States the social, economic, and political climate in Japan differed substantially from conditions in China during the period of Chinese immigration to the United States. Aware of the potential problems of bachelor societies and the deleterious effect on the image of the nation, the Japanese government soon began to encourage married women to join their husbands in the United States. As men established themselves, they sent for the wives they had left behind in Japan. Others returned to Japan to find a mate. Under the Gentlemen's Agreement, the immigration of male laborers was curtailed, but the entry of Japanese women continued to be sanctioned by the U.S. government.

Traditionally, marriages in most Asian countries were considered not liaisons between two individuals but the joining of two families. Often a couple agreed to marry based on family screenings, and they met only at the wedding ceremony. When families lived in different geographic areas, if there was a family match an exchange of photographs was considered sufficient. The "picture bride" system, which emerged as an important vehicle in the emigration of Japanese women in the early twentieth century, was not dissimilar to the arranged marriage. Couples married in absentia, allowing women to emigrate as the wives of men who already resided in the United States.

The economic climate of Japan also lent itself to the independence of women during the late nineteenth and early twentieth centuries. Young women from farm and other rural families were already migrating to urban areas to work as wage earners in textile industries, inns, tea processing, and papermaking. They were also engaged in such labor-intensive fields as coal mining and construction labor, carrying heavy loads on their backs. By 1900, 60 percent of the industrial laborers in Japan were women (Takaki 1989).

Independence and risk taking were much more common among Japanese women than among the Chinese, particularly because the Meiji government in 1872 issued an order that both boys and girls not only must be educated but must be educated together, to become knowledgeable about the ideas of the world. As likely as boys to be literate, and substantially more likely than their Chinese counterparts, girls studied English, Japanese, mathematics, religion, literature, and writing. The emperor encouraged their curiosity and travel abroad, believing that the nation would benefit from the knowledge that the women would acquire. Although many agreed to marry men in the United States, most were drawn not by the prospects of marriage but by the adventure of traveling to the West. On the other hand, emigration was not a choice for some. As the property of her parents, a woman could be given to a family with a son in the United States, and her duty as a wife would require that she migrate to the United States, even against her wishes.

Married Japanese women were not the only women to emigrate. Like the Chinese, several thousand single young Japanese women were lured, tricked, or kidnapped and brought to the United States as prostitutes (Ichioka 1977), while others were already prostitutes in Japan and migrated in hopes of receiving higher wages (Glenn and Parreñas 1996). In fact, in 1900, the majority of the 985 Japanese female immigrants were prostitutes (Ito 1973), part of a large-scale prostitution trade in Japan. During the years 1870 to 1910, thousands of women were sent all over the world, including to the United States, with the profits from their work providing important foreign currency for the modernization of Japan. Politicians defended the practice by associating it with filial piety and patriotism (Glenn and Parreñas 1996). On the whole, however, with later immigration most Japanese women left Japan voluntarily. Many viewed it as an opportunity not only to find adventure but also to shed the gender responsibilities and constraints that they experienced in their homeland. Despite the relative independence of the Japanese woman in comparison to women of other Asian nations, she still had a second-class status and was always viewed as the property, or the dependent, of first her father, then her husband, and finally her son. Emigration of Japanese women to the United States, which had been rapid after the Gentlemen's Agreement, was effectively curtailed with the passage of the Ladies' Agreement in 1921, through which Japan barred the emigration of picture brides.

Another wave of female immigration from Japan followed World War II. Like the earlier Chinese immigrants, these women also skirted immigration quotas by entering under the War Brides Act. But Japanese immigrants at this time were more likely to be married to non-Asian, usually white, GIs. In the 1950s, 80 percent of the approximately 45,000 Japanese immigrants were women, almost all of them wives of U.S. military men they had met during the postwar U.S. occupation of Japan (Nishi 1995).

Reasons for Immigration

Although in 1890, eight years after the Chinese Exclusion Act, only 2,039 Japanese were in the United States, within two decades the number had grown to 72,257. Most Japanese emigrants had been farmers in Japan, and while they came as contract laborers, becoming farmers in the United States was a profound and exciting dream for many (U.S. Immigration Commission 1911). The push factors in Japan included the economic deprivation of the farming community coupled with curiosity and a yen for adventure that was fanned by the mandatory education system and exposure to non-Japanese ideas. The latter also constituted the *pull* to the United States, as did the stories of economic opportunities and possibilities of success. The Gentlemen's Agreement stopped male immigration in 1908, the Ladies' Agreement curtailed female immigration in 1921, and in 1924, when the United States chose to close its borders to all further immigration from Asia by permitting annual entry of only 2 percent of foreign-born individuals of each nationality already residing in the United States in 1890, Japanese immigration to the United States effectively came to an end. Since the Japanese began immigrating in larger numbers only after that date, the number of Japanese residents was small; hence, the Japanese quota under the new law was minuscule.

INDIAN EMIGRATION: 1901–1917

An Overview of the Nation's History

Indian history can be traced back to the highly developed Harappa and Mohenjodaro communities of the Indus and Saraswati Valley Civilization of the period 3100 B.C. to 1550 B.C., which were discovered only late in the first quarter of the twentieth century. They were found to have many of the amenities of city life—baths, markets, palatial buildings, and drainage systems—as well as sophisticated and legendary agricultural and culinary abilities. However, human artifacts dating as far back as 500,000 years have also been found on the Indian subcontinent. The Vedic traditions began in 1000 B.C. This was also the period during which the caste system was established, and it marked the beginning of the Aryan migration into India. The first millennium B.C. bore major implications for Indian society, religion, and culture. With the lives of Gautama Buddha (563–543 B.C.) and Mahavira (b. 599 B.C.) developed two great Eastern religions, Buddhism and Jainism. They influenced the culture and society of India during that period, embodied a strong spirit of philanthropy, and continue to influence India today. Since ancient India was governed not by the state but by society, religion, and culture, its history must be viewed in broader terms than merely from the political perspective. Between the Indus Valley civilization and twentieth-century India lie several periods about which little is known. These periods must have been strongly linked, however, because despite numerous changes, an underlying continuity remains today.

In 326 B.C. Alexander the Great invaded India, Chandra Gupta Maurya established the Indian Empire (the Mauryan Empire) in 300 B.C., and Emperor Ashoka, his grandson, took the throne in 272 B.C., spreading Buddhism through India and beyond its borders, as far away as Egypt and Greece. The first century A.D. was known as the Golden Age of Indian Arts and Sciences. During this time the fine arts, architecture, and sculpture developed and flourished. This period was followed by Muslim invasions and the establishment of the Moghul Empire. Marco Polo (1288 A.D.) and Vasco da Gama (1498 A.D.), from Italy and Portugal, respectively, found their way into India and established a substantial Western influence there. On December 31, 1600, the British formed the East India Company, intended to be a trading company. Though it failed to create trading strength in the East, it nevertheless established British military dominance and political empire.

The directors, based in England, were unable to control activities from afar and had to leave things in the hands of the officers, who, in turn, ceased to focus on trade but made the company a forceful ruler of the Indian subcontinent and other British possessions.

While there were a few wars with the British (the Anglo-Maratha War in 1805 and the Anglo-Sikh War in 1846), it was not until 1857 that Indians made a united attempt to become independent from the British, who had ruled them for more than two hundred years. At first called by the British the Sepoy Riots or the Mutiny of 1857, this conflict now is known as the First War of Independence. Indians constituted 96 percent of the 300,000 in the British army, and the insurrection was stimulated by the realization that their bullets, whose ends they had to bite off before loading, were greased with cow and pig fat. This was an insult to both Hindus and Muslims, since the former are not permitted to eat beef and the latter may not eat pork. It was not just a military revolt but a religious statement. As it spread, it became apparent that it was more a war for independence than a rebellion. Although not successful in driving the British out of India, this conflict made some Englishmen aware that in order for harmony to exist between the small group of ruling English and the Indians, a vehicle for Indian political involvement was essential. The rule of the East India Company ended, and the British government took direct charge.

The Indian National Union was formed in 1885 and soon gave way to the Indian National Congress, which marked the entry of a new educated middle class of Indians into the political structure. With a political voice, the Indians became a united force on several fronts—one with which the British had to contend. A series of violent attacks on Indians, including the infamous and savage slaughter of thousands of Sikhs at a peaceful rally in *Jallianwalla Bagh* in 1919, moved the independence struggle to a different plane as shedding of white men's blood was now considered necessary to atone for the atrocities inflicted on the Indian population.

While the focus on recent Indian history addresses the twentieth century and the freedom movement, the nineteenth century was a time of particular transition for artisans and agricultural workers. The weaving of cotton, silk, and wool resulted in an important textile trade with the world, as did the manufacture of metal, glass, and paper, and the country's agricultural products were superior. The advent of machine-made goods from the West, however, transformed India into a consumer and weakened its presence in the trading world. British policy also barred the country from gaining industrial strength, and Indians turned in greater numbers to rural areas for their livelihoods. The drain on the land became intense, as the population frantically attempted to eke out a living, and these pressures continued into the twentieth century, establishing the foundations of Indian poverty (Nehru 1934).

Population growth in India was not itself the cause of poverty. It was the result of undue pressure on the land, since Indians had to depend on only farming to support their families. Poverty and semistarvation were common, and food supplies were always at the mercy of climate. Famine and disease killed many Indians, but the devastating famine that gripped the country from 1899 to 1902 not only harmed agricultural products but also killed the cattle of many peasant farmers, forcing them into debt.

Indian Emigration to the United States

Although the U.S. Census indicates one Indian in the United States as far back as the first half of the nineteenth century, the first wave of immigration did not begin until 1901 and was very short. Entry was restricted in 1909 and prohibited by the U.S. Congress in 1917. The gender distribution of this group was even more skewed than that of the other groups, with less than one percent of the 6,400 Indians being women. Most emigrants were younger, between the ages of sixteen and thirty-five, and many were married but had left their wives and families behind. Indian tradition, much like Chinese tradition, did not permit women to travel, nor did most husbands have the financial means to bring their wives.

Although from the beginning a number of intellectuals, primarily students, came to the United States and would later provide the community with its leadership (Hess 1998), most of the first wave of Indians came from the northern state of Punjab and were either unskilled or agricultural laborers. The majority had little or no education, and 47 percent of them were entirely illiterate. Most were Sikhs, who wore their hair long and bound in turbans, raising much curiosity, and came to the United States in small groups from villages. Muslims constituted about one-third of the immigrants. Groups of relatives often came together.

The students who entered the United States in the first decade of the twentieth century formed a core of intellectuals who were active on different levels. Several joined forces with political refugees from

India and advocated rights for themselves in the United States. This was also a period during which India's struggle for freedom from the British was in full swing, and the intellectuals and refugees who arrived in the United States directed substantial effort toward their native country's independence. In fact, after 1908, several Indian revolutionaries, attempting to escape imprisonment in India, sought asylum in the United States and launched their movements through established Sikh organizations. By the turn of the twentieth century, at least five hundred traders, merchants, and businessmen were involved in a variety of export-and-import endeavors. Many of these immigrants also supported India's independence movement.

However, it was the devastation of the 1899 famine that forced many in the Punjab who found themselves deep in debt to leave their homeland and seek work abroad. These individuals were the ones who really constituted the wave of Indian emigrants during this period. While some emigrated to Africa and the West Indies, a large number migrated to the United States and Canada. Many, like those from other Asian countries before them, aimed to make enough money to return to India and purchase farmland. The majority settled in the state of Washington to work in the lumber mills and in California to work in agriculture. In 1910 demand for workers on the Western Pacific Railroad increased, and 1,782 Indians were admitted that year.

Emigration was also influenced by other factors. As soldiers in the British army, many Sikhs had traveled to China to help suppress the Boxer Rebellion in 1900, and they returned with tales from the Chinese of the money that could be made in America. Even if young men did not go to China, their experiences in the British army made them aware of the opportunity for excitement and financial prosperity in the United States. However, the decision to emigrate was not an individual one but reflected the joint decision of the family. It was based on the need to supplement family income and fulfill kinship responsibilities. As did the Japanese, the father sent the second son to earn enough money to help offset the debts the family had incurred or the mortgage it owed. Some families even mortgaged part, if not all, of their lands so that the sons could travel to the land of opportunity. The sacrifice and difficulty that the family encountered were considered small compared to the long-term benefits that all would reap.

Although the effects of natural disasters on resources and lifestyle were instrumental in moving a significant number of the emigrants who arrived in the United States at the turn of the twentieth century, those were by no means the only environmental or societal causes. An important factor was the financial difficulties created by British colonial oppression in India. The British prevented nations that they had colonized from developing and progressing, often displacing people from their traditional sources of income and forcing them to emigrate. The perception by many Indian émigrés that they could further the cause of India's independence better from abroad was another impetus for emigration.

The Indian diaspora has long been an integral part of India's historical experience, with migrants spreading across the globe for well over two thousand years. They have sought to settle in other lands for a number of reasons, all involving both push and pull factors. Often moving outside the country's borders to seek jobs, they have been prompted by internal conflicts, perceived oppression by foreign invaders, fluctuations in exploited natural resources, and opportunities available elsewhere.

Reasons for Immigration to the United States

Until 1947, India and Pakistan formed one nation, and East Pakistan did not become Bangladesh until 1971. Hence all immigrants from what currently are three nations were Indians. While political, social, and economic conditions in the homeland, as well as personal and family experiences, may have forced the early Indian immigrants out of India, the majority who arrived in the United States during the early twentieth century came in hopes of amassing fortunes and then returning home—the same plan that brought most other Asians. They left their families in the expectation that they would soon return, and few expected to become permanent residents of the United States. Even students, intellectuals, political refugees, traders, and others considered themselves sojourners who would return home after improving their financial situation, acquiring skills that would be useful in India, or seeing the end of the British colonial era.

As these Indian men arrived at a time of anti-Asian sentiment and immigration policies, they were later either not able or not willing to have their wives join them in the United States. In fact, many returned to India in the 1920s and 1930s. Although several thousand East Asian women did join their spouses under the War Brides Act, India had no military connection with the United States, and thus no wives from India could emigrate to the country under the provisions of this act.

FILIPINO EMIGRATION: 1902–1934 AND 1953–1965

An Overview of Philippine History

The remains of a 30,000-year-old human fossil have been found in Palawan, on the western fringe of the archipelago, suggesting migrations during the last Ice Age, when land bridges connected the islands to mainland Asia. Active maritime trade and migration may have existed in insular and mainland Southeast Asia between 4500 and 5000 B.C. or even as early as 7000 B.C.—a theory based on the most recent radiocarbon dating (Manansala 1999). Archaeological evidence suggests a rich culture with skills in weaving, shipbuilding, mining, and goldsmithing, and trade with other Asian countries that dated back to at least 500 B.C. Links with Hindu empires in Java and Sumatra were instrumental in encouraging exchanges with Indian culture and its incorporation into Filipino social, political, and religious life, including the adoption of syllabic scripts. Early Filipinos, descended from the seafaring Austronesian people of Southeast Asia, grew crops of taro and yams.

By the tenth century A.D., there was significant trade with China, and trade with Arab countries peaked in the twelfth century, resulting in the establishment of a strong Islamic tradition in Mindanao. However, health beliefs and practices included magic-religious elements with strong beliefs in spirits and sorcery as well as the use of herbs and medicinal plants. Despite indications that human presence existed on these islands several millennia ago and that relationships with the archipelago are mentioned among the written records of the Chinese Chou (722 B.C.) and Han (206 B.C.) Dynasties, the first date entered into the annals of the history of the Philippines is March 16, 1521. On this date, Ferdinand Magellan "discovered" these lands, naming them the Philippines, claiming them for the Spanish, introducing Christianity, and attempting to unify them under a central government. Only through the histories and experiences of neighboring nations can the ancient history of the Philippines be reconstructed.

Lack of knowledge about Filipino history may be caused, at least in part, by the deliberate destruction of the ancestral culture by Spanish conquistadors, who viewed its physical manifestations as the work of the devil (Reyes 1993). Oral traditions were demolished when those who knew them were persecuted and killed. During the sixteenth century, Filipino prosperity depended on the exchange of silver from Spain's Mexico colony, which was called New Spain, for silk from

China. Prospects of wealth lured Spanish officials and Chinese entrepreneurs to Manila and resulted in intermarriage and the birth of the *mestizo* classification. This intermarriage and mingling of backgrounds also helped develop a new culture.

The empire of Spain crumbled in 1700, when trade opened and a local wealthy class emerged. Members of that group were sent to Europe for education and were exposed to liberal ideas and the significance of a national identity. In the 1860s discontent with continued Spanish control prompted a peaceful reform movement under José Rizal, but when he was executed for sedition, a revolution began under Andres Bonifacio. In 1898 the United States won the Spanish-American War and purchased the Philippines, Puerto Rico, and several other islands from the Spanish. The Filipinos, who had been involved in a bloody revolution to gain independence from Spain since 1896, were dismayed at the possibility of another colonial period, this time under the Americans. February 1899 marked the beginning of the Philippine-American War, also known as the Philippine Insurrection and the Philippine War of Independence, when fighting erupted between the occupying American army and the Filipino military, led by Emilio Aguinaldo.

The war developed into a savage guerrilla conflict, with wanton violence and slaughter. Destruction of villages, torture, murder of civilians, and mutilations were rampant. Once Aguinaldo was captured in March 1902, the opposition faded, and hostilities died over the next decade. Thus began the colonization and Americanization of the Filipino people. The new link with the United States greatly affected the Filipinos, who were already substantially Westernized because of the Spanish influence and the impact of Roman Catholicism, and it also permitted a steady flow of immigrants from the Philippines. The strong U.S. presence in the Philippine Islands ensured that the natives would become increasingly Americanized.

Following Japan's bombing of Pearl Harbor on December 7, 1941, with little warning or opportunity for American preparation, Japanese ships began attacking American bases in the Philippines. On May 6, 1942, the Americans withdrew from the Philippines, with a pledge from President Roosevelt that the freedom of the Philippines would be restored. Japanese occupation of the islands continued until 1945, however. During this period, beginning with the Bataan "death march," in which 76,000 prisoners of war marched sixty-five miles to a concentration camp and almost one-third lost their lives, the Japanese inflicted great atrocities on their prisoners. In October 1944, after two and a half long years, American troops launched an offensive against the Japanese navy at the Battle of Leyte Gulf. Intense fighting in 1945 forced the Japanese to end their occupation of the Philippines. Although the Japanese occupation was not long, the torture and disenfranchisement of the Filipinos had tremendous ramifications for the population.

Thus, these two wars—the Philippine-American War (1899–1902) and World War II, particularly the period of the Japanese occupation— prompted a push out of the Philippines. Furthermore, the colonization and Americanization of the population enhanced the likelihood of their particular interest in the United States. On the other hand, while large segments of the urban population benefited from the influence of the American presence and economy, there was also evidence of continuing political and economic corruption (Corpuz 1965), poverty (Stone and Marsella 1968), malnutrition (Guthrie 1968), and inadequate access to education (Lightfoot 1973).

Filipino Emigration to the United States

Three early waves of emigration from the Philippines to the United States occurred. The first and second came on the heels of each other, from 1902 to 1910 and from 1910 to 1934. The third came much later, after World War II, beginning in 1953 and lasting through 1965 and into the liberalization period.

The first group of immigrants consisted of students, known as *pensionados*, who returned to the Philippines to contribute to the economic, social, and cultural development of their country. Most of the second group became laborers. Both groups were exposed to Western thought and lifestyles, and although many in the second group came with the expectation of studying, they found the costs of education exorbitant, failed to complete their schooling, and settled into the labor force. Of those who did complete their studies, the majority returned to their homeland to occupy positions of leadership in business and politics. While intellectual aspirations and access to Western education attracted many Filipinos to the United States, their primary motivation, like that of most immigrants, was economic. Job opportunities, especially in the cities of the Philippines, were sorely limited, and each advertisement in the Manila paper attracted a thousand applications. Pay scales were poor, and many sought better opportunities in the West.

A free-trade agreement, particularly in the sugar industry, eased immigration to the United States in the early decades of the twentieth century, but the agreement ended in 1933, when U.S. concern about competition curtailed imports. A large number of Filipino laborers also migrated to the United States, either directly to the mainland or via Hawaii. Most came after World War I, and a disproportionate number were male. Another factor that brought an end to Filipino immigration was the Tydings-McDuffie Act of 1934, which established a U.S. commonwealth status for the Philippines and restricted immigration to the United States to fifty persons annually. No limitation was placed on the number of Americans who could live in the Philippines, however.

A significant proportion of the third wave, the group that came after 1953, was a result of nonquota immigration. These were close relatives of U.S. citizens (including brides of American servicemen), tourists, businesspeople, and students. In addition, the Laurel-Langley Trade Agreement of 1954 gave Filipinos economic rights in the United States and increased access for entrepreneurs. These nonquota individuals often became permanent residents, far outnumbering the quota immigrants. In 1963 immigrants totaled 3,618, while nonquota immigrants and nonimmigrants numbered 13,860 (Kitano and Daniels 1995). This group of highly Americanized and educated people initiated the "brain drain" from the Philippines. While many of them left for countries other than the United States before 1954, changes in U.S. openness to Filipino immigration in that year began the early trickle of professionals into the country (Bello, Lynch, and Makil 1969). The flow of students pursuing higher education was also evident in the 1950s and early 1960s, although a substantial number in this third wave did return to the Philippines after completing their studies.

The Immigration of Filipino Women

Although females and males in the Filipino culture have a more egalitarian relationship than do women and men in most other Asian cultures, the number of women who immigrated to the United States was very small, particularly with the first and second waves. Before the first large group, a few women came to the United States as war brides of Spanish-American War veterans. After that period, there is little information about the women who entered the country. While it is possible that some may have entered as students, it does not appear likely, and if they did, their numbers were disproportionately small.

From 1909 to 1934, close to 120,000 Filipinos arrived in Hawaii under three-year labor contracts, and of these, 7.5 percent were female. It is not clear how many of these women moved to the United States at the end of their contracts. The U.S. Census reveals that in 1930, 67.4 percent (30,470) of the Filipinos in the country resided in California, and of these, 6.1 percent (1,845) were female (Kitano and Daniels 1995). This figure is low compared to the number of Japanese women, although it is a great deal higher than the number of Indians. In 1910 the ratio of males to females was 10 to 1, but by 1920 it had deteriorated to 20 to 1. After 1940 the ratio became more equal at 3.5 to 1 (Agbayani-Siewert and Revilla 1995).

Following World War II, with the Philippines gaining independence in 1946, the annual quota of 100 for immigrants was still decidedly low, but Filipinos who were in the United States were permitted to become citizens. This was followed by the entry of approximately 16,000 war brides of American and Filipino veterans, greatly increasing the numbers of female Filipinos who entered the United States with permanent status.

Reasons for Immigration

The early immigration of Filipinos differed from that of other Asian groups, since the majority came with the aim of acquiring knowledge that could be applied in the Philippines. Of particular interest to them were business practices and democratic principles. Hence, the early immigrants came as educational sojourners, with all intentions of returning. Even the members of the second group, who followed the *pensionados* and then turned to labor when they were unable to complete their studies, had intended to return to the Philippines after immersion in American society.

Among the second wave were those laborers who came specifically to work on the Hawaiian sugar plantations, replacing the Chinese and Japanese workers who eventually moved to the United States. These immigrants were drawn by the economic opportunities about which they had heard. Although the modernization of the Philippines had resulted in benefits for large segments of the population, there were equally large groups in the archipelago who did not have access to the opportunities and experiences of the urban citizens. Thus, like other immigrants, most were drawn for economic reasons. Because they left their women behind, it appears that most anticipated returning to their homeland. The economic and political climate in the Philippines was another factor that pushed them out of the country in search of better options.

KOREA: 1903–1924 AND 1951–1964

An Overview of the Nation's History

Korean mythology places the existence of early Koreans in 7193 B.C., when the Lord of Heaven established a country of twelve nations constituting the ethnic entity *Dongyi*, but the skeletal remains of two children place human life in Korea long before then, during the Paleolithic Period, 400,000 to 500,000 years ago (Eckert et al. 1990). By 2333 B.C., different rulers had annexed territories, introduced medicine, advanced agriculture and animal husbandry, and begun mass production of steel and bronze weapons. The period between 57 B.C. and 680 A.D. is known as the Samguk Shidae or the Three Kingdoms, during which various Korean states battled each other and the Han Chinese for control of East Asia. The Unified Shilla Period (681 A.D.–918 A.D.), also known as the North-South Kingdoms, ended with Korea recognized as an individual state. Korean history begins long after Chinese history but well before Japanese history.

The period of the Koryo Dynasty (918 A.D.–1392 A.D.) was the transition between the Shilla and the Choson—Land of the Morning Calm—Dynasty. During this period the foundations of the Korean identity were set, as were political, social, and cultural changes. While Buddhism was practiced at the time of the Three Kingdoms, it did not receive prominence until the Koryo Period, when it received substantial government subsidies for activities, buildings, and ceremonies. Buddhism also divided into two sects, one that was supported by the ruling dynasty and aristocracy and the other by the local gentry. Results were discord and disunity, with implications for societal functioning. During this period, literature (poetry and essays) and pottery gained interest, and contributed much to the culture.

The Choson Period. It is the period of the Choson Dynasty (1392 A.D.–1910 A.D.) to which historians refer to provide an understanding of Korea. The Choson Dynasty was founded by Yi Sing-Gye, who rose from an obscure military family to become one of the most powerful figures in Korean history. This period, also known as the Yi Period, provided the last "traditional" kingdom before Korea was modernized. The Choson Period had a complex, well-established social structure that permeated Korean tradition through the centuries. Class was hereditary, and at least four distinct classes could be identified: (a) the *yangban*—the elite, who were eligible for high-ranking government service; (b) the *chungin*—the technical experts, translators, scientists, doctors, clerks, who ensured that bureaucratic systems functioned smoothly (but did not emerge as a distinct class until the sixteenth century); (c) the *yang-min*, or commoners—tenant farmers, craftsmen, laborers, and others, on whom society depended daily and who formed the majority of the population, and (d) the *ch'onmin*—the lowest in the hierarchy, who were slaves (freed in the nineteenth century), butchers, entertainers, or prostitutes. During this period, Korea adopted Confucianism as its guiding philosophy, with a strict code of behavior that ensured that women remained in inferior and disadvantaged positions in relationship to males throughout their lives, with obedience to men being paramount.

With the adoption of Confucianism came the end of the power of Buddhism. Behavior was carefully defined in all areas of human interaction, and moral and ethical principles were developed to guide behavior. Foreign policy and cultural identity were influenced by an ideology of *sadae-juui*, or the importance of "Serving the Great," which in Korea's case was China. Though strongly influenced and controlled by China, Korea also developed along autonomous lines. Moving away from the use of Chinese characters in writing, in 1443 it developed the *han'gul*, an alphabet consisting of twenty-eight letters. During the Choson Period the economy was overwhelmingly agrarian, yet the introduction of new agricultural technology, tax collection systems, and currency greatly modified it over time.

Advances in agricultural technology resulted in significant economic improvement for peasants and farmers, and the export of goods to China became common in the seventeenth century. The late eighteenth century saw the beginnings of open-door policies with other countries, and many believed that the strength of the nation could be maintained only through trade with Japan and Western nations. In the late nineteenth century, a number of skirmishes with China led to formal intervention in Korea, sending a resident agent to Seoul. As the increasing corruption and oppression by the Chinese heaped distress on the peasant farmers, Japan's economic penetration further destroyed

Korea's rural economy. The spark that ignited the uprisings of the Peasant Army was an excess of exploitation of the peasant population. About the same time, in the late 1870s, Japan invaded Korea and opened some ports for Japanese trade. Although Korea was a vassal state of China, the latter did not provide assistance, fearing reprisals from the Japanese. By 1882 Korea was completely opened to trade and also became a joint protectorate of China and Japan. The Sino-Japanese War (1894–1895) resulted in freedom from China for Korea, but the Japanese presence remained in the country. Not permitted by Russia, Germany, and France to keep that portion of China that they had conquered, the Japanese prepared for a future successful struggle with Russia, the Russo-Japanese War (1904–1905). Both wars bore implications for Korea, as they expanded the Japanese Empire.

Colonial Korea. In 1905 Korea became a protectorate of Japan, and in 1910 it was formally annexed, marking the end of the Choson Dynasty. Under the first governor general from Japan, the Koreans suffered great oppression and indignities as he attempted to force acculturation into a Japanese identity. Guerrilla bands and the Japanese army locked in violent and bloody struggles from 1907 to 1910. Intellectuals resisted Japanese assimilation and opposed policies throughout the protectorate period. The colonial period lasted from 1910 to 1945, with the end of World War II and the beginning of the Korean War, but national consciousness continued to rise, even as political activism was repressed. By 1945 all area Koreans feared the presence and influence of the colonial police.

As a whole, there are two perspectives on the colonial period: (a) Japan's introduction of modern production, transportation, finance, and education provided Korea with a modern capitalist system, and (b) Japan's exploitation of Korean resources for profit and the control of capital and land by Japanese entrepreneurs placed Korea in semifeudal dependency. It is generally agreed that Japan prevented democratic participation and left Korea unprepared for sudden independence in 1945, resulting in chaos that was not controlled until 1950.

From 1910 until the late 1920s, more than 80 percent of the Korean population was engaged in agricultural work, with the goal of exporting goods to support Japanese consumers. In the meantime, the quality and quantity of the produce declined, and the nutrition of the Korean people appreciably deteriorated. Christianity and Shintoism were introduced, and emigration of males became common. On March

1, 1919, Koreans from all walks of life caught Japanese authorities by surprise as they demonstrated against Japanese rule. While the demonstration was not sufficient to dislodge Japanese rule, in 1920 the Japanese government moved to abandon its military-style involvement in Korea and replace it with a more benign presence, taking into account Korean sensitivities and culture.

The end of World War II meant the liberation of the Koreans from Japanese rule, but it also presented grave economic problems, as Korea had not developed as a self-sustaining unit. The sudden withdrawal of Japan resulted in the collapse of the Korean economy. Furthermore, the nation's division on August 25, 1945, split Korea into an industrial north and an agrarian south, resulting in a dramatic slump in the productivity of both nations (U.S. Department of State 1969). In December 1945, through the Moscow Agreement, the United States, the United Kingdom, the Union of Soviet Socialist Republics (USSR), and later China agreed to establish a trusteeship over Korea and form a Korean provisional government. Lack of agreement led to increasing divisions between Korea's north and south. At the end of 1948 and the beginning of 1949, foreign troops were withdrawn from Korea, and the United Nations (UN) General Assembly declared the Republic of Korea the only legitimate government in the nation. Gradually both the north (supported by the USSR and Eastern Europe) and the south developed separate administrations, and each became increasingly intolerant of political opponents. The thirty-eighth parallel was drawn as the frontier between the two states. Nevertheless, each claimed the whole peninsula as its legal territory. On August 15, 1948, the Republic of Korea was established in the south, and on September 9, 1948, the Democratic People's Republic of Korea was created in the north.

The Korean War. On June 25, 1950, the Soviet-trained and equipped North Korean communist army invaded South Korea in a surprise attack, which the UN Security Council branded as aggression. The south was ill prepared and poorly equipped to counter the attack; Seoul was occupied by the communists within three days, and South Korean forces were isolated in the southeast corner of the peninsula, with the rest of the territory occupied by the North Korean army. The only event that disrupted North Korean plans was the unforeseen intervention of the United States. On June 26, 1950, U.S. president Harry Truman ordered the use of U.S. planes and naval vessels, and on June 30, U.S.

ground troops arrived in Korea. Through the request of the United States and under General Douglas MacArthur, the United Nations Armed Forces defeated the North Korean army, forcing it to retreat, and also took Pyongyang, the North Korean capital. Within a few weeks North Korea was controlled by the United States. In October 1950, however, "volunteers" from China intervened, assisting North Korea in restoring authority. The war lasted until July 27, 1953, with China and the USSR supporting the north, and fifteen UN member nations contributing armed forces and other assistance to the south.

The war reduced the whole peninsula to rubble. Thousands of casualties occurred on both sides, and the possibility of the reunification of north and south grew remote. The Chinese presence continued in North Korea until 1958, and the United States kept troops stationed in South Korea. The generation that survived the war was scarred for life. This war had torn people from their villages and mobilized them into armies and political activism. It also brutally forced them into modernization and paved the way for profound social, economic, and political transformation in both north and south. It permanently separated families and wreaked havoc with individuals' lives. On the international front, the Korean War was the first of a number of battles in the decades-long Cold War, establishing a new environment and atmosphere in relationships among nations around the globe. North and south were so divided that contact between North Korea and the rest of the non-communist world was, for all intents and purposes, completely severed

Republic of Korea.[1] The period between 1953 and 1964 was a time for reestablishing a foundation for Korean society. The first republic of South Korea was led by Syngman Rhee, and most politics in the 1950s either revolved around him or lobbied against him. His ambition for power conflicted substantially with the democratic government he had to adopt to continue to receive U.S. support after 1948. In 1960 concerns about election rigging led to peaceful demonstrations by students that were marred by gunfire and murder by the police. Another wave of demonstrations began, this time by university professors in Seoul. Despite emergency sessions and the resignation of Rhee, difficulties in the economy, problems of government corruption, and deprivation persisted. In 1961 the Military Revolution Committee, under Army Chief of Staff Chang Do-yung, took over the government, declaring a six-point pledge: (a) a strong anticommunist stand, (b) respect for the

UN Charter, (c) closer relations with the United States and other free nations, (d) eradication of corruption, (e) establishment of a self-supporting economy, and (f) efforts for territorial unification and the transfer of power to new and conscientious politicians. A universal free election was held in 1963, and South Korea moved toward growth and development.

Korean Emigration to the United States

By 1882 Korea was completely open to trade and was also a joint protectorate of China and Japan. Thus there existed the possibility of emigration to those two countries. The shortage of laborers on Hawaiian sugar plantations resulted in proposals to attract people from several Asian countries, but the initial attempts in 1896 to recruit workers from Korea were denied by the Korean government. A small number of Korean students, political exiles, *ginseng* merchants, and migrant laborers did arrive in the United States before 1900, but their numbers were negligible. The primary impetus for a large-scale migration was provided by a combination of factors that peaked at the turn of the century. A severe famine occurred in 1901, and an epidemic of cholera took lives and encouraged the more enterprising to look for alternatives outside the country. The government also relaxed its traditionally tight restrictions on emigration, despite the unacceptability of emigration to Korean tradition. In addition, governmental corruption and heavy taxes on the already economically burdened prompted an exodus.

Seven years passed before the first Korean workers arrived in Hawaii. In 1903 they emigrated to work the sugar plantations, and from there some of them moved to California in 1905. Most emigrants were not peasants, but they were from the lower classes and extremely conservative, closely following Confucian ideals that valued land and family. To abandon them through emigration was both unthinkable and immoral (Hurh and Kim 1984), and many Koreans who did emigrate converted to Christianity before leaving Korea, perhaps to reduce the cognitive dissonance evoked by Confucian traditions. Despite these changes, most emigrants maintained the perspective of sojourners and planned, like other Asian emigrants, to return to their homelands when they had acquired enough wealth that they and their families could live in comfort in Korea.

Between 1903 and 1905, the labor migration to Hawaii from Korea resulted in a count of 7,226 Koreans in the United States (U.S.

Immigration and Naturalization Service 1995). In 1905 Japan ended emigration to the United States from Korea. Some accounts suggest that the termination occurred for political reasons when Korea became a protectorate of Japan. Others take the position that the Koreans were so severely maltreated in Hawaii and the United States that Japan and the Korean government intervened to protect them by denying further emigration. The emigrants, thus far, were almost all male and single. Given their sojourner attitude, most did not attempt to assimilate into Western culture, and since plantation life was characterized by racial and ethnic segregation, there was little opportunity to integrate. Emotional bonds with Korea and its traditions led to the picture bride system, and between 1910 and 1924, under the Gentlemen's Agreement between the United States and Japan, 1,100 Korean women migrated to Hawaii and the United States as wives of the Korean laborers (U.S. Immigration and Naturalization Service 1995). Another group that also managed to leave Korea between 1906 and 1924 consisted of about 600 students and political refugees. Before and after the annexation by Japan in 1910, many intellectuals agitated against Japanese rule, and several were kept under close surveillance. A number of these escaped to the United States via Shanghai and continued striving for Korean independence from there.

Although emigration to the United States was stopped for most Koreans by 1905, thousands who were landless or suffering economic deprivation moved to Japan during the period of colonization, starting a substantial Korean community in that country. Emigrants continued to move into other Eastern countries, and there were large migrations to Manchuria and Russia as well. Almost no Koreans immigrated to the United States from 1924 (and the Ladies' Agreement) until 1945, when Korea was liberated from Japanese occupation. Even then, the South Korean government strongly discouraged and restricted all emigration, as it needed its labor force to keep pace with industrialization and urbanization, which was increasing fairly rapidly. It also sought to develop and maintain a large army for its defense against the north, which was now communist North Korea.

Clearly, the immigration to the United States from Korea was small before the Korean War. In the early 1950s, a major Korean emigration to this country began. The destruction and disease resulting from the conflict were enormous and widespread, with an estimated one million civilian and 300,000 military casualties in South Korea alone. In addition, the war left the country with at least 300,000 widows, 230,000 wounded, 330,000 permanently disabled, 100,000 orphans, and one million cases of tuberculosis (Kitano and Daniels 1995; Kim 1988).

Several thousand Korean orphans, war brides, and relatives of Korean American servicemen emigrated to the United States after the war. Between 1951 and 1964, close to 14,027 Koreans settled in the United States (U.S. Immigration and Naturalization Service 1995). Of the some 24,945 children institutionalized in orphanages in Korea, approximately 6,300 were adopted in the United States between 1955 and 1966 through the Holt Adoption Agency, an organization that was specifically interested in placing orphaned Koreans with adoptive parents in the United States. The majority of the orphans were biracial, with American fathers, but about 40 percent were monoracial Koreans. A number of students and other nonimmigrants added 27,500 to the numbers of those who entered the United States during the period.

The second wave of Korean immigrants arrived during the period between 1950 and 1975, when 28,205 Korean War brides arrived in the United States (Kitano and Daniels 1995). In general, that wave was limited to students, war brides, and orphans between 1951 and 1964—before the liberalization of U.S. immigration policies. In the early 1960s, the Korean government became more receptive to the emigration of its nationals, particularly to the United States, and in 1962 an office of emigration was established at the Korean Ministry of Health. With increasing urbanization and overpopulation of Korea's industrial and commercial areas, South Korea began encouraging emigration as a means of population control and a mechanism of establishing and maintaining economic stability (Takaki 1989). So avidly was emigration promoted that private business began offering services to help individuals emigrate as well as to help them acquire skills in construction, automobile and electronics repair, computer programming, and hairdressing, areas that were in high demand outside Korea (Choi 1994).

College-educated Koreans were also lured by emigration opportunities. With the opening of options in other countries and the decreasing availability of career paths in Korea, thousands of young professional and highly educated individuals left their homelands for West Germany, Brazil, Argentina, Canada, and the United States. In addition, a relatively large number of the 1945–1964 immigrants to the United States were students seeking higher education and better economic possibilities. Of these, at least 5,000 remain in the United States today, yet little is known about them (Kitano and Daniels 1995).

Immigration of Korean Women

Beginning with the foundation of the Choson Dynasty in 1392 and continuing for several centuries, Confucian teachings enforced a view that women were subordinate to men. Women therefore enjoyed few human rights. Although they, like women in other nations, formed the foundation of the society, they received little recognition and were in fact systematically denigrated and victimized. The only position of value that they could claim was that of mother to a male child. The lack of credit accorded them permeated the society and still persists today.

Given these conditions, it was rare for Korean women to enter the United States on their own. A few did manage to emigrate to Hawaii as dependents of the men, but little is known of them. Furthermore, since women did not have many rights and through Confucian tradition were expected to be highly dependent on males, it was virtually impossible for them to emigrate independently, even as prostitutes. While a few Korean women might have emigrated as prostitutes, their numbers were lower than those of Chinese or Japanese women who entered the United States in this category. Men, however, had little difficulty bringing wives to the United States through the picture bride system during the first wave of Korean immigration. Therefore, most Korean women entered the United States as dependents. Although the beginning of the first wave of Korean immigration was small and consisted of men, soon after that more than 1,000 women arrived as picture brides, resulting in a higher ratio of women to men among Koreans than among first-wave immigrants from any other Asian country.

Even the second wave of immigrant women from Korea came as dependents of men. Almost all were war brides of American servicemen who had been stationed in Korea. While most American husbands were white and a few were African American, some were also of Korean ancestry. War brides from Korea, particularly those who had married non-Korean men—like the war brides from Japan and the Philippines—were viewed as opportunists, and they found little acceptance in Korea. Unfortunately, the experience of the Korean war bride in the United States was also difficult, for she found little acceptance from the Korean American community and was marginalized by the Euro-American community.

Reasons for Immigration

Korean immigration to the United States, as all other immigration movements, was the result of push factors out of Korea and pull factors into the United States. For the most part, whether migrants were laborers or students, their primary reasons for coming were economic. When political conditions, natural disasters, disease, and other problems in Korea jeopardized survival or made it difficult, Koreans looked outside their national borders for more promising opportunities. The literature on the picture bride system, particularly among the Japanese, reveals that many women chose to marry husbands in the United States, sight unseen, and leave their homelands and all that was familiar, in order to escape economic deprivation and socially constraining conditions. Furthermore, after the Korean War South Korea, unlike other sending countries, made special efforts to assist in the relocation of its citizens by establishing channels through which the appropriate procedures could be followed rapidly and the most applicable tools could be acquired. Thus, the push out of Korea occurred both because of unfavorable conditions in the country and because of the proactive impetus provided by the Korean government.

While a few students, political refugees, and exiles sought sanctuary in the United States after the Japanese occupation and before the Korean War, and hoped to further Korean independence, the majority came because of the opportunities to work on the sugar plantations. The young professional Koreans who immigrated after the Korean War were those who found their options severely limited in their homeland and who chose to apply their skills in Western countries. Despite the migrations, each wave of Korean immigrants to the United States retained bonds to the homeland, which revealed, as it did for every other Asian group, that neither the push nor the pull was extreme enough for most to ensure a permanent emigration orientation. Most immigrants to the United States viewed themselves a sojourners.

Pre-1965 emigration from Asian countries was generally spurred by economic necessity, and entry into the United States was greatly influenced by the economic and social climates in the nations of origin. Strongly discriminatory against people of color, the United States developed immigration policies that sought Asians primarily for occupations as laborers. Nevertheless, whenever the United States opened its borders to Asian emigrants, they tended to avail themselves of the opportunity.

Despite the difficulties, for many the economic possibilities were sufficient to risk all with which they were familiar. In general, however, the majority of the pre-1965 emigrants to the United States were substantially less educated than most Americans. They had low English-language skills, few personal resources, and were dependent on the whims of U.S. nationals. Emigration from Asian countries to the United States during the period between 1840 and 1965 ebbed and flowed based on the needs of the United States economy. After 1965, though immigration policy was still affected by U.S. economic interests, it allowed dramatic increases in the numbers and profiles of Asian immigrants.

3

Post-1965 Emigration:
Changes in U.S. Immigration Policy

*In considering and ultimately passing [U.S.] reforms, policymak-
ers did not pay careful attention to those Asian American and
Asian social forces that Congress and state governments had previously endeavored to hold in check—Asian American family
needs, economic ambitions, and residential patterns. Most policymakers did not understand how the political, economic, and social
dynamics in Asian countries would influence immigration. They
knew little about Asian American communities, Asian countries,
and their relationship, and their analyses by and large were cursory and inaccurate. Asian immigration after 1965 took the
United States by surprise.*

—HING 1995:79

Emigration from Asian nations since 1965 has been spurred not only
by their socioeconomic conditions but also by the opening of immigration policies through the amendments of October 3, 1965, to the
Immigration Act of 1924 and the Immigration and Nationality Act
of 1952. The influx of Asian immigrants may be directly related to
four of the five major changes made through these amendments (79
Statutes-at-Large 911),[1] which

1. abolished the national origins quota system, eliminating national
   origin, race, or ancestry as a basis for immigration to the U.S.
2. established allocation of immigrant visas on a first-come basis, subject to a 7-category preference system for relatives of U.S. citizens
   and permanent resident aliens (for reunification of families) and
   for persons with special occupational skills (needed in the U.S.)
3. established two categories of immigrants not subject to numerical
   restrictions—(a) immediate relatives (spouses, children, parents) of

U.S. citizens, and (b) special immigrants (certain ministers of religion, certain former employees of the U.S. government abroad, certain persons who lost citizenship (by marriage or service in foreign armed forces), and certain medical graduates)

4. maintained the principle of numerical restriction, but expanded the limits to world coverage and limited Eastern Hemisphere immigration to 170,000, with a 20,000 per-country limit. The Immigration and Nationality Act of June 27, 1952, had made all races eligible for naturalization, with an annual minimum quota of 100 per country, but no more than one-sixth of one percent of inhabitants in the continental United States in 1920 whose ancestors were from that country. In 1920, because of restrictive immigration legislation, the number of individuals from Asian countries was minuscule. The 1952 act also set a ceiling of 2,000 for countries in the Asia-Pacific triangle (66 Statutes-at-Large 163).[2] Thus the 1965 amendments to the act had substantial implications for Asian emigration. While conditions in the sending countries may have continued to differ, the opening of U.S. borders to immigration from the Eastern Hemisphere resulted in an unanticipated rate of immigration from Asian countries.

Changes that allowed the immigration of people with special knowledge, skills, and abilities that were needed in the United States and the absence of numerical restrictions on medical graduates further encouraged the immigration of individuals from Asia who had a professional profile that differed from that of the majority of Asians who had immigrated to the United States before 1965. The screening process, particularly in the first decade and a half after the 1965 amendments, ensured that the bulk of the immigrants from Asia were much better educated and were more likely to have already been engaged in professional and managerial occupations than immigrants who had come at other times or from other nations. Not only did they tend to have more education and be more professional than the average immigrant, but they were more educated and professional than the native-born American population.

Another stream of post-1965 immigrants that was also new and of significant size was the group of Vietnam War refugees who came to the United States after 1975 from Vietnam, Cambodia, and Laos. These individuals could change their refugee status to that of immigrant a year after being offered asylum. The majority of them were less educated and possessed fewer skills that were transferable to the U.S. workforce. The third Asian stream, since 1990, has consisted of relatives of earlier migrating Asians who have arrived under family reunification permits and who are not as skilled and educated as the early post-1965 immigrants. A less frequently discussed stream is that of undocumented immigrants—those who enter the United States and remain permanently without the appropriate authorization, but who add substantially to the numbers of immigrants. While a large number of these immigrants are unskilled and slip across the borders illegally, even larger numbers reflect a cross-section of backgrounds. The latter group, called "overstays" by the Immigration and Naturalization Service, comprises those who remain in the United States after their visas have expired.

Although political reasons have spurred some individuals to emigrate from Asian countries, except for political refugees from Southeast Asia, most have left their homelands because of poor economic conditions or situations that would not have allowed them to attain the professional opportunities and satisfaction that might be available elsewhere. After 1965, that "elsewhere" became the United States, which has the opportunities that they seek and has allowed the entry of Asians. Employment options in the United States have increasingly attracted professionals, whereas in the early years of Asian immigration the United States basically recruited laborers.

THE PROFESSIONAL STREAM

The movement to Western countries of Asians trained in such fields as medicine, engineering, and the sciences has been dramatic. During the period 1961–1972 approximately 300,000 professionals migrated from developing countries to Western ones (United Nations Conference on Trade and Development 1975), 65,000 of them coming from Asia to the United States and constituting 72 percent of the professional immigrants to the nation. Although there were only 14,500 Asian immigrants during the period 1961–1965, in 1972 alone there were 16,000 (Ong, Cheng, and Evans 1992). Between 1972 and 1988, the four major sending countries were India, South Korea, the Philippines, and China. These numbers represent emigration to the United States only and do not include emigration to other countries, but it is clear that the composition of the immigrant group changed from laborers to highly trained and practicing professionals.

While the migration of people is affected by the pull factors, there is also a push from the sending countries. The Asian countries have experienced increasing economic development and a corresponding rise in the level of education. More people have attained a college education. In South Korea, for example, the percentage of those who had completed college tripled between 1960 and 1980, to 8.4 percent; in the Philippines 15.2 percent of the population had finished college by 1980. Similar changes occurred in Taiwan and China. As a larger proportion of the population becomes educated, the emigration flow tends to include this group (Ong, Cheng, and Evans 1992).

Many sending nations have been particularly concerned about the change in the emigration flow. Until the 1960s the majority of emigrants tended to be the less educated and the less professional. Those who left to study abroad often returned to their native lands after the completion of their studies, possibly because of a lack of professional opportunities open to them. After the changes in U.S. immigration policies and the rise in professional emigration from Asian countries, however, leaders in the countries of origin began voicing major concerns about the "brain drain" from their lands. The "systematic extraction of talents" from the Asian countries was believed to hurt the economic well-being of those countries. The results of studies that investigated this idea were inconclusive, however, and the concerns declined in the 1970s (Ong, Cheng, and Evans 1992). Although substantial numbers of professionals did leave Asian countries after 1965, the bonds between them and their families remained strong, and the flow of financial support to the sending nations increased with the change in the profile of the emigrants. Emigrants regularly support family members in their home countries, increasing foreign cash flow in those nations. Not only has this continued into the twenty-first century, but along with the great strides in achievement and success among a large segment of the Asian emigrant population has come a sense of social responsibility and philanthropic ideals, resulting in substantial financial support of institutions and charitable causes in the home country (Dugger 2000).

Better education in developing nations changes the economic structure of the nation and both hurts and bolsters the finances of the family (Ong, Cheng, and Evans 1992). While agrarian families can rely on the support of children for an increased income, attending school removes children from the labor force. Education also means more expense for the family, for even if children attend public institutions, the necessary clothing and supplies are costly. Higher education requires even greater expense for the family, since universities are often outside the hometown and families must pay for room and board. College education requires enormous investment—the students must forgo income while they are in school, families must provide monetary and other support, and nations must provide public funds for higher education (Ong, Cheng, and Evans 1992). Yet this investment is believed to pay off in the form of greater output for the nation. If the well-educated citizens leave the nation, however, the direct benefits to the country decline, and it becomes dependent on the indirect support it may receive if these professionals return or if they send a portion of their earnings back to the home country.

When nations are unable to invest precious resources in sufficient quality and quantity of higher education, those who are interested in furthering their careers may seek educational opportunities elsewhere. With the opening of immigration laws in the United States, the influx of Asian students increased dramatically, and the flow continues into the twenty-first century. Many Asian countries now provide superior undergraduate education, but graduate opportunities continue to be relatively limited. Since the 1960s, the majority of students entering the United States from Asian countries have sought professional degrees beyond the undergraduate level. Those who receive professional degrees in their home countries may not recover the cost of their education by practicing in their own lands, or they may not be able to find jobs because of an oversupply of trained professionals there. For some nations, such as the Philippines, the possibility of migration for health professionals led to the expansion of nursing education, as many saw this as a path out of the country. In this case, it was not a surplus of educated health professionals that drove emigration; rather, the likelihood of emigration drove education in the field of health care (Joyce and Hunt 1982). Many health care professionals in the Philippines, particularly physicians, found the pay scale low and alternatives in the United States more attractive, but their migration led to a severe shortage of physicians in their home country.

The demand for physicians and other scientists is no longer as intense as it was in the 1980s in the United States. In the late 1990s and on into the twenty-first century the need for computer personnel became paramount. Technology companies aggressively, and successfully, brought pressure to bear on the Immigration and Naturalization Service to greatly raise the number of H-1 visas, the visa under which temporary workers can enter the United States. Asians, particularly those from China and India, have been actively recruited, and while many came on employment-based visas, with the understanding that they will return, the category allows them to extend their stay in the United States. Thus, with the increasing global demand for computer experts in the late twentieth century, Asian countries began further training their populations in this field. Both Asian and Western nations reaped the benefits as some of these young technocrats emigrated. However, the downturn of the economy in 2001 severely curtailed this flow, and the long-term effects remain to be seen.

REFUGEE AND ASYLEE STREAMS

The United States has always been a refuge for those fleeing from per-secution and until the 1990s accepted the largest number of the world's refugees of any nation (Mayadas and Segal 2000). According to the definition presented in the 1951 convention and the 1967 protocol setting forth the mandate of the United Nations High Commissioner for Refugees, a refugee is

> any person who, owing to a well founded fear of being perse-cuted for reasons of race, religion, nationality, or political opinion is outside the country of his/her nationality and is unable or, owing to such fear or for reasons other than personal convenience, is unwilling to avail himself/herself of the protec-tion of that country.
>
> (UNHCR 1996)

This definition is accepted by the United States Immigration and Naturalization Service as stated in the amended Refugee Act of 1980, which governs the present policy admitting refugees to the United States (U.S. Department of Justice 1999c). An asylee, on the other hand, enters a resettlement country without prior approval, and

> a potential asylee is any person who is in the United States or applying for admission at a port of entry and is unable or unwilling to return to his or her country of nationality because of persecution or a well-founded fear of persecution.
>
> (U.S. Department of Justice 1999a)

In refugee movements, the first wave is usually composed of highly educated, affluent, and well-connected individuals who have resources in the country of refuge. While the move is traumatic, they have the support and the skills to acclimatize themselves to another country and culture. The second and subsequent waves of refugees are usually people from rural backgrounds, and their levels of literacy, education, and skill are relatively low. Moreover, many have skills that are not directly transferable to Western industry, business, and technology. Thus they lack the competencies necessary to adjust to life in today's fast-paced, computer-oriented societies. In addition, the socioeconomic background of refugees varies with the level of economic development in their countries of origin.

Unlike other immigrants, most refugees and political exiles are forced out of their countries. They leave under duress and extreme trauma, with little or no opportunity to prepare for departure. They experience a great deal of stress springing from unfinished business, material and emotional losses, and the uprooting from their homes and countries. Most do not wish to leave their homelands and want to return as soon as possible. Often returning is not an option, and they remain in the neighboring countries to which they initially fled, where the language and culture are often similar to their own. A smaller group is approved for resettlement elsewhere; each year about one million refugees are offered resettlement in third countries. Of these, 10 to 15 percent come to the United States. After a year in the United States, refugees have the option of readjusting their refugee status to that of immigrant. The ceilings set for refugees to adjust their status are independent of the immigration ceilings and the numerical cap for immigrants from that particular region of the world.

FAMILY REUNIFICATION STREAM

Family reunification, a significant direction of the 1965 Immigration Act, with seven of the nine immigration categories based on blood or marital relationships, resulted in a mass migration to the United States. Spouses, children under the age of twenty-one, and parents of U.S. citizens are exempt from immigration quotas. In addition, four of the six preference categories (1, 2, 4, and 5), with their associated annual limits, are family reunification preferences and account for 80 percent of the immigration quotas:

   i. 1st preference: Unmarried children (over age 21) of U.S. citizens—20% annual immigration quota

   ii. 2nd preference: Spouses and children of permanent residents—25% annual quota + percentage not used in first preference

  iii. 4th preference: Married children of U.S. citizens—10% annual
       quota + percentage not used in first three preferences
  iv. 5th preference: Siblings of U.S. citizens—24% annual quota +
       unused percentages from earlier preferences.

While family members of immigrants and U.S. citizens from all nations of the world are eligible, definitions of "family" among Asians resulted in an unprecedented flow of individuals from that continent with the amendments to the 1952 Immigration Act. Among Asians, "family" refers to a much larger group than the nuclear family. Bonds with aging parents are strong. Obligatory and emotional relationships with siblings and married children also remain significant.

The extended family—aunts, uncles, cousins, and even more distant blood relatives—is considered part of the core-family group as well and may be recruited under the 10 percent of the sixth preference category—skilled and unskilled workers in occupations for which labor is in short supply in the United States. They may be sponsored to work in family-owned businesses. It is not the closeness of the blood tie but the bond that defines the relationship. In addition, family sizes in Asia have tended to be somewhat larger than those in Occidental countries, resulting in a higher influx of family-sponsored persons among Asians than among immigrants from other nations. In 1995 the number of family-sponsored immigrants from Asia was 84,177, and the immediate relatives of U.S. citizens, who were exempt from preference limits, numbered 82,944. Together, these two categories accounted for 36.3 percent of the family reunification immigrants from around the globe (Immigration and Naturalization Service 2000).

This segment of the immigrant population has not been limited by professional profiling through immigration policies and hence has tended to alter the face of the more recent Asian immigrant. Many who enter the United States under family reunification preferences do not have the skills, resources, academic and professional training, or other competencies that the majority of the first groups of post-1965 Asian immigrants brought to the United States.

THE UNDOCUMENTED IMMIGRANT STREAM

Undocumented immigrants are those who are present in the United States without the permission of the government. Often described as economic refugees, they flee their countries to escape economic oppression, famine, and drought but do not satisfy the definitions set by the United Nations High Commissioner for Refugees as a group that is persecuted. They do not have the legal documentation to reside in the United States but may have entered the country legally or illegally.

Despite perceptions that undocumented immigrants are those persons who slip across borders without appropriate documentation, the INS (1999) states that 91 percent of all illegal immigrants from Asian countries are "overstays" who fail to return to their homelands when the period of their visas expires. While they continue to reside in the United States, unlike undocumented immigrants who have few resources and cross the borders illegally in hopes of improving their economic opportunities, the "overstays" are often skilled individuals who are unable to find jobs commensurate with their expertise. In order to be employed in such occupations, they must have the requisite papers. Hence, they often work in low-paying service jobs or hold jobs within the ethnic community, usually without health, pension, or other benefits.

ASIAN NATIONS AFTER 1965

China

Between 1958 and 1960, about 20 to 30 million people lost their lives through malnutrition and famine because of Chinese Communist Party policies (Fairbank 1992). Soon after, domestic political and industrial changes became evident, and China became a nation of young people anxious for social and cultural change. In 1969 there were border clashes with the Soviet Union. That was also the year that Lin Biao was chosen as Mao Zedong's successor (but was killed in a plane crash in 1971), and the U.S. trade embargo against China was partially lifted. In 1970 China indicated a willingness to discuss substantive issues at the Warsaw talks, and in 1972 U.S. president Richard Nixon visited China, signifying a realignment of foreign relations. In 1976 one of the world's worst earthquakes shook Tangshan, killing between 300,000 and 600,000 people.

The period between 1966 and 1976, known as the Cultural Revolution, was also Chairman Mao's last decade, and China convulsed with a political struggle that resulted in extreme destruction, violations of human rights, disillusionment with socialist government, and increased dependence on family. The latter part of 1976 saw the defeat of the left wing of the Chinese Communist Party and the return of the right wing, which had been removed from power during the Cultural Revolution. At his death Mao left a China that needed rebuilding, and between 1978 and 1988, Deng Xiaoping turned to rebuilding the party and focusing on the Four Modernizations—in agriculture, industry, science and technology, and defense—which began the reorganization of the economy, society, and culture: (1) The aim of agrarian self-reliance of a community established by Mao was replaced by familial control of farming and agriculture under Deng, and Mao's doctrine of egalitarianism through elementary education, public health, and improved technology led to the entrepreneurial bent of many peasants under Deng and a move away from collective services. (2) Deng dramatically reversed economic policy by opening China to foreign trade, technology, and investment. Earlier, even in the late 1970s, the tendency had been to avoid foreign capital and maintain Soviet-like centralized control. By 1984 fourteen east coast ports were opened to foreign trade and investment. (3) Mao's anti-intellectualism was replaced by Deng's practical focus on facts and the use to which these facts could be put. Technical training was encouraged, and a link was established between research and production. (4) The People's Liberation Army became a part of the political structure, with 55 percent of the membership coming from the military. It was believed in the West that the military was displacing the Communist Party, but in 1969 China focused greater attention on military training, although attempts to separate the party and the People's Liberation Army failed. The most enduring outcome of the Cultural Revolution was education, and it has persisted. University education was supplemented by technical training in institutes as well as literacy and special extension programs via radio and television.

President Richard Nixon's visit to China in 1972 resulted in productive conversations between China and the United States. The last part of the twentieth century saw dramatic changes in the openness of China to trade and free enterprise. In December 1978 the policy of economic self-sufficiency was abandoned, and China began accepting loans and foreign investments, joining the International Monetary Fund and the World Bank, and the Communist Party established four Special Economic Zones for export. With the opening of trade, students and scholars were also granted the opportunity to travel abroad, which they began to do in record numbers as of 1979. By the late 1980s the Politburo decided to allow most commodity prices to be regulated by the market, though concerns surfaced that inflation and price hikes could threaten China's modernization programs.

China's autocracy had gained tremendous strength from Leninism but had managed to stay out of international view for decades. Nationalist troops spent several decades slaughtering between eight thousand and ten thousand Taiwanese demonstrators, and when the People's Republic of China consolidated control between 1949 and 1952, millions of unreported executions occurred. However, the Tiananmen Square Massacre of June 4, 1989—the killing of students who were peacefully demonstrating and calling for democratic freedom, governmental accountability, and the cleanup of Communist Party corruption—was televised worldwide. The electronic media shocked the world by opening its eyes to Chinese repression and violent suppression of its citizens. The reverberations of this massacre were evident in China and around the world for years.

Yet in the 1990s China evidenced the most rapid growth of any major world economy, with an annual average of 11 percent. In a move that resulted in considerable criticism, in 1994 U.S. president Bill Clinton removed the link between China's human-rights record and the Most Favored Nation trade status, and in 1998 China won the world's respect for its economic role in the Asian market crisis. The workforce of China in the 1990s totaled 630 million, with 52 percent in agriculture and forestry, 23 percent in industry, and 14.6 percent in services, including commerce. By 1999 its population had grown to 1.243 billion.

Tradition holds that the Chinese are a nonmigrating people, with the belief that even if they leave, it is because they are driven out and they always intend to return and be buried in the land of their ancestors (Purcell 1965). But the reality is that they have migrated for centuries (Skeldon 1996). In the third quarter of the twentieth century (1950–1978), emigration was restricted. The major migration flows at this time were between China, Hong Kong, and Taiwan. Some movement was seen in the 1950s, when about 11,000 students and scholars were sent to the Soviet Union, and more than 13,000 engineers, technicians, and support staff went to Tanzania to assist with railway construction in the early 1970s.

The momentous decision by the Chinese government to open its economy in 1978 to the outside world increased contact with foreigners and ended several decades of isolationism. With the evolution of free markets, individuals were able to accumulate more personal wealth, which allowed them greater prospects of travel. Travel was further enhanced when in 1985 identity cards were issued to all residents of China. The cards made it easier for them to move from one location to another without having to first obtain permission from their work units or other local authorities. The new Chinese Emigration and Immigration Law allowed citizens to travel outside the country for a number of reasons, including personal ones. It did not result in free travel, however, and although migration has increased since 1979, it is becoming ever more complex. Migrants from China can be divided into four major types: settlers, students, contract laborers, and illegal migrants (Skeldon 1996). Settlers may be either professionals or family members of individuals already established abroad and may be found in the United States. Because of the distance of the United States from China, and despite historical precedent, current contract laborers are less likely to travel to the United States than to neighboring countries. Students and undocumented Chinese migrants are numerous, and refugees of Chinese origin also live in the United States.

Professional emigrants and students. The Cold War that began with the end of World War II saw the movement of elite émigrés out of Nationalist China, and in 1953 about 2,000 visas were granted to Chinese refugees. At that time about 5,000 Chinese nationals who had come to the United States on scholarships from the Chinese government were considered "stranded" when China "fell," and they were granted permanent residency. These two groups of immigrants were significantly different from previous immigrants to the United States in that almost all of them were either university students or highly trained professionals. This was the beginning of the postwar "brain drain," first out of China and then out of other Asian countries.

For later-migrating Chinese, although some indicate that political factors caused the push out of China, the primary reason appeared to be the search for improved economic opportunities. Many indicated dislike of the political system in China and its methods of legislation and control, but the decision to leave the country was not particularly politically motivated (International Organization for Migration 1995). Nevertheless, the Chinese Student Protection Act (October 9, 1992) was passed to protect dissenting Republic of China Taiwanese students who were in the United States, especially in the wake of the Tiananmen Square massacre. This legislation permitted students who entered the

United States between June 4, 1989, and April 11, 1990, to adjust their status to permanent resident, and it resulted in a large increase in the number of Chinese immigrants during that period. The number declined during the mid- and late 1990s, but in 1995 the total was 4,213. It declined to 401 in 1996 and stood at 41 in 1998. Meanwhile, continued opportunities for Chinese professionals in the United States and the availability of second- and third-preference visas for workers have encouraged the continued immigration of professionals and students. Nevertheless, it is still difficult to leave China, and there is still no real freedom of movement despite the increased numbers of emigrants. Furthermore, the migration flows have continued to be heavily biased toward graduate students, professionals, and wealthier people, all of whom tend to maintain contact with their homeland. This group also constitutes a fairly small segment of the total population of China, the majority of which is unaffected by migration.

Chinese boat people. The emigration of political refugees out of China in the 1950s was followed by the flow of less educated and less professional groups, many of whom came not through the legal immigration channels, but illegally in overcrowded boats, leading to the nomenclature of "boat people." This flow of undocumented immigrants continues in the twenty-first century as the media report frequent apprehensions of boats with Chinese peasants off the shores of the United States and Canada. Estimates are that approximately 100,000 people annually were entering the United States illegally from China in the 1990s, and 500,000 Chinese were waiting for opportunities to move to the West from Russia, Eastern Europe, Southeast Asia, and South America. Although those immigrants who attempt to enter by boat garner the media attention, the large majority of illegal entrants arrive via Central America and then travel by land or small plane (Skeldon 1996).

Many who travel to the United States illegally use the services of traffickers and come from the coastal provinces of China. A large number arrive in the United States via Central and Eastern European countries, and many spend several years saving the money necessary to buy their way out of China (International Organization for Migration 1995). Dissatisfaction with living conditions in China and concerns about economic prospects, despite the nation's unprecedented economic boom, motivate the emigrations. As in earlier years, families often pool their resources to send a representative abroad.

China has experienced a resurgence in crime, and the smuggling of individuals to the United States has become a lucrative business, with traffickers charging $30,000 to $50,000 to transport one person. Most men and women thus transported are kept as virtual slave laborers. They must pay 10 percent of the price before boarding the boat, with promises of repayment, in the spirit of the credit system earlier in the last century, once they arrive in the United States. Prostitution and drug smuggling are common means of paying off the high debts incurred in this process.

Media reports and professional literature on undocumented immigrants from China indicate that approximately 100,000 people entered the United States illegally in the 1990s (Skeldon 1996). Nevertheless, the Immigration and Naturalization Service (1999a) did not include China in the top twenty sending countries in its estimates of the illegal immigrant population residing in the United States in 1996. With these numbers, China would place firmly among the top ten countries.

Refugees and asylees. While less is written about Chinese refugees than about other Chinese immigrants to the United States, the U.S. Immigration and Naturalization Service (2000) indicated that between 1961 and 1997, exactly 32,788 refugees and asylees were granted permanent resident status. The largest influx was during the decade 1971–1980, when 13,760 refugees entered the country. In 1997, although only 693 individuals were granted resident status, 2,377 people from the People's Republic of China filed new claims for asylum, and at the beginning of the year 15,068 cases were already pending (U.S. Department of Justice, 1999a).

Family reunification. The pattern of Chinese emigration has been similar for professionals, nonprofessionals, students, and illegal migrants. Usually a male member of the family emigrates first, with the aim of establishing a base from which he can send money to his family and community in China and eventually have his wife and children join him in the foreign country. Thus, even in travel to the United States, almost all categories of recent immigrants have been men, although single professional women and students are increasingly entering the country. If the emigrant is a student or a professional, the time to reunification appears to be less lengthy than if the individual is not a professional, and certainly less lengthy than if the person based in the

United States is an illegal immigrant. Nevertheless, individuals from all groups maintain strong family ties and send money to their families in China as often as they are able.

Changes in U.S. immigration policies that encourage family reunification are resulting in a fairly heavy flow of immigrants from China. In each of the years between 1995 and 1998, between 41,000 and 51,000 legal immigrants entered the United States (U.S. Immigration and Naturalization Service 2000). If immigrants from Hong Kong are included, another 7,000 to 12,000 can be added to these numbers. Many immigrants are relatives of Chinese Americans and Chinese immigrants who may have been in the country for several years or generations. Modifications in immigration policies have begun to affect the profile even of the legal Chinese immigrant. While professionals in the sciences and technology are entering in large numbers, there are large segments of the newer immigrant pool of relatives that are not required to be the professionals needed in the United States in order to enter. Since they come under reunification policies, they do not have to meet the qualifications required earlier of their sponsoring relatives. Many of the immigrants are not only nonprofessional but poorly educated, with little English-language competence.

It is clear, then, that post-1965 emigrants from China represent a bimodal group of educated and uneducated, wealthy and poor, and legal and undocumented migrants. Most are not political refugees; although there are some people of Chinese origin from Southeast Asia who do fall into this category, there are relatively few political refugees from China itself. Most left to better their opportunities. The emigration increased when China adopted a less isolationist policy and as global opportunities became more apparent to the Chinese people. Despite the relatively large numbers of emigrants from China, they represent a very small part of the Chinese population, most of which is not affected by emigration policies or migration flows.

India

On August 15, 1947, India achieved freedom after four hundred years of British rule. In his famous speech, the first prime minister, Jawaharlal Nehru, said, "Long years ago we made a tryst with destiny. . . . At the stroke of the midnight hour, when the world sleeps, India will awake to life and freedom." With the stroke of that hour, the country began reordering political, social, and economic power, and on an international scale, the stroke of that hour marked the beginning of the end of British imperialism. Over the centuries, India has come into contact with many civilizations and has learned to integrate much into its own functioning. Despite gaining its freedom, the nation chose to remain within the British Commonwealth of Nations. It adopted the British system of parliamentary democracy and retained the judicial, administrative, defense, and educational structures established by the British. To date, it is the world's largest democracy, with universal adult suffrage. Its constitution safeguards all people from discrimination on the grounds of race, religion, creed, or gender. It also guarantees freedom of speech, expression, and belief, assembly and association, migration, acquisition of property, and choice of occupation or trade (Ministry of External Affairs 2000).

In the fifty-five years since independence, modern India has emerged as one of the fastest-developing economies in the world. It is the seventh-largest nation in the area and second in population after China, having crossed the one billion mark in May 2000. It is the world's largest producer of rice, and the largest exporter of tea, jute, and computer programs. It adopted a mixed economic policy on a five-year-plan basis, working toward improving both agricultural output and industry. Furthermore, in 1990 it opened its doors to liberalization and trade and currently has a 6 percent annual growth rate. In science and technology, India is beginning to match the West, making great strides in nuclear energy, computer hardware and software, and medical research.

In 1989 the Social Security Fund was established to meet the insurance requirements of the disadvantaged, and in 1999, 2.5 million people received some support under various social security programs. Some of these provide death benefits, others provide coverage for property damage, others provide supplemental hospital care, and yet another, in an innovative attempt to protect female children, provides all girls under the age of eighteen a savings account from which they receive annual unrestricted disbursements.

While there is an India that is highly successful, particularly after the "Green Revolution" of the 1970s that made India self-sufficient in graining and staved off starvation, and while there is an India that is highly forward-looking, there is also an India that is plagued with age-old illnesses and numerous new ones. The nation has been unable to control its population explosion. Rural poverty is extreme, and as migrants move to the cities in search of jobs, the condition of the urban poor deteriorates further. Overcrowding, malnutrition, and disease are rampant. While universal health care is available, preventable diseases persist, and sexually transmitted diseases, including Acquired Immune Deficiency Syndrome (AIDS), are spreading rapidly. Illiteracy is high, and the exploitation of the vulnerable persists. Corruption and bribery are prevalent in all strata of society, and crime organizations are gaining a foothold in large urban areas.

Nevertheless, awareness of social problems and issues affecting the poor, women, and children has increased. Almost 85 percent of the population belongs to oppressed groups, based on caste, class, rural tribe, minority status, or disability, and the government has developed a number of welfare programs to alleviate such oppression and provide assistance in coping with the associated problems. The voluntary sector has also become particularly active, with the establishment of advocacy groups and nongovernmental organizations that address the needs of the disenfranchised.

Defense continues to concern India. The country has experienced several clashes with Pakistan since the initial bloodbaths that resulted from the 1947 partition of India into the two countries of India and Pakistan. A major war was fought in 1965, over the territory of Kashmir, and another in 1971, over East Pakistan, which gained its independence to become Bangladesh. A border war with China in 1962 resulted in lasting suspicion of that country. Skirmishes with Pakistan continue along the Kashmir front, and religious intolerance became more evident in the 1990s than it had been for years since the country's partition.

As the world's greatest democracy and a secular state, India enjoys freedoms not available to many in Asian countries. Nevertheless, because of a number of social and economic factors, a range of opportunities and experiences are unavailable to a large segment of the population. Whether they are among the poor and less educated or among the wealthy, educated, and professional, many perceive opportunities for advancement to be much greater in nations outside India, particularly in the developed Western countries. Although science, technology, and economic opportunities are improving dramatically, and although agricultural developments are consistently progressing, the tremendous overpopulation places constraints on the numbers of people that each industry, profession, or educational institution can absorb.

India has been an open society for centuries, and the migration of its population, unlike that of citizens of other Asian nations, is not a new phenomenon. Indians have long moved to different parts of the world to settle whenever the opportunity was ripe (Saran 1985). The push out of India is generally economic, and the pull to Western countries, likewise, is the possibility of an improved quality of life. Like Chinese immigrants to the United States, Indian immigrants, because of visa constraints, are usually highly professional and educated, family members of U.S. citizens, or undocumented entrants or "overstays."

Professional emigrants and students. From 1965 until 1987 the largest segment of the emigrants from India, particularly to the United States, bore little resemblance to those who came to the United States at the beginning of the twentieth century. No longer was the majority composed of Sikhs, as was the first wave; no longer were they engaged in agricultural work; and no longer were they concentrated on the West Coast. Liberalized immigration laws in the United States and entry criteria effectively limited immigration from India until the mid-1980s to those who were professional or seeking higher education. Thus, the large wave that emigrated from India between 1965 and 1987 was distinctly different from the populations that emigrated to other countries and also different from other groups that have come to the United States. Indian immigrants to the United States during those years did not represent a cross-section of the Indian subcontinent. As a result of personal reasons for emigrating and restrictions on immigrants from Asia, most were the educated and professional elite. India's educational system has a distinctly British orientation, and since the English language is the medium of higher education, most Indians who came to the United States before 1985 were fluent in English and had some exposure to Western values and beliefs.

Early post-1965 immigration opportunities opened the doors particularly to physicians and scientists. Large contingents of Indian scientists began the emigration flow from India well into the 1980s. As in China and other Asian countries, emigration fit into India's modernization efforts; it improved education and, with advances in science and technology, was able to train high-quality professionals in a number of fields. The opportunities for these graduates to apply their skills in profitable occupations were limited, however, and many chose to look outside India's borders for employment. There has long been a tendency of "settler societies" to drain talent from developing countries (Kitano and Daniels 1995). Stevens and Vermeulen (1972) reported that by the beginning of the 1970s, close to 10 percent of the physicians who had been trained in India were practicing abroad, primarily in the United States and Great Britain.

Because India has always had a dual perception of women as both intelligent and dependent, the majority of the country's middle-class women receive college degrees, and many continue with graduate education to establish professions. Thus, while many of the professional emigrants from 1965 to 1985 to the United States were males, most brought their professional wives with them, had their wives join them shortly after they arrived, or, if they were unmarried, returned to India to marry and bring back their new wives. The immigration flow of Indians to the United States since 1965 has been relatively evenly distributed between men and women. Since the 1980s there has been an increase in immigration of single middle-class Indian women seeking graduate education. Most of these, like their male counterparts, find occupations in the United States after they complete their education. Changes in the flow of female emigration reflect changes in Indian society, a greater degree of independence for women, and more recognition by Indian parents that women have the ability to function without a father or husband.

Indian immigrants to the United States tend to be a little older than other Asian immigrants, with a median age of 34.8 years. They are better educated and come from fairly wealthy families in India. Even students who emigrate are more likely to leave India after having completed an undergraduate degree. The tendency to travel abroad for graduate, rather than undergraduate, education results from a number of factors, not least among them the availability of sufficient high-quality undergraduate programs in India. Graduate programs in most fields are relatively few, and opportunities to acquire postgraduate education are better abroad. Thus large numbers of students began entering the United States in 1965 for graduate education. For India, however, this, along with the emigration of professionals, constituted a significant "brain drain," as, despite earlier intentions, the majority did not return after receiving their graduate degrees; instead they found positions in the United States and changed their student visas into immigrant ones as employment became available.

The migration of computer programmers and businessmen and -women burgeoned in the 1990s and continued into the turn of the century. These and other groups of legal Indian immigrants to the United States numbered between 33,000 and 43,000 from the years 1995 to 1998 (U.S. Immigration and Naturalization Service 2000). The training and experience of young Indians in the field of computer technology provided sufficient support for the Indian industry as well as for the foreign one until the end of 2000. The year 2001 saw a dramatic decline in the U.S. computer industry, which has significantly affected the rate of emigration of these technocrats. Future trends in the industry will color immigration patterns for this group. The opening of Indian markets has resulted in an increased flow of entrepreneurs between the United States and India. Not all of them choose to emigrate, for opportunities for success are increasing for many in India, and in many sectors the quality of life in India is superior to that to which they could have access in the United States.

Since there were few U.S. citizens of Indian origin before 1965, the family reunification visa was not applicable to entrants from India. In addition, there were few, if any, individuals seeking amnesty. Thus until the mid-1980s the profile of the Indian emigrant to the United States was that of a person with high professional achievement or of a student seeking a graduate university degree.

Family reunification. Under the family reunification provision of the Immigration and Naturalization Act of 1965 (PL 89–236), U.S. citizens and permanent residents can sponsor their immediate family members for immigration. Since there were relatively few Indian immigrants in the United States before 1965, the provision had little application to this population in the 1960s and early 1970s. Several Indian immigrants of the 1960s, 1970s, and 1980s are now citizens or permanent residents of the United States, are well established economically, and are in positions to sponsor relatives.

Many of these newer emigrants are not as skilled as their sponsoring relatives, and thus the profile of the Indian in the United States since the 1990s has changed. Evidence of the less professional level of Indian migration is apparent in New York, Houston, Chicago, and other major cities. Indians dominate the newsstand industry in these areas, and a large percentage of hotels and motels are owned by Indians. The more recent immigrants from India are often without much education, and many are aging parents of immigrants, with little competence in the English language and high rates of dependency.

Undocumented immigrants. While much media information is available on the illegal entry of individuals to the United States from several
countries, little is known about undocumented immigrants from India.
The estimates of the Immigration and Naturalization Service (2000)
are high, approximately 33,000 in 1996 (eighteenth of the top twenty
sending countries). Reports suggest South Asian human smuggling
rings (Haniffa 2001), but the media rarely mention this, perhaps
because most undocumented Indians are believed to be overstays.
Neither group draws the attention of the public as do the boat people.

These Indians find themselves in the unenviable position of not
having access to professions for which they have been trained. In an
article in *India Abroad*, a newspaper published for expatriate Indians, an
angry young woman complained of the injustice of the plight of undocumented immigrants who are professionally skilled but are denied the
right to work in the United States, when legally admitted unskilled individuals enjoy the support of the welfare system:

> A number of doctors, engineers, nurses, and master's degree
> holders . . . [live] . . . as undocumented people. . . . Doctors may
> be pumping gas, engineers may be selling candies and a nurse
> may be working as a baby-sitter, just for a need of a work permit.
> (DIDI 2000:4)

On the other hand, few Indians leave their country for the United
States as refugees—though at the beginning of 1997 there were 6,801
pending cases of asylum seekers, and during the year another 3,776
individuals made application (U.S. Department of Justice, 1999a).

Despite the persistent perception that Indians have an elite socioeconomic profile, not all Indian emigrants fit that profile. Many of the
Indian emigrants to Commonwealth countries, such as Great Britain,
have very different backgrounds, lacking education and therefore being
forced to take unskilled jobs. In the United States, however, immigration profiling has ensured the professional bent of Indian immigrants,
but family reunification and the continuing entry of undocumented
immigrants can be expected to prolong the downward trend of the
group's socioeconomic conditions in the United States.

The Philippines

On July 4, 1946, the new Republic of the Philippines was inaugurated,
and the nation was free in theory, if not in practice. It remained

economically dependent on the United States. It also had to cope with the ravages of World War II, in which nearly 5 percent of its population was killed or injured, and malnutrition and disease, particularly malaria and cholera, affected large numbers of people. The economy was shattered, farmers and peasants were discontented, a shortage of goods and war surpluses resulted in an enormous black market, and corruption and lawlessness exploded in the nation.

During the Japanese occupation, an important unofficial anti-Japanese guerrilla group emerged through the united efforts of peasant organizations and the outlawed Partido Komunistang Pilipinas that had been established in 1930. The group known as the Hukbalahap (or the Huk) and the new republic were often engaged in confrontation and violence as landlords attempted to reclaim their lands. Relationships with the Huks and the progress of the country were inconsistent under the leadership of Manuel Roxas, the first president of the republic, who was generally inactive. At his death in 1948 Elpidio Quirino became president. He continued the inactivity, and by 1950 the national treasury was empty, government employees had not been paid, official corruption was skyrocketing, and while many Filipino businessmen had made large fortunes, the majority of the population lived in abject poverty and despair. By the end of that year disillusionment with the government was widespread, and the decision to involve the Philippines in the Korean conflict was unpopular. The Huks became a threat to American air, naval, and military bases. To suppress their revolt, the United States provided loans to reorganize and support the Philippine army. Quirino was advised to appoint a former guerrilla leader, Ramon Magsaysay, as the secretary of defense. The choice was a good one, as Magsaysay quickly reorganized the army and by the end of the year had succeeded in disbanding the Huks, who themselves had fallen out of favor with the populace because of their lack of discipline and ruthlessness.

Magsaysay proved to be a dynamic leader, and in 1953 he defeated Quirino in the race for the presidency by an overwhelming majority. Successful in combating the Huks, he also introduced measures to help rural reconstruction, ensure resolution of agrarian problems, and provide tenants assistance with their legal rights. After his election Magsaysay fought to give the masses the right to justice and attempted to remove weakness in the economy. American support was strong, and the Laurel-Langley Trade Agreement of 1954 gave Filipinos the same economic rights in the United States as Americans had in the Philippines.

On the other hand, the defense treaties established between the United States and the Philippines legally bound the Filipino government to continue supporting the presence of large American military bases in Luzon. The dynamism of Magsaysay and his administrative competencies resulted in the successful establishment of a republic distant from communism, but he died in an air crash in 1957, at the height of his popularity.

The Liberal Party regained power in 1961, replacing the Nacionalistas, who returned to office in 1965 with the election of Ferdinand Marcos. He initiated several programs on the improvement of public works, the building of bridges, the establishment of health centers and schools, and the general beautification of the nation. During his first term the rice production was so successful that the Philippines began exporting rice for the first time in many years. The nation was also more involved in world affairs, and the number of communications facilities increased dramatically. Yet problem areas did exist. Corruption in the government was worse than it had been before, crime was on the upswing, the gap between rich and poor continued to widen, and the Huks regrouped to cause unrest and violence in Central Luzon. Furthermore, Marcos's decision to dispatch a contingent of two thousand Filipino soldiers to fight in the Vietnam War—against public opinion and contrary to his position before he became president—resulted in particular dissatisfactions, evidenced by several anti-Marcos and anti-U.S. demonstrations by students between 1968 and 1972. In 1972 President Marcos imposed martial law, shut down newspapers, banned rallies, and began arresting his enemies, including Senator Benigno Aquino, the opposition leader. Aquino was exiled to the United States in 1980 when he developed heart disease, but when he returned in 1983, a military escort shot him in the back of the head as he descended the steps of the aircraft.

When Marcos began his second term in 1969 through a reelection that was believed to have been rigged, the national treasury was empty and the country was faced with dire economic conditions. The prices of most commodities soared, thousands of people were unemployed, the population grew faster than the economy, and the Huks continued to terrorize Central Luzon. Some called this period "the rape of democracy" (Zaide 1970:294), particularly since Marcos was unable to curb the bribery and corruption in the government. The new constitution extended the term of the president to six years, with no term limits.

Marcos's agenda was his own aggrandizement, with little concern for the nation. Through bribery and selective promotions, he brought the armed forces under his personal control. With his wife and friends, he established monopolies and cartels in all areas of the economic structure, depleting the Philippine economy.

The assassination of Aquino reverberated throughout the world despite limited news coverage, and within the nation it caused an uprising against the years of repression. It also precipitated a loss of confidence among businessmen, and as capital began to leave the country, the nation faced bankruptcy (Weir 2000). Concerned about his fading credibility, Marcos announced a new election in 1985, suspecting that the opposition was disorganized and unprepared and that he would once again achieve a resounding victory. However, Corazon Aquino, the widow of the assassinated opposition leader, declared her candidacy for president, and the National Movement for Free Elections, a volunteer group of 30,000, protected the election from the fraud and abuse that had characterized earlier contests. Disagreements between the two parties and their perceptions of the vote counting resulted in about two weeks of violence and dissidence. It became clear that the Marcos regime had lost its power, and the U.S. government sent Marcos a message that if he did not step down there would be civil war. President Ronald Reagan extended an invitation to Marcos, stating that he, his family, and close associates would be welcome in the United States. Corazon Aquino was sworn into office as president on February 25, 1986, and at her insistence Marcos left the Philippines for Hawaii.

Aquino started her presidency during a period of economic impoverishment, yet the mood of the country was optimistic. Beginning with the restoration of the basic civil liberties of free speech, freedom of assembly, and a free press, she completely overhauled the government and the armed forces. A new constitution, ratified in 1987, limited the presidency to a single six-year term. Although Aquino was unable to address the underlying social and economic problems of the nation, and although corruption reemerged as an issue early in her administration (Goodno 1991), she is credited with restoring the Filipino democratic process. She was replaced by Fidel Ramos, a man of integrity who worked to establish economic stability and to improve the energy, communications, and transportation infrastructure, as well as to introduce the economic and financial reforms needed for a competitive industrial economy. When his term expired, popular elections in May

1998 resulted in the selection of the former movie star Joseph Estrada, revealing a secure foothold for democracy in the Philippines (Weir 2000). However, a threat of a coup in January 2001 ousted Estrada, who was increasingly tainted by scandal revolving around bribery, plunder of the economy, and corruption. His trial on corruption charges began on October 1, 2001.

Throughout the problems and progress of the Philippines the United States has been a continual presence. The impact has been ongoing exposure to American interests and lifestyles and a persistent belief in the American Dream. Some Filipinos still consider the benefits of the nation's becoming a U.S. state, believing that such a move would solve many of the nation's ills. The unique relationship between the Philippines and the United States since the occupation by Japan has sustained an interest in emigration. Changes in U.S. immigration policies have fueled the high rates of exit, and most post-1965 emigrants to the United States have been professionals. Political exiles and refugees make up a portion of the emigrants, as well as those who left the Philippines under the family reunification provisions of the 1965 Immigration Act. In 1965 the number of immigrants to the United States was 2,963, in the following five years this number increased to 83,086, and in the two decades from 1971 to 1990, immigrants from the Philippines numbered 855,500 (Kurian 1994). Emigration from the Philippines to the United States since 1965 has been higher than from any other Asian country.

Professional emigrants and students. The emigration of highly educated professionals from the Philippines constituted part of the worldwide brain drain from Third World and developing countries to the developed countries of the West. Trained medical professionals made up a major part of the emigrants. In 1966, 2,474 Filipino doctors resided in the United States (Council on Medical Education 1966), while in 1965, in Manila, the ratio of physicians to patients was 1:671, and in rural areas it was significantly worse, at 1:4,979 (Bowers 1965). During the same period, there were 6,000 Filipino nurses in the United States. The Philippines was one of three developing economies (the others were India and Pakistan) most strongly affected by the brain drain in the mid-1960s (Committee on Government Operations 1968). Between 1966 and 1976 occupational emigrants from the Philippines accounted for approximately 50 percent of all people entering through the preference system and about one-third of all Filipinos admitted to the United States during that period (Liu, Ong, and Rosenstein 1995), with most being health professionals and their dependents. Because of the influx of physicians, particularly from the Philippines and India, and in response to an outcry by American medical graduates who felt ousted because of the increased competition, Congress passed the Health Professionals Assistance Act of 1977, making it more difficult for foreign medical graduates to enter the country.

The U.S. government, however, was not the only institution that affected the emigration of talent from developing countries in the 1960s by providing foreign aid to developing countries that sent highly trained professionals. Academic institutions were major influences on decisions of Filipinos to emigrate. Among those who studied outside the Philippines, 50 percent of the women and 33 percent of the men permanently left the nation, and 7 percent of all graduates of Filipino colleges emigrated (Bello, Lynch, and Makil 1969).

This pattern of professional migration to the United States persisted into the fourth quarter of the twentieth century. Between 1971 and 1985, 36,258 health professionals left the Philippines for the United States. During the same period 12,127 scientists, engineers, and computer scientists entered the United States (Wong 1995b). With severe shortages of nurses and elementary schoolteachers, the United States in 2001 again began actually recruiting Filipinos. It is anticipated that the immigration of Filipino nurses particularly will soar in the near future. Thus this group of immigrants is distinguished from others by high educational levels, lack of ties to pre-1965 immigration, and the tendency to enter the country as families, unlike the earlier emigrants who left families behind and planned to sponsor their entry at a later date.

Family reunification. Reunification of families from the land of origin has been a major impetus for the emigration of relatives of pre-1965 immigrants to the United States. Since the Filipino immigrants of the late 1960s through the 1980s have been here long enough to become citizens, they are also able to sponsor relatives from their homeland. This "chain migration" is evidenced among a large segment of the post-1965 emigrants to the United States (Liu, Ong, and Rosenstein 1995). Family reunification has involved two groups, one consisting of family members of pre-1965, less professional immigrants and the other composed of family members of the highly professional post-1965 immigrants.

Interviews with people before their departure from the Philippines revealed that often the eldest child, either male or female, was the first to emigrate to the United States, thus becoming the first link in the migration chain. An assessment of all family members who could be sponsored (Medina and Nativadad 1985) showed that between 1966 and 1985 those who entered the United States through the preference system constituted 55 percent to 91 percent of the total immigrants from the Philippines, and in 1995 the 40,417 family reunification immigrants accounted for 79 percent of all entrants from that nation. Although "dual chain migration" includes both relative-selective migration and occupational-selective migration, the lengthening of both chains relies on family reunification provisions. Despite the different categories used for the first-link entry into the United States, the immigration of family members increases the chain.

Political exiles and refugees. Current Filipino refugee emigrants to the United States are relatively low. In 1995, the number of refugees admitted was only 80 (Immigration and Naturalization Service 2000). The U.S. Department of Justice (1999a) indicated that only 15 asylees from the Philippines were granted resident status, although in 1997, 3,484 cases had been filed with Immigration and Naturalization Service asylum officers. The number of political exiles was greater during the years of the Marcos regime. Most notable among them were Benigno and Corazon Aquino, who eventually returned to the Philippines. Legal Filipino immigrants constitute a large segment of the immigrant flow from Asia. In the years between 1995 and 1998, 33,000 to 55,000 individuals entered the United States (U.S. Immigration and Naturalization Service 2000).

Undocumented immigrants. Although little in the literature discusses the undocumented immigrant group from the Philippines, the Immigration and Naturalization Service (2000) estimated that in 1996 there were approximately 95,000 undocumented residents of Filipino origin residing in the United States, and the Philippines are the sixth-greatest source of illegal immigration. As with other undocumented residents of Asian origin, the majority are believed to be overstays, and only a small part of the group is believed to have crossed U.S. borders illegally. They are probably visitors, students, or business people with temporary visas, and more likely than not they have an educational and personal resource profile that might be similar to that of legal immigrants. On the other hand, the lack of appropriate papers makes it impossible for them to find occupational positions commensurate with their experience and abilities.

Korea[3]

South Korea since the Korean War has been characterized by two strong, expanding, and opposing forces. The society has been controlled from the top by an increasingly oppressive and systematic authoritarian coalition of political, bureaucratic, economic, and security groups dominated by a dictator. On the other side has been a growing collection of oppositional and confrontational forces both within and outside the political structure. Since the war, three attempts at establishing a democratic government have been made—1960–1961, 1979–1980, and 1987–1988. The first two fell at the hands of ruthless men who gained control of the political system and ended the short periods of freedom (Eckert et al. 1990). The third ended with the presidency of Roh Tae Woo, who moved to eliminate authoritarian and corrupt practices. However, he, too, consolidated his control of the political system. Only in the most recent presidency, that of Kim Dae-jung (1998–), has Korea truly experienced democracy.

From 1948 to 2000, seven men led South Korea. Rhee Syngman (1948–1961), whose tyrannical rule was fraught with corruption, fraud, and coercion, saw the country through the war and eventually gained control of the political system. He was forced to resign because of a nationwide protest against election fraud in 1960, and the dissatisfaction was exacerbated by socioeconomic conditions in which university students were unable to find employment commensurate with their training. For a few months after the fall of Rhee, the nation enjoyed democratic freedom, and restraints on political activity and freedom of the press were removed. However, Park Chung-hee (1961–1979) took control through a military coup, and despite public opposition, he signed the Korea-Japan Basic Treaty in 1965 and excused the Japanese for war reparations in exchange for economic assistance. By 1972 he declared martial law, restricting civil liberties and removing political opponents. But he was able to achieve tremendous economic growth and development, positioning Korea in the international market. Despite this progress, dissatisfaction ran high, and on October 26, 1979, the director of the Korean Central Intelligence Agency assassinated Park, and the acting president, Choe Kyuha (1979–1980), was formally elected. Although he lifted the ban on criticism and dissent, he quickly lost power to General Chun Doo-whan, who became acting director of the intelligence agency while retaining his position as head of the Army Security Command. Demonstrations for Chun's resignation had little impact, and via another coup Chun assumed control and was elected president (1980–1988). Despite his totalitarian rule, he was able to secure $4 billion in loans from Japan, and Seoul was selected as the site for the 1988 Summer Olympics. Under pressure from widespread sources, Chun named his successor, Roh Tae Woo (1988–1993), who, contrary to Chun's expectations, called for democratic reforms and improved relationships with North Korea, Moscow, and Beijing. Seoul also opened diplomatic ties with 43 other countries, resulting in a total of 171 nations. Many criticized Roh's economic policies, stating that although macroeconomic measures indicated growth, the effects on the majority of the population were minimal.

In 1993 power was transferred from a military leader to a civilian, and Kim Young-sam (1993–1998) pledged to build a new Korea grounded in reform and change that would oust misconduct and corruption, revitalize the economy, and enhance national discipline (Hong and Yums 2000). He was unable to fulfill these promises, and corruption and scandals in his family and administration led to his growing unpopularity. Kim Dae-jung assumed the presidency in 1998 in the first peaceful transfer of power between parties through the legitimate political process. Known for his commitment to democracy, human rights, freedom, and justice, Kim Dae-jung was recommended ten times for the Nobel Peace Prize, and on October 13, 2000, the Norwegian Nobel Committee announced its decision to award the prize to him "for his work for democracy and human rights in South Korea and in East Asia in general, and for peace and reconciliation with North Korea in particular" (Cheong Wa Dae 2001).

Kim's "sunshine policy" (now called "engagement") toward North Korea resulted in unprecedented business and cultural links between the two Koreas and encouraged normalization between them. In a congenial, groundbreaking meeting, Kim Jong-il of North Korea and Kim Dae-jung of South Korea spoke in June 2000 about reunification. In August 2000 families who had been separated in the two Koreas were given the opportunity to meet for the first time since the war. And, in Australia, at the 2000 Summer Olympics, representatives from North and South Korea marched together holding a banner with the map of a united Korea.

In the modernization of South Korea during the last quarter of the twentieth century, two social trends emerged—rapid urbanization and dramatic increases in literacy and education. The latter were essential to the former. However, education and increased freedom of thought resulted in open public outrage against authoritarianism and human rights violations. The rapid expansion of the 1980s also brought improvements in living conditions for many South Koreans, and although not all lived comfortably, the homeless population was negligible. The industrial sector employed approximately 46 percent of the workforce in 1988, and agriculture, forestry, and fishing employed another 21 percent. Young people from rural areas migrated to cities, where job opportunities in the industrial workforce seemed more attractive. This movement resulted in a crisis in the agricultural area, and the government began directing funds into improving rural conditions. Many of these efforts were successful at the outset but later fell prey to corruption and fraud.

With general improvements in the economy, job opportunities continued to rise. Expectations of economic reform associated with democracy were not met, however, and the late 1980s saw rising dissatisfaction with working conditions and wages. The number of strikes increased, and large groups of workers emigrated to the Middle East as construction workers.

Health conditions have improved dramatically since the war, and life expectancy has increased by fifteen years for men and nineteen for women. Nevertheless, health problems remain fairly severe, with infant mortality rates significantly higher than those of other East Asian countries. The status of women began improving by the middle of the 1980s, yet even in 1987, women accounted for only 28 percent of the total enrollment in higher education, and only 16 percent of the teachers were women. By 1988, 43.6 percent of the women were in the workforce, but lower-class women continued to suffer. Many turned to the entertainment industry of brothels, bars, massage parlors, and discos. In such environments, the abuse, exploitation, and shame that most Korean women experienced in ancient times persisted.

Koreans, like all others, have migrated to places that offered economic opportunity. While many in the past few decades moved from rural to urban areas within Korea, in the 1980s close to 4 million

Koreans were believed to live outside the country. Approximately 1.7 million lived in China and had assumed Chinese citizenship. In the Soviet Union, there were 430,000 ethnic Koreans, and about 700,000 were living in Japan. By the end of 1988 North America had attracted 1.2 million Koreans. But several thousand emigrated to Central and South America (85,000), the Middle East (62,000), Western Europe (40,000), other Asian countries (27,000), and Africa (25,000). While a number of these individuals emigrated permanently, because of Korea's rapid economic expansion there were considerable numbers of temporary emigrants such as businessmen and -women, technical personnel, students, and construction workers (U.S. Library of Congress 1990). While most return to Korea, it is very likely that large numbers, particularly among the students, will remain in other countries. The number of Korean immigrants to the United States increased dramatically after 1965. This third wave of Korean immigration was so large that in 1975, Korea was one of the three main sending countries (the others were the Philippines and China), and the United States had the second-largest Korean community outside Korea (Hyung-chan 1977).

Professional emigrants and students. A large number of the third-wave Korean immigrants are highly educated, much like other Asians who entered the United States after 1965. Unlike some of the newer Asian immigrant groups, however, the third wave of the Korean immigration pattern has tended to include a large number of housewives and children who have come as dependents of male immigrants. Other Asian groups have included significant numbers of women, but many of them have come either on their own merit or as educated wives of immigrant men and so have been able to become engaged in professional occupations quickly.

The majority of Koreans who entered the United States after 1965 are economic migrants who hoped to improve their economic status. Koreans also emigrated to gain access to a superior education, particularly a college education. While many immigrated as students, a large number of families emigrated in hopes of ensuring that their children would receive quality higher education. In interviews, Koreans applying for visas to enter the United States consistently indicated three aspects of life that they found to be preferable in the United States: (a) higher wages, (b) rewards for hard work and ability, and (c) a more favorable political environment (Insook et al. 1990).

Korean men who emigrated in the late 1960s and early 1970s were professionals who had expected to obtain commensurate positions in the United States, but their lack of language proficiency forced them into low-paying jobs. Immigrants of the 1980s and 1990s learned of the difficulties encountered by those earlier emigrants and left Korea with the intention of beginning their own businesses in lieu of seeking jobs with American companies.

U.S. influences. Individual and economic motives are not the only reasons for the migration of Koreans to the United States. Because of the long-standing military, political, and economic linkages between the two countries since the Korean War, the cultural influences of the United States on the Korean nation have been significant. Even before the Korean War, at the beginning of the twentieth century, numbers of American Presbyterian and Methodist missionaries established schools and hospitals in the country. While this may account for some continuing influx of Koreans to the United States, census data show that in the 1990s Korean immigration substantially diminished.

The strong U.S. military presence in Korea increased the attraction of the United States in a number of ways. Intermarriage between U.S. servicemen and Korean women led to the emigration of more than 3,000 women annually in the 1970s and 1980s. Furthermore, the availability of U.S. television propagating the lifestyle of this nation caught the attention of middle-class Koreans, making them aware that the quality of life in the United States was preferable to that which they had at home (Min 1998). Although Koreans continue to emigrate to the United States, immigration from other nations surpassed them by the mid-1990s. Between 1981 and 1996, 453,018 Koreans emigrated to the United States, making this immigrant group the seventh largest overall, and the fifth among the Asian nations, after the Philippines (843,741), Vietnam (719,239), China (539,267), and India (498,309). In 1996 it became clear that Korea was no longer among the top ten sending nations (Immigration and Naturalization Service 1999b). In the years 1995 to 1998, the numbers of Korean immigrants to the United States dropped below 18,000, dipping to a low of 13,691 in 1998 (U.S. Immigration and Naturalization Service, 2000).

Political exiles, refugees, and undocumented immigrants. Indications are that the number of political refugees and asylees to the United States from the Koreas is very small. In 1995 the Immigration and

Naturalization Service indicated that only five refugee or asylee adjustments were made. On the other hand, the number of undocumented immigrants is thought to be relatively high. In October 1996, 30,000 people entered the country without proper authorization (Immigration and Naturalization Service 1999a). News reports in July 2000 indicated that a number of the undocumented immigrants were elementary school children (Soh, 2000a), those without work permits (Soh, 2000b), and those who were smuggled into the country (Associated Press 2000c). This continued influx of undocumented immigrants is curious, particularly since legal immigration is on the decline.

Family reunification. Among Koreans, as with other Asian groups, the pull of family reunification continues to be a reason for migration. Yet the booming economy in Korea slashed emigration from Korea in the 1990s, and in the 1992–1994 period, not only were overall flows from Korea half those of earlier periods, but the numbers entering under family reunification declined even more steeply. In 1995 family-sponsored preferences and immediate relatives of U.S. citizens totaled only 11,437. With the improvement in the Korean economy, immigration streams are likely to decline further, following the pattern of other countries, including Japan.

Japan

The years immediately preceding World War II saw Japan's movement toward war as it harnessed political and economic factors for expansion. Collaborations with Germany and Italy resulted in a pact against Soviet propaganda and a secret agreement not to help the Soviet Union if any of the three countries was attacked by it. In addition, Japan continued to expand military occupations along the Chinese coastal areas and plains, leading to the China Incident of 1937. Altercations between Japan and China led to the bombing of three Chinese cities, and on August 13, 1937, the terror bombing of Shanghai marked the beginning of a Sino-Japan war that was only called an "incident." No formal declaration of war accompanied these Japanese military activities.

While Japan was expanding its interests in China, it infringed on Western rights in that country, particularly those of Great Britain, which retained strong economic interests in occupied China. In addition, the Japanese moved into Indochina after the end of French control in that country in June 1940, and with the conclusion of the Hanoi

Convention later in 1940, Japan received the right to place troops in northern Indochina. When the Netherlands fell to the Nazis in the spring of 1940, Japan moved into Batavia and by 1942 occupied it. Concurrently, United States–Japan relationships froze over the formulation of a China policy, as the former tried to restrain the latter in an attempt to protect U.S. nationals. Irreconcilable issues provided the backdrop for Japan's decision to go to war.

On December 7, 1941, Japan attacked Pearl Harbor, setting into motion a series of effects not only on Japanese Americans but also on perceptions of Japan in the international political field. During the early years of World War II, Japan enjoyed consistent victory as it speedily occupied much of the Pacific area. Hong Kong, Manila, Bataan, Corregidor, Singapore, the Dutch East Indies, and Burma all fell under Japanese control between December 1942 and May 1943, and Japan turned its sights toward Australia. These swift and decisive victories managed to destroy the myth that whites were the most powerful, and the Japanese were overtly contemptuous and cruel to their Dutch, British, and American prisoners. By 1943, however, international pressure on Japan became intense. Strategies between Japan and Germany were not as well coordinated as were those between Britain, the Dominions and other Allies, and the United States. In addition, China continued to pressure the mainland. The bombing of Japan's industrial plants and its main railway greatly curtailed war production, and when Okinawa was captured in 1945 after very high losses on both sides, the bombing became much more intense, damaging almost all of Japan's large cities. The Potsdam Conference in July 1945 reaffirmed the Allies' intent to eliminate what they termed the "irresponsible militarism" of Japan and called for Japan's unconditional surrender or "prompt and utter destruction." After giving the Japanese ten days, the Allies dropped the first atomic bomb on Hiroshima, the nation's southern army headquarters, on August 6, and the second on Nagasaki, a major port, on August 9. Although the bombs fell on military targets, the primary aim was to break the civilian will to fight and thus to curtail a potentially long battle (Morton 1994). The effects on Japan were devastating. In addition to the physical destruction of the geographic area, people exposed to radiation within five hundred meters were killed, and those at distances of three to five kilometers showed symptomatic aftereffects, including radiation-induced cancers. The estimated death toll in Hiroshima as reported to the United Nations in 1976 was 140,000, and in Nagasaki it was 70,000 by the end of December 1945. People qualifying for treatment under Japan's A-bomb Victims Medical Care Law of 1957 numbered 352,550 in 1990. In the face of such destruction, on August 10 the cabinet asked Emperor Hirohito for his counsel, and on August 14 he decided on unconditional surrender.

The defeat of Japan in World War II was a monumental experience for a nation that for the first time in its entire history found itself invaded and occupied. Thus, the effect of the war was even more traumatic, as the Japanese had always perceived their land as sacred (Morton 1994). Over the next five years a number of changes ensued in the country's government as directives from Washington required demilitarization and democracy. While the former occurred fairly smoothly and rapidly, the latter affected the core of the society, particularly the position of the emperor. At least 5,000 war criminals were tried outside Japan, and 900 were executed; an additional 200,000 were removed from their jobs as bureaucrats, more because of the work in which they had been engaged than because of personal responsibility in war crimes. Despite the international call for an indictment of the emperor as a war criminal, General Douglas MacArthur, the supreme commander of the Allied powers, who was charged with arbitration and rule, showed foresight in retaining the emperor as a symbol of the nation's unity. Emperor Hirohito in 1946 willingly renounced claims to divinity.

On September 8, 1951, the International Peace Treaty, signed by forty-eight nations in San Francisco, brought Japan back into the international fold, officially ending the war for Japan as it regained its independent status. The country was no longer required to pay reparations, and the United States and Japan signed a mutual security treaty. The U.S. occupation of Japan formally ended on April 28, 1952, but it was not until May 1972 that the United States returned control of Okinawa to Japan. In 1989 Emperor Hirohito died, ending the Showa Period and a sixty-three-year reign; his son Akihito was enthroned in January 1989, inaugurating the Heisei Period.

The economy of Japan grew phenomenally in the postwar years. The growth was enhanced not only by governmental and private enterprise but also, in the early years, by U.S. assistance. The overall economic growth rate averaged 10 percent annually between 1950 and 1965. The gross national product, only $1.3 billion in 1946, surged to $167 billion by 1968. Per capita income showed similar gains. Although it plummeted in 1945 to half of its 1934 total, by 1963 it had more than quadrupled. Between 1960 and 1965, the economic growth slowed somewhat, but another five-year boom occurred between 1965 and 1970. Although continuing its agricultural production and output of small businesses, Japan moved to the manufacture of automobiles and tractors and soon included the production of televisions, computers, robots, and other telecommunication mechanisms, leading world production in these areas. By the 1990s less than 10 percent of the nation's labor force continued to work in the primary economic sector of farming, mining, and fishing, and that sector contributed only about 3 percent of the nation's goods and services. The secondary, or industrial, sector comprised about one-third of the workforce, but the majority had moved into the tertiary sector of service, which is highly knowledge-intensive (rather than labor- or capital-intensive). In 1987 Japan's gross national product per capita exceeded that of the United States. Japan became the only modern industrialized non-Western nation and drew on both native traditional and foreign resources in shaping its contemporary national outlook and identity. The dramatic industrial advance of the nation was recognized as an "economic miracle," but it required hard work, concentrated thought and abilities, and considerable sacrifice (Morton 1994).

Particularly supportive of its workers, Japan's economy engendered a level of allegiance not found in most nations. With commitments of lifetime employment, labor unions organized for each enterprise or workplace, a savings plan that allows for investment in the industry, and close cooperation among government, management, and labor, the Japanese workforce and the industry are almost inextricably bound together. While some, particularly those in countries such as the United States where transience is common, may view this as disadvantageous, it has worked well for the Japanese and is consistent with traditions of loyalty and Confucian philosophy. On the other hand, those who left a company were ostracized and could never return. The economy, booming into the late 1980s, crashed beginning in the early 1990s, apparently decimated by several fundamental problems that are equated with traditional ways of doing business in Japan.

The progress of Japan's society has continued rapidly. Heavy emphasis on academic achievement begins in the preschool years with an understanding that education is essential for lifetime success. The role of the mother is that of a *kyoiku mama*, an education mother, and pressures for academic success sometimes overwhelm the child and the family. With population figures escalating from 75.8 million in 1946 after World War II to 123.6 million by 1990, competition is increasingly fierce. Japan's citizens have one of the world's highest rates of longevity, and younger people are postponing the age at which they start a family and also are limiting family size; the "graying of Japan" is under way. It is anticipated that by 2007 population growth in Japan will be negative.

Since World War II, women have made significant advances in freedom and in quality of life, yet they are still far from experiencing equality with men. The traditional role of a woman—marriage, home, children, and minimal interaction with the outside world—is still the rule (Morton 1994). Although most women are better educated than ever before, many enter the workforce before they marry, postponing marriage well into their late twenties. Once they do marry, few have the option for a life outside the traditional pattern, at least until their children leave home. Nevertheless, with fewer children because of easily accessible contraception and abortions, they find more time free from housework. Because of a government ban, the birth control pill was not available to women until 1999, and official family planning methods favored the use of condoms. The ban on the use of the pill and the support of the condom, while enhancing the prevention of sexually transmitted diseases, including HIV (human immunodeficiency virus) infection, did limit the woman's control over her fertility.

Overall, the Japanese people continue to advance, and the route of free enterprise has been very successful. The people are confident and proud of their heritage, culture, and traditions, and travel abroad is commonplace. The quality of life in Japan is high for the majority of people, as are demands for labor. Thus the current population's desire to emigrate is low, as it has been since the 1960s. Japan's Ministry of Foreign Affairs reported in 1999 that there are about 2.5 million ethnic Japanese living outside the country. In addition to second-, third-, and fourth-generation Japanese, many are post–World War II emigrants from Japan who left for Brazil and other parts of South America, in large part through a national policy to reduce overpopulation.

Between 1971 and 1990, the number of Japanese emigrants to the United States was 86,100, less than 1.9 percent of the 4.6 million Asian immigrants during that period. Thus, although the liberalization of immigration policies in the United States led to the influx of Asians, it did not have such an effect on the Japanese, who continued to immigrate at about the same rate (approximately 5,000 annually) as they had since 1952. The U.S. Bureau of the Census revealed in 1993 that of all Asian groups, the Japanese have the smallest number of foreign-born residents—fewer than 33 percent, compared with 65 percent of the total Asian American population. Fewer than 7,000 individuals immigrated to the United States from Japan in the years between 1995 and 1998 (U.S. Immigration and Naturalization Service 2000).

While there may be a few professional emigrants, the majority are students, who anticipate returning to their homeland after they have completed their higher education. Since 1965, the numbers of political exiles, refugees, and undocumented immigrants entering the United States have been negligible. Family reunification may be the other contributor to Japanese immigration to the United States. On the whole, however, emigration from Japan has declined dramatically since the early part of the twentieth century, and there is no indication that this pattern will reverse itself.

SOUTHEAST ASIAN EMIGRATION AFTER 1975

Three countries of Southeast Asia—Vietnam, Laos, and Cambodia—have had particular implications for the United States and for immigration to the country, especially since 1975. Furthermore, unlike emigrants from other nations, most of those who left these three countries fled as refugees, not as voluntary or economic migrants. It is especially important, therefore, to recognize the historical antecedents of these migrations, and although citizens of these lands are grouped together as one people, especially because they were all extensively affected by the Vietnam War (1961–1975), their cultures, their experiences, and their histories differ. Since refugees from Vietnam constituted the largest subgroup of Southeast Asian refugees to the United States, there is an unjustifiable tendency to generalize their experience to the Cambodians and the Laotians. Nevertheless, they do share some experiences, for unlike other Asian groups to the United States, most Southeast Asians came as political refugees until the 1980s. Family reunification efforts under the Amerasian Homecoming Act of December 22, 1987, brought in a number of children of American fathers and Vietnamese mothers, but family reunification streams from the other two nations have been particularly small. They have not been encouraged by immigration policies, and the majority of individuals and families who have been in the United States long enough to sponsor their relatives have not had the financial means to undertake such a responsibility.

The Socialist Republic of Vietnam

Though Vietnam traces its oral traditions to at least 3,000 B.C, its historical presence became apparent about 257 B.C, in the form of a scattering of peoples who were living in the area of what is now Southern China and Northern Vietnam. The small Vietnamese kingdom of Au Lac was located in the center of the Red River Valley and was founded by kings who had reigned over Van Lang for thousands of years. Some archaeological evidence suggests that the people of this area may have been the first in East Asia to engage in agriculture. By the first century B.C, they had moved well into the Bronze Age.

In 111 B.C China invaded and conquered what was known as Nam Viet, absorbing it into the Han Empire and integrating it politically and culturally. Intermittent revolts against Chinese rule may have been temporarily effective, but it was not until the early eleventh century A.D. that Vietnam founded its own dynasty. While Chinese political structures and cultural effects, including Confucianism, were maintained to a great degree, the Vietnamese turned to their ancient experiences to temper the influence of the Chinese. Vietnamese rule under the Ly Dynasty continued until 1407, when China regained control for about twenty years, after which Vietnam reverted to the Vietnamese. In the sixteenth century, however, two opposing aristocracies divided the nation into two zones, and the rivalry between these two groups was exacerbated by the arrival of Europeans in pursuit of wealth.

Early French entrants into the country were missionaries, who nevertheless became involved in political activities. Many were persecuted; some were executed. Cries for support from Paris received little attention until pressure was exerted by commercial and military interests and Napoleon III approved attacks on Vietnam that eventually led to the imposition of French colonial rule. National identity was not destroyed, and anticolonial sentiment was fanned by poor economic conditions, because although transportation and communications improved, the impoverished lives of the masses were not altered. They worked in deplorable conditions in the factories, coal mines, and rubber plantations for low wages, and peasants found they had to pay high rents and had heavy taxes levied on them. The 1920s saw the beginnings of organized nationalist party demands. In 1930 Ho Chi Minh founded the

Indochinese Communist Party but had little success in ousting the French until Japan placed Vietnam under military occupation in 1940 and reduced the French government to a figurehead.

Vietnam War. With the surrender of Japan, Viet Minh forces attempted to establish an independent republic in Hanoi. But the French, unwilling to concede, drove nationalist groups out of the South, and despite attempts to negotiate a solution, war erupted in December 1946 and lasted for almost eight years. At the 1954 Geneva Conference, the French and the Viet Minh agreed to an interim compromise to end the war and temporarily divided the country at the seventeenth parallel into North and South Vietnam. The United States, with the intent of preventing the international spread of communism, became particularly interested in preserving the anticommunist government in South Vietnam. Despite the political protocol that called for national elections to unify the countries in two years, the staunchly anticommunist South Vietnamese president, Ngo Dinh Diem, refused to hold elections. In 1961 U.S. president John F. Kennedy sent military advisors to South Vietnam, but dissatisfaction with Diem and his policies created internal schisms and opened possibilities for North Vietnam's supporters to revolt.

In 1963 a military coup, undertaken with the knowledge and consent of the American Embassy (Zhou and Bankston 2000), overthrew Diem, and with a weaker government in South Vietnam, the communists resumed the revolutionary war. They would have won had U.S. president Lyndon Johnson not decided to prevent the collapse of the Saigon regime by approving intensive bombing of North Vietnam and the sending of combat troops to South Vietnam in early 1965. On February 17, 1967, in a letter to President Johnson, Ho Chi Minh requested that the United States end its involvement in Vietnam and cease its bombing and war atrocities. At the beginning of 1968 the Viet Cong forces in South Vietnam and the Viet Minh army of the North launched the Tet Offensive, shattering American confidence in victory.

Stories of devastation, destruction, death, and war atrocities were prevalent on both sides. Unpopular even in the United States, the Vietnam War continued until 1975, although the leaders of both North Vietnam and the United States changed. With the death of Ho Chi Minh in 1969, Le Duan continued the revolution. In the United States the new president as of 1968, Richard Nixon, had already committed himself to continuing Johnson's policy, though he did begin gradually to withdraw troops from Vietnam.

A peace agreement signed in Paris in 1973 called for the total removal of the remaining U.S. troops from South Vietnam, with a national election agreed upon. This was aborted when on April 30, 1975, the communists seized power in Saigon. They reunited South and North Vietnam in 1976 and renamed Saigon Ho Chi Minh City. More than 58,000 American and 3 million Vietnamese were casualties of the war. Furthermore, the end of the war did not mean the end of violence and subjugation in the region. In 1979 Vietnam invaded Cambodia, and by the mid-1980s, 140,000 Vietnamese troops were stationed in Cambodia and 40,000 more in Laos. By 1990, however, almost all Vietnamese troops had been removed from these countries.

In the wake of the Vietnam War came numerous economic and social problems in all three of the countries that were directly affected by it (Vietnam, Cambodia, and Laos). These problems were further intensified by poor harvests in the following years, and North Vietnam's attempts to nationalize agriculture and business resulted in hostility from the South. A mutual lack of trust and suspicion of the political allegiance of the South Vietnamese resulted in mass incarcerations in "reeducation camps." Even for those who were released from the camps, the experience greatly affected the lives of their families. Finally, the continuing adversarial relationships with neighboring countries depleted Vietnam's resources and minimized the country's ability to reconstruct its institutions and focus on national development.

Political exiles and refugees. Following the fall of Saigon in 1975, refugees from South Vietnam left in several waves. Consistent with patterns of refugee movement, the first wave, in 1975, was composed of government officials, the political and social elite, those with U.S. connections, and people with the professional and personal resources to anticipate the imminent changes and leave before they occurred. Most had access to evacuation arranged by the American military or had their own connections outside the nation. The second wave has become known as the exodus of the "boat people." Large numbers of Viet-namese and Sino-Vietnamese people risked their lives to cross waters in hope of attaining freedom. Crammed into overcrowded, unsafe boats, these individuals suffered starvation, illness, filth, and generally deplorable conditions to leave Vietnam. Many were exploited, raped, and otherwise dehumanized; almost half lost their lives fleeing. The number of boat people who had left Vietnam by 1979 was estimated at 400,000. The majority escaped to the nearby countries of Thailand, Indonesia, Malaysia, Singapore, the Philippines, and Hong Kong (Chan and Loveridge 1987; Caplan, Whitmore, and Choy 1989). The third wave occurred in the early 1980s after the refugee crisis called for a new refugee policy. The 1980 Refugee Act in the United States removed refugees from preference categories for immigration, making them a nonquota group, and indicated that a new cap would be established annually by the U.S. president, based on international conditions and in consultation with Congress.

The Orderly Departure Program (ODP) was created in May 1979 between the United Nations and the government in Hanoi as a temporary solution, and those interviewed and approved by American officials in Vietnam were permitted to leave the country by air for the United States. Most who were approved were former South Vietnamese soldiers who had been in prison or in reeducation camps and their families, and by 1989 more than 165,000 Vietnamese had been admitted to the United States. By the mid-1990s the number that entered under the ODP had increased to 200,000. In addition, in 1989 the United States and the Socialist Republic of Vietnam agreed that those who were in reeducation camps would be allowed to leave Vietnam under the Humanitarian Operation (HO) Program, and more than 70,000 people took advantage of this option.

The emigration of Vietnamese to the United States continues unabated. Between 1981 and 1996, the largest number of refugees came from Vietnam, at 420,178 approximately 30 percent of the total refugee population from around the world during that period. In 1996 alone, the number of approved refugee applications from Vietnam totaled 8,566. Refugees to the United States have the option of adjusting their status to that of permanent resident one year after they have been in the country following the approval of their refugee status. Many become naturalized citizens. However, most have few skills that are applicable in the United States. The Immigration and Naturalization Service reported that in 1997 a total of 33,349 Vietnamese became naturalized citizens of the United States. Of these, 1,840 were in professional or managerial occupations, 13,936 were in sales, service, or factory work, and the largest number, 17,573, listed no occupation.

Family reunification. While the size of the refugee population continuing to enter the United States from Vietnam remains substantial, family reunification also provides an impetus for leaving the homeland. While less information is provided about this group of emigrants, it is clear that the numbers are not negligible. In 1995, when refugee and asylee adjustments in the United States totaled 28,595, another 11,436 individuals were admitted to the country, either under family-sponsored preferences or as immediate relatives of U.S. citizens. The Vietnamese population has now been in the United States long enough to be eligible to sponsor family members. Those who constituted the first wave of refugees from Vietnam are probably in the best socioeconomic positions to sponsor family reunification. A number of the second-wave refugees and those who entered through the ODP and the HO Program have now established themselves sufficiently that they may also have enough financial resources to sponsor relative emigration. Immigrants admitted from Vietnam in 1998, under family reunification efforts, numbered 17,649.

Amerasian Homecoming Act. Amerasian children, the offspring of American fathers and Asian mothers, have always had difficulties in their homelands. American servicemen stationed in Asian countries during the various wars of the twentieth century have fathered thousands of interracial offspring. Most of these children remained in those Asian countries when their fathers left and experienced extreme ostracism and ridicule. Their mothers were seen as little more than prostitutes. Only beginning in the mid-1970s, and with the passage of the Amerasian Homecoming Act (1987),[4] did the U.S. government acknowledge any responsibility for such children. With the cooperation of the government of Vietnam, the U.S. government developed a program aimed at bringing the children of former U.S. servicemen to the United States from Vietnam, whether or not these men claimed their children or their mothers—and the majority did not.

Sorely affected by the U.S. government's embargo after the war, Vietnam also viewed the most undesirable of its citizens, the Amerasians, as an undue burden. With U.S. interest in sponsoring the emigration of these individuals, Vietnam also perceived a lessening of the drain on its resources and the eviction of its unwanted. Thus the Amerasian Homecoming Act became a means for Vietnam to accomplish three things of value to the country: (1) clean the country of social outcasts and criminals, (2) be seen as engaging in humanitarian activities by the international community, and (3) populate a foreign country with refugees who would send as much as 20 percent of their incomes to their family members at home, thereby benefiting the country (Pham 1996).

Amerasian children, most of them with distinctly Euro-Asian or Afro-Asian features, known heretofore as *bui doi* or "dust of life" (trash), suddenly were seen as "golden children." They were now the vehicle by which family members could gain passage out of impoverished Vietnam. Most Amerasians, nevertheless, have had to bribe Vietnamese bureaucrats to have their applications approved, and in order to raise the funds many sponsored strangers as relatives who would be eligible to travel with them. If applicants are rejected, they do not receive a second opportunity to apply to leave the country. Many Amerasians and their families remain in Vietnam, most of them against their choice, because they were unable to raise the money for bribes to have their applications approved.

It is clear that those who left under the Amerasian Homecoming Act had the fewest resources available to them. In addition, their reception in the United States has been less than warm. Most have not been able to find their fathers, and others have been rejected by the fathers whom they were able to locate. The United States has not accepted them as American, as they had anticipated, and the Vietnamese community in the United States projects echoes of the ostracism that they experienced in their homelands. Thus, more than most other Asian Americans, Amerasians as a group have a difficult time resolving the dissonance associated with their exodus. The numbers of those who entered in the initial years were high. Between 1988 and 1993, approximately 17,000 Amerasians and 65,000 accompanying family members were resettled in the United States. Between 1995 and 1998, however, the number of Amerasians admitted dropped to 2,979, and in 1998 only 346 entered. Immigrants from Vietnam between 1995 and 1997 numbered from 37,121 to 39,922, then dropped significantly in 1998 to 16,534 (U.S. Immigration and Naturalization Service 2000). However, in 1998, 12,698 additional refugee applications from Vietnam were approved.

Difficulty in emigration. The Vietnamese government, though claiming to support emigration from Vietnam, has been less than helpful. Concerned about human rights in Vietnam, Congresswoman Loretta

Sanchez of California listed the following concerns in March 2000:

1. The emigration policy of the Vietnamese government still results in far too few people allowed to leave Vietnam due to arbitrary and unfair decisions;
2. An average emigrant must now pay $1,000 in bribes to have access to U.S. refugee programs: 3 times the average annual salary of a Vietnamese worker;
3. A recent report to Congress stated that over 15,000 former U.S. government employees and their families have been denied exit visas...;
4. The Vietnamese government TO THIS DAY continues to block U.S. access to the vast majority of eligible returnees;
5. Those people who were denied exit permits are now being kept off the interview list.

It appears, therefore, that the decline in emigration from Vietnam may well be caused by the artificially erected barriers rather than by a lack of interest in leaving.

Cambodia

Cambodia is the successor state of what was the mighty Khmer Empire, which once ruled the area that includes present-day Thailand, Vietnam, and Laos, its bordering countries. Little is known of prehistoric Cambodia. There is archaeological evidence that before 1000 B.C the inhabitants lived on a diet of fish and rice, and their houses were built on stilts, much as many are today. During the eighth century, known as the Angkorian era, the nation became one of artistic and religious power. In 1431 the Thais invaded Cambodia and caused several dynastic rivalries among the Khmers; war with the Thais continued for a century and a half.

The Spanish and Portuguese also played a part in these wars, as they were active in East Asia. Resentment of them led to the massacre of the Spanish garrison at Phnom Penh in 1599, beginning the reign of a series of weak monarchs until the French arrived in 1863; in 1884 they forced King Norodom into an agreement that made his nation into a French colony. A period of relative peace followed, and even the peasant uprising that occurred in 1916 was considered peaceful. In 1941 the French, assuming that nineteen-year-old Prince Sihanouk would be compliant, installed him on the throne. But that move was apparently an error, for the colonial power soon waned, its demise hastened by the Franco–Viet Minh War that was occurring in the neighboring nations of Vietnam and Laos.

In 1953 Cambodia gained independence from the French, and in 1955 King Sihanouk became the prime minister and tried to keep his country out of the conflicts that were raging in Laos and Vietnam. In a dramatic turn of events, Cambodia was launched into a volatile state in 1970, when Defense Minister and Premier Lon Nol led a coup to oust Sihanouk, who had objected to the U.S. bombing of the Vietnamese in Cambodia, which killed an estimated 500,000 Cambodians. Around the same time, the United States secretly carpet-bombed suspected communist base camps in Cambodia, killing thousands of civilians and dragging the country into the U.S.–Vietnam conflict.

The bloodiest and most oppressive of regimes was installed in 1975, when the Khmer Rouge rebels took Cambodia and named Pol Pot the leader. Their aim was to turn Cambodia into a Maoist, peasant-dominated agrarian cooperative, and they undertook the project with an almost religious fervor by systematically killing Cambodians, particularly the well educated. By 1979 Pol Pot and the Khmer Rouge had forcibly evacuated whole cities and massacred well over a million Cambodian men, women, and children. It is believed that another one million Cambodians died of malnutrition, overwork, and illness. During this period, about one-fifth of the population was eliminated (McDowell 1997). The death toll was not the only legacy of the Khmer regime. Cities were emptied, property was demolished, money became worthless, homes and families were destroyed, and every aspect of life came under the dictates of the government. Without any transition, the occupations of thousands of people, particularly those working in the cities, were changed to farming. It was not until after 1979, however, that those outside Cambodia were to learn of the extent of the devastation inflicted upon the people of that nation.

Between 1979, when the Vietnamese army toppled the Khmer regime but installed former Khmer Rouge commander Hun Sun, and 1997, there was a jockeying for power between Hun Sun and Sihanouk's son, Prince Ranariddh, who had been trained in France and who left to lead a rebel faction against the communist government. While Ranariddh was able to bring some relief from violence between 1983 and 1993, in 1997 Hun Sun led a coup ousting him and ending the short-lived respite from political upheaval and genocide in Cambodia

(ABCNEWS.com 1998). Although Hun Sun was then democratically elected prime minister in 1998, many human rights organizations maintained that the elections were greatly flawed by violence and intimidation. Since then, the political situation has stabilized, although corruption and impunity are rampant.

The primary occupation of the 1998 estimated population of 11.3 million in this small land of approximately 69,900 square miles was agriculture, with the chief products being rice, rubber, wood, corn, and textiles. Literacy levels remain low, at 35 percent, as does life expectancy, at 48 years, and only 36 percent of the population has access to safe drinking water.

Refugees. The flow of refugees from Cambodia began soon after the Khmer Rouge took control of the country. The number of refugees admitted to the United States in 1975 was 4,600. It is assumed that, as with most refugee movements, the first wave consisted of the more elite and those who could foresee the impact of the Khmer regime. Between 1976 and 1978 the admissions numbered only 2,700. The small number suggests that it was difficult for people to leave the country. The exodus truly peaked between 1979 and 1980, immediately after the overthrow of the Khmer Rouge, and from 1979 until 1985 a total of 121,397 refugees were admitted into the United States. The numbers began tapering off after that, dropping to approximately 10,000 in 1986. Between 1991 and 1997, only 208 individuals entered the United States as refugees. By 1996, however, refugees from Cambodia totaled approximately 135,000. The majority came from the agriculture sector, and almost all the women and most men had no more than a third-grade education.

The numbers that entered the United States during the years following the Khmer Rouge occupation are not indicative of the size of the refugee population that made its way to camps administered by the United Nations in Thailand. The UN considered most of them to be "economic migrants" rather than refugees, and therefore not eligible for resettlement in other nations. Consequently, large numbers of the hundreds of thousands of Cambodians languished in these refugee camps for close to thirteen years. During the Khmer Rouge era, about 50,000 Cambodians fled to Thailand, and another 150,000 were estimated to have entered Vietnam. Cambodians who went to France numbered 32,000, and Australia and Canada each admitted 13,000 refugees.

In 1993 the United Nations deemed Cambodia free of political turmoil, the camps were closed, and approximately 370,000 people were
repatriated to Cambodia. In that year the United States also repatriated
Cambodian refugees who had not sought immigrant status. Following
Hun Sun's 1997 coup, 75,000 Cambodians again sought shelter in
Thailand, but a large number returned the following year. Most of the
remaining refugees who have not been resettled have been repatriated,
based on United Nations guidelines.

Nonrefugee migrants. In the United States in 1997, according to
Immigration and Naturalization Service reports, 4,936 individuals of
Cambodian origin became U.S. citizens through naturalization; of
these, 239 were professionals or held managerial positions, while 3,022
listed no occupation on their naturalization papers. Thus it appears that
the number of professionals and students who emigrated in hope of
finding better opportunities in their areas of work was minuscule. There
also appear to be no recent reports of undocumented immigrants from
Cambodia, either in the news media or in government sources. Despite
poor social and economic conditions in Cambodia, considerably fewer
of its citizens are leaving the country for the United States at the beginning of the twenty-first century than in the 1980s and early 1990s.
Other than a small group of individuals who may have entered under
the family reunification provisions of the Amerasian Homecoming Act
of 1987, there have been no "chain migrations" of the sort that were
prevalent among other Asian immigrant groups.

Laos

Laos is a landlocked country in the center of Southeast Asia that over
the course of its history has been influenced to varying degrees by
the bordering countries of Cambodia, China, Burma (Myanmar),
Thailand, and Vietnam. Five thousand or more years ago, it was inhabited by Austroasiatic people, and from the first century A.D. it evidenced
expertise in rice cultivation in addition to pottery making and bronze
work. Beginning in the thirteenth century, Mongols exerted political
influence in the area, and there is evidence of the beginnings of a multiethnic society. In 1985, when the most recent census was conducted
in Laos, approximately forty sizable ethnic groups were counted; by
geographical area, they fall into three main categories: the "lowland"
Lao Loum, who have been the most favored historically; the "midland"

Lao Theung; and the "upland" Lao Sung. The last two groups have experienced a greater degree of discrimination. Among these are the H'mong (231,168 in 1985 [Savada 1995]), who constitute one of the principal ethnic minorities in the higher-elevation areas.

The recorded history of Laos began in the fourteenth century with the Mongol Fa Ngum, the first king of Lan Xang, the name of Laos at that time. Not until 1633, when Laos was united and ruled by its own king, Souligna Vongsa, did the nation experience economic and political stability. This period, known as the golden age of Laos, was short-lived, and the death of the king led to a series of political struggles and the division of Lan Xang. There were conflicts with Burma, Siam (Thailand), Vietnam, and the Khmer kingdom, which continued into the eighteenth century, with the Siamese finally dominating the nation and extending their control into the early nineteenth century. France, which had established a protectorate over Vietnam, became contentious and by the end of the century had replaced Siam and integrated Laos into the French colonial empire, where it remained from 1890 until World War II. However, the French maintained the existing institutions of the nation and permitted the kings to retain their positions, although the French governor general exercised full authority over the kings. At the time of World War II, Japan occupied French Indochina and induced its king, Sisavong Vong, to declare independence from France in 1945 before Japan itself surrendered in the war.

The first large anti-French uprising occurred among the Lao Theung groups from 1901 to 1907, and at least five more movements began and ended between 1914 and 1921. The H'mong, always highly independent, maintained their tradition of rebellion against central governments. In the 1920s successful H'mong uprisings against the French colonial powers resulted in negotiated settlements, and the French later used the H'mong to help subjugate Lao dissidents. Successful farmers, the H'mong not only grew rice and corn and raised livestock but were also major growers of opium, which they used as a cash crop. The French, Japanese, and Americans all benefited from the sale of opium in the financing of their respective interests between the 1890s and the early 1970s (Chan 1994). The independence of Laos from France was formally recognized in 1949, but the country remained a member of the French Union until 1953.

The First Indochina War (1946–1954) was fought primarily in Vietnam, although skirmishes did occur in Laos, as did an unsuccessful attempt of the Vietnamese to gain control of the country in 1953. The 1954 Geneva Conference was convened to settle political issues of both the Korean War and the First Indochina War. A second Geneva Conference on Laos in 1961–1962 was held to reinforce Laotian independence and neutrality, which had not been realized. Political factions within the country continued fighting after 1953, and civil war raged into the 1970s, backed on one side by the United States and on the other by Soviet-supported Vietnam. In the 1960s the United States recognized the superior skill and tenacity of the H'mong and used them extensively as irregular mercenary units. Disproportionate numbers of H'mong were killed during this period (Savada 1995).

During the Indochina War, all warring groups outside Laos found a five-hundred-square-mile region of northern Laos, known as the Plain of Jars, to be a highly strategic location, both centralized and difficult to access. This land had been a battleground for several centuries (Boyne 1999). In the 1960s and 1970s a struggle over this area, now known as the Secret War, involved the U.S. military and was shrouded in mystery, confusion, and tragedy and obscured by years of distorted information. Events revealed that Laos experienced a great deal more of the Indochina War than had been realized. During that time, in that area, an interdependence developed between the Americans and the H'mong. However, the Plain of Jars experienced such tremendous fighting over a decade and a half that the population was decimated and the land and buildings were destroyed. As recently as June 5, 2000, U.S. president Bill Clinton signed the Hmong Veterans Naturalization Act of 2000, stating that it was a "legislative tribute to the service, courage, and sacrifice of the Hmong people who were our allies in Laos during the Vietnam war . . . [and] . . . came to the United States" (1242).

Soon after the fall of South Vietnam and Cambodia to the communists, the Pathet Lao came to power in Laos, proclaiming the country's territorial integrity as well as its independence, sovereignty, and solidarity, and the Lao People's Democratic Republic (LPDR) was established on December 2, 1975, ending the monarchy. Although communist nations do not look favorably upon religion, in Laos 85 percent of the people are Buddhist; the constitution proclaims religious freedom, although the LPDR has attempted to manipulate Buddhism to support its political goals. As a communist nation, in 1975, Laos turned to the Soviet Union and China, which granted aid. With the collapse of the Soviet Union, aid came to an end, and Vietnamese support greatly diminished, requiring that Laos seek help elsewhere. Japan, Australia, France, and Sweden came to the aid of the country in the early 1990s, as did the World Bank, the International Monetary Fund, and the Asian Development Bank. The last three, however, expected reform measures to precede the allocation of funds.

To clearly mark its independence, Laos fought a border war with Thailand in 1988, but in the 1990s relations between the two nations improved dramatically. Nevertheless, news reports in Asian newspapers suggest that Laos continues to doubt Thailand's respect for its borders. Since the introduction of the New Economic Mechanism[5] in 1986, the government has made some headway in improving the lives of Laotians, but the harsh realities and particular idiosyncrasies of the LPDR and the lack of reliable quantitative data make information about economic functioning unclear, and the quality of life is still fairly low, with Laos having one of the poorest economies in the world. The nation's ties with its neighbors were confirmed when it was admitted into the Association of Southeast Asian Nations (ASEAN) in July 1997, yet it continues to be the third-largest producer of opium, heroin, and cannabis.

The population of Laos in July 2000 was estimated to be approximately 5,659,504, with an annual growth rate of 2.9 percent, which is relatively high. The infant mortality rate, at 91.81 per 1,000 live births, is high, but so is the fertility rate, which in 1998 was 5.66 children born per woman. Life expectancy is low, less than fifty-five years, and only 3 percent of the population is over the age of sixty-five. Education and social services, though improving, are still rudimentary, and although the nation made a commitment to five years of universal primary education, limited finances and a lack of trained educators and teaching materials have prevented the implementation of that commitment. Modern health care is severely limited and restricted to the urban areas because of lack of funds, few trained health care practitioners, and difficulties in transportation.

Despite the constant presence of the LPDR government since 1975, there are suggestions that the longevity of the rule has led to a political elite. Human rights activists also point to ruthlessness and genocide, but the U.S. State Department reports no such extremes. Although several political prisoners taken during the 1970s have been released, it is believed that a large number are still being held in Laotian prisons. On October 6, 2000, the Internet Web link (http://www.vientianetimes.com) to the *Vientiane Times*, the English-language newspaper, carried a travel warning from the United States, the United Kingdom, Australia, and Canada: "Warning: Visiting Laos MAY put your life at risk. If you plan to go to Laos, avoid crowds in public places, avoid standing near unattended bags or belongings, avoid night clubs, avoid public transportation." Several bombings were reported by the U.S. Embassy in Vientiane during 2000, and these nations provided cautionary guidelines for travelers, suggesting that Laos continues to experience living conditions that are less than ideal, even for its own citizens.

Economic exploration. Typically, Laotian villagers and sometimes whole villages, have migrated in search of better economic prospects— for example, agricultural areas that had the potential for growing healthier crops. As a semi-migratory people, the Laotians have sometimes fragmented their families and villages in search of better opportunities, although continuing familial ties tend to offset some of the effects of migration. Despite a tendency to believe that refugees and migrants who are dislodged against their will desire to return to their homelands, some evidence suggests that during repatriation efforts many H'mong refugees in Wisconsin did not wish to return to Laos except for short-term visits (Miki 1998). Most continued to believe that they would not be safe if they returned, but, more important, they knew that the quality of life, the economic conditions, and the relatively primitive lifestyle in Laos were a far cry from the comforts and freedom that they had found in the United States.

Political exiles and refugees. When large numbers of Laotians were displaced from their villages during the Second Indochina War, especially between 1960 and 1973, many of them relocated to other parts of Laos either to escape bombing or to get away from the warring factions that were attempting to take control of their residential areas. It is believed that 700,000 people were displaced in one way or another through the war, and though many returned to their villages after the 1973 ceasefire, a significant number chose to remain where they had lived for the duration of the war. A number of families had relocated to refugee sites sponsored by the Royal Lao government, but when the government fell many left the nation for nearby Thailand.

Consistent with the usual flight pattern of refugees, Laotians emigrated in three phases. Royal Lao government officials and the Westernized elite left in the first wave, around 1975. In the second wave, between 1977 and 1981, the refugees were more likely to be villagers who left not so much because of political control measures as in response to the difficulties they encountered with poor weather and ineffective agricultural management by the government. A third wave, which was less rapid, lasted through the late 1980s. By the end of it, about 10 percent of the population, more than 360,000 people, had left the country as refugees. By 1992 approximately 302,000 Laotians had been permanently resettled. Most entered the United States and France, but close to 40,000, mostly H'mong, remained in Thai refugee camps. Although the U.S. Department of State reported that as of December 1998 about 27,846 refugees had returned to Laos since 1980, witnesses, victims, and returnees in Laos reported that about 15,000 H'mong and Lao refugees in Thailand were forced back to Laos from 1989 to 1999 (Lao Human Rights Council 2000).

Unlike other emigrant groups from Southeast Asia, such as the Cambodians and the Vietnamese, the Laotians did not anticipate the need to flee their country. Many of those who would have been political exiles and the elite of the country did not leave. Many were incarcerated, and some continue to be imprisoned into the twenty-first century (Lao Human Rights Council 2000), and genocide persists in the Laos countryside (Pobzeb 2001). Those who did leave, most after the war, were the H'mong, who were assisted by the United States, which felt responsible for including them in the war in Laos. Others were lowland and midland Laotians who fled to neighboring Thailand. Almost all were illiterate agricultural workers; only a few had the skills necessary for adjustment in the United States. Those who had not readjusted their status to permanent residency were repatriated in 1993. The Immigration and Naturalization Service reported that, of those who had become permanent residents of the United States, 8,092 became naturalized citizens in 1997. Of these, 298 were in professional or managerial occupations, and another 3,056 were in sales, service, or factory work, but 4,738 listed no occupation. A 2001 report indicated that 300,000 H'mong were living in the United States and taking advantage of the educational opportunities in the country. At that time 6,500 H'mong American students were enrolled in undergraduate schools, and increasing numbers were going on for graduate education (Pobzeb 2001).

Other Asian Countries

China, Japan, India, Korea, the Philippines, and Vietnam are the Asian nations most often represented by immigrants to the United States.

Even a cursory look at the map of East, Southeast, and South Asia, however, reveals many other countries. Emigrants from these nations are spread around the globe, having left their nations of origin for reasons not dissimilar to those of other emigrants. Their numbers in the United States, though growing, are relatively small, and the nation did not seek to categorize them into their separate nationalities even as recently as the 2000 Census, the results of which are due to be released late in 2002. Fairly large populations of Thais, Cambodians, Laotians, and Pakistanis are in the United States, yet they are rarely counted separately in discussions of Asian Americans. Except for the literature on Laotians and Cambodians, information about other Asians' reasons for emigrating to the United States is sparse, but such information must soon become an area of focus.

In 1997 between 3,000 and 8,000 emigrants from the countries of Bangladesh, Cambodia, Laos, Pakistan, and Taiwan became naturalized U.S. citizens. In 1998 Pakistan, with 13,094 entrants, and Bangladesh, with 8,621, were among the top twenty countries sending emigrants to the United States. In the same year Pakistan ranked sixteenth among the countries that sent undocumented immigrants, with 41,000. Furthermore, relatively little is written about emigration from Taiwan and Hong Kong to the United States. There has always been a tendency to group Asians from these areas with those from the Republic of China, even before 1997, when Hong Kong became a part of that nation.

Large numbers of entrants to the United States—usually students, many of whom adjust their status to immigrant—from Malaysia, Indonesia, Myanmar, Sri Lanka, Nepal, Singapore, and Afghanistan are found in U.S. cities. With the increasing ease of travel and the globalization of almost every aspect of human existence, the relatively small numbers of emigrants from these nations will rise. Thus the Asian American population will continue to grow through birth and through immigration, and it will represent many nations other than China, Japan, Korea, India, the Philippines, and Vietnam.

4

Entry Into the United States and the Nation's Response to Asian Immigration

I am now inclined to extrapolate from my studies the following three conclusions. First, there has been a definite pattern of institutional discrimination practiced by the American judicial system against the Asian immigrant on the basis of her race. . . . Second, immigration and naturalization laws passed by Congress during the period under study (1790–1990) have been discriminatory against the Asian immigrant on the basis of race. . . . Third, racism, be it personal or institutional, as it was practiced during the period under study, was grounded in the human psyche.
—KIM 1994:xi–xii

In a message to the Eighty-ninth Congress on January 13, 1965, President Lyndon Johnson recommended liberalization of existing immigration legislation. After extensive hearings, on October 3, 1965, the president was able to sign into effect the Immigration Act of October 3, 1965. The passage of this act so changed the United States' immigration policy that unprecedented numbers of immigrants entered the country, especially from Asian and Latin American countries, who had up to that time been heavily restricted from entering. U.S. immigration policies were first formulated in response to Asian immigration (specifically Chinese immigration) in the latter half of the nineteenth century. Although earlier there had been some murmurings regarding immigration from Southern and Eastern Europe, there appeared to have been no significant xenophobia or overwhelming need to restrict immigration.

Before 1970, 85 percent of foreign-born residents of the United States were white, while by 1996 the percentage of U.S. residents born in Asia was 26.7 percent (Branigin 1997). The 1990 U.S. Census reported an Asian population of 6,908,638, a 99 percent increase over the 1980 count. The 2000 Census indicated a further escalation to 10,242,998, and it is believed that this figure may be an undercount. The 2000 Census for the first time solicited information regarding biracial and multiracial heritage. If bi/multiracial Asians are included in the count, the numbers increase to 11,898,828. The latest census also differentiated between Asians and Hawaiians and other Pacific Islanders. Until the 2000 Census, Asians and Pacific Islanders were grouped together. The rate of Asian immigration remains high, although it declined somewhat between 1993 and 1998.[1]

Unlike Asian immigrants of previous decades, or even immigrants from other countries, and because of the profile constraints placed on those coming from Asian countries, the majority of post-1965 Asian immigrants has tended to be highly educated and professional, contributing to the stereotype of that group as a "model minority." It is important, however, to put this in perspective and view the history of Asian immigration and specific Asian groups to recognize that legislation and social reaction to this minority have often been intolerant. Violent actions against groups of people are now labeled hate crimes, but early Asian immigrants experienced similar ethnic violence, along with oral abuse and denunciation in the print media. The experiences of abuse and the more recent view of Asians as the ideal minority have shaped the niche of the Asian in the United States.

The numbers and the profile of continuing immigration from Asian countries present both challenges and opportunities for U.S. natives in all sectors. For Asians, the "model minority" stereotype serves as both a compliment and a barrier to healthy inclusion into American society. It camouflages essential issues as well as people who do not conform to this stereotype. Furthermore, the immigration debate is exacerbated by the contributions of Asian immigrants, especially in the face of their phenotypic inability to "melt" into either the dominant European American or the minority African-American society.

While the adaptation of the recent Asian immigrants is eased by their professional achievements, long-standing ethnocentrism and xenophobia among U.S. natives are not easily dispelled. Despite the literature in the last two decades on the history of Asian immigration to the United States, most American history books pay scant attention to it. Little mention is made of the building of the western railroad by

Asians, for example. The first Asian immigrants did begin to arrive at U.S. borders in the 1700s, and significant numbers entered with the Chinese immigration in the middle of the nineteenth century. After the Chinese came the Japanese, Indians, Filipinos, and Koreans; none found an easy transition. Other Asian groups had few members in the United States before the 1965 Immigration Act. Since then, many more of these groups as well as others from the Indian subcontinent and Southeast Asia have added their numbers to those of the original Asian immigrants. This chapter presents an overview of the waves of immigration from Asian countries since the middle of the nineteenth century, providing a comparison of their experiences and the U.S. response to Asian immigration in general and to each immigrant group in particular.

PERIODS OF IMMIGRATION HISTORY

In a democratic society such as the United States, it is believed that national policies reflect the opinion of the majority. H-c. Kim (1994) proposes that congressional legislative action regarding immigration revolves around issues of superiority/inferiority and inclusion/exclusion. These issues, in turn, translate into the quantity and quality of people allowed to enter the country. Early immigration laws reflected the fears of the nation, especially with the increasing Asian presence in the country. Since the mid-nineteenth century, immigration laws have so limited or constrained Asian immigration that they have contributed considerably to the demographic, and hence the social and cultural profile of this population.

Kim (1994:8–9) divides U.S. immigration history into seven periods during which legal measures formally controlled the categories of people allowed to immigrate:

1. The colonial period (1609–1775), during which most immigrants were from the British Isles and the colonies had little effective control.
2. The American Revolutionary period (1776–1840), when European immigration slowed because of war and there were general anti-foreign feelings.
3. The "old" immigration period (1841–1882), during which local governments recruited people from Northern Europe. Chinese were also able to immigrate without much difficulty.

4. The regulation period (1882–1920), when the Chinese were excluded from immigrating. However, large numbers of immigrants were admitted from Central, Eastern, and Southern Europe.
5. The restriction and exclusion period (1921–1952), when a quota system restricted immigration from Central, Eastern, and Southern Europe, and when all Asians were excluded from admission because of their ineligibility for U.S. citizenship.
6. The partial liberalization period (1952–1965), when Asians were assigned the same quota as those from Central, Eastern, and Southern Europe, and were also allowed naturalization.
7. The liberalized policy period (1965–present), when the quota policy was repealed to allow entry to immigrants from Third World countries.

ASIAN IMMIGRATION

The Staggered Waves

The literature suggests that "waves" of immigrant groups from different nations have entered the United States during distinct periods with the goals of improving their lives and/or escaping unsatisfactory conditions in their countries of origin. Diverse Asian groups came in identifiable phases and either remained in the country or returned to their own nations, depending on the nature of the social and economic opportunities or barriers they encountered. Historical information on immigration from Asian countries after the middle of the nineteenth century is readily available. The first immigrants to arrive in substantial numbers were the Chinese, who came between 1848 and 1882; in 1882 they were barred from further entry. The Japanese began immigrating shortly after the Chinese were excluded, and despite restrictions that specifically targeted the Japanese, this population continued to grow as a female immigrant flow began to replace the male one. In 1923 further restrictions prevented Japanese entry. Because of the number of females who came to the United States between 1907 and 1923, however, the Japanese could establish families. After 1923, despite the decline in Japanese immigration, the birth of a large second generation established and perpetuated the Japanese American population.

A relatively large group of Indian males entered the United States between 1901 and 1911 as laborers; these men were regarded as the least desirable of all the immigrants thus far to the United States

(Kitano and Daniels 1995). Yet their numbers soared until 1917, when additional exclusionary measures enacted by the U.S. Congress effectively curtailed all further immigration from India and most other Asian countries. Distressed by their experience in the United States, close to 3,000 Indians returned to their homeland between 1920 and 1940. In the 1920s and 1930s, Filipino immigrants constituted the next Asian wave, one that began even in the face of the 1924 exclusionary actions by the U.S. Congress and peaked between 1932 and 1934. Because of the unique political relationship between the Philippines and the United States, Filipinos were not legally perceived as aliens and were not subject to the political sanctions imposed on other Asian groups.

The first immigrant wave from the Philippines occurred between 1902 and 1910 and was composed of students who were sponsored by the U.S. government. Even after financial support for the program declined, a number of Filipino students arrived in search of academic advancement. Thus a second wave of Filipino immigrants entered after 1910. Many were students, but more of this group were laborers who came to the United States via Hawaii upon completion of their labor contracts there. By 1935, however, the anti-Asian sentiment in the United States extended to them as well, and Congress passed resolutions that provided free passage on army transportation to encourage them to return to the Philippines. After that, until the end of World War II, little migration occurred from the Philippines.

Following a pattern set by the Japanese and the Filipinos, Koreans migrated primarily to the Hawaiian Islands, beginning in 1903, to work on the pineapple plantations. A smaller number did immigrate directly to the United States, however. Most of the early immigrants were males engaged in plantation labor, but over the course of the next decade and a half, "picture brides" and political refugees constituted the majority of the immigrants. Many of these early migrants to Hawaii moved to the mainland in time. By 1930 about 2,000 were believed to be living in California. A second wave of immigrants from Korea arrived between 1951 and 1964, during and after the Korean War (1950–1953). The close military, political, and economic ties maintained between the United States and South Korea encouraged resumption of immigration. The group that came at that time represented a heterogeneous collection of wives of American servicemen, war orphans, and students.

Thus the primary Asian immigrants to the United States before 1965 were the Chinese, Japanese, Indians, Filipinos, and Koreans.

While individuals from other Asian countries may have been in the United States before the liberalization policies of 1965, there is a paucity of literature about them, and data through the U.S. census are scanty. Furthermore, although Turkey, countries of the Middle East (West Asia), and the former Union of Socialist Soviet Republics (USSR) are a part of the Asian continent, they are rarely so perceived.

Laws That Have Significantly Affected Asian Immigration

Over the past 150 years the U.S. government has passed laws to control immigration in general and the immigration of specific groups in particular. Although legislative actions were directed toward regulating immigration in the nineteenth century, those that had the most impact, especially on Asians, began with the Chinese Exclusion Act of 1882, which barred the entry of laborers from China for ten years. This act was extended until 1892 and then made "permanent" in 1902. When President Theodore Roosevelt negotiated the Gentlemen's Agreements of 1907 and 1908 with Japan, Japan agreed to cease issuing passports to laborers. Less than ten years later, Congress passed the Immigration Act of February 5, 1917 (commonly known as the Barred Zone Act), which enumerated the classes of people who were ineligible to enter the United States. Among them were those who were natives of a zone defined by latitude and longitude; the geographic area identified became known as the Asiatic Barred Zone, and the act clearly became the Asiatic Barred Zone Act.

Under the Asiatic Barred Zone Act, the only Asians allowed entry into the United States were Japanese and Filipinos. The more restrictive Immigration Act of 1924, commonly known as the Quota Immigration Law, the Nationality Origins Act, or the Japanese Exclusion Act, was subsequently passed. This legislation effectively curtailed the immigration of the Japanese, but natives of the Philippines, because of their unique status as U.S. nationals, were able to continue entering the United States between 1902 and 1946. Finally, the Tydings-McDuffie Act of 1934 ended even this immigration (Kim 1994).

Laws minimized Asian immigration from then until the partial liberalization period (1952–1965), which began with the passage of the highly comprehensive McCarran-Walter Immigration Act. All aliens admissible for immigration were classified either as quota immigrants or nonquota immigrants. Despite continuing quotas for different countries, the nonquota immigrants (spouses and unmarried minor children of U.S. nationals) greatly increased the number of immigrants. Furthermore, all races became eligible for U.S. citizenship, reflecting a significant change in the long-existing legal attitudes toward people of color.

The October 3, 1965, act finally liberalized immigration and repealed legal discrimination because of race, gender, nationality, place of birth, or place of residence; it benefited many, especially those of the Asia-Pacific triangle. It established a preference system with eight categories and an annual quota of 290,000 persons; up to 20,000 from any one nation were allowed entry. This quota did not include spouses and unmarried minor children of U.S. citizens and thus permitted the annual number of immigrants to be substantially larger than the number specified.

The United States first allowed refugee entry in 1946, after which several refugee acts were passed, beginning with the Displaced Persons Act, under which refugees entered the United States as immigrants. The Refugee Relief Act of 1957 allowed refugees to enter either as parolees or under a statutory refugee status, with the right to adjust their status to permanent residency later. In 1975 the United States passed the Indochina Migration and Refugee Assistance Act, which was amended to become the Refugee Act of 1980. This act conforms to the 1967 United Nations Protocol on Refugees, exempting refugees from the worldwide annual quota and allowing them to adjust their status to that of permanent resident after one year in the United States. At the beginning of each year, the U.S. president and Congress review worldwide refugee conditions and determine the number in need of resettlement and of special concern to the United States. During 1980 a limit of 234,000 refugees was established, of which the Carter administration reserved 169,000 for refugees from Southeast Asian countries. Since then, the number has gradually decreased; the ceiling for refugee admissions in 1997 was 78,000 (U.S. Department of Justice 1999).

The Swell

The Immigration Act of 1965 rescinded the national origins system, replacing it with annual quotas for the Eastern (170,000) and Western (120,000) Hemispheres. Legislators assumed that this plan would redress injustices against Southern and Eastern Europe. The intent of the act was not the increase of Asian immigration. In addition to placing high priority on the reunification of families, it prioritized the entry of both professional and nonprofessional workers who were believed to be in short supply in the nation.

While the United States wanted to be seen as the "egalitarian champion of the free world" (Hing 1995:79), it was unprepared for the unprecedented numbers of Asians who entered its borders between 1965 and 1980. American policymakers and American society had little knowledge of either the effects of political, social, and economic factors in Asian countries or the strength of family and community relationships in Asian cultures. Once immigration laws were relaxed in the United States, these factors combined to escalate the flow of immigrants from several Asian countries as individuals left unsatisfactory environments in search of better opportunities. Definitions of "family" also differ between the United States and many Asian countries. The family boundaries in the latter are more encompassing, as obligations and affections bind extended family members in these collectivist societies. Asian, more so than European, commitments to extended family members are more likely to result in chain migrations, in which immigrant families acquire permanent residence, and then citizenship, often specifically in order to sponsor other eligible relatives.

The United States also prioritized the entry of workers who were in short supply in the nation. This, combined with the resources available to potential migrants in their home countries, resulted in an influx of professionals and students seeking graduate education. These upwardly mobile groups hailed primarily from Korea, China, the Philippines, and India. Thus, because of both the liberalization of the immigration laws and the modified established priorities, the more recent Asian immigrants presented a profile vastly different from that of the majority of earlier immigrants from Asian nations: a large majority of these later immigrants were professional and highly educated.

Furthermore, as a result of the Vietnam War, Southeast Asian refugees from Vietnam, Laos, and Cambodia fled their native countries to escape communist regimes. Many sought refuge in the United States, and by 1980 this refugee group exceeded one million (Laufman 1986). The first of these refugees arrived in 1975, after the fall of Saigon, and in 1976 the United States admitted 100,000 Southeast Asian refugees. In addition to accepting refugees from Southeast Asia, in 1982 and 1987 the United States passed humanitarian legislation designed to enable Amerasian children whose natural fathers were U.S. citizens—often from the armed services—to enter the country. Children who qualified for benefits under this law were those fathered by U.S. citizens and born in Cambodia, Korea, Laos, Thailand, or Vietnam after

December 31, 1950, and before October 22, 1982. They suffered such extreme racial discrimination and ostracism in their own lands because of their mixed heritage that their basic housing, medical, and nutritional needs went wanting. By October 1991 a total of 18,280 Amerasians (primarily from Vietnam) had taken advantage of the Amerasian Homecoming Act of 1987 and migrated to the United States.

The Immigration and Naturalization Service (INS) also has responsibility for assessing asylum cases. Asylees, or potential asylees, are any persons *who are already in the United States* and are unable or unwilling to return to their homelands because of a legitimate fear of persecution. This definitition differs from that of the refugee, who is a person who has been granted refugee status *before being admitted* into the country. The INS is charged with determining whether or not the asylee should receive the protection of the United States. According to the Refugee Act, an individual's current immigration status is irrelevant to that person's claim as an asylee. No limit is imposed on the number of individuals who may be granted asylum in the United States. To apply for permanent residency, they need only reside in the United States for one year after being granted asylum.

Two other groups qualify for entry under the refugee policies and are exempt from the national quotas. These are refugee-parolees and parolees. The former group constitutes applicants who were qualified for conditional entry into the United States between February 1970 and April 1980 but could not be approved because of inadequate numbers of visas available for skilled workers, professionals, and other workers needed by the United States. These people were paroled into the United States under the authority of the attorney general. Parolees are those who appear to be inadmissible to the inspecting officer but who are allowed to enter the United States under emergency or humanitarian conditions or when their entry is deemed to be in the public interest. The parolee status is a temporary one, and parolees are required to leave the United States when the conditions requiring their parole no longer exist.

Despite the liberalization of immigration laws and the nation's policies toward refugees and asylees, there are a number of other immigrants to the United States who do not come through the legal channels. Known as "undocumented" immigrants or "illegal aliens," these persons enter the United States by crossing the border without the permission of the appropriate authorities. The most typical way of entering for the undocumented group, however, is to stay beyond the period specified by visa allowances; about 40 percent of the population enters in this manner. The remainder enters surreptitiously across land or water borders. According to the INS, it is this latter means of entry that is the most publicized. The combined numbers of these two categories of undocumented immigrants is estimated to be well over 5 million. While the largest numbers come from Central and South America, the INS (1999a) estimates that at least 250,000 from Asia have entered in this manner, with the leading countries being the Philippines (95,000), Pakistan (41,000), India (33,000), and Korea (30,000). Nevertheless, it is impossible to determine an accurate estimate for the size of this undocumented group.

Clearly, since 1965 the liberalized immigration laws and refugee policies have made it possible for more people to enter the United States more easily than ever before. Because of social, political, and economic conditions in many Asian countries, the opportunities offered by the United States, and the collectivist Weltanschauung of most Asians, the attraction of Asians to the United States has been phenomenal. Other major factors contributing to the swell of Asians in the United States are family reunification and the birth of the second generation. Asian immigrants before 1965—except from Japan—were overwhelmingly male. After 1965, the family reunification provisions and the entry of professional workers equalized immigration opportunities for women. The contemporary flow of immigration to the United States is predominantly female and, as such, has significantly influenced the growth of Asian families. U.S. census figures indicate that Asians continue to be the fastest-growing minority in the United States, both by immigration and by birth, into the twenty-first century.

EARLY ASIAN IMMIGRATION

The Chinese and Japanese

The presence of Asians in the United States was recorded by the U.S. Bureau of the Census as early as 1820, when there appears to have been one immigrant from China and another from India (Kurian 1994). The first Asian group to immigrate in substantial numbers was the Chinese. While some Chinese presence was identified in northeastern U.S. cities such as Philadelphia and Boston (Kitano and Daniels 1995), the Chinese arrived in larger numbers in the middle of the nineteenth century to mine gold in California and subsequently found employment in other labor-intensive occupations. These immigrants were perceived as "sojourners," with plans to stay in the United States only temporarily, as they had left their wives and strong family ties in China and had traveled because of economic opportunity or necessity. Their unsatisfying experiences in the United States and their inability to find acceptance resulted in their return to their homelands but may have been misinterpreted as a lack of desire to bring their families to the United States or to immigrate permanently (Ng 1994).

The Chinese began arriving in the United States in the 1840s, drawn to California by tales of gold and economic plenty. Some did, indeed, work in the gold mines, but they were met with hostility from the white miners. The 1850s saw an appreciative increase in numbers, and contrary to popular beliefs about their acceptance in the first few years of their immigration, they were now targeted by both legal (the 1850 Foreign Miners Tax) and vigilante (anti-Chinese riots) actions by the white miners. Despite the difficulties they experienced, their numbers continued to rise, for they were being actively recruited to join the labor force. They fulfilled the need for laborers in railroad construction, but they also worked in laundries and as domestic help. Their willingness to work diligently, their capability, and their acceptance of lower wages than the whites made them essential to Californians. They were considered less demanding and more dependable than other workers in the country. More than 225,000 Chinese immigrated to the United States between 1850 and 1880, most of them from two small communities in Southern China, and males outnumbered females by more than fifteen to one. And while Chinese indentured slave labor and the "coolie" industry were common in other parts of the world, the Chinese arriving in the United States were voluntary immigrants, eager to participate in the newfound wealth of the Western states. Although many of them might have borrowed heavily in China to pay their way, they were never coerced into traveling to the United States.

Voluntary migration also occurred from Japan to the United States around the turn of the century. Transient travelers from Japan were found in the United States beginning in the middle of the nineteenth century—visitors, students, merchants, and officials. Although at least one small Japanese colony did exist in California in the 1870s—composed of political refugees from the Meiji Restoration[2] in Japan—it did not survive long (Kitano and Daniels 1995). Since emigration from Japan was not encouraged, few Japanese left the country until 1884. Toward the end of the nineteenth century, large groups of Japanese immigrants went to Hawaii as indentured or contract laborers to work on the plantations. By 1890 about 12,000 were believed to be residing in Hawaii and about 3,000 in the United States. Because of their dissatisfaction with contractual failures, however, some returned to Japan and others migrated to the mainland United States. At the same time, large numbers of Japanese migrated directly to the western United States. Many came as sojourners, with every intention of returning to Japan, many others came with the aim of establishing permanent residences, and still others returned to their country because they were unable to fulfill their expectations. Like the Chinese, most of the first wave of Japanese to immigrate were young men who came in the 1880s. By the end of the decade they had created a Japanese bachelor community on the West Coast. The European American population in the United States initially welcomed the Japanese, considering them different from the Chinese yet sharing the characteristics of diligence, dependability, and willingness to work for lower wages than white workers. Like the Chinese, most of the Japanese came with the intention of acquiring some wealth to send to their families in Japan, whether or not they themselves intended to return. Unlike the Chinese, however, who came from two small sections of China, the Japanese immigrants were drawn from several different rural areas.

U.S. Reaction to Early Chinese and Japanese Immigration

A view of U.S. responses to immigrants over the last two centuries reveals the decidedly xenophobic reactions of early settlers. Most of the literature on Asians in the United States discusses the anti-Asian sentiments evident among the native population, but not much of it details the extent of the verbal and physical assaults that many Asians experienced. Clearly the violence to which they were subjected was not isolated. Perhaps intolerance toward difference is intrinsic to human nature—a cursory look into the history of any nation will reveal processes of systematic and institutionalized discrimination against one group or another. Suffice it to say that the United States, despite being a nation of immigrants, has traditionally shown fear or dislike of the newly arrived once they achieve a visible presence. Evidence of this attitude can readily be discovered throughout U.S. immigration history, beginning against the continental Europeans, who were not British, moving to immigrants from Southern Europe, and continuing to other non-English-speaking peoples.

The United States initially welcomed immigration from both China and Japan. The Chinese were considered more attractive laborers than the whites, and unhampered by familial responsibilities, they were available to work longer hours or relocate as needed. Employers also warmly received the Japanese, who were strong, healthy young men (Hing 1995). The immigrants' move to the mainland from Hawaii was a step up, as they exchanged their indentured positions for more independent agricultural work, aiming to become self-employed farmers.

While the Chinese were welcomed by several U.S. labor employers in the middle of the nineteenth century, negative and stereotypical images of the Chinese people and culture had already been propagated via the printed media through American traders and merchants (Kim 1994). They were portrayed as dishonest, xenophobic, cowardly, having several vices and suffering from technological and military backwardness. Thus the Chinese found themselves caught in contradictory perceptions of them as honest and reliable yet cunning and untrustworthy, a situation that resulted in a national uneasiness with respect to them and friction between a desire for their labor and resentment at their presence.

Chinese women did not travel with their men. Several cultural barriers prevented their migration. Among them were the taboo against single women traveling alone to distant places and the need for married women to stay at home to care for children or members of the extended family and to ensure that the adult sons would return to the parental home (Takaki 1989). Despite these barriers, Hawaiian plantation owners encouraged immigration of the wives, even paying their way, for they believed that the presence of the wives would provide the men with stability and support. Unlike the Hawaiian employers, whose attitudes regarding the immigration of women were based on self-interest, the California employers thought their interests would be best served by ensuring that the laborers remained temporary and migratory. Single men without encumbrances formed a mobile workforce that could move to new construction sites or new harvesting areas. Furthermore, the physical conditions in the areas where the Chinese laborers worked would have been difficult for women and children.

White settlers in California felt that the presence of increasing numbers of Chinese workers threatened their own livelihoods, and U.S.

policies, reflecting their concerns, were designed to keep out Chinese women. On the census manuscripts before 1875, most Chinese women in the United States identified their occupation as "prostitute"—many family members actually sold their very young daughters into prostitution. In the absence of a stable family life and a normal community, Chinese immigrants found themselves in predominantly male company. Without Chinese women, and because of antimisogyny laws, they turned to prostitutes. Since they were denied entry into the social activities of the natives, they occupied their nonworking hours by gambling, drinking alcohol, using drugs, and frequenting brothels, behavior that promoted increasingly negative stereotypes about the debauchery of the Chinese and their lack of moral fortitude.

In reaction to the threat experienced by the white settlers, the perceived amoral lifestyle of the Chinese immigrant, and the growing anti-Chinese sentiment, the U.S. government began to institutionalize the xenophobia. The 1790 Nationality Act limited citizenship through naturalization to free white people and thereby effectively excluded African Americans and Native Americans. In the process, it also excluded, by definition, the naturalization of the Asian. In 1870 when Congress extended the act to naturalize aliens from Africa, it deliberately excluded the Chinese because of their "undesirable qualities" (Hing 1995). Although most historical accounts of Chinese immigrants and the policies leveled against them begin with the Chinese Exclusion Act of 1882, restrictionist movements started well before (Hing 1995).

The 1882 act had the most impact on Chinese and other Asian immigrants. Although it ended the immigration of the Chinese, their absence from the labor force created an entry for the Japanese. Thus the early Japanese, like the Chinese, worked in physically difficult, low-status, and poorly paid occupations. While the Chinese were employed in mining, agriculture, and railroad construction, the Japanese worked primarily in agriculture and railroad construction.

Movements toward modernization in Japan ensured that most Japanese had received some elementary education, which garnered them a modicum of respect among the whites. Most important, however—and dramatically unlike the Chinese—the Japanese had behind them a government that inspired and demanded growing recognition and that sought to ensure that the human rights of its nationals were not violated (Kitano and Daniels 1995). While the Japanese government's concern was not sufficient to negate the xenophobia in the

United States, it was able to politically arbitrate it until 1924. By then, the male-dominated flow of the Japanese immigrants had changed to a female-dominated one, which led to changes in the demographic constitution of the Japanese community and allowed the development of a native-born Japanese American community.

In 1908 the United States and Japan signed the Gentlemen's Agreement, under which Japan consented to no longer send laborers to the United States. The U.S. and Japanese governments, however, agreed on efforts to stabilize the Japanese men who were already residing in the United States, concurring in the belief that if the men were established and self-supporting, they could bring their wives and other family members. U.S. legislators did not understand the implications of such an agreement or the Asian definition of "family," and so they were not prepared for the stream of Japanese who emigrated to the United States. Several Japanese immigration organizations emerged to expedite immigration under the new laws. These organizations also were instrumental in developing creative channels for immigration; for example, in order to illustrate the financial stability required to support a wife in the United States, several Japanese men would pool their resources to demonstrate a sizable bankroll. Likewise, because the United States had little knowledge of the arranged-marriage system that was prevalent in Japan and many other Asian countries, men in the United States and women in Japan were able to marry sight unseen through the "picture bride" system. After exchanging photographs, the couple would be either engaged or married by proxy, making the women eligible to immigrate. Similarly, since men could bring in their dependent children, many men sponsored "paper sons," who were either unrelated to them or only distantly connected; the young men merely provided documents of evidence that they had fathers in the United States and they were thereby eligible to immigrate.

Since the Japanese were able to marry and establish their own families, they could avoid the kinds of antisocial activities into which the Chinese laborers had been drawn, and their patterns of family stability precluded the stereotypes that plagued the Chinese. Nevertheless, anti-Japanese sentiment appeared to be unavoidable. Discrimination against Japanese immigrants was publicized and became of governmental concern when in 1906 the San Francisco School Board attempted to force Japanese children to attend the segregated school that had been established many years previously for the Chinese. They increasingly encountered racism, particularly from those who felt that the Japanese were depriving them of their livelihoods by working for lower wages. The Japanese, like the Chinese, were rejected and isolated, and they began to rely heavily on each other to survive, to find employment, and for social support. This very cohesiveness, imposed upon them by the larger society, resulted in accusations that they could not assimilate. The increased hostility from the white society caused the Japanese to cling to each other even more and to strengthen their ethnic communities. Some immigrant Japanese gave up trying to become a part of the United States and returned to Japan. Others remained but were bitter about the experience and their exclusion from mainstream society. Many had both consciously and unconsciously adapted themselves to the customs and ideals of the United States, yet despite their attempts to assimilate they found that they were not accepted.

SMALLER-SCALE EARLY ASIAN IMMIGRATION

Indians, Filipinos, and Koreans and U.S. Reactions

The literature suggests that Indian (Chandrasekhar 1982), Filipino (Cordova 1983), and Korean (Conroy 1960) immigrants, like the Chinese and Japanese, were found in the United States in small numbers in the early and middle part of the nineteenth century. In fact, isolated individuals and small communities originating in India, the Philippines, and Korea are known to have been in the country as early as the mid-eighteenth century. Although the U.S. census identifies at least one Indian at the time of the first census in 1820, Filipinos were not identified as a separate group until 1936, and the Koreans not until 1948.

The Indians

Although India is a complex of ethnic diversity, as is China, most early immigrants from India to the United States came from one region—the Punjab—and most of them were Sikhs. They arrived in Washington to work in the lumber industry and in California to work in railroad construction. There was also a smaller group that consisted of middle-class students, political refugees, and the elite. Immigration records indicate that by 1910 close to 5,000 Indians had entered the country. Soon after they began in the railroad industry, many moved to agricultural work, first as laborers and then as proprietors. Like the early immigrants of other Asian nations, the overwhelming majority were male sojourners.

Of the 5,800 Indian immigrants between 1901 and 1911, only 109 were female; by 1920, with the continuing immigration, about 8,000 men had entered the United States. Most indicated that they were married, although their wives were abroad, and most sent significant portions of their income home to India.

Although the Indians came without wives and many worked as laborers, they did not form ethnic enclaves as did many other Asian immigrant groups. If ethnic solidarity existed, it was not in the form of geographic clusters. This group of Asian immigrants also represented another facet in Asian immigration to the United States—they were "dark Caucasians" (Takaki 1989). In the absence of Indian women, many Indian laborers married Mexican women, but these marriages were often fraught with difficulties because of the extreme cultural differences, and at least 20 percent of them ended in divorce (La Brack and Leonard 1984).

The Indians who were neither laborers nor farmers became involved with and affected U.S. society in two other ways unlike other Asians. Perhaps because of their Caucasoid backgrounds, some of the early middle-class immigrants who settled in major areas of the East Coast were able to practice their professions, and some married white women. In addition, an elite group of activist students and other leaders in the Indian community developed the Gadar freedom fighting movement for India. Referred to by American historians as the Hindu Conspiracy, the organization, based in San Francisco, aimed to overthrow the British raj in India. This group was violent and managed to marshal arms to transport to India, but most of its members were apprehended and many were executed. Although it was a very small group, it exacerbated perceptions of Indians as violent.

Though Indians in the United States were called "Hindus," a third of the group was Muslim and the majority was Sikh—readily identifiable by the turbans worn and the full beards sported. Initially viewed as being "picturesque," they were soon called "niggers" (Takaki 1989). Despite their Caucasian features and their brown skin, they were more frequently associated with the Chinese and Japanese, and unacceptable characteristics were ascribed to all the groups. Unlike the Chinese, the Indians were viewed as sullen and uncompromising. They were blamed for the violence directed against them, as were the Japanese.

The presence of Indians caused considerable confusion among white Americans, who recognized them as Aryans. Like the Chinese and

Japanese, they were willing to work for low wages and hence were viewed as dangerous rivals by the white working class, who often victimized them. The Asiatic Exclusion League,[3] formed by a group of white workers in 1905, denounced these immigrants as dirty, lustful, and diseased (Takaki 1989). In 1907, 700 Indians were driven across the border from Washington into Canada by hundreds of white workers. Such vigilante mass expulsions of Indians from one community to another occurred more than a few times. Once again, legislative action reflected societal attitudes—between 1908 and 1920 immigration denied entry to almost 3,500 Indians on the grounds that they would become public charges.

The Filipinos

In the early twentieth century, the influx of Filipinos was sudden and large. In 1910 a mere 406 Filipinos, primarily government-supported students, were on the mainland. By 1920 there were 5,603 Filipinos in the United States, and by 1930 their numbers had increased to 45,208. The Philippine-American War (1899–1902), known in the United States as the Philippine Insurrection, ended with the Philippines becoming an American colony and the natives becoming U.S. nationals. Therefore, although this group was Asian, it was different from all other Asian populations because its members were recognized as U.S. nationals. In addition, American influence in the Philippines ensured that the citizens were able to speak English and that they were considerably more knowledgeable about the American way of life than were their counterparts from other Asian countries. Because of the Philippines' three-century experience as a Spanish colony, the majority of the citizens were Catholic, and all were heavily influenced by the Spanish culture.

Between 1900 and 1930, then, two waves of Filipino immigration to the United States took place. Although some Filipino women arrived as war brides of Spanish-American War (1898) veterans, the first wave began arriving in 1903. It was small and consisted of government-supported students, known as *pensionados*, who studied at such high-profile universities as Harvard, Stanford, and Cornell. Most of them returned to the Philippines to assume leadership roles in the Philippine political, economic, and social systems (Agbayani-Siewert and Revilla 1995). Of those who did not return, a large segment blended with the second wave of immigrants, who arrived after 1910.

This second wave came in the wake of the *pensionados*, some with hopes of acquiring a U.S. education. These immigrants, however, did not receive government support; they soon found the cost of education prohibitive and turned to the labor force. The majority of young men who arrived in the second wave were seeking employment. Because of the Chinese Exclusion Act, which barred Chinese immigrants, and the Gentlemen's Agreement, which prevented additional Japanese labor migrants, the United States found itself in short supply of cheap labor. A large number of Filipinos migrated first to Hawaii, then to the mainland once their three-year contracts in Hawaii had ended. Another group came directly to the United States from the Philippines. In Hawaii, the Filipinos were pitted against the Japanese workers by plantation owners, but this rivalry was carefully regulated to prevent violence and disruption in productivity. Labor contractors regularly pitted different ethnic groups against each other to break the strikes that desperate farmworkers had begun staging in an effort to improve their working conditions. In the United States, however, the Filipinos competed with a racist white working class and were often the targets of a violent backlash.

Early Filipino immigrants to the West Coast, like other immigrant laborers, were almost all bachelors. The Filipinos, many of whom had been peasants and agricultural workers in the Philippines, could work in seasonal farming and move from one community to another, harvesting crops as needed. They were stereotyped as good for "stoop labor." Since they were smaller in stature than white men, it was believed that they could stoop more easily. Greatly exploited, they worked under deplorable conditions, for long hours, and in unhealthy circumstances. Despite their status as U.S. nationals, the American labor unions not only did nothing to improve their situations but actually worked to exclude them from the United States, believing that they competed with whites for scarce jobs.

The literature indicates that Filipino bachelors in the United States, especially in the absence of Filipino women (who numbered 7 to every 100 males), were very attracted to white women. As U.S. nationals, and because they were more knowledgeable about American society and culture than were other Asians, they were able to compete with white males for these women. Filipinos actively sought white females, and in dance halls they could pay ten cents (of their daily one dollar income) for a dance with a white woman. In addition to such transient contacts, many were able to establish more lasting relationships, some of which led to marriage. Even if the girl's family approved, however, social and legal forces still sought to curtail such relationships. In the late 1920s a series of bloody anti-Filipino race riots occurred, stemming from economic rivalry and sexual jealousy. In 1933, in response to public outcry, miscegenation statutes were modified to forbid marriages between whites and Filipinos, which, until that time, had not been covered. White men believed that white women were not safe from Filipino men and needed to be legally protected from them.

Among the laws enacted was the Tydings-McDuffie Act of 1934, which ended Filipino immigration. Strongly debated, this act was passed six years and one presidential veto after it was initiated. Through it, the Philippines were promised independence in 1945, but among other provisions was the statement that "the citizens of the Philippine Islands who are not citizens of the United States shall be considered as if they were aliens" (Kim 1994:117). This part of the act effectively influenced the economic status of Philippine immigrants, and although many had been employed in the American merchant marine, they were dismissed in 1936 when Congress passed legislation requiring that 90 percent of the jobs be filled by U.S. citizens. With a new quota of only fifty, immigration from the Philippines virtually stopped until the end of World War II. Such an act, in fact, was not necessary. The flow of immigrants had stemmed as word reached the Philippines that the United States was no longer the Promised Land. Labor disturbances coupled with the unemployment and suffering of Filipinos on the West Coast greatly diminished the Filipinos' attraction to the United States (Takaki 1989). During the period between 1934 and 1953, the heavily male Filipino population aged and declined.

In 1946, as a reward for loyalty to the United States against Japan, Congress made Filipinos eligible for citizenship, and President Truman doubled their annual immigration quota to one hundred. During the period between 1953 and 1965, the thirteen years of the McCarran-Walter Act, annual Filipino immigration should have totaled 1,300. However the Immigration and Naturalization Service recorded 32,201 immigrants from the Philippines. This figure represented another wave of immigration, in which more nonquota immigrants—wives and children—and an even larger number of nonimmigrants—students, businesspeople, and tourists—arrived in the United States.

The Koreans

Koreans, though also found in the United States in the late nineteenth century, have a relatively recent history in the country, since a significant number migrated only after the Korean War (1950–1953). In fact, U.S. immigration records did not count the Korean presence until 1948, and literature about their experiences before 1965 is scant compared with that on other Asian groups.

Like the Japanese and the Filipinos, Koreans were recruited to work in the Hawaiian sugar plantations, and between 1903 and 1905, some 7,200 Koreans immigrated there. Most were young males who came as sojourners, with every intention of returning to Korea as soon as they had accumulated enough money. They arrived as contract laborers and were in fact little better than indentured servants. They worked for seven years at wages substantially lower than those paid to American workers and under less than satisfactory working conditions, including long and grueling hours. Although they were from the lower classes, they were not peasants, who in Korea were very conservative and believed that immigration was immoral (Hurh and Kim 1984). The majority was from Seoul, Inchon, and other urban locations, whereas many other Asians had come to the United States from rural areas. Like the Filipinos, however, the Koreans had been heavily influenced by American Christian missionaries, and 40 percent of the immigrants had been Christian even while in Korea. They were unlike the Filipinos in that they were not well versed in the English language and had not been culturally Westernized.

A small group of Koreans did immigrate earlier to the United States, with some literature indicating that in 1930 there were fewer than 2,000 Koreans in California. Koreans who came between 1906 and 1923, when Asian immigration was banned, were composed of two groups—picture brides and students and political refugees. This second group of intellectuals, students, and political exiles played a major role in organizing the Korean community and directing activities toward Korean independence. Most of the pre-1906 immigrants to both Hawaii and California were single males, who were later allowed to bring their picture brides from Korea. Often there was an age difference of a decade or more between the man and his young wife.

Koreans in the United States in the early years found themselves in a particularly awkward position. Korea had been taken over by Japan,

and many of these individuals had been involved at some level in organizing to free Korea from Japanese rule—yet when they arrived in the
United States, they were officially represented by the Japanese government. The Japanese government intervened on their behalf when they
were mistaken for Japanese by an angry white mob, but the Koreans
rejected the assistance of the Japanese consul general in Los Angeles
who stepped in to protect "the Japanese nationals." The Koreans were
most offended by the tendency of U.S. natives to call them Japanese,
especially since they had been fighting the Japanese for so long and perceived them to be the enemy. The Koreans, along with the Filipinos,
eagerly joined U.S. war efforts against Japan. Since many of them spoke
Japanese, they were an invaluable asset to the U.S. government. One
fifth of the Los Angeles Korean population joined the California
National Guard. Elderly Korean women and men also joined the war
effort, with women serving in the Red Cross and men volunteering as
emergency fire wardens. Their involvement in the war effort generated
substantial support for them among white Americans.

The next wave of Koreans to the United States was a somewhat
larger group, and their numbers increased substantially between 1950
and 1964, especially after the Korean War, with immigrants numbering
15,050 and nonimmigrants numbering 27,459 (Min 1998). Most
Korean immigrants at this time were the war brides of American servicemen (more than 40 percent [Min 1995; Shin 1987]), war orphans,
and students. The literature suggests that they were expected to blend
into U.S. society before they had an opportunity to become acculturated, and many were isolated and unhappy. In addition, many U.S.
servicemen stationed in Korea adopted some of the hundreds of thousands of children who were orphaned because of the war and brought
them to the United States. The Holt Adoption Agency was also responsible for the entry of some 6,000 children during this period; the
majority of them had American fathers—46 percent were white and 13
percent were black (Kitano and Daniels 1995). A considerably larger
number of nonimmigrant Koreans also entered the United States,
particularly students whom U.S. servicemen had helped or those who
sought the educational and professional opportunities about which they
had learned through the military aides in South Korea. Thus it was the
established connections between the United States and Korea that were
primarily responsible for the immigration flow to the United States
between the Korean War and the liberalization period.

THE JAPANESE INTERNMENT

While the early Asian immigrants from China, Japan, India, the Philippines, and Korea shared many similarities, the first generation of Japanese immigrants, called the Issei, was decidedly different. This group came from a country with a strong government that was willing to advocate on its behalf. The majority of the immigrants had some elementary education, and while most began their lives in the United States as laborers, many soon became farmers and proprietors. Those who resided in urban areas became small-business owners and catered primarily to the Japanese ethnic community.

Furthermore, many women and children arrived as "picture brides" and "paper sons," fostering the development of the Japanese American community and the birth of the second generation, the Nisei. By virtue of their birth in the United States, the Nisei were U.S. citizens, eligible for many opportunities denied to their parents, who were "aliens" ineligible for citizenship. Most were highly acculturated to the American culture, and a large proportion availed themselves of the opportunities to attend university. Beginning to form a middle class, they entered the professions of law, medicine, and dentistry. Many distanced themselves from the Japanese culture, much to the dismay of the Issei, on whom they were still economically dependent. Nevertheless, the dominant American society did not accept them as Americans, and they continued to be subject to prejudice and discrimination. Reports abound of highly educated Nisei who, despite college degrees and professional credentials, could find no positions in the majority society and had to continue to work in the ethnic areas.

Psychologically devastating but consistent with the continuing perception of Japanese Americans as foreigners, immediately after the bombing of Pearl Harbor by the Japanese on the morning of December 7, 1941, all Japanese Americans were targeted as "enemies." Pearl Harbor was the U.S. center for military action in the Pacific, and it was almost completely destroyed, resulting in intense U.S. anger against the Japanese and serving as the impetus for the U.S. entry into World War II. The United States would later drop two atomic bombs, on Hiroshima and Nagasaki, prompting Japan to surrender on August 14, 1945.

On the night following the Pearl Harbor attack, the systematic internment of the Japanese American population commenced. First the Federal Bureau of Investigation took into custody those of Japanese background who had connections with the Japanese government. They were presumed guilty by association, and most often were the Issei leaders. At the beginning the government differentiated between those Japanese who were "aliens" and those who were U.S. citizens, but the distinction was soon abandoned, and all people of Japanese origin, regardless of age, occupation, or gender, were rounded up and herded to internment camps. This irrational and methodical exile and incarceration of more than 112,000 Japanese Americans not only made their history in the United States unique but also revealed a degree of xenophobia that overrode the natural and legal rights of a large portion of this population.

Disagreement exists about whether or not these "internment camps" were concentration camps. Suffice it to say that they were camps created to confine and segregate innocent people whose common trait was their ancestry. Surrounded by barbed-wire fencing, the interned risked being shot and killed by armed patrol guards if they sought to leave the camps. Although about 10,000 people who lived further east and others who were able to move before the spring of 1942 in response to rumors that Japanese Americans were at risk avoided incarceration, they lived in fear that they too would soon be identified as enemies and suffer the same fate. Despite the internment, in 1944 the draft was reinstated for Japanese American men, and approximately 25,000 served in the U.S. military in dangerous capacities. On the other hand, some resisted the draft because the internment violated American principles; these men were tried, convicted, and sent to federal penitentiaries.

The Issei never recovered from the shock of what they perceived as the American betrayal. Although they had always hoped to become "American," they soon learned that because of the great cultural differences and the tremendous discrimination, that goal was not an option for them. When they were finally given the opportunity of becoming U.S. citizens in the 1950s, it was too late to significantly change their lives. They had developed a parallel community, in which not only businesses survived but also the services that they needed. Japanese American doctors, realtors, and businessmen met the needs of the Japanese community, thus minimizing dependence on mainstream organizations.

THE LIBERALIZATION PERIOD, 1965–PRESENT

While some modifications are continually made to the Immigration Act of October 1, 1965, it remains the primary directing force of the INS.

It set the annual immigrant quota at 290,000—170,000 for the Eastern Hemisphere and 120,000 for the Western Hemisphere. INS specifications of the worldwide level of immigration and the selection procedures are detailed in Title II of the act (INA: ACT 201), as is the preference in allocation of immigrant visas (INA: ACT 203). Even more significantly, while INA: ACT 202 identifies the numerical limitation for any foreign state, it also includes a nondiscrimination clause that states: "No person shall receive any preference or priority or be discriminated against in the issuance of an immigrant visa because of the person's race, sex, nationality, place of birth, or place of residence."

The Immigration Act specified that spouses and unmarried adult children of U.S. citizens are exempt from the numerical quota and established a preferential system for the allocation of entry visas. Some modifications have occurred since the original 1965 act, through the Immigration Act of 1990, which restructured the immigrant categories of admission. In many important ways, however, the 1965 act has remained substantively the same, and it is clear that system allocations are not based on the prevention of entry of Asians. The 1998 fiscal year limit was 675,000, and the following categories are currently identified:

FAMILY SPONSORED IMMIGRANTS (480,000 ANNUALLY)

1. Unmarried sons and daughters of citizens (23,400 annually)
2. Spouses and unmarried sons and unmarried daughters of permanent resident aliens (114,200)
3. Married sons and married daughters of citizens (23,400)
4. Adult brothers and sisters of citizens (65,000)

EMPLOYMENT-BASED IMMIGRANTS (140,000 ANNUALLY)

1. Priority workers (40,040)
   a. Aliens with extraordinary ability
   b. Professors and researchers
   c. Certain multinational executives and managers
2. Members of the professions holding advanced degrees (40,040)
3. Skilled workers, professionals, and other workers (40,040)
4. Special immigrants, usually refugees adjusting their status (9,940)
5. Employment creators, "investors" (9,940)

DIVERSITY (55,000 ANNUALLY, EFFECTIVE 1995)

Nonpreferential immigrants ineligible under the other categories

ASIANS IN THE UNITED STATES SINCE 1965

Once the barriers were removed from Asian immigration, those who had not been able to bring their immediate relatives into the country filed immigration visas for them, rapidly exhausting the annual allocation for each country. Within a few years, a long backlog of applicants and a waiting list of several years, sometimes close to a decade, had built up.

Thus the 1965 act gave priority to the reunification of families and to both skilled and unskilled workers needed in the United States. In 1960 the Asian population numbered about 923,000 (U.S. Bureau of Census 1975), and by 1990 (see table 4.1) the figure was nearing 7 million. The 2000 Census revealed numbers close to 12 million, and it is believed that there may have been an undercount.[4]

The flow of immigrants from different countries varies annually, but there appears to be a fairly consistent pattern. The Immigration and Naturalization Service in May 1999 reported that during fiscal year 1998 Asian immigration was 219,696, or 33.3 percent of all immigrants. The Asian countries sending the largest numbers of immigrants were China (5.6%), India (5.5%), the Philippines (5.2%), Vietnam (2.7%), Korea (2.2%), Pakistan (2.0%), and Bangladesh (1.3%). Refugees approved from Vietnam and other Asian countries are not included in these numbers, but the ceiling for them in 1997 exceeded 14,500 (East Asia 10,000; Near East and South Asia 4,500). In contrast to the dramatic increase in immigration from most Asian countries since 1965, however, Japanese immigration declined and the number of Japanese entering the United States is relatively small. Although the 1990 Census reported a Japanese American population that was the third largest among the Asian groups, two-thirds of these were native-born, compared with less than 40 percent of other Asians (Nishi 1995). The large numbers represent an Asian group that is well into the fourth and fifth generations in the United States. The 2000 Census reveals a dramatic decline in the size of this population as fewer individuals immigrate, some return to Japan, and the older generations begin to die. Although the 1990 Census reported a population of 847,562, the 2000 Census reported a decline to 796,700. The Japanese group fell from the third position to the sixth among all Asian groups. While the groups holding the first five positions each had an immigrant population well above one million, the Japanese numbered well below 800,000.

Table 4.1.

ASIAN POPULATION (1990 AND 2000)*

Population	1990 Number	1990 Percent	2000 Number	2000 Percent
Total Asian population	6,908,638	100.0	10,242,998	100.0
Chinese	1,645,472	23.8	2,432,585	23.8
Filipino	1,406,770	20.4	1,850,314	18.1
Japanese	847,562	12.3	796,700	7.8
Indian	815,447	11.8	1,678,765	16.4
Korean	798,849	11.6	1,076,872	10.5
Vietnamese	614,547	8.9	1,122,528	11.0
Laotian[1]	149,014	2.2		
Cambodian[1]	147,411	2.1		
Thai[1]	91,275	1.3		
H'mong[1]	90,082	1.3		
Other Asian[2]	302,209	4.4	1,285,234	12.6
Pakistani[1]	82,904	1.2		
Indonesian[1]	27,634	0.4		
Malayan[1]	13,817	0.2		
Bangladeshi[1]	13,817	0.2		
Sri Lankan[1]	13,817	0.2		
Burmese[1]	6,909	0.1		
All other Asians[1]	14,508	2.1		
Two races (total U.S.)[3]	6,368,075	100.0		
White/Asian	868,395	13.3		
Black/Asian	106,782	1.7		
Asian/Pacific Islander	138,802	2.2		
Asian/Other	249,108	3.9		
Asian and bi/multiracial[4]	11,878,828	100.0		

*Source: U.S. Census Bureau (1990, 2000). Census 2000 figures still incomplete at the time of this printing and will be available for public distribution in late 2002.
[1]Data for these groups not yet published.
[2]In Census 2000, the category of "Other Asians" also included individuals reporting two or more Asian groups.
[3]This information was not solicited for the 1990 Census. Does not include either Asians of two or more Asian groups nor does it include individuals reporting three or more races.
[4]Includes total of all individuals indicating any Asian heritage.

The Immigration and Naturalization Act and its modifications and the Refugee Act and its modifications have had significant impact on the arrival of Asians in the United States. Because of the stipulations of each category of acts, however, the profiles of Asians entering the United States under each group have substantially differed. The reasons they left their countries of origin differ, the intrapersonal resources they bring with them differ, and the receptions they receive in the United States differ. Their personal profiles, their experiences, and their acceptance greatly affect their adjustment. Most recent East and South Asian arrivals have had the professional skills and resources to adapt to life in the United States, while the majority of Southeast Asian refugees have not had these capabilities.

Kitano (1991) suggests that prejudice is maintained through stereotypes, while discrimination is tied to legislation and usually leads to disadvantage. While still embodying prejudicial attitudes and institutionalized discrimination, the United States, perhaps more than any other country in the world, engages in unprecedented attempts at pluralism, which emphasizes the preservation of ethnic differences and recognizes the complex mix of various populations. By seeking pluralism, the nation is attempting to equalize opportunities across racial groups and minimize xenophobia.

Discrimination ensures inequality by preventing access to superior education, sufficient income, and adequate housing, which then diminishes one's ability to meet daily needs. The resulting stress and subsequent family dysfunction can lead to antisocial behavior, which reinforces stereotypical perceptions of poor adaptation and increases prejudice and discrimination. These, in turn, ensure the cycle of discrimination and dysfunction and maintain the "culture of poverty," which is transmitted across generations. Since prejudice is an attitude, it is perceived to be less damaging to a group than is discrimination, despite the strong link between them (Kitano and Daniels 1995). Eradication of prejudice cannot be legislated, but antidiscrimination measures can be implemented through legislative efforts. While this approach may ensure a modicum of equality, it can also exacerbate prejudicial attitudes.

Although the Asian community was segregated and isolated in the first half of the twentieth century, since the beginning of the liberalization period, it has been allowed access to opportunities in the dominant society. This change, coupled with the increased professionalism of second- and third-generation Asians (particularly the Nisei and Sansei) and the screening of post-1965 immigrants, has led to the establishment and success of large numbers of Chinese, Japanese, Koreans, Filipinos, and Indians.

The academic attainment levels of these five groups were above the national average in 1990,[5] with 78 percent of all Asians aged twenty-five and over having completed high school. The national average was 75 percent. Sixty-seven percent of all Asians and 60 percent of all Asian women were in the labor force, as compared to 65 percent of all Americans and 57 percent of American women. Furthermore, in part because of higher levels of education, Asians were more likely to have professional specialty occupations (31.2% versus 26.4%) and technical jobs (33.3% versus 31.7%) than the general population, with a higher per capita income ($14,143 versus $13,806) in 1990. Overall, Asians, when compared to the national norms, appear to be more economically successful. They often have won the reputation of being the "model minority," which in the twenty-first century translates into the recognition that they are economic successes and therefore constitute a group to be emulated. This view represents a change from the original idea that the model minority is a group that is well behaved and therefore is to be emulated by other minorities.

It is important to recognize that while several Asians, especially those from East and South Asian countries, have made significant achievements in many professional areas and have therefore been able to establish comfortable lifestyles, this outcome has resulted not only from their own abilities and capabilities. Certainly their abilities are instrumental in allowing them to meet academic expectations and professional standards. As history has shown, however, not all those who are blessed with academic abilities have been able to participate in the opportunities offered by the dominant society. The experience of the Nisei in the 1930s and 1940s testifies to this. Although they were highly educated, with college degrees from such notable institutions as Harvard and Stanford, they could not find jobs commensurate with their degrees and found themselves confined to the ethnic community.

Despite the opening of opportunities for Asians in the professional, technological, and academic worlds, they continue to believe that in order to compete for jobs they must attain credentials that surpass those of whites. Hence, they are constantly compelled to excel. While that drive may be rooted in their family values and in the selectivity of their immigrant group through immigration policy, the family directive to surpass the whites in competence is also based on the disparity between the employment and salary scales of Asian Americans and those of white Americans, for Asian Americans are paid significantly less than whites in similar occupations and positions (U.S. Bureau of the Census 1998c). Equal opportunity efforts do not extend to them, as they are not seen as an oppressed minority. So although they are counted as minority members in an organization's personnel count—and so meet some expectations for minority representation—they do not fill any quota requirements, nor are they able to fill positions reserved for minority candidates. To compete for positions that are open to whites, they must outperform white candidates, as they must compensate for their ethnicity that does not fill legislative quotas.

The impetus to excel and the increased rewards for excellence, in the form of professional and economic opportunities, have resulted in the superior performance of many Asian Americans. Like the cycle of poverty, there appears to be a cycle of opportunity. As Asians evidence high levels of ability, they are provided opportunities to put their ability to use and are awarded recognition. With their successful performance, they are further reinforced by additional opportunities. As a "model minority," they are perceived as being competent, and adaptable, and well adjusted economically, socially, and emotionally. Perhaps they are now viewed as the well-adjusted model to which all minorities, and perhaps even the majority, should aspire.

The stereotype of model minority can also have a halo effect, in that all Asians are perceived as being competent and aspiring and therefore may be afforded opportunities based on the expectation that they will perform with greater diligence than non-Asians. This view is a visible shift from the earlier half of the century, when Asians were regarded with mistrust and dislike. In fact, in California's Silicon Valley, Asians— particularly Indians—are considered an asset because, according to Sabeer Bhatia, the founder of Hotmail.com, "the history of Indian entrepreneurs in the [Silicon] Valley speaks for itself" (Haniffa 1999a:34). It is not that there were no Asians earlier who were successful in the Silicon Valley, it is that only recently have Asians been viewed as an asset rather than as competition or threat. Ultimately, what appears to matter to the present U.S. society is the individual's ability to meet and—even better—to surpass expectations. For Asians, merit is more readily rewarded in the contemporary United States than ever before, certainly substantially more than it was before the 1950s.

The experiences of the Indian immigrants suggest that the success of an individual or a group depends not only on the capabilities of that individual or that group but also on the readiness of the dominant society to recognize those abilities, acknowledge them as being of value to the well-being of the society, allow them to be utilized, and reward the employees for their contribution. For this, the current dominant U.S. society deserves credit. It came a great distance during the latter half of the twentieth century from the oppressive xenophobia that resulted in the early legislative measures to limit Asian immigration and the barriers that prevented Asian economic and professional achievement.

Although professional success has secured for immigrant Asians the reputation of being a model minority, some express the experience of social discrimination substantially more frequently than economic discrimination. As the second generations of these newer groups of immigrants reach adulthood, there may be considerable differences in perceptions—both of them and by them. Increasing numbers of them report that they have non-Asian friends, and interracial marriages are common.

The general public's overwhelming perception of Asian Americans is that they constitute a model minority, are professionally successful, and, according to their own cultural notions of health, are well adjusted both emotionally and mentally. While such a stereotype may be an asset to some, several theoreticians and researchers believe that, contrary to being a compliment, the view of Asians as a model group is racist and presents barriers to a large segment of the Asian American constituency. Although many among the Chinese, Japanese, Indian, Korean, and Filipino immigrants have now had the opportunity to excel in their chosen professions and to do well economically, some encounter the glass ceiling, meaning that the very top echelons of corporate or professional life are not accessible to them. Women in the United States have long recognized and struggled with this barrier. Because of the model stereotype, the majority population is skeptical about the validity of claims regarding discrimination and violence against Asians (Delucchi and Do 1996). However, in the wake of the September 11, 2001 terror attacks, this is changing.

The achievements of a large number of Asian Americans, moreover, obscure the economic, health, emotional, familial, and social problems that significant numbers of people from this group continue to experience in the United States. Such difficulties characterize the lives of some

South and East Asians, but especially those of the most recent Asian immigrant group, the Southeast Asians from Vietnam, Laos, and Cambodia, most of whom arrived under refugee status and live below the poverty line.

Southeast Asians

As a result of the Vietnamese War, large numbers of Southeast Asian refugees fled communist regimes, and many sought refuge in the United States. The total population of this refugee group (also known as "Indochinese" refugees) now stands at well over one million. The first wave—highly educated, affluent, and well-connected individuals who rapidly adjusted to Western society—began arriving in 1975, after the fall of Saigon.

The U.S. Refugee Act of 1980 provides for federal programs to assist refugees through the Office of Refugee Resettlement. The programs—English-language instruction, job training, medical care, and so on—are designed to promote self-sufficiency. The primary goal is to help refugees become "economically self-sufficient" in the shortest possible time; they are defined as economically self-sufficient if they are not receiving welfare benefits. A number of studies suggest, however, that many refugees in the United States manage to reach only a low economic status. A significant proportion receive public assistance and live well below the official poverty level long after they have been determined to be economically self-sufficient (Bach 1988; Office of Refugee Resettlement 1991), and most of them spend a greater percentage of their income on housing than do other groups, yet they live in significantly more crowded conditions (Potocky 1996; Vu 1990).

Furthermore, economic self-sufficiency does not necessarily resolve cultural, economic, and social problems (Mayadas and Segal 2000). Unlike the elite of the first cohort, the second and subsequent groups of refugees from Southeast Asia have been fishermen, farmers, peasants, and laborers, with low levels of literacy, education, and skills. Despite U.S. resettlement programs, they experienced significant difficulties acclimatizing themselves to life in the fast-paced, computer-dominated environment of the United States during the last quarter of the twentieth century. The skills they bring with them have not been directly transferable to Western industry, business, and technology, and their inability to speak English has been a major deterrent to finding and retaining jobs. Thus, the number of Southeast Asians with marketable or employable skills is limited. As a result of these factors, this group of Asians has been dependent on external aid for longer than the Refugee Resettlement Program envisioned (Law and Schneiderman 1992).

Despite basic similarities, Vietnamese, Laotians, and Cambodians do originate from diverse nations, with diverse cultures. Because the majority arrived in the United States as a result of the Vietnam War and under the Refugee Act, they tend to be perceived as one. The communities that they have established in the United States, however, are not integrated into one Southeast Asian community, and their processes of adjustment to the United States do differ. It is important to recognize, on the other hand, that barring repatriation efforts that were directed specifically toward the Laotians in the 1990s, the majority of Southeast Asian refugees have had a similar history and experience in the United States and have often been treated as a uniform group by the United States legal and social systems.

Before 1975 few Southeast Asians lived in the United States. In the 1950s the number of immigrants from Indochina totaled 179, and by the 1960s the number had increased to only 3,503 (Tran 1998). While in 1974 there were 18,558, mostly Vietnamese immigrants, the 1990 Census reported more than one million, but after the Amerasian Homecoming Act, the numbers continued to rise annually, resulting in a count of more than one million for the Vietnamese population alone (table 4.1). Using data from a number of governmental sources, Rumbaut (1995) presents a breakdown of refugee and nonrefugee immigration from Cambodia, Laos, and Vietnam, revealing the largest numbers of entries during 1980 and 1981. Between 1975 and 1992, 147,460 refugees arrived from Cambodia, 230,023 from Laos, and 653,521 from Vietnam. In addition, 173,896 nonrefugee immigrants entered from Vietnam (including 55,985 Amerasians between 1989 and 1992).

When the South Vietnamese government collapsed on April 30, 1975, more than 100,000 Vietnamese from all walks of life escaped to the unknown in search of safety. The United States responded by ensuring that its navy, stationed in the Pacific, rescued the refugees, and the first group arrived in the United States, despite the general reaction of the public that they should neither be admitted nor allowed to remain. The views of the U.S. population and the U.S. government clearly differed with regard to settling the Indochinese in the country. The public was opposed, yet the government felt a moral obligation to permit these refugees to enter, and the influx has continued since 1975.

Rumbaut (1995) reflects that this group of refugees had a unique legal and political status, and therefore they were allowed access to public assistance to which other immigrant populations were not entitled. Many Americans, over the years, have voiced dissatisfaction with the continuing stream of Southeast Asian refugees. Some believe that they compete for a limited number of jobs; others resent the use of taxpayers' money to support them. Longer-established and oppressed minorities feel the more recent refugees are diverting limited minority resources.

Other Asian Groups

Patterns of migration have indicated that as a particular group settles in a nation, establishes roots, and becomes economically solvent, it begins procedures to bring in other family members from the home country who may not have been eligible, or able, to enter on their own. Family reunification guidelines of the INS and employment-based visas have allowed all immigrants, including Asians, to send for family members and other community members to work in ethnic businesses. Hence, the earlier guidelines and the absence of potential support in the United States ensured that most Asian entrants between 1965 and 1985 were highly qualified professionals. The latter half of the 1980s and the 1990s saw a distinct change in the sociodemographic characteristics of immigrants from this continent. While a large percentage of those who enter are still highly educated and professionally qualified, a substantial number lack the skills necessary for survival and adaptation in the United States. Therefore, East and South Asians are increasingly becoming part of the U.S. welfare population.

In addition to the Southeast Asian refugees, the INS reports that a number of Asians from other countries continue to seek refugee status on an annual basis. In 1998, 5,795 applications came from China and 2,664 from India. Another substantial number is that of undocumented aliens, most of whom are overstays. Frequently they are visitors or students who would not be permitted to remain in the United States because they do not meet immigration requirements, and theoretically they are ineligible for employment.

The U.S. society is concerned about immigration, and the government is ever more cognizant of the drain on resources for U.S. nationals when immigrants require public assistance. Before 1996, legal immigrants were eligible for most forms of public assistance as soon as they were granted permanent residency in the United States. The Personal

Responsibility and Work Opportunity Reconciliation Act of August 22, 1996, established restrictions on the eligibility of legal immigrants for means-tested public assistance[6] and broadened the restrictions on pubic benefits for illegal aliens and nonimmigrants.[7] This measure has substantially affected the health, education, and economic benefits available to large segments of the newer immigrant groups.

Thus, while entry into the United States may have been easier in the last quarter of the twentieth century, it is also more difficult to survive without the personal and professional skills and resources that help the immigrant to adapt to societal expectations and standards. In recent years, although it is no longer legal or politically correct to be prejudicial and discriminatory—particularly in employment—it is clear that xenophobia continues to be rampant in the U.S. society. News reports are replete with violence perpetrated by members of the white society on ethnic Americans, and they are also filled with reports of violence by members of one ethnic minority group against those of another.

Once called discrimination or prejudice, violent acts against a group because of its race, ethnicity, or other differentiating characteristic are now designated as "hate crimes." Despite the illegality of harming a person because of race, belief, or sexual orientation, such incidents continue to be common. It is ironic that it was necessary to enact such a specific law, especially since some existing laws already protect individuals and their property from violation. While news reports and research suggest that the frequency of hate crimes against Asians is quite high (Chan and Hune 1995; Chen and True 1994; Leung 1990; Min 1995), the general public may be less sympathetic to violence against Asians because of the image of the model minority (Delucchi and Do 1996). On the other hand, the low number of reports made to the Department of Justice (DOJ) suggests that though such acts do occur, they are reported infrequently. Of the 11,039 victims identified as having been assaulted because of bias motivation in 1996, 544 (4.92%) were Asian. Damage against property was reported less often by Asians (120 of 3,120 reported incidents). The inconsistency between the numbers of reports to the DOJ and the news report suggests that it is not the frequency that is low but the reporting. Given the current racial climate in the United States, the relatively few reports of hate crimes—11,039—imply that either such violence is not reported or the investigator is not sensitized to the issue and does not categorize the assault properly.[8]

Since the September 11, 2001, terror attacks on the World Trade Center and the Pentagon, people of South Asian descent have been increasingly targeted, assaulted, and, on occasion, killed as hatred for the perpetrators of the attacks has become generalized by many to people of brown skin.

RACIAL DISCRIMINATION AND PREJUDICE

There is no doubt that discrimination and prejudice are prevalent in the United States. While race and ethnicity are major reasons for discrimination, the human species across the globe has always discriminated against others who were dissimilar. Discrimination cuts across all peoples and areas of life, and deplorable stereotypes exist with respect not only to race but also to gender, age, disability, class, and numerous other factors. Xenophobic discrimination based on race, ethnicity, and national origin can be found in all nations. Extreme forms have resulted in measures leading to "ethnic cleansing" and civil war, but an examination of any nation will reveal at least one group that consistently and systematically experiences both social and institutional discrimination.

In these first years of the twenty-first century, many nations of the world are experiencing civil strife. In September 2000 the "hot spots" were identified as Africa in general—but particularly Eritrea and Ethiopia, Sudan and Sierra Leone—Indonesia (including East Timor), Colombia, the Balkans, Chechnya, and Liberia (U.S. Committee for Refugees 2000). Other nations that are not engaged in internal warfare nevertheless have their share of difficulties as intolerance and discrimination pit one group against another. Occidental countries continue to resent the presence of people of color. Some developed countries have so controlled indigenous peoples that they have unequal access to the resources available to the majority of the citizens. People who because of political history and colonialism reside in the lands of the colonizers are relegated to second-class status. In other nations, people of lower class are so bound that they have no opportunity to escape the lifestyle to which they were born. Discrimination appears to be endemic in human societies; it is used by the powerful and the "haves" to control and victimize the "have-nots." While this certainly does not excuse the injustices perpetrated by one group upon another, it does point out that the United States has not cornered the market on discrimination and prejudice.

The United States, a nation composed of immigrants, is one of the most multicultural societies on earth, and the profile of immigrants since 1965 clearly indicates that it is becoming more diverse. Because of its theoretical position affirming the equality of all people and its laws passed to protect that equality, the United States has built-in mechanisms to combat racism and prejudice. While institutional racism persists, there are avenues to address it. In many other nations, not only does institutional racism exist but there are few ways by which to challenge it. Most Asian Americans, however, continue to be bound by Confucianism and a belief in structure, power, authority, and clearly defined relationships—cultural factors that make them less likely to avail themselves of the existing means of confronting inequities.

The historical experience of a group affects the definition of the individual, as do the unique experiences of that individual. Early representations of Asian Americans portrayed them as shifty people with low moral standards, but also as hardworking and able to outperform native-born Americans. The new image of Asians as the model minority reflects the stereotype of a highly accomplished and hardworking individual. The label of "model minority" was imposed on Asian Americans during the Civil Rights Movement of the 1960s, during which they were identified as the quiet people who did not draw attention to themselves and did not challenge the status quo. In addition, different Asian groups bring different resources to the United States, which affects the dominant culture's perceptions of them. This, in turn, affects Asian Americans' definition of self. The recent view of Asian Americans as highly successful and overachieving serves as a self-fulfilling prophecy for many but is detrimental to others who are unable to live up to the expectation. Certainly, in Asian countries not all Asians are highly successful and competent.

While the definition of self comes from within the individual, it is to a large extent a reflection of the perceptions of others that are communicated to individuals throughout their lives. The increasing pluralism of the U.S. society and the greater exposure of individuals to people of diverse backgrounds have allowed a growing acceptance of difference at the outset of the twenty-first century than ever before. On the other hand, awareness of diversity does not result in blindness to difference, and the acceptance of difference among peoples means there is less pressure for individuals to attempt to assimilate into the dominant society. A disadvantage of increased acceptance of diversity and the inclusion of all minority groups in all aspects of U.S. society is evident in the backlash of disapproval from some constituents, especially when that disapproval is manifested in hate crimes against minorities. For example, the greater numbers and visibility of Asian Americans have been accompanied by an increase in violence directed toward them.

The dichotomous changes in the United States, with more recognition of the multicultural nature of the society and its attempts to address institutionalized discrimination, accompanied by an increase in intolerance and prejudice against Asian Americans serve to strengthen the sense of self but also complicate the already complex task of defining an identity. Defining who they are in American society is particularly difficult for Asian Americans, most of whom look very different from the dominant population, as well as from those of other minority groups, and who also retain a strong allegiance to their countries of origin.

Asian Americans have gained the dubious reputation of being the model minority. They contribute to the economy and work diligently to adapt to U.S. expectations. Nevertheless, some of them do not have the resources to live up to the image, and they are therefore victimized by this very stereotype. Regardless of how much they adapt and adjust, regardless of whether they are first- or fourth-generation Asian Americans, they are different in color and features from the Euro society, and their appearance continues to generate distrust among some.

The historical and current experience of Asians in the United States clearly illustrates the fact that this is a group that constitutes a number of cultures, each of which differs from the others and also within itself. The conditions under which each group left its country of origin can be correlated with the resources it brought to the United States. The resources can also be correlated with the stipulations placed on particular groups when they entered. The extent to which they have been able to adjust and be successful has been a result of the competencies they brought with them as well as of the willingness of the native population to allow them access to available opportunities.

As the fastest-growing minority, both by birth and by numbers of immigrants, Asians are becoming a significant presence in all areas of U.S. society. Many have made their mark in professional arenas, while others have learned to adapt and behave as does much of mainstream America. Some have had to become dependent on public assistance. Opportunities were limited for the pre-1965 immigrants and their children. They have improved considerably for later groups of Asians who have entered the United States. Children of the post-1965 immigrants, along with the small second and third generations of earlier Asian groups and the relatively large Nisei and Sansei, are increasingly American in values and behavior. It is these later generations that are a blend of the Asian and American cultures. It is they who are truly adapting to U.S. society by participating not only in the economic and professional spheres but also in the political, judicial, and social sectors. Their choices and their lives reflect their allegiance not to their parents' countries of origin but to the United States.

5

Asian Adjustment

People may start in an ethnic enclave, but they move to the sub-urbs, and their children speak English and their grandchildren intermarry . . . and that process is as old as America itself.
                                                                    —Sharry 1999

Perceptions of adjustment have differed over the years. In the view of early assimilation theorists, as well as some contemporary ones, a well-adjusted immigrant is one who assimilates into the dominant society by assuming the values, attitudes, culture, and behaviors of the majority group. The ideal is that all people should melt into one pot, which is necessary to enable equal access to resources for all. However, not all immigrants can or wish to pursue this route to assimilation. Others may wish to assimilate, but because of their reception in the host country they may not be permitted to do so. Such external factors as skin color, language, and religion can temper assimilation. In fact, it is unclear what assimilation means in light of the increasingly diverse groups that are entering the United States. Unlike most countries, the United States is truly multiracial, multiethnic, and multicultural, and over the years this has had a substantial impact across groups.

Melting pot theories assumed assimilation of factors unrelated to physiology, but they must have recognized that phenotypic characteristics would not sanction blending with the white society. Nevertheless, while there is still great debate about the presence of immigrants, Americans are becoming more tolerant of both immigration in general and immigrants of color in particular. In 1992 close to 70 percent of the Americans polled indicated concern about immigration and the possibility that those of European descent would lose their majority status, but in 1997 only 59 percent indicated such concern. Furthermore, in 1992, 62 percent believed that too many immigrants were entering from Asia, but in 1997 only 41 percent expressed that belief (National Immigration Forum 1997). It will be interesting to see if polls taken in the wake of the September 11, 2001, terror attacks reveal a reversal of this trend. Concern about immigration is also age-related, with groups over the age of fifty more likely to believe that immigrants of color threaten the majority status of whites (51 percent) than those under the age of forty-nine (32 percent). Despite increased tolerance of diversity, 79 percent of the respondents to the National Immigration Forum (1997) nevertheless supported a "melting pot," believing that the country's unique character is its ability to absorb all cultures and blend them into one.

Perceptions of successful adjustment, then, differ among the general population, contemporary immigration theorists, and the immigrants themselves. It is clear, however, that adjustment is not synonymous with assimilation. It must be measured first in terms of the life satisfaction of individuals and the extent to which they have been able to realize the aspirations that drew them to this "land of milk and honey." Second, adjustment should reflect adoption of the basic concepts of American life—equality under the law, due process, and economic opportunity (National Immigration Forum 1999a). On the other hand, it would be erroneous to view adjustment outside the context of assimilation processes as proposed by Gordon (1964). When separated from issues of race and phenotype, the extent to which immigrants make, and are permitted to make, a commitment to the nation at all levels—cultural, economic, social, and political—is also significant.

A large number of Asian immigrants, especially in the last quarter of the twentieth century, entered the United States hoping to improve their economic opportunities by seeking either higher education or professional advancement. Also during that period, refugees from Southeast Asia, seeking to escape persecution in their home countries, arrived in the United States. While many of the latter group live below the poverty line, some report that their situations in the United States are substantially better economically and in terms of physical and emotional safety (Segal 2000a, 2000b). Another factor that affects the extent of adjustment and acculturation to U.S. values and style of life is whether Asians in the United States are of the immigrant generation or of the second, third, or fourth generation. It is also more difficult to identify typical U.S. values and lifestyles, as they have become an amalgamation of several cultures.

The 2000 Census indicated a general population of approximately 281,421,906. Of these, 97.6 percent indicated that they were of a single race; 75.1 percent were white, 12.3 percent were African American, 3.6 percent were Asian and Pacific Islander, and 0.9 percent were Native American. These figures do not differentiate among the variety of groups that indicate ethnic differences in the white population. While the census estimates do break down numbers of Latinos into whites and blacks, they do not differentiate among European immigrants, or those of European ancestry, who bring with them a variety of cultures and values that are distinct from those of the traditional dominant culture—the Anglo-Saxon Protestant. Hence, it is not uncommon for theoreticians and researchers to shy away from using values and norms as indicators of adjustment. More observable factors are considered to be measures of successful integration—commitment to American society through citizenship, home ownership, English-language acquisition, and intermarriage (National Immigration Forum 1999a). Yet these indicators do not provide sufficient understanding about the intangible values that define a culture and a society. Current Asian adjustment in the United States must therefore be assessed by looking at a number of different factors: (a) economic, educational, and professional achievement, (b) ethnic identity and issues of race, (c) social and cultural values, (d) familial, gender, and community norms, (e) physical and mental health, and (f) antisocial behavior and deviance.

ECONOMIC, EDUCATIONAL, AND PROFESSIONAL ACHIEVEMENT

Economic Profile

The National Immigration Forum reports that, based on 1996 data released by the U.S. Census Bureau, immigrants and their children bring long-term economic benefits to the United States as a whole. As a group, immigrants raise the incomes of U.S.-born workers by at least $10 billion annually. This estimate is, however, conservative, for it does not include the effects of immigrant-owned businesses and highly skilled immigrants on overall productivity. The National Research Council of the National Academy of Sciences estimated that typical immigrants and their children pay an estimated $80,000 more in taxes than they will receive in public benefits over their lifetimes. Furthermore, since on the average, foreign-born naturalized citizens have higher adjusted gross incomes than do native-born Americans, they typically pay more in taxes each year. Immigrant businesses also provide a source of economic and fiscal gain for U.S. citizens—for example, immigrant-founded high-tech firms hired thousands of U.S. citizens through the year 2000.

Most immigrants' earnings increase over the course of time as they climb the U.S. economic ladder. Though many come as students, refugees, or young professionals and may be a drain on public assistance programs during their early years in the country, they do bring with them a wealth of resources, often professional but also personal, that help them achieve their dreams. Since they are usually a young population, in the prime of their working years, they are able to contribute substantially to the Social Security and Medicare systems.

Overall, Asians rank higher than most ethnic groups in the United States in terms of family income, level of education, and occupational achievement. Yet their ethnic backgrounds and immigration circumstances differ so substantially that these achievements vary across groups in the Asian American population. And within specific groups, there appears to be an economic polarization, with clusters near the top in the professions and business ownership and at the bottom in service fields and other low-status jobs (Marger 2000). The median family income in 1995 was $46,360—slightly higher than the median income of white families, which was $45,020 (U.S. Bureau of the Census, 1998a), and in 1997 it was $51,850 to the whites' $49,636 (U.S. Bureau of the Census 1998b). These figures can be deceptive, however, for the typical Asian American household may include several earning adult members, whereas the typical white household has only one or two.

When median incomes of individuals rather than families were compared, the income of whites with a high school degree ($31,120) was higher than that of Asians with a similar level of education ($25,320). Likewise, whites with a bachelor's degree earned more than did Asians ($42,050 versus $37,040). Asian women with college degrees earned about the same as their white counterparts, but Asian men earned $82 for every $100 earned by white males (U.S. Bureau of the Census 1998a). Reflecting economic polarization, in 1995, 14.6 percent of Asians lived below the poverty line, compared with 8.5 percent of whites, despite higher educational levels and a similar median family income (U.S. Bureau of the Census 1998a), suggesting that a greater number of members in one family relied on that income. By

Table 5.1.

ASIAN AMERICAN MEDIAN FAMILY INCOME*				
	All	Native Born	Foreign Born	Percentage in poverty
All Asians	$41,583	$50,513	$40,011	11.4
Chinese	41,316	56,762	37,966	11.1
Filipino	46,698	42,114	47,595	5.2
Japanese	51,550	52,728	47,836	3.4
Asian Indian	49,309	38,256	49,567	7.2
Korean	33,909	42,427	33,401	14.7
Vietnamese	30,550	23,819	30,621	23.8
Cambodian	18,126	21,974	18,063	42.1
Hmong	14,327	22,171	14,272	61.8
Laotian	23,101	20,795	23,144	32.2
Non-Asians	35,108	35,451	30,354	9.9

Source: Race and Ethnic Relations: American and Global Perspectives, 5th ed., by M. N. Marger © 2000. Reprinted with permission of Wadsworth, an imprint of the Wadsworth Group, a division of Thomson Learning.
*2000 Census data will not be available until late 2002.

1997 the percentage of Asians living in poverty increased to 15 percent (U.S. Bureau of the Census 1998c). In the early 1990s approximately 25 percent of the Vietnamese lived below the federal poverty level, as did 33 percent of the Laotians, 50 percent of the Cambodians, and 66 percent of the H'mong (Rumbaut 1995).

Thus, although U.S. government data suggest a high level of income for Asians, it becomes clear that it is still lower than that of the average white person. On the other hand, a closer look at income data reveals further discrepancies in income levels of Asians from different countries, and differences within Asian groups between those who are native-born and those who are foreign-born (table 5.1).

Overall, in 1993, the Japanese, Asian Indians, and Filipinos had the highest median incomes. Chinese income was substantially higher than that of the Koreans or of the Southeast Asian groups. On the average, it was about $5,000 lower than that of the Filipinos. Laotians earned less than half of what Filipinos and Indians did, while the income of the H'mong and Cambodians was about a third of that of Filipinos and Indians. Income levels also differed between native- and foreign-born

Asians. In general, the populations that had been in the United States the longest—the Chinese, Japanese, and Koreans—had higher median incomes among native-born individuals. The Filipinos, Indians, and Laotians who were foreign born and entered after 1965 had higher family incomes than did their native-born counterparts. A deviation from this pattern was found among the H'mong and Cambodians, also relatively recent arrivals; among them the native-born group had higher incomes.

Reasons for these variations are many. The long-established Asian groups are now in their second and subsequent generations and have had the opportunity to become more acculturated and to avail themselves of the resources necessary to succeed. Therefore, although many of these groups came to the United States as laborers in the latter part of the nineteenth century and the first half of the twentieth century, their second and subsequent generations have progressed and excelled. The newer groups, barring the Southeast Asians, were more carefully screened through the visa eligibility requirements of the 1965 Immigration Act and have been both a larger and a more professional group. The Southeast Asians, most of whom came with few transferable skills, have had greater difficulty acclimating to life in the United States and have been forced into low-paying positions. Children of Southeast Asians are more likely to secure somewhat higher-paying jobs than their parents, since they have acquired English-language skills and higher academic education.

English-language facility is an important mediator between immigrant entry and immigrant success. As a primarily monolingual country, the United States has few opportunities to offer those who are unfamiliar with the English language. Of the monoracial Asians in the United States, approximately 3,400,000 (33.3%) reported to the 2000 Census that they spoke English "less than very well."

While most Indians in 1990[1] spoke English in their homes, almost all other Asian groups spoke an Asian language (table 5.2 [U.S. Department of Commerce 1998]). Since the official language of India is English, a legacy of British occupation, and since most higher education in India is conducted in English, this group of Asians is the most proficient in the language. Indians tend to use English more readily with their children, who are more comfortable with English than with the native tongue of their parents. Despite the Americanization of the Philippines, 66 percent of Filipino Americans speak their native language at home.

Table 5.2.

ASIAN LANGUAGE SPOKEN AT HOME
AND ABILITY TO SPEAK ENGLISH, 1990 CENSUS*

	Asian Language Spoken at Home	Do Not Speak English Very Well	Linguistically Isolated**
	Percentage	Percentage	Percentage
Total Asian	62.2	56.0	34.9
Chinese	82.9	60.4	40.3
Filipino	66.0	35.6	13.0
Japanese	42.8	57.7	33.0
Asian Indian	14.5	31.0	17.2
Korean	80.8	63.5	41.4
Vietnamese	92.5	65.0	43.9
Cambodian	95.0	73.2	56.1
H'mong	96.9	78.1	60.5
Laotian	95.6	70.2	52.4
Thai	79.1	58.0	31.8
Other Asian	21.0	49.9	30.2

Source: U.S. Department of Commerce (1998).

*2000 Census data will not be available until late 2002.

**No one over the age of fourteen years speaks English very well.

Educational Levels

Higher education is valued as the route to success and therefore is stressed among Asians. While the academic achievement levels of Asians continue to reinforce the image of the model minority, it is important to recognize that most East and South Asians who have come to the United States since the 1960s have been highly educated and professional. Hence it is not surprising that they would expect the same of their offspring. This emphasis on schooling is not something that Asian immigrants acquire after they arrive in the United States. Most East and South Asians, particularly the Chinese, Japanese, Filipinos, and Indians, also emphasize education in their homelands. Especially in societies where the population is high, where the resources are scarce, and where professional opportunities are limited, education is paramount. When quality higher education is also limited, competition to excel at younger and younger ages, despite the accompanying stress, is believed to be essential. In Japan and India, for example, children attend school for long hours and then receive private after-school tutelage in the evenings and on weekends, sometimes as early as in kindergarten. Furthermore, since parents always hope that their children will do better than they have and Asians recognize that minority status in the United States is a liability, they stress higher and higher levels of academic achievement in order to level the playing field for their children. Referring to the Japanese experience—although the observation is applicable to all Asian American groups—Nishi indicates that the majority society fails to understand this "unusual reliance on education for social mobility" (1995:118).

Overall, educational attainment remains high for Asians; in 1996, 90 percent of the men over the age of twenty-five and 80 percent of the women had completed high school (U.S. Bureau of the Census 1998a). Though education is highly valued in Asian communities, the educational achievement of different groups varies dramatically. In 1990 Asian men had a higher high school graduation rate than women (82 percent versus 74 percent); in contrast, the graduation rate of the total U.S. population was lower than that for the Asians, but the percentages of males and females who graduated from high school were about the same (76 percent versus 75 percent). Substantial differences were also evident among Asian groups. Eighty-eight percent of the Japanese graduated with high school degrees, while only 31 percent of the H'mong completed high school, and 86 percent of Japanese women had high school degrees, compared with 19 percent of H'mong women (U.S. Department of Commerce 1993). Such discrepancies are evident beyond high school as well. By 1990, 38 percent of Asians had a bachelor's degree or higher, compared with 20 percent of the general population, with Indians having the highest rates and Cambodians, Laotians, and H'mong having the lowest (U.S. Department of Commerce 1993). In addition, although native-born Filipino Americans do somewhat better than whites, they lag behind many other Asian groups, especially at the college level. There is some suggestion that this may be because they are more acculturated to the American style of life and value system and believe that education is not necessarily the only key to success (Agbayani-Siewert and Revilla 1995).

What is less widely known, however, is that significant discrepancies often exist even within a particular Asian population. Despite their high mean academic achievement, Chinese are found disproportionately at the lower end of the educational spectrum, with about 26 percent not having graduated from high school, compared with the 22 percent 1990 dropout rate for whites. Chinese who do not complete high school (17 percent) are almost twice as likely to have less than a ninth-grade education as whites who do not complete high school (9 percent) (Wong 1995).

In general, however, many Asian immigrants to the United States already have earned undergraduate and graduate degrees (Marger 2000), and many nations perceive the emigration of their educated elite as a flight and a brain drain. In the late 1960s and early 1970s India and the Philippines sent more professional immigrants to the United States than did any other country. The irony of the Asian experience is that despite their superior academic accomplishments, many Asians are unable to achieve occupational and income levels commensurate with their education.

Professional Achievement

Significant numbers of Asians contribute to the United States and to the world after immigrating—in science, education, the arts, the social sciences, technology, and other fields. Though some do attain prominence in their fields, national recognition for their achievements is rare. The changes in immigration flow have meant that the Asian American community is becoming more and more bipolar, with one segment being highly educated, affluent, and well adjusted to American society, while the other is not well educated and has low levels of income and close ties to traditional culture.

Table 5.3 shows the Asians who were included in a list compiled by the National Immigration Forum (1999b) of immigrants living in the United States who have made substantial contributions to the country, its economy, its culture, and its science.

Though by no means exhaustive, this list illustrates the range of areas in which Asians in the United States are making their mark. Since 1999 Asian Americans have been unsurpassed in their contributions to the burgeoning industry of information technology.

Ong, Cheng, and Evans state that the "migration of Asians trained in technical fields is the most important component of the total global migration of scientific, technical and professional workers from developing to developed countries . . . [and] favors the highly educated" (1992:543). Between 1972 and 1988, approximately 200,000 Asians

Table 5.3.

A FEW ASIAN IMMIGRANTS IN THE NEWS

Name	Profession	Country of Origin
Dr. David Ho	Scientist/AIDS researcher	Taiwan
Zubin Mehta	Conductor	India
Midori	Classical violinist	Japan
Yoko Ono	Vocalist/songwriter	Japan
Seiji Ozawa	Conductor	China (of Japanese descent)
I.M. Pei	Architect	China
Jhoon Goo Rhee	Judo expert	Korea
Shoji Tabuchi	Country/Western entertainer	Japan
David Sun	Cofounder, Kingston Technology	Taiwan
Chang-Lin Tien	Chancellor, U.C. Berkeley	China
John Tu	Cofounder, Kingston Technology	China
Charles B Wang	CEO, Computer Associates, International	China
Wayne Wang	Film director	China

Source: National Immigration Forum (1999b).

with training in the sciences entered the United States from India, South Korea, the Philippines, and China. Clearly these numbers reflect not only the push from the countries of origin but also the pull from the United States, which liberalized immigration policies and identified areas of skill for visa eligibility. The very process of training highly educated people transcends national boundaries and cultures, involving both a shared body of knowledge and a shared style of thinking, which forms a transnational subculture that serves as a foundation for an integrated labor market (Ong, Cheng, and Evans 1992). The globalization of professions, the development of telecommunications, and the availability of information through the electronic superhighway have allowed the establishment of a common base of knowledge, values, and skills in a variety of professions, and this has served to make transitions across nations easier and to establish a mechanism through which potential immigrants can identify available opportunities in the United States.

The occupational distribution of post-1965 Asian immigrants differs substantially from that of the general U.S. population. Perhaps as a reflection of the immigrants' education, the distribution is skewed toward professionals, executive managers such as proprietors, and white-collar workers. Labor force participation rates for Asian males are slightly higher than the United States average, and higher than those for any other ethnic category. This group also has lower rates of unemployment than does the general population. Partly because of their higher educational achievements, many Asian immigrants are more occupationally advantaged than their non-Asian counterparts (Wong 1998). About 22 percent are involved in professional occupations, compared with 13 percent of the non-Asians, with all groups—other than Southeast Asians—having a higher representation than non-Asians. The profile of the Southeast Asian differs from that of most other Asian groups. Employed Southeast Asians are twice as likely as the general population to have jobs as factory workers and laborers, and they are less likely to be self-employed than are other Asian Americans (Rumbaut 1995).

Since the early 1990s, however, Southeast Asians as a group show higher rates of labor force participation and decreasing unemployment rates. While welfare dependency appears to be associated with residence in California for many Southeast Asians, 18 percent of all Southeast Asian refugee families were economically self-sufficient within one year of arriving in the United States, and some had never used public assistance (Bach and Argiros 1991). Like the success of Asian immigrants from South and East Asia, the socioeconomic positions of Southeast Asians reflect their social backgrounds. The lack of education, absence of English-language skills, and negligible exposure to Western ways have served as liabilities to second- and subsequent-wave refugees who have not had access to the economic and professional opportunities available to other Asians.

With the increase in unemployment in the mid-1970s, the federal government severely restricted the admission of a number of occupational immigrants, especially discouraging alien health care professionals by removing physicians and surgeons from eligible categories of labor certification. Since then the U.S. Department of Labor has also curtailed other types of employment-based immigration by declining to issue visas to many individuals who were qualified. Ironically, despite the continuing availability of a number of employment visas, the INS reported in 1999 that the quota was not filled for this category of immigrants, perhaps suggesting that people from other countries now have many alternative and attractive options. Furthermore, the majority of Asian immigrants (85 percent) since the mid-1980s have arrived on the basis of family reunification efforts. These two factors have led to a decline in the rate of professional immigration, with more Asian immigrants across all groups reporting lower levels of education and more of them clustering in local labor markets and lower-skilled jobs.

Reports of the professional achievements of Asians in the United States increasingly recognize that not all Asians reflect the image of the model minority. Society is becoming more cognizant of the difficulties encountered by Southeast Asians as they seek employment and adjustment. Overall reports of other Asian groups present aggregate data, albeit separated by country of origin. However, such data do not reflect the discrepancies within each subgroup of the Asian American population between those who are successful and those who are not.

While the majority of native-born Chinese have white-collar occupations (77 percent compared with 59 percent of whites) and are twice as likely to be in professional occupations, this pattern is not reflected among foreign-born Chinese. The foreign-born Chinese present a bipolar occupational pattern, with workers clustering in professional occupations and low-paying service jobs, with few in between (Wong 1995a). Although they are more likely than whites to be involved in professions, they are also more likely to be dishwashers, waiters, and other low-status service providers. Such bimodality of occupational distribution is evident also among native-born Japanese; they consistently polarize in professional/technical areas at the upper level and in labor and service at the lower level (Nishi 1995). The Filipino population also shows bipolar distributions, with differences between foreign- and native-born Filipinos. Substantially fewer native-born Filipinos hold managerial and professional positions than do foreign-born ones, perhaps reflecting differences in overall educational levels of the two groups (Agbayani-Siewert and Revilla 1995). While Indians do not evidence quite the same bipolar distribution as do the Chinese and Filipinos, the 1990 census reported that 7 percent were living at the poverty level—the same percentage as white families. Among Koreans, data on recent immigration patterns show that the immigrants of the 1970s were from the middle and upper-middle classes in Korea, but now it is Koreans from the lower socioeconomic classes who are coming to the United States to improve their lives (Min 1995). Family reunification immigrants from Korea, as from other Asian nations, also represent a lower socioeconomic background than that of the earlier immigrating professionals. The Filipinos show bipolarity between the native-born and the foreign-born groups. The Japanese American community does not indicate the same extent of bipolarity as do other groups and reports a relatively high percentage in professional and managerial occupations (37 percent) compared with the total U.S. population. Nevertheless, Japanese Americans have a much lower representation among professionals than do Asian Indians at 44 percent and Pakistani Americans at 45 percent (U.S. Bureau of the Census 1993a).

The majority of immigrant Indians tend to pursue the same professions that they had in India, yet those who are for some reason unable to do so open their own businesses or become self-employed consultants. This group is also well represented in the hospitality industry of hotels and motels—more than half of all motels in the United States are owned by Indians (Varadarajan 1999). In general, Korean, Indian, Chinese, and Japanese Americans are much more involved than other Americans in small, family-run businesses—ethnic restaurants or grocery stores, for example—which can employ most members of the family. Such family-owned businesses promote independence and social mobility, especially when English-language proficiency is lacking. Furthermore, labor costs are lower, little capital is needed, and discrimination from the dominant economic sector is minimized. Unlike other Asian immigrants, Indians and Pakistanis are also involved in some aspects of the automobile industry—as taxi drivers and owners, as gas station and car-repair-shop owners. Many post-1965 Korean immigrants, despite good qualifications, were unable to find professional positions, partly because of a lack of English proficiency and partly because American firms did not recognize their Korean professional certifications (Min 1995). They were therefore forced into low-status, low-paying, menial jobs. Many turned to small business, but unlike other groups, they have tended to cater to minority clientele and have experienced a high level of economic segregation.

A disheartening report by the Center for Immigration Studies (Haniffa 1999b) suggested that newer immigrants are likely to be poor and remain poor, with each successive wave faring worse. These immigrants have a higher poverty rate, higher levels of unemployment, less education, and larger families than the native-born population, and it is more likely that more of their children will grow up in poverty. Many of these immigrants are recent Latino or Asian immigrants.

As has been shown, sociodemographic data suggest a bipolar distribution of professional achievement among and within many Asian groups. While certain groups tend to be more educated, acculturated, and successful, others tend to be less educated, more isolated, and more dependent on public assistance. Despite the economic and professional success of a large segment of the Asian American community, it is underrepresented in important administrative, executive, and managerial positions in both the corporate and the public sectors. Though many Asians progress through a professional hierarchy, regardless of the Asian group to which they belong, nearly all appear to encounter the "glass ceiling," rarely being selected for the highest-ranking positions in any enterprise. Those who make hiring and promotion decisions may believe that the Asian employees do not possess the communication and negotiation skills necessary for top-level positions, because of Asian perspectives on authority and socialization, or perhaps they are perceived as docile employees who lack leadership qualities (Min 1995). At any rate, they are underrepresented in leadership positions, even in organizations where they are well represented professionally. Furthermore, Asian Americans, unlike African Americans, Native Americans, and Latino Americans, are not identified as an oppressed minority and are not eligible for affirmative action benefits.

ETHNIC IDENTITY AND ISSUES OF RACE

While the concept of ethnicity has replaced that of race, it means a great deal more than race, which is an anthropologically specified phenotype. Ethnicity involves unique cultural traits that include behavior, religion, and language, as well as a sense of community or belonging. Sociologists suggest that the combination of these two features, race and ethnicity, set people apart from each other, especially to the extent that they retain the behavior, religion, and language of their specific groups and to the extent that they identify themselves with a particular group and remain separate from others. Commitment to an ethnic identity is believed to be an important criterion for positive adjustment, ego development, and self-esteem among minorities in the United States (Phinney 1990).

Over time in a multicultural society, it is common to have an exchange of behaviors and an integration of differing attitudes and languages. As subsequent generations grow together and blend their attitudes, values, and beliefs, certain aspects of the culture become less divisive. Yet if the group continues to maintain its sense of community as being distinct from others, ethnic identity remains intact. In addition to an individual's or group's definition of ethnic identity, that identity is also dependent to a large degree on whether the dominant society allows the group to retain or lose it. Ethnicity can serve as a mechanism of inclusion or of exclusion. An ethnic group may hold more closely to its cultural traits if it is insecure about its position in the larger society, if the larger society ridicules or rejects it, or if it feels a sense of pride in retaining its ethnic identity. On the other hand, people may seek to emulate the majority for the very reasons described above if retaining cultural traits makes the immigrant group appear too different from the dominant group.

In the early twentieth century, the Nisei[2] tried desperately to lose their cultural traits and blend in with the Euro population, much to the dismay of the Issei.[3] Their efforts made little difference in their acceptance by the larger U.S. community, however, and they were forced to remain within the Japanese ethnic community. Clearly, with Asians, cultural traits and a sense of community were not the only factors that were instrumental in ensuring the persistence of ethnic identity; phenotype also played a role. Although the Nisei were American by birth, they were never recognized as other than Japanese—a fact that was forcefully underscored by their internment.

The role of ethnicity and ethnic affiliation differs among groups, individuals, and periods in history. For some people and groups it may be a primary determinant of behavior, while for others it may be less important. In a multiethnic society such as the United States, it is often used as a basis for ranking, and—especially among people of color—one is treated according to the norms of one's ethnic group, with all its accompanying stereotypes and expectations. Thus, regardless of whether individuals' behavior is determined by ethnic affiliation or identity, ethnicity can still be a dominant force in their lives, influencing relationships within the dominant society and in their own ethnic groups.

Theories of identity and ethnic identity abound as psychologists and sociologists wrangle with the knotty issue of how people define themselves, how that definition guides their thoughts and actions, and what the implications are for relationships with others who have both similar and different identity constructs (see, for example, Marger 2000; Sue, Mak, and Sue 1998; Uba 1994). As with most psychological constructs, models of identity development and change are difficult to conceptualize and develop systematically. They are even more difficult to measure empirically, although Sue, Mak, and Sue (1998) identify instruments that have adequate reliability and validity in measuring ethnic identity among Asian Americans. Nevertheless, it may be most prudent for purposes of our understanding of Asian identities to focus not on theories of ethnicity or methods of empirical or qualitative research but on how Asian identity differs from U.S. identity and the extent to which Asians subscribe to one or both identities. Based on this simple description of identity, the focus is on (a) awareness of ethnicity, (b) adoption of ethnicity, and (c) application of ethnicity (Uba 1994). Awareness assumes knowledge of attitudes, values, and beliefs, and adoption requires consciously integrating these parameters into daily life.

Attitudes toward ethnicity vary among and within individuals, groups, and the larger society. For Asians, ethnic identity may also be closely linked with whether they are foreign-born immigrants or second-, third-, or fourth-generation U.S.-born. The extent of acculturation can clearly affect identity, in terms of both definition of self and the degree to which one displays the behaviors consistent with the ethnic identity. In general, however, the greater the exposure to the majority culture in areas of residence, schooling, and occupation, the more likely it is that ethnic identity will accommodate surrounding behaviors and attitudes. Hence, members of families that live in ethnic enclaves tend to have a stronger allegiance to ethnic identity than those scattered throughout areas of majority residence.

The extent of adherence to ethnic identity depends on a number of factors, not least among which are personality and the value the family places on ensuring that ethnic identity is maintained and transmitted to subsequent generations. For example, although the Issei were strongly Japanese, the Nisei noted the discrimination and isolation they experienced and, in hopes of gaining greater acceptance, consciously sought to separate themselves from as much of their Japanese heritage as possible (Takaki 1989). The Japanese are often regarded as representatives of assimilation, whether or not they truly reflect patterns of assimilation among Asians in the United States. However, because of early Japanese female immigration, the Japanese are the only Asian group that has been here long enough to establish families of several generations. The first generation, the Issei, were the least likely to assimilate, to acculturate themselves to U.S. society. The second generation, the Nisei, attempted to truly assimilate but found that they were not accepted. This discrimination was tragically reinforced during the internment

period. The third generation, the Sansei, have integrated even more
into U.S. society by marrying non-Japanese, yet some of the Sansei have
also reinforced their heritage by learning more about their origins. Some
researchers have raised questions about whether the Japanese will be
able to maintain their culture in the United States into the fourth
generation, the Yonsei, while others are convinced that despite their
extensive assimilation into mainstream U.S. culture, the strength of the
Japanese culture is such that Japanese Americans are not losing all their
distinctive cultural traits and identities (Marger 2000).

Foreign-born Asians are much more likely to have a strong ethnic
identity than are the second or third generations. Yet there is a suggestion that in present-day America, a nation that at least pays lip service
to the value of multiculturalism, it is more acceptable for the second
and third generations to integrate their ethnic and American personae
to form new cultural norms. Universities are offering more courses on
Asian studies and Asian languages, and U.S.-born Asians frequently
enroll in such courses to learn more about their cultures. While this is
consistent with findings that third generations tend to become more
interested in reviving their ethnic identities (Masuda, Matsumoto, and
Meredith 1970; Phinney 1990), it now appears that second-generation
Asians, once they have left the confines of the home environment to
attend college, seek knowledge about the cultures of their parents; while
they attempt to assimilate during their adolescent high school years, in
their late teen years they seek a more holistic understanding of themselves, reflecting Erik Erikson's (1963) fourth stage of development and
identity formation. This response is contrary to the experience of the
Nisei and the Sansei. That Asian American youth are motivated to learn
about their backgrounds and that universities provide them opportunities to so do reveal a significant societal recognition and acceptance of
multiculturalism and the importance of understanding differences.
Such courses do not specifically aim to teach the second and third generations about their own cultures; rather they target all students to
increase awareness of the multiethnic nature of the country.

Unlike European ethnics, whether they are native- or foreign-born,
Asians, as people of color, are almost always defined by their Asian back-
grounds. At least while they are in the United States, they are Asian
Americans, not merely Americans. Yet most grow up believing that
European phenotypes are the ideal. Thus fair skin, light hair and eyes,
tall stature, and muscular build are valued by most Asian cultures, and

even more so by Asian Americans. Hair dyeing, skin bleaching, colored contact lenses, and eye surgery have all found their way into the lives of youth in Asian countries, reinforcing the value that Asians and the world continue to place on these Occidental measures of beauty. Asian features are also associated with the stereotype portrayed in Western literature and in the entertainment industry of Asians being buffoons, villains, or geniuses. Rarely are they represented as ordinary people living in the United States. Even in Asian countries, the ideal features appear to be European American—fair skin, light hair, and large eyes. A group of activists in the United States has stressed the importance of developing toys with Asian characteristics (Tawa 1999). It helps Asian American children understand that their features are also valued and that they may love and play with dolls with which they can identify.

Clearly, despite the degree to which the attitudes and values of Asians become acculturated to those of the United States, their physical characteristics always set them apart, and their ethnic identity is thrust upon them, regardless of their degree of conformity to ethnic norms. That foreign-born Asians and native-born Asians of the same age often have little in common underscores the impact of acculturation. On the other hand, second-generation Asian Americans with parents from different countries find much in common with each other as they struggle with cultural values and family norms.

Ethnic identity thus reflects a number of factors: the extent to which the ethnic group, in general, has been in the United States, the generational status of the individual in question, social acceptance of the ethnic group, exposure to ethnic and dominant culture identities, and personal and family experiences. Consequently, it is not possible, in the early twenty-first century, to determine the degree to which Asian Americans, particularly native-born Asian Americans, define themselves along ethnic lines.

TRADITION IN SOCIAL AND CULTURAL VALUES

Asian groups substantively differ among themselves and must not be identified as one group. They do, however, share social and cultural values that serve to determine goals, guide behavior, and maintain harmony within society. A major emphasis in most Asian cultures, particularly East and Southeast Asian ones, is the avoidance of all conflict—at the individual level, the family level, the community level, and the societal level. By developing and abiding by strict rules of conduct,

Asians remove a great deal of the ambiguity in any situation and increase the likelihood that interactions will be smooth. The source of these norms may not be the same in every culture (i.e., historical experience, religion, oral tradition), but the outcomes are similar.

Common Cultural Qualities Among Asian Groups

Chung (1992) lists a number of shared behavioral norms that cross cultural origins:

- filial piety
- direction of parent-child communications
- self-control and restraint in emotional expression
- respect for authority
- well-defined social roles and expectations
- shame as a behavioral influence
- inconspicuousness and middle position virtue
- awareness of social milieu
- fatalism
- communal responsibility
- high regard for the elderly
- centrality of family relationships and responsibilities

Each of these norms has been explored and discussed in international, cross-cultural, and American literature over the years. Acculturation to U.S. society has modified the extent to which each plays a role in the lives of Asian American families, yet there are sufficient indications that even into the third generations, as with the Sansei, these values guide behavior. For example, individuals may behave in a more "Asian" manner when they are interacting with members of their own ethnic group and in a more "American" fashion with non-Asians. It may therefore be worthwhile to identify these areas of behavior, many of which are closely interwoven, and recognize that they may have substantial implications in social, professional, economic, and all other interactions with the dominant society even for Asians who have resided in the United States for several years or who were born in the country.

Filial piety. For Asians filial piety means the respect, honor, love, and obedience that children owe their parents. It is a duty and an obligation; parents must be obeyed regardless of the child's assessment of the situation. In the traditional Asian family, filial piety involves unquestioning obedience, as the parent is expected to be the most knowledgeable and responsible for the well-being of the child. This continues into adulthood and through the lifetime of the child. Children also represent social security for the parents and are responsible for their care when they age. Even after the death of the parent, veneration continues in the form of ancestor worship, as in East and Southeast Asian countries, or as a continuing respected presence symbolized by enlarged and garlanded photographs, as in South Asian cultures.

Direction of parent-child communications. Consistent with filial piety is the unidirectional communication between parent and child. Information and direction are given to the child by the parent. Children are not expected to have ideas or suggestions that are of import, and they are not involved in decision making. This becomes especially evident in traditional patterns of arranged marriages, in which parents select a mate for children after exploring available options and the qualifications—familial, social, economic—of a number of potential spouses. It also is evident in career choice, as parents steer children toward careers considered appropriate, in light of both the status associated with the careers and the potential earning power of an individual in that profession. Inclusion in family businesses is an option for many Asians who are trained from an early age to work with other family members.

Self-control and restraint in emotional expression. In general, individuals are expected to control their emotions. The open display of both positive (happiness, pride, love) and negative (grief, anger, hatred) emotions is unacceptable. There may be appropriate times and places to express such feelings, or they may be evidenced through ritualized religious or creative activities. When they are expressed spontaneously, it is expected that they will rapidly be brought under control, since strong expression of feeling may be viewed as exhibitionism and the inappropriate drawing of attention to oneself or one's group.

Respect for authority. Consistent with the ideals of filial piety, one imbues persons in authority with all five bases of power (French and Raven 1968). People in authority are able to reward and punish, and they have legitimate power that has been given them because they are in such a position. In contrast to French and Raven's theory, however, the individuals in authority do not achieve expert and referent power because of their own personal accomplishments or qualities. Those qualities are ascribed to them *because* they are in positions of power—or perhaps they are believed to be in positions of power because they have those qualities. Hence authority is not questioned, and Asians are taught to honor and obey those in authority, not only because they have the power to control through external reinforcers but because they are believed to be wise and knowledgeable.

Well-defined social roles and expectations. Roles and responsibilities are clearly defined. Males are generally expected to assume the instrumental roles involving task accomplishment and women the nurturing roles to maintain relationships and family functioning. Roles and expectations within the family are clearly defined along lines of gender and age. Status and responsibility are also so defined, with males and elders having more importance and impact than women and youth. While this is true within the family, it is also generally true within the community and the society, with business and governmental authority and decision-making power lying in the hands of males and elders. As women reach elder status, and if no men of their generation are still alive, they garner more power than they can have when men of their cohort are present.

Shame as a behavioral influence. Behavior and attitudes are never simply a reflection of oneself. If an individual violates prescribed norms, it is considered a disgrace, and not only is it a disgrace for the individual but it is a reflection on the entire family. Children learn at a very young age that if they misbehave or do not live up to the expectations of the family, the entire family is affected. This may merely mean that the whole family is embarrassed, it might involve the loss of family status in the community, or it could even mean ostracism of the family from participation in societal activities. Thus, shame is a strong mechanism of control and influences Asian individuals throughout their lives.

It is well known that family relationships are strong and well defined. Similarly, Asian commitment to colleagues, superiors, and work environments is expected to be akin to their commitment toward their families. Members of the work environment become "like family," and one's behavior becomes more than a reflection on oneself and one's family; it is also a reflection of the organization or company for which one works. Thus shame controls behavior beyond the home and into the workplace.

Inconspicuousness and middle position virtue. It is important not to draw attention to oneself, and it is necessary to be moderate in ideas, expectations, and behaviors. All excesses are to be avoided. An individual who is able to blend into the social fabric of society or into the group by being consistent with its norms is believed to be the ideal member. Extremes in thought, word, or deed may not only draw attention to oneself but also may increase conflict and discomfort and bring shame to family or community.

Awareness of social milieu. The expectations and norms of any given situation are important in guiding behavior. A particular behavior may be more appropriate in one situation than in another, and the environmental circumstances, or the social milieu, dictate what is expected. Therefore, when Asian Americans act more "Asian" with their own community members and more "American" in the workplace, they are merely fulfilling the expectation that they conform to the milieu of a given time and place.

Fatalism. Many Asians are fatalistic, in that they believe that what is destined to happen will happen. While this does not mean that they merely wait for things to occur, they do believe that their ability to control their destinies is limited. They do establish goals and directions, yet if they are unable to accomplish them, or if they experience a loss, they do not necessarily place blame on either themselves or others; rather they accept the outcome as one that was preordained. While Westerners may perceive this as passive, it also is a highly effective coping mechanism, especially in societies where behavior is clearly delineated, options are restricted, or resources and opportunities are scarce.

Communal responsibility. Just as individuals are extensions of the family or the work environment, and their behavior shames or enhances the group in which they have membership, the group or the environment is responsible for them. Raising a child, then, becomes not only the responsibility of the parents but also the responsibility of the entire family, including siblings and extended family members, as well as of the community. Within the boundaries identified (such as family, community, work environment), successes and failures are experienced by the entire community. The community provides financial, social, and emotional support for its members, and individuals or families have a right to expect such support from their community.

High regard for the elderly. Asian societies believe that with age comes wisdom. Life experiences and having survived the roller coaster of life provide knowledge that is unavailable to younger people. The elderly do not have to prove themselves, nor do they experience a loss of status as they retire from the workforce. Status is bound not only to professional position and achievement but also to age and a belief that during the process of life one has contributed to the enhancement of some aspect of society, from rearing children to the governing of the nation. The elderly are revered and helped when they are in need. Their views are valued as products of a lifetime of experience and lifelong learning. Until recently, the life span was relatively short and the elderly were few in number; consequently they were even more honored.

Centrality of family relationships and responsibilities. The importance of the family cannot be overemphasized: The family is the central focus of the individual, who is an essential extension of the family. Intrafamilial relationships are paramount, and expectations are that the family member will be totally committed to its development, preservation, and protection from external influences that might be seen as harmful. Role responsibilities are established across generations, between genders and age groups. Each individual serves as a representative of the family, and each individual has a part to play in the improvement of its position in the community. Family problems are resolved within the boundaries of the family, and the guidance of older members is sought in making decisions and in coping with prickly situations. Family dynamics, economic conditions, illness, and mental health are handled within the family. When the designated individual, usually the eldest male, is unable to provide guidance or is the source of the problem, the next eldest male assumes the responsibility. Clear lines of authority and responsibility, deference and compromise are established. Disagreements are not expected to be voiced, and the good of the family must supersede the desires of any one individual or subgroup within the family.

Asian Cultural Traits and Values . . . Shared

Much is written about the cultural traits and values around which Asians and Americans differ. In addition to physical differences, it is believed that these cultural differences are what define individuals of each society and make it difficult for them to understand each other.

A close look at these traits brings into focus the impact of others in defining and circumscribing Asian behavior. Despite the tendency for Asians, and perhaps non-Asians also, to identify these as *Asian* cultural values, on closer inspection even the most casual reader must note that to some extent *all* these values are important in *all* societies. They are neither unique to Asians nor absent in the American world; what may differ is the degree of pressure to adhere to these values and the social implications of violating them. In fact, these are all human values, and as social animals human beings must adjust to living in harmony with social and physical environments. Thus, individuals and ethnic groups may fall along a continuum on the significance of these values in determining their attitudes and behaviors, as is indicated by a hypothetical diagrammatic example below:

This diagram illustrates that while obedience, respect, and obligation toward the parent are paramount to Asians, such qualities are also important to Americans. A similar continuum can be devised for every value that has been discussed, for each one is common to all human beings who must live in a social context, who are interdependent, and who do not have absolute control over their environments.

The extant literature would lead one to believe that all Asian cultures and all Asians are collectivists, value family, adhere to a hierarchical structure of relationships, strive toward harmony, are self-effacing, and so on. Conversely, it would appear that Euro-Americans are individualists, focus on the individual rather than the family, are egalitarian in relationships, challenge when necessary, and seek to be noticed. It is erroneous to assume that the norms of the respective cultures truly and completely guide behaviors. Certain groups may fall further toward one end of the continuum, while others may fall closer to the opposite end, but all the values and behaviors identified as Asian are also appreciated by Americans.

Both Asian and Euro-American societies expect obedience, respect, honor, and love of the child toward the parent. The difference may be in level of expectation. Although parent-child communications are more bidirectional in American families, children hesitate to openly express themselves with parents, and most parents clearly direct their children. While Americans permit self-expression, it cannot be excessive or destructive. Jubilation and anger are both frowned upon. Americans expect authority to carry respect, and social roles and family responsibilities are clearly defined, although Americans are more willing to tolerate less than strict adherence. While "shame" may not be used as a behavioral influence, "guilt" is an emotion that Americans report experiencing when they fail to fulfill expectations.

Generally, Americans also assume middle-of-the-road positions in ideas and behavior, and rarely do they wish to make a spectacle of themselves. While in the United States it is necessary to discuss accomplishments in order to advance professionally, an individual who consistently seeks to be noticed often loses acceptance. It is important also to be aware of the social environment and environmental expectations in the American culture. Insensitivity to it can result in conflict and affect social relationships and professional progress.

Furthermore, although Americans would not say they are fatalistic, many believe that it is not possible to change the course of events, an attitude that is certainly reflected at every governmental election, when less than 50 percent of the registered voters actually vote. Communal responsibility is evident as people assist each other with child care, help others in sickness or distress, show social responsibility, and provide volunteer services.

While the elderly are often valued less than is preferred, they are not maltreated. They are helped by their children, other family members, friends, and even strangers. Though they do not have the same status as they do in Asian cultures, in the earlier half of the twentieth century they were more respected than they are at the beginning of the twenty-first century. Finally, family relationships and responsibilities are important to Americans as they rear their children and help them to make sound decisions about their futures. The boundary of the family may be smaller than it is with the Asian family, but it is not unusual for aging parents to be cared for by their children.

Although Americans may be individualistic, most do not make decisions that are divorced from the needs of people in significant relationships with them, whether in the home or in the workplace. Likewise, Asians do not base all decisions for self-advancement on the achievement of group goals. On the other hand, to advance and grow in the United States it is essential for Asians to promote their own goals and expectations. Asians do engage in behaviors that are usually ascribed to Euro-Americans, but they view such behaviors in light of their own cultural norms. When individual Asians leave their home country for the United States, seeking the higher education that will allow them to advance professionally, they view it as a step that raises the status of the entire family, while Americans perceive them as individuals who are taking advantage of opportunities unavailable in their homelands. If these individuals do not return to their families or do not provide financial or other assistance to their families in the home country—or even if they do—it is difficult to argue whether such immigration reflects a collectivist orientation or an individualist one.

Differences Between Asian and Euro-American Cultures

Chung (1992) draws on existing literature to describe differences between areas of substantive variations in perceptions and patterns of behavior between Asians and Euro-Americans. Among these, he specifies the cultural context, the relationship between the individual and the environment, and patterns of association.

Cultural context. Asians differ from Euro-Americans in the importance that they place on the context of situations (Chung 1992). The identity of the former is bound up inextricably with the identity of the group, while the identity of the latter is a reflection of the individual persona (Triandis 1989). Social and cultural conditions that surround members of Asian cultures are of great importance in the understanding of a message. Frequently, oral communication is not direct, requiring that recipients of messages interpret nonverbal behavior, interpersonal status, and a host of other variables. Americans are more likely to phrase the content of a message to convey exactly what is meant; the focus is on objective information, and there is less need to interpret surrounding clues.

The individual and the environment. Reflecting the concept of fatalism, Asians believe that they are an elemental part of the environment and that they do not control it but are more often controlled by it. The Chinese theory of yin and yang—(the negative and the positive)—has influenced much of Asian thinking, and living in harmony with nature underlies the traditions of Hinduism, Buddhism, and Confucianism. Furthermore, the need to live in harmony is extended to social and interpersonal environments, and traditional norms are established to ensure that such harmony exists. Being a part of a whole is the cornerstone of much of Asian thinking, and it is important to be self-effacing. Self-expression and individuality are of supreme value among Americans, and the appearance of commanding one's environment is lauded.

Patterns of association. Asian cultures are allocentric, or collectivist, while Euro-American cultures are idiocentric, or individualistic (Hofstede 1980; Triandis et al. 1988). The focus of the former is the advancement of the group, while the focus of the latter is the development of the individual, or the individual unit—the nuclear family. Because of the Asian group identity, much personal effort is devoted to the development and maintenance of social relationships that are expected to be lifelong. American identity is individual, and so strong social relationships are not as essential. Asians are process-oriented, while Americans are task-oriented; goals and tasks are likely to be accomplished more rapidly by Americans, while Asians focus more on the maintenance of human relationships in the process of accomplishing the task, thus prolonging goal attainment. Among Asians, social relationships are hierarchically ordered, while among Americans, all people are more equal and each has the right to make decisions. Finally, Asians tend not to participate in voluntary activities. While they will commit themselves completely to their families and their companies, they are less likely than Americans to participate in the political process or voluntary social activities. Low levels of participation may be a reflection of cultural and political factors, perhaps fears of the ramifications of such participation, or of increasing competition and conflict.

Changes in Traditional Values

Several authors have discussed multiple levels of enculturation (socialization), which contribute to the development of personal attitudes, values, and behaviors. Influences stem from ethnic cultural values, local and regional values of the country of residence, social influences, family values, and life experiences. National culture is assumed to be the primary determinant of individual behavior (Segal, Segal, and Niemczycki 1993), yet the behavior of immigrants is tempered by the values of the host country and the opportunities and obstacles they experience. Furthermore, second and subsequent generations are often truly bicultural, as they are reared in Asian homes yet spend most of their waking hours in Euro-American organizations.

The following now well-known list of cultural differences (fig. 5.1) was drafted in 1978 by a group of Vietnamese refugees in the United States who were suffering culture shock (Chung 1992:41):*

DIFFERENCES BETWEEN EAST AND WEST	
East	**West**
We live in time.	We live in space.
We are always at rest.	We are always on the move.
We are passive	We are aggressive.
We accept the world as it is.	We try to change it according to our blueprint.
We like to contemplate	We like to act.
We live in peace with nature.	We try to impose our will on nature.
Religion is our first love.	Technology is our passion.
We delight to think about the meaning of life.	We delight in physics.
We believe in freedom of silence.	We believe in freedom of speech.
We lapse in meditation.	We strive for articulation.
We marry first, then love.	We love first, then marry.
Our marriage is the beginning of a love affair.	Our marriage is the happy end of a romance.
Love is an indissoluble bond.	Love is a contract.
Our love is mute.	Our love is vocal.
We try to conceal it from the world.	We delight in showing it to others.
Self-denial is a secret to our survival.	Self-assertiveness is the key to our success.
We are taught from the cradle to want less and less.	We are urged every day to want more and more.
We glorify austerity and renunciation.	We emphasize gracious living and enjoyment.
Poverty is to us a badge of spiritual elevation.	Poverty is to us a sign of degradation.
In the sunset years of life, we renounce the world and prepare for the life hereafter.	We retire to enjoy the fruits of our labor.

*Chung, D. K. (1992). Asian commonalities. In Furuto, S. M. et al. (eds.), *Social Work Practice with Asian Americans*, p. 41. Copyright © by Sage Publications, Inc., reprinted by permission of Sage Publications, Inc.

Most apparent in these differences are the internal locus of control of the American and the external locus of control of the Asian, as illustrated in the values of passivity and self-denial among Asians and assertiveness among Americans. Not mentioned among the differences is the collectivist orientation of the Asian and the value of subordinating oneself for the group versus the individualist orientation of the American and the value of assertively pursuing personal goals.

Though the list does identify real differences between Eastern and Western values, it was written from the perspective of those suffering from culture shock and has overtones of disapproval of American values. Nevertheless, both ways of viewing the world have assets and drawbacks. The collectivist approach ensures strong family and group commitment and cohesiveness that help shape identity and minimize conflict and confusion about future directions. On the other hand, it often requires the individual to sacrifice any hopes, dreams, and wishes that are inconsistent with those of the group. The individualist orientation of the American allows individuals to pursue their goals and achieve personal satisfaction, but in the process they often must branch out from the family and group and become less interdependent, which in turn reduces group and family commitment and support.

Despite their ties to Eastern values, Asians, particularly Asian women, are finding that their lives in the United States and the opportunities to escape the tight controls of tradition are both a blessing and a bane. The ability to decide what is best for oneself and one's children without direction from the family or from the society is highly liberating, but it also means a loss of the strong traditional network that can provide consistent, ongoing support and guidance. The freedom to be one's own person comes at an additional cost for Asians, who must balance the collectivist orientation into which they have been socialized. Obligations and responsibilities to the elder generation and to the extended family in general persist, not only accompanying immigrants to the United States but also being transmitted—although in a somewhat modified fashion—to U.S.-born children.

In recent years, second- and third-generation Asian Americans have moved on the continuum toward their American counterparts in their values. Although second- and third-generation Asian Americans of Chinese and Japanese descent in the early and middle years of the twentieth century, who were allowed little social and professional interaction with the dominant community, may have been more strongly influenced by Asian than by American values, studies of the current second and third generations are finding substantially more assimilation, with the third generations being almost entirely "American" in their attitudes, values, and behaviors.

MODIFICATION OF FAMILIAL AND GENDER NORMS

Through the process of immigration the family, gender roles, and community norms change dramatically. New immigrant family patterns emerge that are a blend of the old and the new and are shaped by both the cultural meanings from the nations of origin and the social, economic, and cultural forces in the United States (Foner 1997). The traditional Asian family structure provides stability, interpersonal intimacy, social support (Segal 1998), and a relatively stress-free environment (DeVos 1978) for its members. However, immigrant and refugee experiences cause major disruptions in family life and create pressures that destabilize established family relationships and hurt role performance. In the traditional Asian patriarchal joint family, the age, gender, and generational status of individuals serve as the primary determinants of behavior and role relationships. While Asian countries may draw on a variety of Confucian, Buddhist, Hindu, and Muslim principles, there is great similarity in the definition of role relationships among family members. Interdependence is fostered, self-identity is inhibited, and a conservative orientation, resistant to change, is rewarded. Children are valued for their ability to contribute to the economic survival of the family and to provide security for parents in their old age.

A major issue in immigration is the disruption of the extended family structure. After immigration, ethnic families in the United States in many cases serve as surrogate families, meeting the needs for both emotional and material support, but they cannot totally substitute for the natural family (Lum 1992). Furthermore, because children and youth rapidly become more fluent in English and quickly adopt patterns of the United States, a role reversal often occurs within the family. The children frequently act as the English-language negotiators, and in so doing they may be viewed as undermining the authority of their elders and threatening the Asian value of filial piety. Generational conflicts arise because Asian families rely on traditional hierarchical authority, demanding respect and obedience from their children. In becoming acculturated to U.S. norms, Asian children also learn the competing values of independence and assertiveness and begin to challenge their parents, causing increased conflict within the family.

Gender Roles

The traditional Asian family clearly defines the role of the male, particularly the father and the eldest son, as those with the most authority and primary responsibility for maintaining the family. Even in the United States, among most Asian immigrant families, the adult male members of the family continue to be the primary wage earners, decision makers, and protectors of the young, the women, and the elderly. Filipino family structure, however, departs from this pattern. Role relationships between the genders are much more egalitarian, and power and decision making are distributed fairly evenly. Furthermore, while the elders are respected, they do not hold the same status in Filipino society as they do in other Asian cultures, for age is not automatically associated with authority.

The fact that increasing numbers of Asian women are highly educated professionals who work outside the home might suggest their emancipation from traditional role behaviors, but any such assumption is faulty. Similar family patterns can be found among educated immigrant Asians and agrarian Asian refugees in the United States. While educated immigrant Asian wives, such as those from India, may work outside the home, gender role relationships established before they entered the United States are maintained. Asian immigrant women continue to be primarily responsible for all domestic tasks; working-class Asian women also face a lack of services such as child care, and therefore suffer the dual burden of long working hours and traditional household responsibilities.

A divergence from the patriarchal pattern is found among Filipino immigrants. Filipino American women are likely to work outside the home both for cultural reasons and to increase the family income. Filipino culture not only encourages but also expects women to be wage earners. Furthermore, marital relationships are more egalitarian; Filipino women share a more equal status with males than do females in other Asian nations. Perhaps this is a result of historic, precolonial, or U.S. influence in the Philippines, or perhaps it is intrinsic to the belief that recognition, deference, and opportunities should be accorded to any family member, regardless of gender, who is able to heighten the family's status. The majority of the women work outside the home, and both native- and foreign-born women are active participants in the economic role. Most of the foreign-born women, particularly those who are nurses, took advantage of the liberalized 1965 immigration policies and have continued to work in the United States as they did in the Philippines. Role relationships between men and women among this group of Asians have not changed dramatically, since interpersonal relationships between husbands and wives were not dissimilar pre- and post-immigration.

The most significant change is seen among the less educated immigrants and the refugees. Korean women in the United States, who in their native country would have remained at home to tend to the family, are forced into the labor force so that the family can become economically viable. Many work in family-owned businesses, and most work longer hours outside the home than do American women, yet their active economic role has not resulted in particular change in their marital relationships. Most Korean women, regardless of their employment status, perform traditional homemaker responsibilities, and many suffer from overwork, stress, and role strain (Choi 1994; Hurh and Kim 1988).

In many nations, when women work outside the home, it is primarily to supplement the husband's income or to meet their own career goals. The male is usually the breadwinner and the decision maker. Unlike most Asian male immigrants to this country, who consciously make a decision to move and have some idea of what to expect, Asian male refugees come to the United States with few other options. Many find that they are ill equipped with the skills necessary for success in the United States, and issues of pride and honor prevent them from accepting menial and low-paying jobs. As a result, women are forced to seek employment outside the home in order to ensure some income. Women, unlike men, are often ready to accept the menial jobs that the men reject—jobs as domestic help, jobs in fast-food restaurants, and jobs in other minimum-wage occupations. Such situations increase the woman's contact with the dominant culture, allowing her to become more comfortable in the host country than her husband and to become the negotiator for the family, assuming more decision-making power and responsibility. This combination of economic and personal independence allows women to challenge patriarchal authority (Okihiro 1996). The result is further restructuring of the traditional power distribution between husband and wife.

Thus, while gender role expectations between women and men are fairly similar across Asian cultures, in the United States they are modified and begin to vary widely based on class of origin, current class, ethnic group, generation (Root 1998a), and immigration status. Traditionally, marriages were utilitarian and arranged to ensure progeny and transmission of culture and wealth. Role relationships within the family, between genders and between parent and child, could continue to be clearly defined along traditional role expectations. As Asian American youth acculturate themselves to American values, they are no longer prepared to marry for utilitarian reasons, and love and friendship become critical requirements for entry into marriage (Root 1998a). However, there is some suggestion that Asian American men, even into the second and third generations, continue to hold traditional role expectations of their wives, even as the women's definition of themselves and their roles begins to change; this may account for the higher rate of interracial marriage between Asian women and non-Asian men than between Asian men and non-Asian women (U.S. Department of Commerce 1993).

Gay and Lesbian Asian Americans

Studies of the Asian American gay and lesbian population are limited and rarely appear in the mainstream literature on Asian Americans. Perhaps their absence reflects not an oversight but a difficulty in acknowledging the presence of this population. In Asian countries, though there is some recognition that there might be gay or lesbian individuals in the population, their numbers are not acknowledged and they appear to have little or no visibility. In the United States, however, there is clearly a large gay and lesbian population that identifies itself as such, regardless of how the populace feels about this group. Consequently, there may be greater opportunity for ethnic minority members to have a voice. Being both an ethnic minority and a homosexual, however, can present a double, or even triple, handicap. One is marginalized in society because of ethnicity and is discriminated against because of sexual orientation. In addition, an Asian American who is gay or lesbian may not be assured acceptance by the gay or lesbian community, which must also face its own feelings about ethnic minorities. Minority gays and lesbians find themselves a minority within a minority. For this group, establishment of a healthy identity can be an even more difficult process than it is for either a white gay or lesbian individual or a heterosexual minority person.

The heterosexual society frequently views gays and lesbians as people who flaunt their sexual preference, but those who identify themselves as gay or lesbian are concerned not only about sexuality but also about finding a partner who fulfills their emotional, affiliative, affectional, and spiritual needs (Hirshberg 2000). Until recently, there have been no adequate role models for homosexual individuals. The media responded to public preferences by avoiding presentation of this population as other than pathological. When a popular comic strip, *For Better or Worse*, which is carried by most major U.S. newspapers, revealed that one of its teenage characters was gay, many newspapers refused to print it for fear of offending public sensitivities. Until very recently, literature, media, and the community provided few images for gay and lesbian people that were not the stereotypical effeminate male and masculine female, and family and school discussions never touched on the topic of gay and lesbian identity. Even the military's "don't ask, don't tell" policy reinforces society's need to avoid recognition of this group.

Thus, throughout their development, gays and lesbians, almost all of whom grow up in heterosexual homes, find no one with whom they can identify. Often, because of the society's general perceptions and reactions to this population, they learn to "hate themselves even before they know who they are" (Hirshberg 2000). Unlike other minorities who are at least accepted within their own communities, gays and lesbians are minorities within their own families, and often their family members unwittingly discriminate against them. In Asian families, discussion of sex and sexuality itself is taboo (Segal 1998). Girls are expected to be virgins, and any exploits of boys are not acknowledged. Homosexuality is not only not discussed, it is a non-issue (Liu and Chan 1996). Therefore, gay or lesbian Asian Americans experience feelings far outside the imagination of the average Asian family, and Asian American gay or lesbian children must develop two parallel minority identities, which, in turn, interact to affect social and emotional growth and development (Chung and Katayama 1999). The personal stories of Filipino gay men (Manalansan 1997) and lesbian women (Lipat et al. 1997) reveal that they, like other gays and lesbians, have to struggle with issues such as "coming out" and identifying themselves as gay or lesbian. They must also find a community in which they feel comfortable, decide on the extent to which they will be visible, find partners, and deal with their families (Almeida 1996).

Chan (1997b) proposes that to some extent the Asian American community's "don't ask, don't tell, don't know" attitude toward sexuality as an aspect of one's identity allows a greater range of acceptable behaviors. The show of affection between two individuals of the same gender is not automatically interpreted as a homosexual liaison. While this approach may allow gays and lesbians to display some affection in public, it does not acknowledge the existence of intimacy. Asian American gays and lesbians must weigh the extent to which they can remain a part of their particular subgroups against the extent to which they wish to join the gay and lesbian population. While there appear to be few studies of this issue in the United States, studies of Asian gays in Australia reveal that their needs are different from those of the Euro-Australian gay community. The distance created between them and heterosexuals in the Asian community results in a loss of connection with a support network that is not easily replaceable because of cultural differences (Ridge, Hee, and Minichiello 1999; Sanitioso 1999). The experience of Asian American gays and lesbians may well reflect that of their counterparts in Australia, and the lack of recognition of their presence in the United States serves to further marginalize them.

Position of Elders

Traditional Asian norms stress veneration of the elderly, associating longevity with knowledge, wisdom, and experience. It is also the responsibility of the young to care for the elderly, and the eldest son and his family (or sometimes the second son) are traditionally the primary caregivers. Little literature is available on Asian elderly in the United States because most of the Asians in the country are still young. The few studies that have been conducted have primarily been on the Chinese and the Japanese, who have had the longest period of residence in the United States. The literature reveals that many Asian elderly suffer fallout from the "model minority" stereotype. Since they are perceived as belonging to an advantaged minority group, few services and opportunities are available to them. Since in their youth most of them had less access to education and the other opportunities now available to Asian Americans, they tend to have lower-status jobs and lower incomes than the rest of the aging population (Wong and Ujimoto 1998).

The Asian American elderly, like the rest of the Asian American population, are a heterogeneous group (table 5.4). Regardless of their length of time in the United States, however, Chinese and Vietnamese

Table 5.4.

	SIZE OF ASIAN AMERICAN ELDERLY POPULATION*		
	Total Population	Age 65 or Older	Percentage Age 65 or Older
Chinese	1,645,472	133,977	8.1
Filipino	1,406,770	104,206	7.4
Japanese	847,562	105,932	12.5
Asian Indian	815,447	23,004	2.8
Korean	798,849	35,247	4.4
Vietnamese	614,547	18,084	2.8
Cambodian	147,411	3,724	2.5
H'mong	149,014	3,697	2.5
Laotian	90,082	2,535	2.8
Thai	91,275	1,416	1.6
Other Asian	302,209	7,901	1.7

Source: U.S. Bureau of the Census 1995 (Wong and Ujimoto 1998).
*2000 Census data will not be available until late 2002.

elderly are more likely to live in poverty than are other Asian elderly (Lee 1992).

Most Chinese, Japanese, and Filipino elderly came to the United States as young immigrants themselves or are of the second generation. The elderly among the Koreans, Indians, and Southeast Asians are more likely to be the aging parents of those who immigrated after 1965, now joining their children and grandchildren in the United States. Larger percentages of immigrants from Asian countries than from any non-Asian nation are over the age of 65. Elderly parents of immigrants must also cope with many of the same cross-cultural stresses experienced by their children, particularly with regard to familial relationships and changed roles between themselves and their adult children. In the traditional Asian family, parental authority remains intact for the lifetime of the parent. With immigration, aging parents are removed from their financial resources as well as their social and emotional supports. With their dependence, they lose much of their authority.

Often isolated and vulnerable (Ishii-Kuntz 1997), the elderly are dependent physically, financially, socially, and emotionally on the adult children who become the decision makers for them. This role reversal results in personal and cultural conflicts, both for the aging parent and for the adult child. When the adult immigrant children are themselves struggling financially and culturally while trying to become established, difficulties of the elderly are exacerbated. Furthermore, in a culture where individualism and the nuclear family are the norm, and where youth is valued over age and productivity over wisdom, the position of the elderly in the immigrant household becomes tenuous. They are no longer able to provide insight and direction—indeed, much of what they have experienced seems irrelevant in U.S. culture. Successful adjustment of elderly Asians in the United States is found to be positively correlated with level of education, length of residence in the country, and a multigenerational household (Kiefer et al. 1985). If they have the tools to adapt to the new lifestyle, transition is easier. It appears that it is the elderly who must adjust to the new roles, for their children and grandchildren who are already struggling with bicultural issues often more easily accept the changed position of the elders. While the Asian American elderly are a heterogeneous group, most despair at the erosion of their traditions and are saddened by the diminished respect for the elderly and filial piety and obedience, many are isolated from their contemporaries, and a large number are dependent on their adult children.

Studies of Asian families often use superficial measures of acculturation, such as change and facility in use of U.S. language, dress, and arts and crafts (Yee, Huang, and Lew 1998). Thus, what appears to be a total acculturation of a group into the family norms of the dominant society is often only an external and observable form of assimilation. Many additional issues develop as the Asian family evolves, integrating American and Asian values. American norms and behaviors are not sufficient to replace the long-established traditions of Asian cultures and soothe the ensuing difficulties. Such well-established patterns are not readily substituted, and many long-range ramifications of the changes affect the very construct of the Asian family.

Family problem-solving skills, the role of culturally determined emotional responses, social support practices, and responses to life crises are deep-seated patterns, cultivated over generations (Nishi 1995). Major familial decisions may still not be made within the boundaries of the nuclear family. Input from the extended family may be requisitioned before decisions are made. Furthermore, behavior is situation-specific, adapted to the demands of a particular social and environmental context. For example, Indians may speak English and wear Western attire in the work environment, yet use their native tongue and dress in Indian clothes in social situations with other Indians. Deep-seated values and behaviors, transmitted across generations for centuries, provide a sense of familiarity and stability to a group. These are less easy to shed than are the superficial and observable phenomena that make interaction with different people easier. Thus variables that have been used to measure acculturation or adjustment, such as those suggested by the National Immigration Forum (1999a), may not in fact measure acculturation; they may merely reflect a commitment to life in the United States.

PHYSICAL AND MENTAL HEALTH

Much literature in the 1980s and 1990s has focused on the health, particularly the mental health, of Asians, reflecting work with refugees from the Vietnam War era. These refugees evidenced a range of psychological and psychosomatic ailments in addition to their physical health problems, and it became apparent that traditional Asian treatment was not always consistent with U.S. medical practices.

Physical Health

A significant concern among immigrants is their physical health, and this is an area in which they must make substantial adjustments. Immigrants, as all Americans, are affected by the U.S. health care system, its resources, and its costs. A large proportion of immigrants and refugees join the millions of Americans who are without adequate health care. They are also drawn to traditional beliefs about health care that conflict with U.S. medical approaches.

Access to the U.S. health care system is influenced by a number of considerations, among them the exorbitant costs, the restrictions imposed by managed-care insurance companies (Yoder-Wise 1999), and the limited access to health insurance experienced by many immigrants. In addition, changes under the Welfare Reform Act of 1996 make it difficult for more recent immigrants to access either Medicare or Medicaid. Legal immigrants must wait at least five years to be eligible for Medicare, and "means testing" for Medicaid no longer signifies assessing the assets of the individual applying for Medicaid; rather, it assesses the assets of the individual's sponsor. This system virtually ensures that the applicant will not be eligible for Medicaid, yet the sponsor, usually an immigrant family member, can rarely afford to pay out-of-pocket medical expenses. Hence, since many immigrants are uninsured, they avoid using health care services. Recently enacted federal welfare and immigration reforms can greatly increase the health vulnerability of large segments of the immigrant population by limiting access to health and social services (Weitzman et al. 1997). The University of California at Los Angeles Center for Health Policy Research revealed that with the decrease in public insurance, the number of uninsured Asian Americans increased (Dutt 1999). Indians and Filipinos had the lowest uninsured rates (20 percent), while Koreans had the highest (40 percent).

Moreover, in the process of accessing health care, immigrants often lack adequate English-language skills to communicate symptoms and experiences. They also find that cultural factors such as shyness, politeness, and gender may make appropriate diagnoses and treatment of illnesses difficult. For example, the Vietnamese often use the word "ya" to indicate respect; it does not necessarily mean affirmation or agreement as it would in English. A physician's misunderstanding of this usage can prevent adequate communication with the patient (Lindsay, Narayan, and Rea 1998). Even though many low-income Asian women are eligible for publicly funded health benefits because they meet the income requirements, they do not avail themselves of the benefits because of the maze of paperwork and their fears (whether warranted or not) of deportation (Dutt 1999).

Poor examination facilities overseas often allow immigrants with infectious diseases to enter the country. Immigrants from Southeast Asia have the highest incidence of tuberculosis (TB). The World Health Organization reported 7.96 million new cases of TB in 1997, half of them in Southeast Asia. India, China, Indonesia, Bangladesh, Pakistan, and the Philippines had the highest incidence rates (Reuters 1999b). Other commonly occurring problems are malnutrition, vitamin deficiency, and iron deficiency (Ackerman 1997). Between 1978 and 1985 most of the Southeast Asian ethnic groups were at high risk for poor infant health, teenage pregnancy, and pregnancy among unmarried women (Rumbaut 1995). It is increasingly apparent that immigrant families often have special health care needs. They are a diverse population that comes with numerous risks to physical health and functioning, many of which may be unfamiliar to U.S. health care providers (Weitzman et al. 1997).

Among many Asians, preventive medicine is not practiced, and minor ailments are apparently ignored. Certain forms of touch may be deemed inappropriate, for example. The Vietnamese believe that the head is sacred and when it is touched a vital life force can escape; therefore a patient may shy away from a physician seeking to touch the head or face as part of an examination. The Vietnamese may use herbal medicines or home remedies such as hair pulling, cupping (which involves placing a suction cup on the skin), pinching, and scraping (of the skin) to treat certain ailments (La Borde 1996)—traditional home remedies that are likely to be unfamiliar to American health care providers. Some such remedies cause scabs and bruises, and American physicians may easily mistake them for signs of abuse (Look and Look 1997).

Indians, likewise, may be affected by traditional beliefs. Although more likely to be familiar with modern medicine, and hence amenable to it, some Indians may still resort to traditional Ayurvedic medicine, which includes the use of herbal medicines, diet, skin therapy, and spirituality. In Indian culture, possessing sufficient self-control to deal with strong feelings is considered essential to the physical health of the body (Mahat 1998). Touching, especially cross-gender touching, is considered improper and invasive, particularly for Indian immigrants who are not well educated. Among the general pool of Indian immigrants to the United States, who are highly educated and Westernized, many are physicians themselves and barriers to medical care may not be insurmountable for them.

Given the increases in the elderly Asian population, some of them native U.S. citizens and others immigrants who are joining their families, health care providers must be especially cognizant of their unique needs and the cultural barriers that may impede delivery of services and compliance with treatment. The literature indicates that Asian elderly underutilize health care services, but this does not necessarily indicate greater physical health. While many of the Asian elderly are as healthy or more healthy than whites, numerous pockets of Asian seniors are both poverty-stricken and in ill health (Tanjasiri, Wallace, and Shibata 1995). Aggregate data in this area of physical health, as in many other areas, reveal that the average Asian elderly person is in good health. Such mean data, nevertheless, cloud the bimodal distribution of socioeconomic status and the associated ill health of the poor Asian elderly.

In addition to the barriers encountered by many Asians that may prevent them from receiving adequate health services, the model minority image can also impede access. This image excludes many Asians from the social services that they may desperately need, and it also assumes that they do not engage in high-risk behavior. Hence, they are rarely believed to be at risk for sexually transmitted diseases, for example. Women in general, and white and Asian women in particular, often are not diagnosed and therefore fail to receive treatment, because they do not fit the stereotype of people at risk. Physicians are much less likely to offer white and Asian women an HIV test or ask them about their sexual history than women of other groups. These women learn of their infection only after taking an HIV test because of pregnancy, a job or insurance change, or after a partner becomes ill (Reuters 1999a). While the incidence rate of HIV infection among Asians is believed to be low, between 1991 and 1996 the number of diagnosed AIDS cases more than tripled among Asian Americans, from 1,130 to 3,826. Despite its occurrence among this population since awareness of AIDS emerged in the early 1980s, cultural beliefs and stereotypes have presented barriers to effective education and prevention efforts, thus increasing the level of risk (Mui and Reid 1999).

Failure to discuss sensitive subjects makes prevention and intervention especially difficult. Topics such as sex, drug abuse, homosexuality, and death are often taboo among Asians. In such a cultural environment it is of utmost importance that health care providers become aware not only of the unique needs of Asians but also of the emotional and cultural factors that may prevent compliance with suggested remedies.

Mental Health

Substantial differences exist in definitions of mental illness between Asians and Americans. Fulfilling obligations in life by working hard and providing for the family are signs of mental health in the Asian culture. Frequently, Asians believe that organic factors or external environmental variables, rather than intrapsychic difficulties, cause mental disorders. Somatization of psychological problems, cited by numerous researchers, is most plausible if the cause is believed to be organic or external to the individual. Since Asians view psychological problems as physical, if they are sufficiently disturbed by negative feelings or emotional problems they tend to seek the help of physicians, acupuncturists, and spiritual healers. In general, however, most Asians attempt to deal with psychological problems without seeking professional help, instead relying on family members for support. Family members, in turn, may protect the individual, for mental illness can be regarded as a disgrace to the family and discussing such problems with strangers, such as psychologists, is viewed as inappropriate.

Nevertheless, mental health providers in the United States do indicate that Asians show symptoms of mental disorders similar to those experienced by non-Asians. Depression, psychoses, paranoia, schizophrenia, emotional turmoil, unhappiness, and so on are prevalent among Asian populations, regardless of whether they seek professional help for them or not. Chun et al. (1998) propose the VULNERABILITY ➡ EXPERIENCE ➡ MANIFESTATION ➡ PREVALENCE model[4] for the understanding of psychopathology among Asian Americans. In their review of the literature, Chun et al. (1998) cite biological differences and responses between almost half of all East Asians and Caucasians studied, to alcohol intake or to some psychotropic medications, suggesting greater biological vulnerability under certain circumstances. Other research on neonates revealed differences in temperament between Chinese Americans and Caucasian Americans, with the former being able to calm themselves more readily than the latter.

Vulnerability. The limited research on biological vulnerability reveals substantial evidence of a link between environmental stress and increased risk to mental health for Asian Americans, particularly for Southeast Asian refugees, most of whom experienced tremendously turbulent conditions in their homelands and throughout their transition to the United States. The stress does not abate when they arrive in the United States, either. Cultural conflicts, language difficulties, financial strain, absence of familial support, and prejudice and discrimination exacerbate any already existing mental health problems. For example, Chinese who are more recent arrivals to the United States, especially those who are in the first five years of residency, display greater levels of depression than Chinese immigrants who have been in the United States longer (Ying 1988), although the former have a higher academic achievement. Differences are also apparent among the recent immigrants. When social class is controlled, the differences in levels of depression between recent Chinese arrivals and longer-established ones are insignificant. Hence, academic achievement should not serve as the sole measure of adjustment. Koreans, the most recently arrived Asian immigrants, who have few English-language skills, exhibited greater levels of depression than did other Asian groups—yet this result appeared to be correlated with age and whether their knowledge of the United States was accurate before they immigrated (Kuo and Tsai 1986). Indians, often believed to be among the most acculturated of Asian immigrants, also report depression and isolation (Juthani 1992). Increasingly frequent news reports of suicide among young Indian immigrants and literature on family violence underscore the fact that mental health needs among this population are not being met (Segal 1998).

The most well-documented evidence of mental illness among Asian Americans has emerged from studies of Southeast Asian refugees. The extent of their traumatization has been well established, as most experienced the loss of family members, homes, property, and lifestyle in their countries of origin. Most reported experiencing or being witness to murder, rape, torture, starvation, solitary confinement, and other war atrocities (Chun et al. 1998). A report by the United Nations indicated that well over 40 million of the world's refugees run a high risk of depression, anxiety, and posttraumatic stress disorder (PTSD) (Mitra 1995). PTSD may manifest itself through somatic ailments, such as chronic headaches and backaches, low energy, and weakness (Foulks, Merkel, and Boehnlein 1992), which are more acceptable in Asian society than is depression or PTSD.

Experience. It is essential to understand how stress is experienced and how mental illness is viewed among Asians. While there is acknowledgment of emotional difficulties and depression and recognition that these may be caused by pressures and problems, some Asians believe that these conditions are the result of genetic or organic factors. Asians who have lived in the United States for a fairly long time may be more likely than recent arrivals to ascribe psychological problems or mental disorders to factors unrelated to physiological sources (Loo, Tong, and True 1989). Often Asians will somatize psychological issues, since seeking physiological treatment is more acceptable than is the display of psychological weakness. The intertwining of psyche and soma leads to a different conceptualization of mental illness among the Chinese (Chun et al. 1998) and other Asians, and methods of coping then differ from American mechanisms.

Manifestation. A number of studies suggest that psychological difficulties may be expressed differently by Asians and by Euro-Americans. The intertwining of the mind and body seems to play a more significant role in understanding mental illness among Asians than among Americans. Depression appeared to be correlated with gastrointestinal problems (Marsella, Kinzie, and Gordon 1973) or general feelings of ill health, such as aches, weakness, and fatigue, more often for Asians than for Caucasians (Cheung, Lau, and Waldmann 1981). While the perceived connection between mind and body may be the main reason that Asians focus on the physical rather than the emotional difficulties that they experience, researchers suggest that the stigma attached to mental problems may prevent individuals from reporting them. Thus, though many Southeast Asian refugees continue to suffer PTSD fifteen or more years after the Vietnam War, its manifestation in this community is still physiological. One must be careful, however, of somatization theories, for they perpetuate Asian stereotypes (Rumbaut 1985). With increased focus on holistic health in the United States, the health and mental health fields are becoming more cognizant of the impact of physical health on psychological functioning and, conversely, the effects of psychological health on physical well-being. It may be paramount that in order for providers to best serve the needs of human beings, they must address both their physical and mental health needs simultaneously, in a systematic manner.

Prevalence. Researchers and practitioners share the viewpoint that prevalence studies of the mental health needs of Asian Americans may be less than adequate because this group tends to underutilize mental health services. Whereas disproportionately large percentages of Caucasian Americans utilize inpatient psychiatric services, disproportionately low numbers of Asians do so (Flaskerud and Hu, 1992; Sue and Sue 1987). According to some estimates, 45 percent of Filipino American girls have contemplated suicide (Wolf 1997). Studies suggest that although Asians may have multiple mental health needs, they turn to family and personal supports, seeking to mobilize their own resources and avoiding mental health services, which are stigmatized (Segal 1998). Only when mental illness becomes very severe do Asians turn to professionals for help, which means that the Asians in the mental health system are those who are the most severely afflicted (Sue and McKinney 1975). Their reluctance to use mental health services reflects cultural values of avoiding shame and maintaining family integrity, but studies show that Asian Americans, and more specifically Asian immigrants, have a higher level of stress and other mental health problems than do white Americans (Hurh and Kim 1990; Ying 1988). The logical conclusion is that the use of mental health services is not an adequate indicator of the prevalence of mental illness among Asian Americans.

PROBLEMATIC BEHAVIOR

Substance Abuse

Most studies of alcohol use and misuse and drug abuse among Asian populations have found that Asian Americans have higher abstinence rates and lower rates of drug use than do other ethnic groups (Zane and Kim 1994). Yet other indicators suggest that the abuse of substances may be on the rise and that there are differences in the use patterns among Asian groups (Varma and Siris 1996). Males generally consume more alcohol than do females, which may well reflect international consistency in differences in gender socialization. Chinese men report the least drinking among the Asians, while Japanese males report the most; Filipino women report the least drinking, and Japanese women the most (Klatsky et al. 1983). This may be consistent with patterns in Japan, where alcohol consumption is fairly high among both men and women. In the Klatsky et al. (1983) study, foreign-born Asians tended to drink less than did their native-born counterparts; however, Kitano et al. (1992) found that foreign-born Japanese drank more than did those born in the United States.

A number of studies have looked at the drinking patterns of Asian Americans, but the focus has usually been on individuals who have been identified to have an alcohol dependency. The number of individuals treated is usually low, and not proportionate to the population, leading to the belief that alcoholism is low among Asian Americans. While that may in fact be an accurate assessment, it is important to bear in mind that Asian Americans tend to underutilize health care programs, especially mental health programs (Zane and Kim 1998). Therefore it is difficult to determine whether the available studies accurately reflect the prevalence of substance abuse. It may be that as individuals experience stress, prolonged poverty, and emotional discomfort, and do not find ways to cope with these problems, their acceptable social drinking becomes chronic. Prevalence studies on alcoholism and substance abuse among more recent Asian immigrant populations, such as Southeast Asians and South Asians, appear to be lacking, but Southeast Asians have been identified as showing heavy use of alcohol and illegal substance abuse (Erickson 1997; Makimoto 1998).

Criminal and Gang Behavior

The image of the model minority is sometimes challenged by statistics related to criminal and gang behavior. The number of arrests of Asian Americans, especially among the youth, has generally increased (U.S. Department of Justice 1996), and national concern has arisen about the rise in Asian gangs. Asian gangs, particularly Vietnamese, Chinese, and Korean ones, are the most insidious and brutal, usually preying upon their own ethnic groups (English 1995), and it is difficult to identify them, because unlike Euro-American and other non-Asian ethnic gangs, they do not leave a mark of victory or any other identification.

Many of the young people involved in gang behavior, particularly Vietnamese youth, are those who have difficulty in adjusting to life in the United States and also experience tremendous family conflict because of changes in role behavior (Furuto and Murase 1992). Gang membership affords them a sense of fellowship and belonging (Cassidy 1995), and they mention poverty and a desire to get money quickly as their reasons for joining. Their prime targets are other Southeast Asians, who often keep gold or money in their houses, as is common in their home countries, and who also do not trust or understand the American banking system. Because of their fear of the police and reprisals, the victims rarely report the robberies.

Youths may also join gangs to find protection from other gangs, to gain the support of a team, and to find some of the benefits of a family, since the gang functions very much like the family, with a strong concept of unity, hierarchy, and structure. Gangs may include both genders, or they may be gender-specific. Some of the well-known Southeast Asian gangs in Orange County, California, are all male, with names like the Natoma Boyz, the Chosen Brothers, and the Nip Family (many also have associated female groups), and others are all female, such as the Innocent Bitch Killers, the South Side Scissors, and the Midnight Flowers. Girls who have been sexually victimized find gang protection a more supportive alternative to the family. Sexual purity is so important in most Asian cultures that girls who have been forced into sexual and illegal activities believe that they can no longer be accepted by their families (Cassidy 1995).

Every year the INS returns some nonimmigrant aliens to their home countries for a variety of reasons. In 1997, 1,738 Asians were deported, and of these, 646 were deported for criminal offenses.

Country by country, the largest numbers returned for criminal offenses were from the Philippines (171), Pakistan (61), Korea (57), the People's Republic of China (45), and India (32).

Family Violence

Believed to be from cultures that stress family unity and integrity, role relationships, and harmony, Asians are stereotyped as experiencing little, if any, family violence. Issues of physical violence among these groups have essentially gone unnoticed by researchers and social service providers. However, there are sufficient reasons to believe that this is a grave oversight. Theoreticians and researchers around the globe have consistently stated that family violence is not limited to any ethnic group or socioeconomic class, and the evidence suggests that the weak and dependent in any society are vulnerable to victimization by the more powerful and independent. The wealth of international publications on family violence suggests that family violence is prevalent in all nations. There is no reason to believe that once Asians come to this country they will not inflict harm on their own family members. On the contrary, it might be argued that the additional pressures of adjusting to a new environment, experiencing new role relationships, and having to deal with varying norms and expectations, exacerbate the stresses experienced by a family and therefore increase the tendency to lash out at those who are closest and least likely to retaliate.

The traditional Asian family structure provides stability, interpersonal intimacy, and social support, and most immigrants and refugees from Asia reflect a traditional group orientation with a hierarchical family power structure and clear role definitions. Authority is gender-based, with males in instrumental roles and females in nurturant roles. As we have seen, however, immigration experiences cause major disruptions in family relationships and affect role performance. Women are likely to find jobs as domestic workers, and so they become the bread-winners and are exposed to the extrafamilial environment. Children go to school, and in that environment they move rapidly toward Americanization. The male, however, is often left at home in a state of bewilderment (Espiritu 1997; Hirayama 1982). Furthermore, Americans and Asians may have very basic differences regarding perceptions of the parent-child relationship (Ahn 1994) and the spousal relationship (Espiritu 1997), especially with regard to issues of dominance and submission. Changes in parenting styles and role relationships greatly increase the stresses that many Asian immigrants experience in the process of adaptation (Tran 1998).

Spousal abuse. Traditional gender roles between men and women are severely threatened once Asians arrive in the United States. Disadvantaged immigrant women have been found to be more employable than men (Espiritu 1997), and because of the significant decline in income level for a large segment of the immigrant male population, women must work for the family to have enough resources (Glenn 1983). The result is a loss of status and power for a number of men, both in public and at home, and it proves a great challenge to their patriarchal authority, sometimes leading to spousal abuse and divorce (Luu 1989). Chin (1994) provides an explanation of spousal assault that is couched in the unique cultural circumstances of Chinese immigrants in the United States.

Despite the paucity of empirical literature on the prevalence of spousal abuse among Asian American populations, it would be a mistake to assume it does not occur. In addition to the increased stresses experienced by Asian immigrant families, cultural norms of protecting the family, tacit acceptance of abuse, and lack of knowledge and trust of the justice system and social services in this country make it virtually impossible for Asians to report domestic violence (Root 1998a). Nevertheless, some studies that have focused on Asian subgroups have found that spousal abuse is more prevalent than is generally recognized. Most of the empirical literature on Asian wife battering appears to have studied Korean families (see Lum 1998 and Root 1998b). However, the dearth of literature on the abuse of women in other Asian groups must not be interpreted as evidence that such abuse is nonexistent. Rimonte (1989) reported that a women's shelter in Los Angeles served 3,000 women between 1978 and 1985; one-third were Korean, another third were Southeast Asians, and the rest were of different Asian groups. She found that most of these women were afraid of reporting the abuse for fear of being deported if they separated from their husbands. Immigration laws have since changed, and they no longer need to fear such reprisals. Other studies have also found that Southeast Asian women are abused (Bui and Morash 1999; Segal 2000b), yet many fear calling authorities because they experienced severe indignities and war atrocities at the hands of authorities in their home countries (Rozee and van Boemel 1989; Tien 1994). While studies of spousal violence generally focus on the abuse of women by their husbands, in an exploratory study with a nonclinical sample of Vietnamese subjects, the men reported more frequent physical aggression by wives (Segal 2000b). Although there were several methodological issues that emerged in this study, it may be worth assessing the impact of role reversal and shifts in power in immigrant and refugee families when studying the direction of violence.

Ho (1990) used the focus group method to explore attitudes toward domestic violence among Chinese, Vietnamese, Cambodians, and Laotians, revealing a tendency among all ethnic groups to accept male privilege and dominance, including varying levels of acceptance of spousal abuse. While sufficient anecdotal evidence suggests that spousal violence is prevalent among families that lack the resources to acclimatize themselves in the United States, until recently less was known about this phenomenon among South Asian immigrants who appear to be well educated and established. However, male privilege is intrinsic to these cultures also, stress can originate from a variety of sources, and family violence appears to cut across all groups and socioeconomic strata. The number of women's shelters specifically for South Asian women in large urban areas is on the rise (Segal 1998). South Asian women are particularly vulnerable to both physical and sexual abuse, they hesitate to speak of it, and they often see no recourse or escape (Abraham 1999; Mehrotra 1999). There appears to be no literature on spousal abuse within the Japanese American family, yet its prevalence is beginning to be disclosed in Japan (Kozu 1999; Yoshihama and Sorenson 1994). This conflicts with the early findings of Kumagai and Straus (1983) that there was no domestic violence among the Japanese or the Indians, although it was prevalent among American populations.

Although poverty and stress exacerbate family conflicts, it is important to recognize that spousal violence is not inevitable in poor families. Since a major focus of social services is intervention in family dysfunction, when problems are recognized there is a tendency for professionals in the field to present them as commonplace. Nevertheless, it is becoming evident that wife battering, while not extensive in the Asian culture, is also not unknown, though it is a problem that has generally been well hidden by the Asian American community. Consequently, it has been overlooked and underestimated by researchers and practitioners in the field of family violence. The overarching finding appears to be that despite evidence of physical violence, most Asian women choose not to seek help. This is consistent with the findings of most literature on battered women, regardless of ethnicity.

Child abuse. Socioeconomic and sociocultural changes are correlated with increases in child maltreatment, but most often the increases in child abuse are attributed to breakdowns in traditional values and practices. As Asian children become more rapidly acculturated into U.S. society, intergenerational tension and alienation between children and parents often increase. Sometimes internal conflicts become manifested in gang membership, drug abuse, juvenile delinquency, and running away (Furuto and Murase 1992; Ingrassia et al. 1994). Parents may resort to physical discipline that is not acceptable in the United States but is sanctioned in the country of origin (Ahn 1994; Furuto and Murase 1992). Child abuse among Asian Americans has received little attention, but the physical abuse of children may be more common among Asians than among the general U.S. population (Ima and Hohm 1991; Jung 1998). The Los Angeles County Department of Children and Family Services reported a gradual increase in Asian intakes referred for child abuse between 1989 and 1996, with 60 percent being reported for physical abuse in 1996 compared to 26 percent in the general U.S. population (Jung 1998). Corporal punishment is acceptable among Southeast Asians. Much akin to the Western saying of "spare the rod and spoil the child" is the Vietnamese proverb "When we love our children, we give them a beating; when we hate our children, we give them sweet words" (Freeman 1989:28; Ima and Hohm 1991). While the Vietnamese in the United States may believe that the "American way" of disciplining is different from the "Vietnamese way," they may still use the latter (Segal 2000a). The attitudes of Chinese American parents are more similar to those of Chinese immigrants than to those of Caucasians, and the likelihood of physical punishment and shouting is greater among the Chinese groups than among the Caucasians (Chiu 1987; Kelley and Tseng 1992; Lin and Fu 1990). In general, research suggests that Asian American parents retain attitudes and childrearing patterns consistent with their unique Asian cultures (Lee and Zhan 1998), and they consider physical discipline an appropriate form of social control (Kibria 1993; Rimonte 1989; Uba 1994).

Although in the United States child abuse is found across all economic and ethnic groups, studies suggest that the physical abuse of children may be more prevalent in conditions of poverty, as many of the environmental circumstances of potential abusers are concomitant with poverty. These circumstances may include financial stress, less opportunity to escape from childrearing, less inhibition to express and discharge aggression, and greater cultural approval for harsh discipline (Gil 1973). A large number of Asians live below the poverty line. In addition, in the absence of the extended family and other supports to share in child-rearing, many Asian families get little respite. Corporal punishment is also viewed as an acceptable, if not preferred, means of discipline for many Asian groups, perhaps increasing the children's vulnerability to parental abuse. While literature is beginning to emerge about the mal-treatment of Asian women, information about child abuse among Asian Americans is severely limited, and what information is available is restricted primarily to the Southeast Asian population (Ima and Hohm 1991; McKelvey and Webb 1995; Segal 2000a).

Elder abuse. Although Asians emphasize the veneration of elders, which in conjunction with filial piety requires the support and care of aging parents, elder abuse among Asians is on the rise (Rittman, Kuzmeskus, and Flum 1999). With increases in life span, more chronic and debilitat-ing illnesses, rising costs of maintaining an elderly person, and decreases in support systems—especially the absence of the extended family, the stresses that caregivers experience are unanticipated. When families' resources are stretched beyond their abilities to care for their vulnerable elderly, particularly in the context of acculturative stresses that new immi-grants experience, elder abuse can occur (Yee, Huang, and Lew 1998). A group found to experience more pressure than others in a variety of areas is the Vietnamese. Despite the paucity of literature about family relation-ships, indications are that the elderly, like women and children, are vulnerable to maltreatment (Le 1997). In addition, Pablo and Braun (1997) found that the abuse and neglect of Korean and Filipino elderly are of growing concern, yet Korean American elderly are either more tolerant of potentially abusive situations or less likely to perceive situa-tions as being abusive than are other groups (Moon and Williams 1993).

Higher rates of suicide have been found among elderly Asian American women, particularly the Chinese, than among other groups (McIntosh and Santos 1981; Yu 1991), although the precursors of these rates were not explored. While there is little clear indication of abuse in this population of Chinese women, studies indicate that elder abuse is cause for concern among the Chinese in Hong Kong (Ywan 1995).

Elderly Asian Indian women were found to be less likely to request support from their children or help in dealing with chronic illness, even though they had spent several years of their lives caring for their grandchildren (National Asian Women's Health Organization 1996). Disproportionately large numbers of Asian Indian women lived alone, a pattern inconsistent with that found in the home country. Yet there is indication that abuse of elders is on the rise both in India (Segal 1999; Shah and Veedon 1995) and in the United States (Nagpaul 1997). Among Asian Americans who are generally successful and ought not to feel as many stresses as those who are not as financially and professionally secure are the Japanese Americans. Yet, like the South Asians, elderly Japanese Americans are also becoming victims of abuse (Tomita 1998)

Sibling, filial, and daughter-in-law abuse. Studies of family violence pay little heed to three additional relationships in the family—relationships that have the potential to become violent. Sibling abuse, filial violence, and daughter-in-law maltreatment are rarely discussed in professional literature yet are reported regularly in the popular literature and through the news media.

Sibling abuse, abuse perpetrated by one child on another in the family, has received little attention in the West, and in most nations it is excused as a normal part of growing up (Wallace 1999), but Gelles (1997) calls siblings and parents the hidden victims of family violence. Most literature on family violence omits these forms of violence, yet reports indicate that in the United States parents consider sibling abuse the most common form of family violence and one of concern (Straus, Gelles, and Steinmetz 1980), and recent incidents of patricide in the United States suggest that filial violence is a greater problem than has heretofore been recognized.

Older Asian children often assume parental responsibilities for their younger siblings, and frustration, along with other issues of cross-cultural adjustment for Asian American youth, may increase levels of maltreatment of younger children in Asian American households. Segal (1999) suggests the occurrence of sibling and filial violence in India, though families are hesitant to discuss the latter. Likewise, in Japan violence perpetrated against parents by children has been identified by several researchers as an emerging social problem (Crystal 1994; Gjerde and Shimizu 1995; Kumagai 1983). Neither sibling abuse nor filial violence among Asian Americans has been studied or documented, but the absence of data does not indicate that the problem does not exist.

Another phenomenon that has received little attention in the United States, perhaps because of cultural differences between Eastern and Western norms and the preponderance of nuclear households, is the abuse of women by their in-laws, particularly by the mother-in-law. The literature makes occasional reference to it (Dasgupta and Warrier 1996; Huisman 1996; Lum 1998), and it has been found to occur in Asian countries (Segal 1999), especially those with joint or extended family systems. Nevertheless, there has been little recognition of it in the United States, perhaps because the authority of in-laws is relatively limited in the American family. However, Asian in-laws, many of whom reside with their sons, continue to wield power over their sons' wives, which may be misused to control and abuse their daughters-in-law.

Why does family violence exist? There are a number of theories about family violence, many of which focus on the individual psychological problems of perpetrators, victim characteristics, and environmental circumstances. Other theories suggest that the cause of family violence lies in the structure of society (Connors 1989), which is both a product and a reinforcement of the unequal distribution of power between men and women, between adult and child, and between the powerful and the vulnerable. Patriarchal values support female inferiority and are transmitted to younger generations, with family violence tolerated as a male prerogative to control the dependent (Carrillo 1992; Heise, Pitanguy, and Germain 1994). Most theories on the structure of family violence tend to agree that when society tolerates physical violence as a mechanism for conflict resolution, and when it accepts male authority and superiority in decision making within the home, it provides the ideal blueprint for family violence. In most Asian cultures, traditional norms that condone violence, themes of the sanctity of the family, and patriarchal privilege (with perceptions of women and children as the property of their husbands and fathers) have dominated family relationships and prevented societal recognition of, or intervention in, all areas of family violence. This context is reinforced in the United States, as Asian American victims still seek to protect the privacy of the family, and researchers and practitioners are lulled into the false belief that family violence among Asians is negligible.

COMMITMENT TO AMERICAN SOCIETY THROUGH CITIZENSHIP, HOME OWNERSHIP, ENGLISH-LANGUAGE ACQUISITION, AND INTERMARRIAGE

While acculturation and professional success are good indicators of how well a group has adapted to life in the United States, these measures do not reveal the group's level of commitment to the country and offer no guarantee that once individuals have achieved some identified goal—especially if they are voluntary immigrants—they will not return to their home countries. Commitment can be measured by a few factors that suggest that the immigrant plans to establish roots in the country. The National Immigration Forum (1999) found that adopting U.S. citizenship, purchasing a home in the United States, learning the English language, and marrying out of the ethnic group were all indicators of permanence. Many of these forms of commitment may occur in tandem, further ensuring the resolution not only to stay in the country but to become part of it.

Rate of Naturalization

If the commitment of immigrants to this country can be measured by the rate of naturalization, one would have to say that the degree of commitment is high. Becoming a U.S. citizen is a proactive step that in most instances[5] requires individuals to consciously renounce the citizenship of their birth. Immigration itself does not require such renunciation, nor does it necessarily reflect a commitment to the United States, since it is often a response to pressures in the home country (National Immigration Forum 1999a). In 1990, 76.4 percent of immigrants who had been in the United States for forty years were naturalized. The longer the immigrants are in the United States, the more likely they are to become U.S. citizens, and because of anti-immigration sentiment in both the social and the political arenas since the middle of the 1990s, there has been a significant move toward naturalization since 1996. Many have become citizens as soon as they have become eligible,[6] and others who earlier chose not to renounce their citizenship of birth have recently taken this step. Foreign-born Asians have a higher rate of naturalization than do foreign-born Latinos (the other large immigrant group since 1965). While two-thirds of each immigrant group has been in the United States long enough to qualify for citizenship, 38.4 percent of the Asians are naturalized, but only 18.3 percent of the Latinos have become U.S. citizens (U.S. Bureau of the Census 1998a).

Home Purchase

The purchase of a home is the largest investment that most people will ever make, and it indicates the accumulation of a substantial amount of wealth. Almost all home buyers in the United States purchase homes through mortgage loans, with payments usually distributed over fifteen or thirty years. After extensive reviews of the potential buyers' assets, mortgage companies determine whether particular buyers have sufficient assets and adequate income to be good risks. Purchase of a home suggests a long-term commitment to a geographical area, since a large proportion of one's assets is thereby tied to the area and one is receiving a steady income from it. For both native-born and foreign-born Americans, home ownership is a symbol of stability, permanence, and faith in the future (National Immigration Forum 1999a), and for immigrants it is a visible sign of commitment to living in the United States.

The 1990 Census revealed that within twenty years of arriving in the United States, 60.9 percent of all immigrants were living in purchased homes, and within twenty-six years, of the larger immigrant groups, more than two-thirds had bought homes. The housing industry since 1991 reports substantial boosts in sales to minority and immigrant groups (Thompson 1998), and mortgage lenders are beginning to court immigrant business (Buckley 1998; Wise 1997). Few lenders previously believed that immigrants' purchase of homes would match that of native-born Americans, but an examination of trends reveals that most immigrants begin their lives in the United States in central city areas and move to the suburbs as they acquire more assets (Schneider 1998; Wilson 1997). Clearly, not only are theoreticians and governmental bodies interested in the home ownership patterns of immigrants, but so are mortgage lenders, indicating that they, too, are confident that immigrants have made a long-term commitment to the nation. A 1999 report on Home Mortgage Disclosure Act data shows that home-purchase loans for Asians increased 13 percent in 1998 (Thomas 1999), reinforcing patterns of commitment.

English-Language Acquisition

The acquisition and use of the English language is another means of measuring adaptation and commitment to living in the United States. Many immigrants are already proficient in English when they arrive. Census Bureau data reveal that approximately 25 percent of new immigrants come from nations in which English is either the dominant or the official language. Even when it is not, many immigrants are able to speak English, and more others are able to read and write it, although they have had less opportunity to speak it. Recent immigrants are more strongly motivated to learn English than were earlier ones, and they are

believed to be making the transition more rapidly than earlier generations. Data on immigrants show that the longer they are in the United
States, the better they speak English; however, these results are correlated with age, education, and socioeconomic status (National
Immigration Forum 1999a). While some immigrants work at more
than one job, often within the ethnic community, and do not have the
opportunity to learn the language, they are the exception. The National
Immigration Forum (1999a) reported that more than 50 percent of
immigrants who had been in the United States for five years reported
speaking English well in 1990, and more than 75 percent who had been
here for ten years reported the same. Fewer than 2 percent of the long-
established immigrants reported not speaking English, and they were
usually part of the elderly immigrant group who resided with adult
immigrant children. Interestingly, some of these data conflict (see table
5.2), as a large number of the Asian immigrants in both the 1990 and
the 2000 Censuses reported speaking their native language at home and
many reveal that they are linguistically isolated.

Loss of native-language capability is occurring more quickly
between current generations than it did with earlier immigrants (Portes
and Schauffler 1996; Stolzenberg and Tienda 1997). This certainly
holds true for Asian American children. The 1990 Census reported that
98.3 percent of them spoke English "well," "very well," or "exclusively."
Previously it had taken three or more generations for native-language
loss, as most immigrants to the United States retained their native languages for daily use and acquired English merely to survive. Their
children would be bilingual, gradually losing their language as they
grew older, and the grandchildren would speak only English (National
Immigration Forum 1999a). Now, as most immigrants are becoming
bilingual themselves, their children tend to use English as their primary
language (Yee, Huang, and Lew 1998). A longitudinal study conducted
by Michigan State University and Princeton University of second-
generation children found that immigrant children preferred English to
their native languages and, on the average, performed better academically than did children who had native-born parents (*Los Angeles Times*
1997). Similar patterns of language loss and academic performance are
found among Asian American children. Such preference for the English
language should help to dispel concerns among the general population
that English will lose dominance and immigrant children will drag
down national test scores.

Intermarriage

Marriage between members of different groups is both a transcendence of ethnic segregation and the forging of an American identity that is distinct from the ethnic American identity of subgroups (National Immigration Forum 1999a). It not only attests to a newly formed American identity but also loosens ethnic and cultural ties with the parental generation, making an even stronger statement of adaptation and commitment to the United States.

Antimiscegenation laws and attitudinal barriers were at one time sufficient to prevent interracial marriages. Despite changes in laws, non-Asians and Asians alike frowned upon alliances with out-group members—marriages to those not of the same ethnic group. Interracial marriages are described as those between Asians and non-Asians (Kitano, Fujino, and Sato 1998), but most studies of interracial marriages include marriages between members of different ethnic and different Asian groups.

Some Asian groups have been in the United States longer than others and also arrived under varying historical conditions, hence patterns of behavior and intermarriage may differ. In addition, cultural and family differences will affect the tendency to marry outside the group. Kitano, Fujino, and Sato (1998) report a number of studies of out-marriage among Asians, and indicators are that the frequency has gradually been increasing. Thus, there appears to be more widespread acceptance of the American culture and society by immigrant generations and of Asians by the native population.

Both foreign-born Asians and foreign-born Latinos have higher rates of intermarriage than do U.S. Euro- or African Americans, and intermarriage rates for second and third generations of the former two groups are extremely high (National Immigration Forum 1999a). Analyses of data from the 1980 Census found that 25 percent of all married Asians were in interracial marriages, 90 percent of them to non-Asians (Lee and Yamanaka 1990). Yet the 1990 data seemed to suggest that percentages of interracial marriages (between Asians and non-Asians) had decreased, out-marriages (between Asians from different ethnic groups) had increased, and the social distance between Asians and Americans had increased (Lee and Fernandez 1998).

These figures seem to contradict other data stating that intermarriages are on the rise. Population profile data from the Census Bureau in 1998 found that one-fifth of all married Asian women chose a spouse of a different race or ethnicity, nearly twice the rate among Asian men overall. In addition, fully 30 percent of married Asians between the ages of 15 and 24 have found a spouse of a different group (Suro 1999), yet a disproportionately larger number of the interracial marriages of Asians have been with European Americans, rather than African Americans (Suro 1999). The native-born are much more likely than immigrants to intermarry, but even for immigrants the prevalence of intermarriage steadily increases with the length of time spent in the United States.

While intermarriage is on the rise between Asians and non-Asians, the frequency of marriages outside the Asian community has consistently been greater for all ethnic groups of Asian women than for men—almost two to one. By the third generation, 41 percent of Asian American women have intermarried (National Immigration Forum 1999a). Intermarriage is a very delicate matter in Asian communities. Many Asian men experience strong underlying resentment about the large number of Asian women who seek husbands outside the ethnic community (Suro 1999).

Theoreticians and researchers suggest that acculturation is not unidirectional. In the process of adapting to the United States, ethnic groups introduce the United States to their own traditions, values, and styles of life. With increases in global communication and international travel, Euro-Americans are beginning to value a variety of patterns of behavior, eating, and dress. Increasing societal acceptance of diverse options lowers pressure for ethnic groups to assimilate to all Euro norms. Beyond the outward indices, trends show that assimilation by the white culture is also under way as it begins to embrace family values that are basic to Asian and Latino societies.

6

Public Policies:
Social Welfare, Housing,
Education, and Criminal Justice

The placement of decision-making authority in government not only facilitates the creation and enforcement of rules, it also creates a mechanism for defining, seeking, and hopefully achieving collective goals intended to benefit the entire society. . . . These authoritative decisions on behalf of society [constitute] "public policy" . . . [and] society is affected not only by the actions taken by government but also by governmental inaction.

—SMITH 1993:1–2

Public policies in the United States may be federal, state, or local. Governing or affecting almost all areas of public life, they have implications for immigrants as well as for nationals, often serving as the economic and social pulse of the nation. Usually grounded in the majority's values and ideologies, they touch all aspects of life and serve to regulate patterns of behavior, distribution and use of resources, provision of services, and a host of other activities considered important for the functioning and well-being of the society.

Some public policies particularly affect immigrants and Asian Americans, because of their immigrant status, because of sociocultural differences that influence styles of behavior, or because of a combination of these factors. Clearly, the primary ones with implications for a number of Asian immigrants are immigration and refugee policies. In addition to affecting immigrants (or potential immigrants) themselves, they also affect Asian Americans with family members or other contacts who are allowed, or disallowed, entry into the United States.

Also among the national public policies that are of major concern for the largest number of Asian Americans are (1) social and family welfare policies, (2) housing policies, (3) educational policies, and

(4) criminal justice policies. While not designed particularly for immigrants or Asian Americans, they substantially color the daily lives of Asians, as they do for all Americans. When policies do not effectively address the problems of a particular population, an exploration of reasons is warranted. Furthermore, when policies do meet needs, it behooves policymakers to understand the ingredients for success so that it may be replicated. Policy analysis has a number of facets, not the least of which are the value-laden underpinnings and historical context of the development of a particular policy. This book examines the major dimensions of the problems the policies were designed to address, discusses the goals of particular policies, and examines eligibility requirements in order to assess the benefits, provisions, and services that are of specific import for the Asian American community.

DEFINING PUBLIC POLICY

Drawing on a number of sources, Koven, Shelley, and Swanson (1998:3) identify at least six definitions that are applicable to public policy:

1. Actions intended to accomplish an end
2. Whatever governments choose to do or not to do
3. An authoritative allocation of values though [*sic*] governmental activity
4. All governmental action
5. A program of goals, values, and practices
6. A standing decision on the part of those who make it and those who abide by it.

Clearly, these definitions are all-encompassing and suggest the far reach of governmental control, which can identify activities that are prohibited, establish penalties, and identify qualifications for engaging in particular activities. Nevertheless, environmental factors, societal conditions, and general attitudes and values are not static. Democracies pride themselves on their responsiveness to public opinion and need and current political philosophy, and the policies set by democracies are dynamic and modifiable through appropriate processes. Similarly, since policies can be changed or adapted to particular societal needs, and because the United States is so heterogeneous, policymakers are constantly confronted with competing goals, such as external security, internal order, justice, general welfare, and freedom (Merriam 1945). Yet the U.S. government's system of checks and balances attempts to ensure, if it is possible, that policies are made or amended only with deliberation and foresight.

The triad of government's branches—legislative, judicial, and executive—enact laws, establish the constitutionality of those laws, and sign or veto them. Furthermore, the individual in the presidential seat often has a great effect upon the direction and scope of public policy, through either proactive initiatives or vetoes of legislative action. Not only is the public pulse significant, but so are the leanings of the president (Jansson 1999). This factor can have special significance for immigrants and minorities in the United States. The courts have increasingly gained power as they arbitrate whether decisions taken by the legislative branch are consistent with constitutionally established rights and directions. Unlike those who serve in the other branches, the members of the judicial branch, notably the federal-level U.S. Supreme Court, are not as subject to public pressure. While state and local judges are elected, the nine federal judges are appointed by a president for life, regardless of changes in other government areas or offices. Consequently, the president who is able to replace through appointment Supreme Court justices who have retired or died, can indirectly have tremendous long-term impact on legislative actions. For example, Presidents Nixon, Reagan, and Bush were able to change the liberal bent of the Supreme Court with the appointment of more-conservative individuals. At least three of the nine members of the current Supreme Court are expected to announce their resignations between 2002 and 2006, allowing President George Bush, who took office in January 2001, to have an important say in determining the profile of the next Supreme Court.

While policymaking is especially important in directing action, within the framework of the policy administrators are responsible for implementing its provisions. These individuals are in positions of authority because of their knowledge and skills, and they are charged with translating policy into action. They wield considerable power and discretion, especially when they interpret directives that are vague or ambivalent. Another group, the front-line practitioners, are the ones who actually turn policy *into* action, which may or may not be entirely consistent with the directives of the policy or the administrative interpretation. In the end a difference often exists between the public policymaking and the policy implementation.

If public policy is not sensitive to the needs of immigrant and minority communities, then discretion in interpretation becomes moot. Koven, Shelley, and Swanson (1998) propose a model of policymaking as influenced by three factors—rationality, power, and ideology. Experts in the area lend rationality by providing practical information to guide decisions; interest groups and influential parties may affect decisions by lobbying, voting, courting public opinion, and contributing to the political campaigns of those who support their interests; and philosophies and values of democratic societies contribute to the development of policies as they help to put specific people into office or vote to implement particular policies that reflect their beliefs about what constitutes justice.

SOCIAL AND FAMILY WELFARE POLICIES

Often developed in response to social problems, social welfare policies are designed to allocate or reallocate societal goods, services, and opportunities, with the goal of enhancing the social functioning of all citizens. While social welfare is grounded in altruistic ideals that promote the care and well-being of the less fortunate, it is also seen as a necessary tool for the survival and maintenance of society. If the disadvantaged have their basic needs met, they will be less likely to cause agitation about the unequal distribution of resources (Kingdon 1999). Policies that require the redistribution of resources and opportunities are also means for rectifying past injustices, particularly those that have been racist (Lieberman 1995; Quadagno 1994), and sexist (Gordon 1994; Mink 1995), as some consider the Social Security Act of 1935 to be. Social welfare policies are ideologically based and usually reflect the social values of the decision makers, who in a democracy are believed to represent the values and norms of the society's majority. One major issue is whether social welfare should be normative or remedial, whether it should be institutional or residual. Often governments and nations differ on their opinions and actions, some believing that social welfare should be institutional and available to all people, and others, such as the United States, generally supporting the notion that most social welfare programs should be residual and designed to assist those who are unable to meet their needs through their own resources. Often policy decisions and institutional legacies of one era continue to shape and constrain policy development in subsequent periods (Skocpol 1992).

History of Family and Social Welfare Policy

American Poor Laws during the colonial period were modeled after the English Poor Laws, which differentiated between the "deserving" and the "undeserving" poor. The former were poor children, the elderly, and the disabled, while the latter were the "able-bodied" poor. Local governments raised monies to assist the "deserving" poor and to establish workhouses for the "undeserving." The "undeserving" also included those who were alcoholic, mentally ill, or indolent and refused to work. The concept of poverty as the responsibility of the local government gained general acceptance in the nineteenth century when most states passed laws that established poorhouses as the primary care facilities for the needy. This perception and treatment of the poor and needy persisted until the Depression. Identification of individuals as being deserving or not was based on a moralistic belief that poverty was the result of individual deficiencies and a just reward for lack of productivity and personal actions.

This view did not recognize environmental and social factors that prevented groups of people from working or developing the skills necessary for the employment arena. On October 24, 1929, known as "Black Thursday," the U.S. stock market crashed, marking the beginning of the Great Depression, which lasted until the United States entered World War II in 1941. Although there had been other periods of depression during the late nineteenth and early twentieth centuries, they were not comparable to the Great Depression, which marked one of the bleakest periods of the American economy. It was only after millions of hardworking, heretofore successful people lost their jobs, businesses, or farms, that individualistic explanations of failure were replaced by a recognition of systemic causes of poverty. Although voluntary agencies—the economic welfare of the 1930s—attempted to assist those affected by the Depression, they found that the impact was so far-reaching that they did not have adequate resources to cope with the crisis.

President Herbert Hoover was unable to change the course of the Depression by relying on the voluntary social welfare sector. He believed that federal relief would weaken the social fabric of the society and harm the efficacy of the government. When in 1932 he was forced to propose an unemployment assistance program that was subsidized at 80 percent by the federal government, it was too little, too late. Hoover's inaction led to the landslide victory for Franklin D. Roosevelt in the 1932 election. When Roosevelt (FDR) took office in 1933, more than 33 percent of the labor force was unemployed, and one in every six families was dependent on outside assistance. He instituted job programs for enormous numbers of the jobless, assistance to the destitute became a national issue, and millions of federal dollars were spent for public welfare assistance. At this point, social welfare became a federal concern.

Through President Roosevelt, several acts were passed that affected society in a number of areas, including public works, relief, employment of youth, labor standards, banking insurance, and social security. The Great Depression encouraged Americans to reevaluate ideologies and assumptions about the organization and responsibility of society and to make major changes in the mode of government. Between 1933 and 1939 Roosevelt created programs to address the economic crisis—programs of relief, recovery, and reform; the combination of these programs was known as the New Deal. The aim of the New Deal was to stimulate industrial recovery, assist Depression victims, guarantee minimum living standards, and prevent future economic crises. The federal action that was initiated during this period was unprecedented in scope and raised many controversies about the appropriate role of government and the extent and nature of its involvement in the lives of private citizens.

The highlight of FDR's administration and his New Deal was the passage of the Social Security Act in 1935. It created (1) a national old-age insurance program, (2) aid to dependent children, assistance for maternal and child welfare services, vocational rehabilitation for those with disabilities, aid for the visually impaired, a plan to strengthen public health services, and (3) a federal-state unemployment system. Each of these provisions, though since modified, has persisted into the twenty-first century and has benefited innumerable individuals and families.

Following World War II, a strong antiwelfare reaction resurged, and for many years no new welfare programs were proposed. In 1950 the Social Security Act was amended to cover the mother, or any other needy adult, with whom a child was living. Other amendments increased the level of governmental involvement in the lives of the poor, and further amendments in 1956 required states to provide casework and social services to needy families. The 1962 amendments allowed people to qualify for aid based solely on need. Before these changes, governmental workers were permitted to make surprise visits to homes to ensure that those who were receiving aid were not engaging in "immoral behavior." Finally, in the 1970s, the federal government became a major player in the family issue of abortion. Until this time, states had been allowed to decide the circumstances under which a woman could obtain an abortion. In the 1973 landmark Supreme Court case of *Roe v. Wade*, the majority argued that the Due Process Clause of the Fourteenth Amendment (the right to privacy) protected a woman's freedom to choose whether or not to have an abortion during the first trimester of pregnancy.

Welfare continued to be of concern for the Nixon, Reagan, and Clinton administrations. Under Nixon's proposed Family Assistance Plan (FAP), every unemployed family could receive federal relief that was equivalent to approximately two-thirds of the 1969 poverty level. In order to be eligible, however, the able-bodied, including women with children over the age of three, would be required to work or to be enrolled in a job training program. Most of Nixon's proposed plan was rejected by Congress, but the Supplemental Security Income (SSI) program was adopted in 1972. Reagan reassessed the welfare state, believing that the federal government's expenditures for social welfare should be minimal, that only those who were "truly needy" should receive benefits, and that welfare assistance should be provided only on a short-term basis. The Reagan administration was professedly committed to removing governmental involvement in the family and reestablishing family values by promoting self-reliance, adopting the position that welfare should provide a safety net, not a way of life. Interestingly, Reagan's proposals of the "workfare" program and the repeal of the Aid to Families with Dependent Children (AFDC) program finally were realized in 1996 under the banner of "Welfare Reform" in the administration of Bill Clinton.

On August 22, 1996, Clinton signed a new welfare bill, the Personal Responsibility and Work Opportunity Reconciliation Act, that ended more than sixty years of guaranteed help to the nation's poorest children through the AFDC program. It placed a five-year lifetime limit on payments to families, giving states the power to run their own welfare and work programs. States that did not comply with federal guidelines ran the risk of losing some of their grant funding. This bill was recognized as the biggest change in social welfare policy since the Great Depression, and Clinton was lauded by many for a policy that provided opportunity but expected responsibility in return. Others called Welfare Reform and its enactment "a moment of shame" (Marion

Wright Edelman, president of the Children's Defense Fund), an "unconscionable retreat" (Christopher Dodd, chair of the Democratic National Committee), and "[not] welfare reform, [but] welfare denial" (Paul Simon, senator from Illinois) (Clines 1996). Welfare Reform is reminiscent of Wilensky and Lebeaux's classic typology of social welfare systems, which contrasted the *residual* and *institutional* approaches to providing assistance (Wilensky 1965). The former provides a safety net for the poorest in the society, while the latter affords basic support to the entire population. The U.S. welfare state, unlike many European ones, has always taken the residual approach, not dissimilar to its historical tendency to provide reactive, remedial assistance for a variety of problems such as illness, substance abuse, and family violence. It has devoted little effort and resources to the *prevention* of problems and has not yet truly recognized that the economic, social, and psychological costs of remediation are significantly higher than those of prevention.

The Effects of the Social Security Act on Asian Americans

Amendments to the Social Security Act of 1935 currently provide for (1) a combination of old age and survivors' insurance (OASI) and disability insurance (DI), known as OASDI, (2) unemployment insurance, (3) federal assistance to the elderly, the visually impaired, and those with disabilities under the Supplemental Security Income (SSI) program, (4) public assistance to families under the new Temporary Assistance to Needy Families (TANF) program, (5) federal health insurance for the elderly (Medicare), and (6) federal and state health assistance for the poor (Medicaid). While some Asian Americans and immigrant Asians benefit from the services delivered through the Social Security Act, their use differs from that of the rest of the population, both because of their sociodemographic characteristics and because of the changes in eligibility requirements enacted by Congress in 1996. Differences also exist in welfare participation rates among immigrant groups from different countries of origin. These are related to characteristics of the sending countries, such as national output and income inequality (Borjas and Trejo 1993). An immigration policy that delineates the characteristics of the nonrefugee immigrants that the nation will admit also filters out many individuals who may become welfare-dependent.

In 1996 about 15 percent of all Asians in the United States had an income below the poverty line (Hooper and Bennett 1997). Nevertheless, not all of those who were eligible accessed the available range of welfare services, for a number of cultural reasons, among them shame in seeking assistance from outside the family and fear and distrust of governmental authority. Although some signs of increased poverty rates and increased use of welfare, such as SSI and food stamps, are evident among new immigrants, the decline in immigrant quality has been greatly exaggerated. Working-age Asian immigrants and refugees who have been in the United States for ten years or more are much less likely to receive welfare than are natives (Ross-Sheriff 1992). Data from studies of Southeast Asian refugees do indicate that many do not experience a level of economic well-being equal to that of the U.S. population as a whole, and at any particular point in time a significant proportion of this group is indeed receiving public assistance (Potocky 1996).

The policy of the Refugee Resettlement Program in the United States is to promote economic self-sufficiency within the shortest time possible after a refugee enters the United States. This goal is accomplished through the coordinated use of support services and cash and medical assistance. Under the existing policy, the federal government provides means-tested eligible refugees with cash and medical assistance, through SSI and a modification of the old AFDC program, and monetary assistance through the first thirty-one months. Those who are not eligible for these programs receive Refugee Cash Assistance during the first eighteen months after their arrival.

Economic self-sufficiency usually means the ability to get and maintain a job. Many immigrants are forced to accept low-paying, menial positions, especially when they come to the United States with skills that are not transferable or when they have no English-language competence. Operationally, sufficiency can be defined as having an income above the poverty level set by the government. In reality, however, that income level may not be sufficient to meet financial needs (Law and Schneiderman 1992). In fact, it appears that a significant number of refugees who are officially considered "self-sufficient" are actually below the poverty level (Office of Refugee Resettlement 1991). Because of the short period during which they can receive assistance (eighteen months), the aim of many resettlement agencies is to place them in the labor market as soon as possible, but that does not necessarily result in sufficiency. The length of time a refugee has spent in the United States is the most significant factor in accounting for variations in economic self-sufficiency. The Refugee Resettlement Program aims also to influence English proficiency, vocational skills, access to the labor market, and welfare benefits. Because most in the refugee population are eager to be self-supporting, however, they tend to look for jobs as soon as possible, rather than devoting time to improving vocational skills or English proficiency, both of which require inordinate amounts of time and commitment.

A report released by the Department of Health and Human Services (1995) revealed that the longer refugees remain out of the labor force, the less likely they are to begin a job search or find jobs in a subsequent year. Most moves into the labor force occur within the first two years, and for those who are not employed during that period, the probability of entering the job market declines steadily. Without provisions ensuring that refugees will be successful in securing employment, however, welfare dependency is prolonged. In fact, Southeast Asian refugees, particularly those in California, experience the worst economic conditions of any ethnic group: lower employment, higher poverty, higher public assistance, and lower earnings income (Potocky 1996). According to the 1990 Census, the poverty rate for the H'mongs was 63.6 percent; for the Cambodians, 42.6 percent; for the Laotians, 34.7 percent; and for the Vietnamese, 25.7 percent.

The other group of Asians that tends to use governmental assistance is the elderly. Many Asian Americans have inadequate income and poor health but have no information about public assistance. According to reports from the late 1970s, more than twenty years ago, the Asian American elderly tend to have lower-status occupations and lower incomes compared with the total aging population (Special Services for Groups 1978). The rapid growth of the Asian American community since then is reflected in birth data as well as immigration figures. The INS reports that current numbers of Asian elderly immigrants are significantly greater than those of non-Asian elderly immigrants. In the 1980s and 1990s a substantial number of Asian American elders joined their adult immigrant children, and many, lacking income and resources, have become dependent on public assistance. At the very least, they subscribe to Medicare, and often to SSI. Immigrants who enter the United States after age fifty-five are significantly more likely to use welfare than are immigrants who arrive during their prime working years. It is often not the difference in Social Security benefits that distinguishes between the younger and the older immigrants, or even low income or poor labor market performance—it is the decision to apply for benefits (Hu 1998). As in other areas of adjustment, Asian

Americans remain a heterogeneous group. Those from different ancestries do not share the same experiences, and while elders from all Asian ancestries are dependent on public assistance, the Chinese and Vietnamese elderly are more likely than others to live in poverty (Lee 1992).

Though the Asians most likely to use welfare services are refugees and the elderly, the changes brought about through Welfare Reform have meant that many of the more recent immigrants, a large number of whom are elderly, are no longer eligible for assistance. The Personal Responsibility and Work Opportunity Reconciliation Act (PRWORA) of August 22, 1996 (110 Statutes-at-Large 2105), lists the following restrictions for "qualified" immigrants who entered the United States after August 22, 1996:

Barred from SSI and food stamps

Subject to a 5-year bar on non-emergency Medicaid, the Child Health Insurance Program (CHIP), and TANF.

After 5-year bar, subject to deeming for the above programs. Exemptions for one year for some battered spouses and children, those at risk for going hungry or becoming homeless.

After 5-year bar, states still retain option to determine immigrant eligibility for TANF, Medicaid, and social service block grants.

The changes mandated through PRWORA effectively bar qualified needy families, the elderly, and women with dependent children from applying for assistance. While census reports indicate that the number of Asian female-headed households is small, the number of needy families and elderly is sizable.

Furthermore, undocumented or "non-qualified aliens" are barred from most federal, state, and local public benefits. The INS is required to verify immigration status in order for aliens to receive federal benefits, a provision that appears to target immigrants of color, both legal and undocumented, who are readily identifiable and therefore are most frequently challenged about the authenticity of their papers. It also results in the discriminatory practice of questioning natives of color who are visibly different from either Europeans or African Americans.

Child Welfare Policy and Asian Americans

Concerned with the care and protection of children, early child welfare efforts focused on protecting and boarding orphaned or unwanted

children. The 1916 Child Labor Act prohibited the interstate transportation of goods manufactured by children. The Social Security Act
of 1935 introduced the AFDC program and Maternal and Child
Welfare Services (child protection services), which effectively shifted
child welfare services from the private, voluntary sector to the public,
governmental arena. Since the 1960s, the primary emphases of child welfare services have been child protection, foster care, adoptions, and Head
Start. The 1974 Child Abuse Prevention and Treatment Act sought to
identify and provide services to children who suffered nonaccidental
injuries, those who were chronically neglected, and those who were sexually and emotionally abused. Foster care is an alternative for parents
who are unable, or unwilling, to provide care for their children. Children
are placed in homes of other families, and their care is subsidized
through governmental funds. For children who do not have parents, or
for children whose parents wish to relinquish them, adoption is a permanent option. Finally, the Head Start program seeks to provide early
educational opportunities for children in poor communities. With the
termination of AFDC, it is anticipated that the burdens to single-parent
families will increase, and so will the need for child welfare services. The
absence of subsidized day care creates a burden for all families, but particularly for the working poor. Although the United States purports to
protect and promote the welfare of all children, child welfare policies
tend to be directed primarily toward disadvantaged children, and "disadvantaged" is defined using criteria that do not include the needs of a
number of children. Furthermore, even children who are "disadvantaged" by governmental standards, especially under Welfare Reform, are
less likely to benefit from governmental "care and protection."

Although it is generally recognized that Asian Americans depend
less on social welfare services than other ethnic groups, 3 percent of the
population does receive TANF and certainly would use Medicaid services. This group, like the majority group, is clearly affected by Welfare
Reform and may have even fewer personal resources than others do to
make a successful transition off welfare. The implications for the quality of care that their children receive can be substantial. Gersten (1996)
indicates that welfare dependency among refugees continues to be a
serious problem, especially in states such as California, which had the
highest AFDC payments. The answer may be not Welfare Reform but
programs such as the 1985 Wilson/Fish Amendment to the Refugee
Act, which allows refugee resources to be directed to voluntary agencies

to provide services to refugees. This plan does not, however, answer the question of welfare dependency for those Asian Americans who are not refugees but need more assistance and are likely to fall through the cracks that have emerged because of the combination of Welfare Reform and the Wilson/Fish Amendment.

Relatively little is known of child maltreatment in the Asian American population. Since the primary focus of child welfare policy is on child protection and the perception persists that Asians are family-oriented, there is little awareness that some Asian American children require public protection and that prevention and education efforts must target Asian families as well as others. Rimonte (1989) suggests that to interpret the dearth of information about family violence in the Asian community as a positive reflection on cultural values would be a misdirected use of cultural sensitivity. A number of researchers have documented a high tolerance for corporal punishment as a form of social control in most Asian cultures (Dunphy and Mera 1991; Ima and Hohm 1991; Kitamura et al. 1999; Lum 1998; Samuda 1988; Segal 1995).

Asians in the United States also indicate a greater acceptance of the use of physical punishment for discipline (Ho 1990; Hong and Hong 1991), and Asian American children and young adults report a higher level of physical abuse than do Euro-Americans (Meston et al. 1999). Despite the acceptance of corporal punishment as a disciplinary strategy and the prevalence of abuse in Asian countries (Ahn 1994; Furuto and Murase 1992), few researchers have sought to explore its occurrence among Asian Americans. Since Asians tend to avoid contact with majority social service agencies, the U.S. society's perception that Asian family values preclude family violence has been reinforced. The few studies that have explored the issue show that corporal punishment is common among Asians in the United States (Ima and Hohm 1991; McKelvey and Webb 1995; Segal 2000a). Child welfare policy and services must be made cognizant of the occurrence of abuse in this population, especially considering the long-term dysfunctional psychosocial correlates of childhood abuse. Outreach efforts must take into account variations in cultural patterns of childrearing, but extreme cultural relativism must not allow U.S. child welfare policy to overlook harmful practices.

The Welfare of Asian Women

Financial self-sufficiency and health care aside, a major concern for welfare is the frequency with which women experience domestic violence.

A number of theories of family violence focus on individual psychological problems of perpetrators, victim characteristics, and environmental circumstances. Other theories suggest that the causes of family violence lie in the structure of society (Connors 1989), which is both a product and a reinforcement of the unequal distribution of power between men and women.

Although empirical studies regarding spousal violence in the Asian American community are sparse, this should not be interpreted as indicating that abuse does not exist. Cultural factors and traditional taboos conspire to keep such violence out of the view of the public. The privacy of the family and the importance of its good name make it especially difficult for any woman to report abuse (Root 1998a), and Asian women are less likely than any other group to report intimate family violence. Survey data indicate a low incidence of spousal abuse among Asian Americans (Tjaden and Thoennes 1998) although there is some evidence that domestic violence is substantially higher than is reported to the Department of Justice. Eighty percent of the participants in Yoshihama's (1999) study of Japanese American women stated that they had experienced violent actions at the hands of their male partners, but only 61 percent defined those actions as abusive. Indian American women also reported the experience of abuse, and they included verbal, emotional, and economic abuse along with physical violence (Mehrotra 1999).

Despite the paucity of empirical literature on violence against Asian American women, it is known that violence against women inflicted by their intimate partners continues to be a leading cause of injury and death worldwide (Mills 1996), and its prevalence is noted also in Asian countries (Associated Press 2000a; Kozu 1999; Segal 1999). When male dominance is woven into the fabric of the culture, as it is in most Asian societies except the Philippines, the values are transported along with emigrants to their new host countries. Especially when immigrant men are not able to assimilate into the dominant culture—as has been the case for many Asians in the United States—entrenched cultural patterns of interaction persist through generations. Hence, U.S.-born women of Asian ancestry may be as much at risk for domestic violence as are Asian immigrant women. Furthermore, although the United States is less patriarchal than Asian countries, its underlying social constructs still denigrate the position of the female while allowing male superiority. Males are still expected to be more dominating, strong, assertive, and aggressive than are women.

Spousal abuse is a major problem in the United States, one that cuts across all ethnic groups and socioeconomic levels. Likewise, it is a cause for concern in the Asian American population, and increasing numbers of shelters are being established and utilized by women in this population who have finally decided that wife battering is unacceptable (Lum 1998; Segal 1998). Among all Asian women, however, refugee women constitute a group at greater risk, yet they are even less likely to seek extrafamilial help if they are being abused at home. A new phenomenon that became common among a number of Asian groups in the last decade of the twentieth century and has continued into the twenty-first is that of the "mail-order bride," a means of acquiring a wife that is similar to the "picture bride" system at the end of the nineteenth century and the beginning of the twentieth century among the Chinese, Japanese, and Koreans. Most frequently, Filipino women immigrate to the United States to marry European American males, or Chinese women come to marry Chinese American men. The Filipinos are often stigmatized by the Filipino American society and exploited by the American husbands (Ordonez 1997); among the Chinese there is a high incidence of wife battering (Chin 1994).

All advocates for women in the United States already recognize that most women tend to hide their experience of abuse, believing that they somehow provoke it. A number of women feel they can trust the men who say they will not harm them again, while others are afraid that if they do report the abuse they will be hurt even more severely. Many continue to love their abusers and hope for their reform. It is time for policymakers to recognize that although Asians tend not to discuss family problems, the problems do exist. Outreach efforts and awareness programs should help Asian American men recognize that they must not abuse their wives, and the women should recognize that such treatment is not their just due. As the Asian American population grows, overlooking the experience of a large number of Asian American women can have long-range ramifications on the society, in terms of their mental health, their productivity in the workforce, and their child-rearing capabilities.

Asian American Elderly

In the United States—and in many other countries—improved nutrition, better health care, and overall enhanced quality of life have allowed life expectancy to increase significantly. Yet, because of societal expectations, most people retire at the age of sixty-five, and many find themselves living on a fixed income and being faced with annual inflation. As people age, they find themselves becoming increasingly dependent on family members and societal resources for their financial, social, and physical needs. In a culture that is particularly youth-oriented, there is little room for elderly who appear to have outlived their usefulness to society.

In contrast to the U.S. culture, all Asian cultures stress respect for the elderly and filial piety. Regardless of how many generations of Asians have lived in the United States, these core values persist. While in European cultures, the vast majority of the elderly live with their spouses or alone, most Asian elderly live with their children, usually in the home of the eldest married son. In Asian countries the male children bring their wives to live in the ancestral home and the parents retain the prerogative of decision making, but in the United States the aging Asian parents move into the homes of their children. Such choices may necessitate the abdication of power and adjustment to the expectations and values of the children. Thus, although Asian elderly and their married children still live together in the United States, when the home is that of the children, family dynamics are altered. The elderly begin losing the asset that Asian cultures have always promised them— authority. While many Asian American elderly experience a great degree of dependency in such a situation, elderly Asian immigrants who enter the United States to be close to their children often become extremely dependent upon them. These individuals usually have few financial assets or income and little social or emotional support from anyone other than their children. They face daunting language barriers and acculturative stresses, and they are confined to their home because of a lack of transportation or access to activities outside the home. Such total dependence on their children makes Asian American elders in general, and immigrant Asian elders in particular, highly vulnerable.

Elder abuse, recognized only relatively recently even in the Western Hemisphere, emerges as an issue that has implications for social policy (Hugman 1995). Though identified in the media earlier (Gargan 1981), in the United States in 1987 it was termed "domestic elder abuse," or the form of maltreatment experienced by elders at the hands of those who have special relationships with them, specifically spouses, siblings, children, or other caregivers in the home. Elder maltreatment may include physical abuse and neglect, sexual abuse, emotional abuse, abandonment, and also financial exploitation. It is now becoming apparent that the abuse of elders is much more frequent than had been believed. Pillemer and Finkelhor (1988) reported a prevalence rate of 32 elderly people per 1,000, with men and women equally victimized, although the latter suffered more serious abuse. In recognition of the need for policy to protect vulnerable elders, the Older Americans Act of 1965 was amended in 1992, combined with other advocacy instruments, and placed in Title VI—Vulnerable Elder Rights Protection Activities (Netting et al. 1995). Nevertheless, the National Elder Abuse Incidence Study revealed that approximately 500,000 elderly were identified as abused and neglected in domestic settings in 1996, and it further estimated that for every report to Adult Protective Services, more than five cases were not reported (Cyphers 1999). While causes of the problem may involve caregiver stress, impairment of the dependent elder, intergenerational transmission of aggression to resolve conflict, or personal problems (SLIK Designs 1996), among Asians the license to abuse may be compounded by the changed status (dependency) and longevity of the elderly. U.S. social policy is only just beginning to awaken to the fact that the very large numbers of aging "baby boomers" are going to be a force with which to reckon (Chapin 1999), as their composition is highly diverse and their needs are widely varied.

Social Welfare Services in the Asian American Community

In general, Asian Americans' use of social welfare services is limited because of a lack of knowledge, a poor level of trust, and a tradition that prevents them from seeking services outside the boundaries of the family and community. Many may not avail themselves of the financial assistance programs to which they are entitled through the Social Security Act. Social welfare providers may need to increase their awareness of eligibility, and through sensitivity to cultural barriers, encourage Asian American clients to apply for these assistance programs. Community contacts and educational programs through local ethnic organizations may increase the level of awareness of and access to Social Security and welfare benefits for those who are eligible.

It may be more difficult to encourage the Asian American elderly to become involved in family intervention programs, however, since participation in any such programs to address family dysfunction runs counter to Asian beliefs and traditions. In cultures that advance collectivism, in which the needs of the family group supersede individuals' needs, power and authority are hierarchically determined by age and gender, and philosophies place the locus of control outside oneself, assistance in the psychological and social areas of functioning may not be considered acceptable. Indian, Chinese, and Japanese philosophies guide a large part of Asian American psychology, and this must be understood by those who engage in the delivery of services.

Indian psychology. Four basic concepts undergird much of Indian psychology and behavior: (1) *Dharma*, the codes of conduct that define goodness, maturity, and appropriate behavior; (2) *Karma*, the propulsion from previous incarnations, present deeds, and future destiny; (3) *Maya*, the illusion of real knowledge and its causes; and (4) *Atman*, the person as a part of the ultimate cosmic unity (Pedersen 1991). Buddhism stresses inner harmony and psychic consciousness as the key to freedom, with four noble truths: (1) suffering is intrinsic to life; (2) the desire to live is the cause of rebirth; (3) annihilation of desire ends suffering; and (4) escape is through the eightfold path of righteousness (Pedersen 1991).

Chinese psychology. Though influenced by Buddhist philosophy, Chinese behavior is tempered by the practical and clearly defined guidelines of Confucianism that describe the five basic social relationships (between sovereign and subject, father and son, elder and younger, husband and wife, friend and friend) and a belief in the order and harmony of nature in Taoism. Cognitive structures in Taoism are built to view life holistically in a system of balances and the forces of yin and yang. Adherence to the guidelines can provide harmony and equilibrium for the individual.

Japanese psychology. Influenced by both Indian and Chinese philosophies, the Japanese expanded their reach through the Zen perspective, which states that persons are emancipated from the dual bondage of subjectivity and objectivity of mind and body and are awakened to their own true nature (Pedersen 1991). Relationships here also stress the group, rather than the individual, and behavior is guided by hierarchy. Of significance is the Japanese identification of themselves according to the current frame of reference, rather than according to individualized attributes. At all times, it is the role relationship of the moment, rather than individual characteristics, that guides behavior.

Implications of psychologies for the use of services. Most Asian psychologies are patriarchal, with a highly organized hierarchical structure
that defines behavior and roles. This, coupled with a belief in an external locus of control and a group orientation, greatly influences the
extent to which Asian Americans make use of social services that are
designed to change established patterns of family behavior. In situations
in which people are victimized, the perpetrators believe it is their right
to control others, while victims concur and also believe that they cannot
control their own destinies. In working with Asian American populations, then, social service providers must first raise awareness among Asian
Americans through community education that family violence is dysfunctional and should not be accepted. If Asian Americans seek services
or, more likely, are referred for services, cultural variables that prevent
compliance with intervention must be addressed with sensitivity and
empathy. Unless and until Asian Americans believe that social welfare
services will not further destroy their families or challenge and denigrate
their traditions, it will be difficult to provide assistance that can relieve
daily pressures and resources that can lead to an improved quality of life.

HOUSING POLICIES

The first national housing legislation was introduced as the Housing
Act of 1937, intended to give financial assistance to states that would
enable them to provide safe and sanitary housing to low-income families. A number of additional acts followed, all with the aims of improving housing options for Americans and addressing the availability of
mortgage loans for a large number of poor people and disadvantaged
neighborhoods. Clearly, in the present day the most glaring housing
problem facing the nation is the increasing numbers of homeless individuals and families, but there is still a great need for the provisions of
the first act, for many people of low income, those on public assistance,
the working poor, and even a large segment of the middle-class population experience difficulty in finding and maintaining adequate, affordable housing. Public assistance for housing and public housing were
intended at their inception to serve as intermediate measures for the
working poor, who were expected to purchase their own private homes
at some point. These measures were never intended to serve as final or
permanent solutions to the housing problem.

The Cranston-Gonzales National Affordable Housing Act of 1990
had six specific goals, intended to benefit those of low and moderate

income. It was the first housing legislation in more than a decade that sought to (1) decentralize housing policy, (2) develop and implement housing services with the help of nonprofit sponsors, (3) link social services more closely to housing assistance, (4) encourage home owner-ship for low- and moderate-income people, (5) preserve existing federally subsidized housing, and (6) initiate cost sharing between governmental and nonprofit organizations.

Despite difficulties for some families, as a whole housing in the United States has steadily improved since 1937. Home ownership rates are relatively high, having climbed from 44 percent in 1940 to more than 64 percent in 1995 (Karger and Stoesz 1998), and the 2000 Census reported that the number of houses being bought continued to rise through the 1990s. Furthermore, new homes are mostly single-family dwellings, larger and with more amenities than ever before (U.S. Bureau of the Census 1991). Housing costs are the single largest monthly expense in the budgets of most families and are often paid before any other bills, including food, clothing, and health care. In 1999, 66.8 per-cent of the total population reported home ownership (U.S. Census Bureau 2000), but further investigation shows that at least two-thirds of poor homeowners spend between 30 percent and 50 percent of their income on housing, and 20 percent to 35 percent of moderate-income homeowners spend a similar amount (Lazere et al. 1991). These figures do not include the escalating costs of utilities (electricity, gas, water) and property taxes. Although most U.S. families own their own homes, a large number are renters, and the problems experienced by low-income renters have reached crisis proportions. Many poor families live in deplorable conditions, and when they do live in adequate facilities, they spend a disproportionately large percentage of their income on housing. A variety of socioeconomic factors have led to a dramatic decrease in low-cost rental units, resulting in the largest shortage on record of afford-able housing units (Karger and Stoesz 1998).

Many who cannot afford to pay the costs of housing are forced to join the ranks of the homeless. The most visible among the homeless population live in streets, parks, transportation terminals, abandoned buildings, and automobiles, sometimes moving from public or private shelters to emergency housing placements. No longer is the homeless population limited to men, substance abusers, "bag ladies," or the men-tally ill. The very poorest in society are frequently the unemployed, female-headed single-parent families with young children, women and children escaping from domestic violence, the retired poor on fixed incomes, and runaway and "throwaway" children (those who have been ejected from their homes by their parents). Some of the homeless are individuals and families who take temporary shelter with friends or family members, moving from location to location as necessary. In 1987 the McKinney Act, signed by President Ronald Reagan, created more than twenty programs to meet the housing, health, mental health, education, and other needs of the homeless. Housing reform proposals aim to address the housing crisis for low-income families, but homelessness and housing problems are an integral part of poverty, and their eradication will ensue only from fundamental change in larger areas, such as income support, social services, and employment training programs.

Initially, nations believed that the state had little role in the housing sector, but by the middle of the twentieth century the governments of most industrialized countries had assumed some responsibility for adequate housing for most of the population and attempted to meet some of the housing needs of the poor (Castles 1998). Although housing assistance falls within the purview of the modern welfare state, the incidence of home ownership also reflects the capacity of individuals to provide shelter for their families and themselves without public intervention. For many, home ownership is seen as the basis for the creation of a property-owning democracy (Castles 1998), forcing a continuing dilemma regarding the extent of governmental involvement. Title 12, Chapter 13 of the United States Code Service provides authorization for home ownership assistance by supporting periodic payments to mortgagees and to manufactured-home buyers (12 USCS §1715z [1999]). Assistance is accomplished through payments on behalf of homeowners, with preference being given to low-income families who "without such assistance would be likely to be displaced." Rent supplements are also provided for qualified lower-income families (12 USCS §1701s [1999]).

Financing and affordability are the primary concerns about U.S. housing policy, but displacement and discrimination are also cause for alarm. Those who are homeless are displaced from their residences not merely because of a lack of funds but also because a number of socioeconomic factors have led to that point. Discrimination and segregation in housing raise concern. Housing is segregated along both socioeconomic lines and race and ethnic lines. In addition to providing support for their members, ethnic communities often develop because their members are denied access to predominantly white middle- and upper-middle-class residential areas. Racism, so deeply ingrained in U.S. history, is embedded in the culture and the nation's institutions (Zarembka 1990). Discrimination in housing may extend beyond racism to those who have disabilities, children, and nontraditional families.

The civil rights movement of the 1960s was successful in getting the Fair Housing Act (1968) passed, although it did not have the impact on discrimination and segregation that was expected, since it failed to address the systemic, institutionalized nature of housing discrimination. No enforcement mechanism was in place, and Congress mistakenly assumed that the housing market was basically nondiscriminatory. The 1988 amendments to the 1968 act added enforcement provisions and provided a venue through which to file suit, to be awarded damages, and to impose civil penalties on defendants.

Residential Patterns of Asian Americans

The real difference in location and quality of housing adds to the extent of segregation between a particular minority group and the dominant society. Asians generally live in major urban and suburban areas of the United States, especially on the East and West Coasts. While the Chinese, Japanese, Koreans, and Southeast Asians tend to live in relatively segregated ethnic neighborhoods, Indians and Filipinos select housing based on the quality of life that they seek and the distance from work. However, this pattern may soon change, for large numbers of the more recent Indian and Filipino immigrants are less educated and are nonprofessionals. Ethnic enclaves are developing, particularly in the Indian community, as patterns of adjustment become increasingly bipolar, with the educated more readily accepted by, and accepting of, U.S. culture and the less educated working and living in the rapidly growing ethnic locales.

Low-income Asian Americans, like other low-income people, are burdened by cost, overcrowding, and poor housing quality, as well as discrimination and segregation. In 1997 about 1.5 million Asians were living below the poverty line (Dalaker and Naifeh 1998). This rate (14 percent) was slightly higher than the 13.3 percent for all Americans and substantially higher than the rate for whites (8 percent). Nevertheless, in 1999, 53.1 percent of the Asian American population were homeowners, up from 50.8 percent in 1996. Also in 1999, 70.5 percent of the European Americans and 46.3 percent of the African Americans were homeowners (U.S. Census Bureau 2000).

An alternative to home purchase is home rental. While many professionals in transition or those who are frequently relocated select rental housing, disproportionately larger numbers of poor families live in rental facilities. Of these, 80 percent live in rental housing and struggle with problems such as the necessity of spending more than 30 percent of household income on housing that is often inadequate, with incomplete plumbing, ineffective heating and electricity, structural and maintenance problems, and overcrowding (Karger and Stoesz 1998), and there continues to be a shortage of affordable rental housing. In 1995, 5.3 million families with very low incomes (households with incomes below 50 percent of the median income for the area [U.S. Housing and Urban Development 1998]) who rented spent more than half their income on housing or lived in substandard housing, but received no governmental assistance. If slightly more than half (53.1 percent) of the Asian American population are homeowners and one percent are homeless, that means approximately 45 percent must be renters.

Despite evidence that 14 percent of the Asian American population live below the poverty line, the percentage of the homeless who are Asian American is small (one percent)—substantially smaller than the proportion that are African Americans (53 percent), European Americans (31 percent), and Latinos (12 percent) who compose the homeless population in the United States (van Wormer 1997). Nevertheless, it is expected that the influx of individuals who are not as skilled as the earlier post-1965 immigrants and the increasing numbers of women and children who are leaving their homes because of family violence will add to the numbers of the homeless Asian American population. Asian Americans are also more likely to be renters and live in substandard housing. That 14 percent of the Asian population lives below the poverty line, that only 1 percent is homeless, and that housing comes at such a high cost all suggest that poor Asian families may be pooling their meager resources to maintain their living environments. The 1990 Census data reinforce this hypothesis of pooled resources among the Asian poor, revealing that Asian American households include more individuals than do the households of other groups. While there may be a tendency to assume a larger family size, larger households reflect not more children but the sociocultural practices among Asians of maintaining the extended family structure and of including unrelated people in the household. Large households suggest, furthermore, that while homelessness may not be a problem, overcrowding and inadequate living facilities are common, and that, in turn, has implications for this population's health, education, and family functioning.

Anti-Asian discrimination in housing is not uncommon; it has been a social reality through much of U.S. history, resulting in the segregation of Asians as early as 1879. Certainly the government no longer attempts to separate Asian Americans from the majority population, and the Fair Housing Act prohibits segregation based on race and ethnicity, but discrimination regarding housing against Asians is still evident throughout the country (Young and Takeuchi 1998). A review of fair housing audits conducted across the United States between 1977 and 1983 found that Asian Americans, like other minorities, face considerable prejudice when seeking information from real estate agents regarding available housing (Yinger 1988). Overt discrimination has occurred in the form of flyers distributed in neighborhoods in New York and California, encouraging the boycott of Asian businesses and realtors that sold homes to Asians (U.S. Commission on Civil Rights 1992). Vandalism, harassment, arson, and other racially motivated intimidation have prevented Asians from living in particular communities or have threatened their residential arrangements (U.S. Department of Justice 1999b).

Housing Programs

In 2000 housing programs fell into five categories: (1) Section 202 housing provides funds for new construction and rehabilitation of existing buildings specifically for the aged and the disabled. (2) Section 235 housing focuses on the middle-income renter, providing new construction subsidies for this group. (3) Section 8 housing provides rental assistance and subsidy for low-income renters. (4) The Farmers' Home Administration (FmHA) provides low-interest loans for new construction for rural low- and middle-income people. (5) Public housing provides new construction and rentals that are federally funded for low-income people and administered through local housing authorities.

Asians evidence a bimodal housing pattern both across and within subgroups. While the educated, professional, and well established are able to purchase their homes and achieve a standard of living consistent with the majority population, the large number of immigrants and refugees who have low levels of education and poor English-language skills must manage in overcrowded and less than satisfactory conditions. The data that indicate that only 1 percent of the Asian population is homeless and that large numbers own their own homes make it less likely that Asians will become beneficiaries of the housing policies that have been developed to benefit low- and moderate-income families.

Ratner (1996) identified four major shortfalls that, if corrected, would allow more minorities and immigrants to become homeowners: (1) lack of appropriate, affordable housing; (2) limitations of existing financial avenues; (3) poor knowledge regarding home purchase, credit, and credit judgment; and (4) cultural gaps, misunderstanding, and biases that distance these subgroups from mainstream lending institutions. Furthermore, the cultural tendency of Asians to avoid authority and to make as few waves as possible may set up a situation in which they do not avail themselves of the housing assistance to which they are entitled and which they may desperately need. As large numbers of Southeast Asians and Chinese continue to live in less than desirable facilities, it becomes particularly important not only that they be made aware of housing assistance, but also that they be taught how to negotiate access to these resources.

Clearly, the accomplishments of governmental housing policy are tempered by the reality that even though it is not a permanent solution to housing problems, it demands long-term involvement. Housing is expensive, requiring the commitment of a sizable portion of governmental resources. Currently, federal low-income-housing policy continues to be marked by severe inadequacies. Although many low-income families, those on public assistance, and the working poor do benefit from public housing and housing assistance, these venues do not adequately address all the issues, assist a large enough segment of the population, including needy Asian Americans, or provide long-term solutions to housing crises. An adequate housing policy must address a combination of issues, particularly cost burden, overcrowding, and housing quality, while providing opportunities for true housing choice that ends discrimination.

EDUCATIONAL POLICY

The national policy with respect to equal education opportunity [20 USCS §1221–1(1999)] states:

> Recognizing that the Nation's economic, political, and social security require a well-educated citizenry, the Congress (1) reaffirms, as a matter of high priority, the Nation's goal of equal

education opportunity, and (2) declares it to be the policy of the United States of America that every citizen is entitled to an education to meet his or her full potential without financial barriers.

This policy clearly states the importance of preschool, primary, secondary, postsecondary, and occupational education for all Americans. Not only does it address the needs of the majority population, but it also stresses responsibility to, and adequacy of, education for children with special needs: those who have disabilities, those who are economically disadvantaged, those who are racially or culturally isolated, those who need bilingual instruction, and those who are gifted and talented. The policy also attempts to ensure that nonpublic primary and secondary education provides alternative educational experiences and options to parents in guiding their children's development. The national policy also recognizes the importance of developing, expanding, and implementing educational opportunities for adults at the basic and secondary education equivalency levels.

Referring to federal immigration policies, Congress specified in 20 USCS §7402 (1999) that the collection of language-minority Americans in the United States speak almost all the world's languages and that there are ever greater numbers of children and young people of limited English proficiency. These children face numerous challenges in their efforts to receive adequate education and become an integral part of U.S. society. Because of poor evaluation measures, they are often placed in segregated programs, including special education classes. There is a shortage of teachers and staff who are qualified to serve them, and their parents often lack English proficiency and are unable to effectively participate in their children's education. For this reason, the Congress recommended that elementary and secondary school education be strengthened with bilingual education, language-enhancement, and language-acquisition programs. Congress also proposed an emergency immigrant education policy to help the large number of immigrant children who lack English-language skills to make the transition. The U.S. government holds education to be one of its most "sacred government responsibilities" (20 USCS §7541 [1999]), and it is evident that U.S. educational policies recognize the importance of education for all children and expect at least a high school level of academic competence for all people.

Despite policies to ensure academic competence, discrepancies still exist in the public's perception of the quality and efficacy of American education. Many believe that education in the United States holds lower standards than that of many other nations, but it nevertheless provides children with knowledge superior to that of the past (Koven, Shelley, and Swanson 1998). Perhaps this incongruity can be explained by the disparities in education across the nation, and even within a region. Much funding for the educational system is tied to taxes, which are tied to income levels, housing quality, and standards of living. Poor urban and rural areas do not have the resources to attract quality teachers, access sufficient technology, or provide adequate physical environments that are conducive to learning. Disparities in the literacy levels of young Americans (Murnane and Levy 1992) may be partially explained by such socioeconomic factors as children living below the poverty line and in female-headed families. African American and Latino children often test lower than Euro students, and children whose parents have a college education score better on standardized tests than those whose parents have not attended college. A key to improved educational attainment is providing all students with challenging curricula and improving socioeconomic variables for disadvantaged children.

Other factors may also affect the quality of education, among them poor hiring decisions, societal attitudes of discrimination and isolation, social problems of school violence and poor discipline, and corrupt administrators. Certainly, then, educational policy is a necessary but not sufficient condition for ensuring that all children and adults meet basic literacy levels.

As a "sacred governmental responsibility," education is recognized as having practical value. It is a vehicle through which a society transmits its knowledge, values, traditions, and norms to subsequent generations, with the intent of perpetuating society as it is currently understood. Not merely altruistic, the government's responsibility and interests are reflected in one of the eight goals of Public Law 103–277, the Goals 2000: Educate America Act, signed into law on March 31, 1994, by President Clinton. Goal 5 specifies that "every adult American will be literate and will possess the knowledge and skills necessary to compete in a global economy and exercise the rights and responsibilities of citizenship." For the nation to compete in the increasingly global economy, its citizens must have the competencies necessary for advanced technical education and specialization. Commitment to education is a commitment not only to individuals but also to the economy and society through the services provided to individuals. An educated workforce is necessary if modern economies are to remain productive and maintain their vitality (Castles 1998).

In his final State of the Union address, on January 27, 2000, President Clinton identified four initiatives specifically related to education: (1) improvement in early education by expanding the Head Start budget by $1 billion and establishing a $600 million fund to improve child care and early childhood education; (2) improvement of teacher quality with the assistance of a $1 billion grant package; (3) an increase in school accountability with a grant of $250 million to be used to substantially improve those schools that are failing or to close them and $450 million for bonuses to schools that evidence dramatic improvement in student performance; and (4) a reduction in class size, to be achieved by hiring 100,000 new teachers through a $450 million increase in the budget. The implementation of such ambitious initiatives with the associated funding could have substantial impact on the quality of public education offered to both American and immigrant children. The president's further goals to work toward ending poverty and violence aimed to allow children who are living in less than adequate conditions access to environments that are more conducive to learning.

These initiatives were directed toward the improvement of educational opportunities for all Americans, including minority and immigrant children. Although the overwhelming perception of Asian Americans is that they value education and are high academic achievers, data from the U.S. Bureau of the Census reveal a bimodal distribution that clusters around the high end and the low end of achievement, often differentiating among various Asian subgroups. While a disproportionate number of Asians hold advanced degrees and attend prestigious universities, a disproportionate number also fail to achieve a high school education (table 6.1).

Furthermore, indications are that Southeast Asians over the age of seventeen who arrived in the United States between 1978 and 1982 have a relatively low level of education, with fewer than 15 percent having attended college (table 6.2).

The myth of the universally excellent scholastic ability and academic success of Asians has been a disservice to this very diverse population. More recent data show continuing variations within this group and across subgroups. The Educational Testing Service (ETS) reported in 1997 that Asian Americans represent a mixture of extremely successful students and a large undereducated class with low socioeconomic status.

Table 6.1 Asian American Educational Levels*

EDUCATIONAL ATTAINMENT, AGE > 25 YEARS (in Thousands) / SELECTED ASIAN POPULATIONS*** (in Thousands)**

Educational Attainment	Total U.S. Population	Asians	Chinese	Filipino	Indian	Japanese	Vietnamese	Korean
Total (>25 years)	158,694	4,158	1,809	1,717	1,017	1,007	961	784
Percentage	100.0	100.0						
Elementary (total)	10.6	12.4						
0-4 years	2.4	5.3						
5-7 years	3.8	4.4						
8 years	4.4	2.7						
High school (total)	49.6	34.4						
1-3 years	11.0	5.8						
4 years	38.6	28.0						
College (total)	39.8	53.2						
1-3 years	81.4	14.2						
4 years	12.7	23.3						
Graduate school 5+years	8.8	15.8						
< High school graduate			19.1	11.0	11.0	9.3	29.0	27.7
			23.5	19.6	16.9	31.9	30.5	29.7
Some college			13.9	22.4	13.3	25.1	19.4	17.1
4+ years college			43.5	47.1	58.8	33.7	21.1	40.6

*2000 data available late 2002.
**Gall and Gall (1993:193).
***U.S. Census Bureau 1990.

Table 6.2 Education levels of Adult Southeast Asian Refugees 1982

Levels of education (over 17 years of age in percent)	Vietnamese	Chinese (from Vietnam)	Laotian	Total
No formal education	1.6	6.5	21.0	8.3
Elementary	34.5	50.3	56.6	44.2
Secondary	27.4	24.0	12.2	22.2
High school graduate	22.6	15.5	4.9	15.9
Some college	13.8	3.7	5.1	9.2

Source: Office of Refugee Resettlement, 1985

Seventy-nine percent of South Asian and 69 percent of Korean high school seniors scored above the 50th percentile on reading ability for all U.S. high school seniors. Yet only 50 percent of Filipino, 46 percent of Chinese, and 43 percent of Japanese scored above this level. The results are surprising, since the second and subsequent generations are larger for the latter group than for the former, and one would expect greater English-language comprehension among U.S.-born Asian Americans. Southeast Asians scored the lowest, with only 32 percent performing above the 50th percentile. Japanese, Chinese, Koreans, and South Asians all evidenced a high level of math competence (from 73 percent to 84 percent scored above the 50th percentile), but Filipinos and Southeast Asians performed only at the 52 percent and 43 percent levels respectively (Hudson 1997). Such differences are evident across the board, at the high school level and at the middle and lower school levels (Gall and Gall 1993).

The United States holds sacred the right to a public education for every child through high school, including minority and immigrant children who might have special needs that must be addressed so that they may compete effectively in a society that increasingly requires academic competence. But perceptions of Asians as model minorities, high academic achievers, and members of advantaged groups prevent a large part of the Asian American population from accessing a quality high school education. The dropout rate is high, especially in areas that have greater concentrations of Southeast Asians and Filipinos, and few programs target their needs.

It is often believed that standardized tests discriminate against those who have not had a number of opportunities or those who have not been able to participate fully in the mainstream culture. In other words, standardized tests are biased against those who do not belong to the majority Euro-American culture. As shown earlier, however, test results for Asians follow a bimodal distribution. When Asians are studied as one group, they cluster at the high end of a scale or at the lower end. Those at the high end perform as well as or better than Euro-Americans do on standardized tests. Now the Educational Testing Service is considering adopting a weighting measure that would equalize the scores of those who are more advantaged and those who are less advantaged.

Many Asians highly value education and invest heavily in their children's education both financially and through personal involvement. ETS believes that because of criteria that place Asian children at an advantaged level, the scores of many of them who are applying for college entry should be scaled down in reports to these institutions. While it is laudable to give the disadvantaged increased opportunities in order to level the playing field, such strategies punish those who have made the most of the advantages they have had—for not all advantaged children invest the effort necessary to attain success.

To this end, in October 1999 the College Board pulled Asian Americans out of the minority category in a study of academic achievement, placing whites in one category, Asians in another, and African Americans, Latinos, and Native Americans as minorities. Asians were removed from the minority category because of the College Board's view that they outperform the other three groups (Rodriguez 1999). This aura of academic success masks the frequency with which many Asians, particularly those from Southeast Asia—Cambodians, the H'mong, Laotians, and Vietnamese—are struggling and performing poorly in school. The perception that all Asians are educational high achievers has sometimes prevented many students from receiving much-needed services and support. Averaging Asians into the larger group of whites can be devastating, because even the limited programs and scholarships that are currently available to them will be diverted to other identified minorities. This was apparent when Bill and Melinda Gates announced that their foundation's $1 billion gift for minority college students would be disbursed through African American, Native American, and Hispanic education funds (Varner 1999). While it was not the intent of the Gates Foundation to exclude Asians, the decision about how the funds are to be administered certainly deters potential Asian applicants.

Mark Della, an administrator in the Seattle public schools, indicated that he was confident that Asian students would nevertheless continue to receive college assistance from the usual source—other Asians (Varner 1999). This, too, suggests that the majority society feels little responsibility for helping Asians in the educational arena. Reminiscent of early-twentieth-century Asia experiences, they must turn to their own group for assistance, while other minorities can rely on funding from majority sources. The Foundation Center, a New York–based organization that classifies every grant over $5,000 reported to it, revealed that foundation grants to Asian American organizations between 1983 and 1990 ranged from a low of 0.12 percent to a high of 0.20 percent of the total annual amount. Of this low percentage, only 4.0 percent was granted to education for Asian Americans (Asian Americans and Pacific Islanders in Philanthropy 1992).

In addition to denying services to deprived students, this perception has encouraged another form of discrimination. Because Asians are regarded as overrepresented in higher education, particularly in the prestigious East and West Coast schools, and because they are overrepresented in the fields of science, technology, and increasingly in business, quotas have been set for the acceptance of children of Asian descent into these colleges. Unlike quotas for other minorities that allocate spots with the aim of attracting students and increasing their access to excellent universities, the quotas for Asians are set to prevent more than a specified number of qualified applicants from being offered admission. Regardless of their eligibility and the availability of openings, their Asian descent disqualifies them from entering. Furthermore, because of the quota system, Asians are no longer competing against the general applicant pool; they must compete against other Asians for the limited spaces allocated to their minority group.

Public policies may need to ensure that Asians are not moved to a separate, nonminority status that further deprives them of the support and services they need at all levels of the educational system. English as a Second Language (ESL) programs must not only be made available but should be actively offered to all non-English-speaking Asians through outreach efforts. Education policies should include provisions that encourage Asian and other immigrant families to become familiar with the U.S. educational system and understand the resources and support services that can enhance the academic success of students. Programs such as Head Start must reach out to all urban children, because not only do they give children an opportunity when they are very young, but they ensure that parents begin to recognize the importance of education in this technological and information age. Statistical data indicate that those Asians who are less advantaged and less established tend to live in urban areas. As they become more settled, they are likely to move to suburban locations (Gall and Gall 1993). If educational policies, especially those that target the less advantaged populations of society, were to include outreach efforts for Asian populations as well, the bimodal distribution issues would be addressed, and those at the lower end could receive the assistance necessary to bridge the gap. At the level of higher education, educational policies must prevent discrimination against those who are perceived as being advantaged, for leveling the playing field should not entail penalizing high achievers. It may be better to address those factors that are concomitant with low educational achievement or aspiration—such as poverty, stress, poor self-esteem, and environments that are not conducive to learning—and thereby improve opportunities for underachievers.

CRIMINAL JUSTICE POLICY

All societies respond to norm defying behavior through sanctions. . . . In Western cultures, irrational deviance is usually understood as a mental health matter, while anormative behavior on the part of a rational actor falls under the purview of law enforcement.
—KARGER AND STOESZ 1998:358

Crime policies, much like other policies, have the dual purposes of prevention and remediation. Criminal justice policies seek to deter crime and provide sanctions against it, with the ultimate aim of controlling its occurrence. However, criminal justice policies do not—and cannot—remain static, for the array of problems changes over time. Crime and criminal activity change in nature, incidence rate, and scope, as do the ideologies that drive the administration of justice policy.

Crime is a complex of many elements, with such variety that the average individual in the United States believes that criminal activity is on the upswing, but statistics from the Department of Justice (2000) indicate that crime in the nation has steadily decreased since

1993. Although crime itself is declining, as is the likelihood that most Americans will experience it, fear of crime is on the rise. Violent crimes such as rape, robbery, assault, and homicide are decreasing, but the underclasses are more likely than other socioeconomic groups to be victimized by these crimes. Two important points become apparent: criminal behavior changes over time, and the changes hold different implications for different groups in society (Walker 1998). Besides victimization of people, other areas of concern are crimes against property, the misuse of guns, and the sale and use of illicit drugs.

The challenge for policymakers is to determine what measures must be taken to address the problem. Their policies are informed by the prevailing ideologies and the current level of acceptance of particular activities. Since the 1980s, the gap between liberal and conservative policymakers has closed; most politicians who identified themselves as liberals have adopted most of the traditional policy agenda, including advocating the presence of more police and a higher level of incarceration, and some traditional conservatives have begun supporting the legalization of drugs, ordinarily a liberal proposal (Walker 1998). While society tends to be in agreement about certain activities—for example, robbery and homicide are clearly unacceptable—differing opinions emerge about such issues as the legalization of drugs, the age at which alcohol can be consumed legally, and gun ownership. The function of the administration of justice is another area of disagreement. While some believe the justice system should deter criminal activity, others, particularly those who have been victimized, prefer that it be a means of vengeance and retribution.

Despite the decrease in crime over the last two decades of the twentieth century, the United States still reports far more episodes of serious crime than any other industrialized nation. While burglary has declined, the murder rate is still very high. At approximately 20,000 murders annually, it is ten to twenty times higher than the rate in all other industrialized countries and most developing nations (Federal Bureau of Investigation 1997; International Crime Victim Survey 2000). As these statistics suggest, the crime problem in the United States is really one of violent crimes such as robbery (which in this country is much more likely to involve firearms and therefore to have graver consequences) and murder.

The most significant development in criminal justice since the 1970s is the war on crime, which has placed heavy emphasis on incarceration.

This includes the popular "three strikes" law, an anticrime measure mandating life imprisonment of those convicted of a third felony. The incarceration rate in the United States is extremely high, three times that of Canada and four times that of Japan. Almost three-quarters of a million individuals are on parole, and almost three million more are on probation (Bureau of Justice Statistics 1998). The enormous numbers have so overloaded the criminal justice system that it is sometimes unable to fulfill its basic functions (Walker 1998), and overcrowding in prisons is a chronic problem.

In exploring criminal justice policies, the most significant question to ask is whether there is a correlation between changes in policy and criminal activity. The "war on crime" and its counterpart to deter drug trafficking and use, the "war on drugs," have promised unrealistic outcomes. War implies a goal of victory, and the victory—namely, the eradication of crime—is virtually impossible. Walker (1998) suggests that it would be more appropriate to develop policies that set goals to decrease crime to a "tolerable" level. Another of the difficulties of considering these issues is that basic assumptions regarding the control of crime, the administration of justice, and the human psyche differ between liberals and conservatives. Many conservatives believe the death penalty deters crime, yet there is no conclusive evidence that it does; and most liberals believe treatment will cure crime, yet the literature reports only limited effectiveness of intervention programs (Walker 1998).

Conservative crime control policy is based on the premise that criminals lack self-control, succumb to their passions, and break the law. Free will, rational choice, and moral responsibility are the guideposts of conservative policy, suggesting that potential criminals weigh the costs and benefits of their behavior before they break rules. If the costs are not high, there is little to deter them. Liberals, on the other hand, view crime in a social context, believing that antisocial behavior is the effect of external influences such as the family, the peer group, a lack of economic opportunities, and discrimination (Walker 1998). Clearly, policies and programs vary according to the political climate of the time, and liberals and conservatives, with such disparate perceptions, are likely to develop quite different policies. Conservatives emphasize criminal law, stressing that anyone who violates the rules of society should be punished. Liberals, on the other hand, underscore the significance of criminal procedures, out of a concern to ensure that the power of governmental officials is limited (Walker 1998).

Some others believe that the criminal justice system is not a just system. Those who are most frequently targeted by the criminal justice system are people (particularly males) of color and poor people. Department of Justice statistics have consistently shown a disproportionately high rate of African American and Hispanic incarceration, and many in the public call for reforms to eliminate the racial profiling responsible for the skewed rates of incarceration. The criminal justice system also penalizes those who are poor by handing them much longer sentences and affording them fewer opportunities to have those sentences commuted for shorter ones or to be paroled; at the same time, those with status and power are absolved or receive minimum sentences, many of which do not have to be served in their entirety. Citing the Watergate roster published in the *Washington Post* on June 17, 1982, Reiman (1996) revealed the unequal justice in the system. President Richard M. Nixon was pardoned. Of the twenty co-conspirators, nineteen were given prison sentences. Of these, fourteen served less than the minimum time, while two others spent no more than three months above the minimum period, and substantially (several years) less than the maximum. If they had been among the poor or disenfranchised, they would have had very different experiences. It appears that two systems of justice are operating, both of them less than just: one underpenalizes the elite, and the other overpenalizes the already disadvantaged.

Interestingly, although crime rates have been gradually dropping among both adults and youth, the government has redoubled its efforts at law enforcement. Belief in the benefits of removing criminals from society ensures that incarceration will continue to rise and jails and prisons will continue to be filled beyond capacity. Perhaps the purpose of criminal justice now is not to arbitrate punishment in relation to the crime (Karger and Stoesz 1998) but to incapacitate high-risk offenders selectively (Freeley and Simon 1992).

Immigrants and Crime

Almost always xenophobic, native-born Americans have tended to distrust all immigrants, including whites from outside their borders, and with the influx of immigrants of color, fears have become institutionalized. Nonwhite and non-European immigrants have long been suspected of contributing to the demise of U.S. morality, unity, and stability and have often been viewed as inherently criminal (Lamm and Imhoff 1985). Perry (2000a) suggests three categories of immigrant offenders—illegal immigrants, criminal aliens, and organized crime groups.

Illegal, or undocumented, immigrants may be those who enter the country illegally or those who are described by the Immigration and Naturalization Service as "overstays," whose visas to stay in the United States have expired. By definition, because they do not possess the appropriate papers to reside in the country, both these groups of undocumented immigrants are criminals; in 1995 they were estimated to number approximately five million (Bureau of Justice Statistics 1996). Undocumented immigrants do not belong to the category of criminal aliens who are noncitizens convicted of felonies, drug trafficking, firearm offenses, or offenses endangering national security. Criminal aliens are usually in the United States legally, as permanent residents or on valid visas. The majority of criminal aliens are charged with drug trafficking offenses—85 percent of the noncitizens in federal prisons and 45 percent in state prisons—but most are drug users and small-scale dealers (Dunn 1996).

Organized-crime groups in the United States have developed an international dimension, with a cross-section of the new immigrants represented. While many of their members are immigrants, a large number are nonresidents with the explicit purpose of expanding the domain of crime groups in their own home countries by using cultural and social bonds as bait to attract U.S.-based individuals (Marshall 1997). Many Asian crime organizations began as political or community-oriented groups, others developed from street gangs, and more recently they have begun to resemble organizations that are created around criminal activity (Perry 2000a). Asian syndicates control much of the drug smuggling, prostitution, and other illegal markets in parts of the West and East Coasts (Tranton and Lutton 1993).

Asian American Criminal Offenders

On the opposite side of the model minority myth sits the stereotype of the Asian as mysterious, devious, and fearsome (Perry 2000b). Often confused with the reality of Asian criminal activity, this stereotype is reinforced by media images of Asians as violent gangsters and martial arts experts. What is known about Asian criminal activity in the United States belies the perception of Asians as inscrutable and unscrupulous.

Most often, the offenses for which Asian Americans are arrested are public order offenses, such as being argumentative and engaging in fights in public places, and are consistent with the reasons for their arrests throughout the twentieth century (Perry 2000b).

The more serious crimes committed by Asians tend to be associated with group efforts, and crimes associated with lucrative sources of revenue (i.e., prostitution, smuggling) are also particularly enticing to Japanese, Chinese, and Vietnamese crime groups. In fact, there appears to be consensus that Asian organized crime is accelerating faster than such crime in any other cultural group (Ho 1998; Mann 1993), and its members consist of both immigrants and U.S.-born Asians.

Violent crimes associated with Asian Americans involve protection of illegal markets (Marshall 1997). A consistent flow of women from Asian countries, and also from South American countries, is managed through Asian organized crime. On August 20, 1999, the organized-crime task force in the U.S. attorney's office reported the indictment of thirteen members of a smuggling group that had recruited between five hundred and one thousand women from Asia who agreed to pay $30,000 to $40,000 to be smuggled into the United States. Payment was to be made through bonded prostitution, with 30 percent of the women's earnings to go to the brothel and 70 percent to the smugglers until the amount was paid (Booth 1999). News reports in the late 1990s and into the twenty-first century frequently indicated that smuggling of Chinese and South Asian boat people into the United States continues.

Asian organized-crime groups are the most violent criminal enterprises in most Chinatowns across the nation, and they pose a particular challenge to law enforcement because of the diversity of their involvement in revenue-generating illegal operations and also because of the language and cultural barriers (Lindberg et al. 1997). While the literature suggests that Asian crime groups are substantially different from other gangs, it indicates that Chinese and Japanese organized crime resembles its European and African American counterparts in a number of characteristics. All of these operations are well structured and hierarchical, require sworn secrecy and loyalty, demand absolute obedience to superiors, maintain control through the use of fear and violence, and involve themselves in racketeering (Jan 1993). Most often their victims are also Asians who live within the Asian community; since they have not truly infiltrated the larger society, they may not yet have warranted the attention that has been received by Western organized-crime groups like the Mafia.

The youth counterpart of adult organized crime is gang affiliation, and the rise in Asian youth gangs has troubled policymakers, particularly since the late 1980s and through the 1990s. While such gangs are sometimes linked with Asian organized crime, they are more often independent of it (Perry 2000b). In Chinatowns children are running away and often finding their way into gang membership, criminal activities, and violent behavior. Chinese gangs are highly structured, with a commitment both to gang warfare and to generating income through robbery, burglary, extortion, and protection (Chin, Fagan, and Kelly 1992). Vietnamese gangs are prevalent in California, New York, and Texas, but they also exist in other parts of the United States. They are especially volatile, less hierarchical than Chinese gangs, and usually victimize other Southeast Asians (Dao 1992; Mydans 1991). Unlike the adult organized-crime groups, these youth gangs consist primarily of recent immigrants, reflecting the marginal status of many in this group and their inability to adjust in the United States (Perry 2000b).

Despite general perceptions that Asian gangs consist of youth who are unable to assimilate into the U.S. mainstream and are frustrated because of their inability to be successful through legitimate means (Cowart and Cowart 1996), the evidence indicates that most Asian gang members do not belong to exclusively Asian gangs, and that gangs have a strong homogenizing effect. There is remarkable similarity between gangs regardless of ethnic composition (Knox and McCurrie 1997). Some suggest that rather than those who are marginalized, those who are more assimilated are the ones who join gangs (L. C. Lee 1998). Noncultural explanations, such as a positive attitude toward gangs and their proximity to the youths' residential environment, may predict gang involvement better than do cultural factors (Kent and Felkenes 1998).

The arrest statistics of the Department of Justice (1988, 1992, 1996b) indicate that arrests of Asian Americans under the age of eighteen have steadily increased, while arrests of those over eighteen have remained stable. Offenses contributing to this increase are crimes against families and children, curfew violations, embezzlement, gambling, robbery, running away, and rape (Lee and Zahn 1998). The numbers of alcohol- and drug-related violations are substantially lower among Asian American youth than among European Americans or other minority youth (Walker, Spohn, and DeLone 2000), perhaps because of high levels of parental disapproval and control (Gillmore et al. 1990).

O'Kane (1992) proposes an interesting theory of immigrant adjustment based on an alternate route to the achievement of the American Dream. He suggests that the criminal road to prosperity allows each new immigrant group to oust its predecessor from the leadership of organized crime. The evidence does show that historically, different ethnic groups have acquired wealth through criminal activity and then gradually, through successive generations, have moved into the mainstream of middle-class America. Thus, the grandchildren of today's drug kings and gang leaders will be an integral part of middle-class society because of organized crime.

In general, Asian Americans do not constitute a significant proportion of the prison population, but they are often involved in criminal activity through organized crime. While other groups of color (African American, Latino American, and Native American) are overrepresented in the nation's prisons, Asian Americans are underrepresented, at 1.6 percent in the federal system and 0.6 percent in the state system. Similar rates are reported for female Asian Americans (1.8 percent and 0.4 percent, respectively [Department of Justice 1999a]).

Since the small amount of existing literature on criminal behavior among Asian Americans has focused on organized crime and gang activities, the criminal justice system is becoming more vigilant about those issues, yet it has been extremely slow to identify and intervene in domestic violence. The little awareness and focus that does exist regarding domestic violence has been evidenced in the field of social welfare services by the establishment of shelters in many large cities with substantial Asian populations. Still shrouded in the myth of the model minority, Asian Americans continue to be viewed by many, including the criminal justice system, as too ideal to engage in family violence, a perception that is further reinforced by this minority group's conspiracy of silence.

While most women, and others who are battered in the family, are loathe to report violence against them by family members, all Asian cultures put a premium on family image. Many in the dominant society do not report violence, for a number of reasons: fear of the perpetrator; lack of resources if the perpetrator is removed from the home or if the victim leaves; a misguided sense of duty; a sense of responsibility for incurring wrath; and love and hope. It is ingrained in the Asian psyche from an early age that one does not disgrace the family by sharing its woes or troubles with outsiders. In some Asian cultures this attitude is reinforced by religious and philosophical beliefs that the ability to endure suffering is a positive trait (Ho 1990) and that to have to suffer is one's fate or karma resulting from deeds committed in a past life. The literature, however, reveals that domestic violence is prevalent among Asian American groups and is steadily growing (Dasgupta and Warrier 1996; Rimonte 1989; Segal 2000b; Song 1996; Yoshihama 1999). Given the patriarchal nature of most Asian cultures, and all the psycho-social-religious contingencies, it is not surprising that the larger population remains ignorant of the occurrence of domestic violence. Although the criminal justice system has made great strides since the early 1990s in intervening in the area of domestic violence in general, it has not included the Asian American community in its purview.

The needs of Asian Americans are beginning to be recognized in the context of criminal justice, but the process is complicated by Asians' general mistrust of legal authority. This attitude is especially evident among recent immigrants from countries where autocratic regimes are in power, those who have experienced the atrocities of war, or who have suffered personal violations by those in power. It may also be true of other Asian groups that put little faith in the effectiveness of the law. Among many first-generation Asian immigrants, language barriers may prevent the communication of concerns.

The mutual mistrust between service provider (law enforcement) and service user (either offender or victim) in the criminal justice system is probably significantly higher than in any other provider-user relationship, regardless of ethnic differences, but ethnic differences exacerbate the problem. McShane (2000) recognizes this issue, saying:

> Different cultures, different languages, and different appearances all create barriers to the successful operation of the criminal justice system. When citizens interact with the criminal justice system, there is often tension, fear, and conflict. Victims, witnesses, offenders, parents, and criminal justice personnel must all coordinate together effectively to resolve issues of crime and justice. The quality and success of each interaction is dependent on each person's perception of the system's legitimacy.
>
> (p. 207)

Whether criminal justice policy in relation to Asian Americans is grounded in liberal or conservative ideology, it becomes imperative that it include an awareness of the barriers that prevent effective application. The criminal justice cognition must go beyond identifying the problems as being related only to organized crime and gang behavior. Domestic violence must also be recognized. Though there is not much discussion in the criminal justice literature about alcoholism and illicit substance abuse among Asian Americans and the associated problems that are evidenced in the rest of society, there is sufficient literature that suggests substantially high levels of adult abuse of these substances. Perhaps this issue has not claimed attention because it may be associated with Asian-on-Asian crime, rather than crime that infiltrates the larger society. Or perhaps it reflects the continued perpetuation of the model minority myth.

Prevention, rehabilitation, and/or correctional efforts require that the criminal justice system, like other systems, become aware of the effects of culture and the diversity of experience in understanding problems and offering assistance in the Asian American community. Public policy in the criminal justice system, more than any other system—and particularly because of the high level of mutual mistrust—must ensure that Asian American representation in the workforce is increased. Its current level is low, even in areas with high Asian American concentrations (Perry 2000b; Stokes and Scott 1996). Recruitment efforts will require that myths be dispelled and outreach efforts be made to attract Asians to careers in the criminal justice field. Such inclusion can reduce the mistrust of Asians within the workforce and the mistrust of the criminal justice system among Asians. Effectiveness in prevention, rehabilitation, and correction will be significantly improved if criminal justice both understands the unique impact of Asian cultures and is perceived as having that sympathy through its inclusion of members of that group among its workers.

Workforce training and cultural awareness, including an awareness of both the unique and the disparate experiences of the various Asian groups, can enhance the efficacy of all criminal justice policies. Such training must include issues of verbal and nonverbal communication, as these go beyond language differences and affect the system through stereotyping, ethnocentrism, and inappropriate humor (Nielsen 2000). Like other individuals, personnel in the criminal justice system experience anxiety, uncertainty, and discomfort in communicating with strangers. Yet the power they can wield by their very presence imposes the responsibility to handle negative emotions effectively. It is therefore the obligation of the criminal justice system to ensure that its personnel have the skills to learn about the motives and behavior of the people whose lives they affect, even if those people belong to relatively powerless groups (Nielsen 2000).

Furthermore, a disparity often exists not only between criminal justice workers and offenders but also between criminal justice personnel and victims. This disparity exists regardless of cultural differences or similarities; it is simply inherent in the relationship. The individual who has been victimized is frequently different from the person processing the claim in many ways—age, socioeconomic status, life experience, training, resources, family structure, and others. Thus the two people perceive each other and the situation differently (Morgan and Perry 2000). When such different perceptions are compounded by cultural and language differences, mistrust is once more exacerbated.

To ensure that the criminal justice system becomes more effective with Asian Americans in providing preventive services, intervening in organized crime, raising awareness of domestic violence, and providing services to victims of crime, criminal justice policy must see that the mechanisms for cultural awareness and Asian inclusion are in place. These mechanisms must heighten the consciousness of criminal justice personnel, and they must also ensure that the process is reciprocal, so that Asian Americans can value and use effectively the range of services offered by the system.

Inclusion of Asian Americans

Sensitivity to Asian American needs will be advanced most rapidly if this population is represented in the policy and services arena. Asian Americans have traditionally shied away from professions in government, public policy, law, and social services, focusing rather on technology, medicine, engineering, business, and the sciences. The dominant society has also been less than forthcoming with invitations to Asian Americans to join the workforce in these fields. Advocates cry for the inclusion of Asian Americans in decision making, but the effort must have a dual focus. While calling for cultural sensitivity and including Asian Americans in the policy and service areas, it must also call upon Asian Americans to take up the challenge and join U.S. society in professionally influencing policies and programs that affect not only Asian Americans but American society as a whole.

7

Public Policies:
Health, Mental Health,
and Substance Abuse

*Managed care . . . refers to a variety of organizational and finan-
cial structures, processes, and strategies designed to monitor and
influence treatment decisions. . . . Some reflect concern that
service changes being put in place are more motivated by cost-
reduction than by a desire to improve services.*

—MECHANIC 1999:151

Access to quality physical and mental medical care is of universal
concern. While the United States is a leader in quality health care,
accessibility is often limited to individuals with financial resources.
Those with adequate health care coverage through either public (Medicaid and Medicare) or private insurance programs receive at least basic
care, but a large segment of the population is not covered by private
insurance and is not eligible for public insurance coverage. The health
care needs of this group are high, but frequently go unmet. Immigrants
and refugees find the health care system complex and intimidating, and
they may avoid even those services that are available to them.

Even if they have the resources and the ability to access health and
mental health services, immigrants and refugees must perceive the
system as being unsympathetic to their particular needs and lacking
awareness of differences in cultural practices. In an already perplexing
system of service delivery, poor understanding between patient and
service provider exacerbates potential problems.

HEALTH POLICY

*The United States is the only country in the developed world,
except for South Africa, that does not provide health care for all its*

citizens. The absence of such universal coverage is even more shock-
ing when it is realized that most of the developing countries, poor
as they are, still manage to provide health care for all.
                                                          —AYERS 1996:xii

The national policy on education holds the education of every citizen
(or U.S. resident) as paramount and views it as a universal right. It is the
responsibility of the government to ensure that all individuals be
encouraged to reach their full potential without financial hindrances.
Educational policy is so firm on this point that children between the
ages of six and sixteen who do not attend school violate the law and
merit legal disciplinary action.

No such expectation is present in the country's health policy statements. Health care services are not considered a fundamental American
right but a commodity to be allocated and rationed in the market (Ayers
1996). While education is the right of all, health care—particularly
quality health care—is often the privilege of those who can afford it.
The nation believes that its economic, political, and social security is
bound to the level of education of its citizenry, but such perceptions do
not extend to concern about the nation's health. If significant numbers
of people do not have access to health care, however, the nation's economic and social functioning can be seriously affected. In a nation
concerned with "liberty and justice for all," a health policy that denies
equal access to health care breaches basic tenets. Moves toward health
care reform reflect the belief of many Americans that it is inappropriate
and unfair to tie health care access to socioeconomic status.

The questions that drive public health care policy, like other policies, reflect the prevailing ideologies of the society. The first and most
important question is whether all Americans should have access to basic
preventive and curative care. Few would contest that it is in the best
interest of the nation as a whole. The second, equally important, question has to do with the extent of the government's responsibility in
providing health care to those who cannot afford it. It is about this
responsibility that the nation is divided, and it is about this that the
issue of health care reform caused major debate in 1993 and 1994.
Health care now constitutes the single largest industry in most developed countries, and because of the size of the health care sector and the
sharp escalation of costs in recent decades, controlling the public health
budget has become a major public policy concern (Castles 1998).

Most Americans access health care through the support of employment-based or public insurance programs. Yet in 1995, 40.6 million
people (15.4 percent of the population) lacked any form of coverage
(Weinberg 1996). For those living in poverty, the rate was 30.2 percent.
Until recently, health insurance programs did not cover preventive care.
The result was that the system incurred greater expense because individuals were more likely to become ill with ailments that would have
been preventable. Because of health policy and legal prohibitions
against denying care to those who go to emergency rooms, the uninsured tend to overutilize that source of care. Hospital emergency rooms,
however, merely stabilize uninsured persons, rarely admitting them,
since the hospitals would have to bear the costs.

Only about 25 percent of health care costs are paid for directly
by consumers. The remainder is covered by private insurance, public
assistance plans, and direct public provision of services (Karger and
Stoesz 1998). It is easy to see, then, that health policy is inexorably
linked to health care financing. The literature on health policy focuses
not on health care itself but on the expense of care and how that is
met. Without doubt, science and technology are making major strides
in improving the health and longevity of the population, and U.S.
knowledge of medicine and interventions is the best in the world.
Substantial funds are available to pursue the research that will keep the
nation on the cutting edge of medical advances, and few would disagree
that it is vital to channel funds for that purpose. There is, however, no
such unified agreement about who should bear the expenses for maintaining or restoring good health—specifically, what is the government's
responsibility? Until agreement on governmental responsibility occurs,
and until the general public truly recognizes the importance of good
health for its citizens as both a moral obligation and an economic benefit to society, U.S. health policy will not support equal access to health
benefits for all.

In 1994 President Clinton proposed to the Congress health care
reform that guaranteed universal employer-paid health insurance.
Congress was not unenthusiastic, especially since the plan was presented
simultaneously with welfare reform that would ban open-ended welfare
entitlements. Welfare reform was enacted in 1996, but the health insurance proposal lost momentum in 1994, and after that the president
pursued only incremental changes. In his State of the Union address on
January 27, 2000, Clinton revisited the issue, proposing a three-point

plan to manage health care: (1) the unfinished "patients' rights" legislation of 1999; (2) a ten-year, $110 billion program to lower costs of health insurance and make quality insurance easier to obtain; and (3) a $28.7 billion allocation over ten years for the expansion of health insurance options for people who find it difficult to get coverage.

Had it passed, the patients' rights legislation would have guaranteed access to specialists and emergency rooms and would give patients the right to challenge the decisions of health plan administrators. It would have extended the same benefits to those who are unable to pay and who are on public assistance programs. The second proposal would have allowed coverage for at least five million people who are currently uninsured and would also expand insurance options for millions of others. The third would have provided assistance for the elderly and others for whom Medicare might not be sufficient, including covering the costs of prescription medicine, which are now finally covered for some. In addition, it would have provided insurance options for those who are between employment or those who are in the process of leaving welfare to begin work. The Republican response was less than enthusiastic, for while they could laud the aim to improve health care, they were concerned that the plan could not be implemented without excessive federal spending and burgeoning new bureaucracies.

Numerous arguments have been presented both for and against health care reform. One major debate revolves around whether the United States needs nationalized health care and often cites the Canadian and British health care programs as examples. Proponents believe that nationalizing health care would eliminate the need for the entire private insurance industry and do away with a large proportion of doctors' office costs and hospitals' administrative expenses. Distribution of funds would be based on health needs rather than on market-driven forces, and the elimination of corporate profits from the sale of health care would make this money available for expanded health services and research (Himmelstein and Woolhandler 1994). A counterargument holds that the socialized medicine systems of Canada, Britain, and other developed nations are inadequate and that less governmental intervention is the key to quality care. With national health care, the demand skyrockets, as there is no need to resist going to a doctor or hospital even for the most minor ailments, such as the common cold. The result is deteriorating facilities, poor diagnostic services, overburdened physicians, and long hospital waiting lists.

Many in the United States who have had personal experience with either the British or the Canadian system report a better quality of care in those two nations than in the United States (Bernard 1994). The British system provides free and comprehensive health care coverage, including diagnostic, therapeutic, preventive, rehabilitative, environmental, and occupational health care. Included also are free dental and vision care. While there is some private insurance coverage through employment, the majority is publicly funded. In Canada, a single-payer national health care system is in place, with states responsible for ensuring delivery of health services and paying providers according to the guidelines of the federal government. Under such a system, the practice of private medicine could continue, but private health insurance coverage would not. A social work educator, well versed in both U.S. and British health policy and programs and with personal experience in February 2000 with both systems, revealed that hospitalization and quality of care in Britain are more humane and more responsive to the needs of patients than in the United States (Elliott 2000). The hospital environment is pleasant and clean, two nurses attend the patient, ensuring that there are no errors in treatment, pain control is high on the list of medical priorities, the patient's emotions are considered, and attention is paid to the needs of the family. After benefiting from this high-quality care, patients can walk away from the hospital unconcerned about costs. And because preventive care is free, there is less need to use the more expensive curative medical services. In Britain, medical insurance is provided for the majority of individuals through their employment, but it is worth noting that private hospitals sometimes do not have the range of resources and services that are available in the public hospitals.

In any medical system there must be a rationing of services. Only in the best of all possible worlds would all medical treatment be available to all people. Resources are not limitless, health care providers are finite, and time is a confounding factor. Regardless of arguments that rationing is inhumane and unethical, it is unavoidable; what is inhumane and unethical is rationing based on socioeconomic status—which happens in the United States. Services are rationed vertically and are available to those who can pay. In Britain services are rationed based on need and the critical nature of that need (Elliott 2000). Diagnostic tests may not be ordered in Britain to the same extent as they are in the United States, but in the latter, tests may frequently be used to hedge against malpractice suits. In another difference between the two systems, in Britain, high-level technology and treatments are usually not employed when a patient is terminally ill. The practice of taking "extraordinary measures" to prolong life—such as using respirators and feeding tubes—is more common in the United States than in Britain. Ironically, many people in the United States are signing "living wills" that instruct caregivers to allow them to die rather than initiating life-prolonging measures that carry a multitude of financial, social, and emotional expenses. It is peculiar that the health care system should prompt people to write directives to avoid treatments that will prolong but not improve the quality of their lives, while others who desperately need health care are denied it for lack of resources. In nations with socialized medicine there might be long waiting lists for elective treatments and surgery, yet those in critical need receive immediate care. Conversely, in the United States, the uninsured who require critical care are usually stabilized by private hospitals. The United States may have believed that it was providing a modified form of socialized medicine when it established health maintenance organizations (HMOs), but HMOs gravely curtail patients' freedom of choice. In Canada, primary and emergency care, which are universally insured, are readily available, and no financial or administrative barriers prevent patients from seeking services from a physician of their choice. They are not assigned one from a pre-approved list. The emotional security for those in nations that provide universal health coverage lies in the knowledge that no illness, regardless of how catastrophic, will result in financial disaster.

Health Care Coverage for Asian Americans

U.S. health policy, which allows health coverage for many, but not for all, has particular implications for those in poverty, those who are near poverty, and those of low socioeconomic status and income who are self-employed. The last group is the least likely to be able to afford private insurance coverage, yet it is ineligible for means-tested coverage[1] such as Medicaid. The continuing perception of Asians as a model minority and the tendency to view them as one group once again serve as a barrier to the development of policies and programs that address their needs. In discussing those who are underinsured and uninsured, Karger and Stoesz (1998) indicate that the noncoverage rate is higher for minorities. In 1995, 14 percent of the white population was not covered by any form of insurance, including Medicaid. During the same year, 21 percent of the African American and 33 percent of the Hispanic populations were not covered. Despite the size of the Asian population and despite its rapid increase—as noted in the authors' own statements—they failed to mention that in that year 17.8 percent of the Asian American population had no coverage—and by 1997 the percentage had increased to 18.8 percent (Centers for Disease Control 2000).

The omission of data about needs in the Asian American community reflects an alternative form of bias. Researchers, practitioners, and policymakers fail to recognize that this is a not a uniform, one-dimensional group. While the proportion of insured Asians, such as Indians, is higher because many in this group are in professional occupations that provide employer-paid insurance coverage (Dutt 1999), a significant number of Southeast Asians lack coverage (Gall and Gall 1993). In some states, such as California, where there is a large Asian population, a disproportionate percentage of Asians are uninsured. A report by the Asian Pacific Islander American Health Forum, a non-profit health advocacy group, revealed that 24 percent of the Asian American and Pacific Islanders in California were uninsured in 1997. Indians and Filipinos have among the lowest uninsured rates, at 20 percent, and Koreans have the highest, at 40 percent. The Chinese rank second highest at 30 percent, with Southeast Asians at 23 percent and the Japanese at 17 percent (Dutt 1999). All these Asian groups in California, furthermore, have a higher uninsured rate than do the whites, at 14 percent. The tendency for self-employment among Asians and the exorbitant costs of private insurance may well be correlates of poor insurance coverage. Their income levels and their age make them ineligible for both Medicaid and Medicare. Further data indicate that new immigrants are likely to be poor and stay poor because they have higher levels of unemployment, less education, and larger families than do native-born groups (Haniffa 1999). Asians compose one of the largest immigrant groups, and this suggests that their percentages of uninsured will continue to rise.

The implications of health policy for Asians are not limited to issues of coverage. A number of other cultural and educational concerns confound their access to health care services. Health policy must focus not only on who is covered but also on how services are utilized. Currently, general access to health care services is fraught with problems for many immigrant groups, and the access problems are exacerbated by the implementation of the 1996 Federal Welfare Reform law (H.R.

3734). Responsibility and financial risk for immigrants have moved from the top level of government (federal) to the lowest level (county) (Riedel 1998). Under this structure, each county must ensure that its policies in delivering services reflect awareness of the unique needs of immigrant groups. Another essential component of effective health care policy is research effort that recognizes the interaction of race, ethnicity, nativity, and health (Hummer et al. 1999). Health policy must also be driven by how, when, and why health services are used—or not used—because of a mix of cultural effects.

Invariably, the most vulnerable and dependent members of any group have access to the least resources. Policymakers must take into account the particular needs of children, the elderly, and those with disabilities among the Asian American populations. Multicultural awareness and policies that address the diversity of issues must be integrated into health care policy so that not only is lack of insurance removed as a barrier to health service access but so are cultural factors. In California, for example, many low-income women are unaware of their eligibility for Medi-Cal (California's equivalent of national Medicaid) and healthy-family programs, and an even larger proportion of immigrant women are unaware of or intimidated by the system. Not only is there a high uninsured rate among Asians in California, but even those who are eligible for public health care do not seek it because of the morass of paperwork required to qualify for eligibility and the fear of deportation. Women and children, more often than men, are likely to deprive themselves of health care services under such conditions (Dutt 1999).

Because the Asian population is relatively young, with a median age of 31.7 years and a mean age of 32.7 years (U.S. Bureau of the Census 1999), most policies and programs targeting Asians have been geared toward age groups under 65. The elderly portion of the Asian population, however, is rapidly increasing; in fact, this is the fastest-growing racial group among all those aged 65 and older in the United States. On this measure, as in other areas, a bimodal distribution is evident—the good health of some groups, such as the Japanese, masks the ill health of others, such as the Southeast Asians. Furthermore, many of the immigrant Asian elderly have substantially fewer economic and social resources than their white counterparts or the elderly of other minority groups (Tanjasiri, Wallace, and Shibata 1995), and they may not be familiar with, or willing to take advantage of, the services for which they are eligible. While most may use Medicare benefits, they may not be aware of Medicaid eligibility, and they may not apply for Medicaid benefits, instead struggling to meet the 20 percent of their medical expenses that Medicare does not pay. Although some among the Asian elderly participate in Medicare and some are enrolled in Medicaid, the numbers are apparently very small, since the 1997 National Health Interview Survey did not report their presence in the aggregate data. In 1991 the United States Bureau of the Census recorded 514,000 Asians over the age of sixty-five, and in 1990, 12.1 percent were living below the poverty line (Bennett 1992). Since then, these numbers have increased, but even though the elderly Asian poor constitute a growing population, they are not significantly visible to the governmental health insurance programs, which fail to identify elderly Asian Medicaid clients—although they do report Medicaid use by Asians under the age of 65.

Despite the many problems, U.S. health policy does ensure that most of the basic health care needs of a large segment of the population are met. Medicare, Public Law 89–79, was attached to the Social Security Act on July 30, 1965, and provides prepaid hospital insurance for the elderly, as well as voluntary medical insurance. Most Americans over the age of sixty-five are automatically entitled to Part A of the Medicare program, which is compulsory hospital insurance and covers 80 percent of all costs. The federal government through Medicaid pays the remaining 20 percent that is not covered by Medicare if the beneficiary is on public assistance. Part B is a voluntary supplemental medical insurance plan for seniors who are eligible for Part A benefits, and approximately 96 percent of all seniors who are enrolled in Part A also enroll in Part B. This covers outpatient services, doctors' office visits, and diagnostic tests, and so on. In 1997, 20.7 percent of all the elderly had only Medicare, while a further 7.8 percent had coverage through both Medicare and Medicaid. The rest were covered by Medicare as well as private insurance or insurance through a place of work (Centers for Disease Control 1999b).

Although the nation attempted to provide health care for the elderly and the poor through the Kerr-Mills Act of 1957, it was not mandatory, and many states chose not to participate in it. However, President Lyndon Johnson, identified health policy as a priority and signed Medicaid and Medicare programs into law in 1965 (Marmor 1973). Medicaid became, and continues to be, the largest public assistance program in the nation. In 1997, 22.9 million people (10.7

percent of the population) under the age of sixty-five were covered by Medicaid. In the same year, roughly the same percentage of the Asian population in this age group (10.3 percent) received Medicaid benefits. Medicaid is funded through matching federal and state funds, with states paying approximately 43 percent of the costs. States also participate in setting benefit levels, and some may provide more coverage than others. Four major gaps exist in Medicaid coverage: (a) the low limits allowed for assets, (b) the states' refusal to adopt most or all of the Medicaid options, (c) the gaps in coverage for the elderly and disabled, and (d) the general ineligibility of many poor single people and childless couples.

U.S. health policy must be modified to ensure universally affordable and accessible quality health care. A large number of Asian Americans are financially stable and have adequate or good health care coverage through their places of work and/or through private insurance. In 1997, 68 percent of the Asian population under the age of sixty-five had private insurance, and 60.4 percent had coverage through the workplace (Centers for Disease Control 1999a). Since in the same year 29.1 percent either had no insurance or had only Medicaid, those with nongovernmental coverage had more than one form of health insurance. Asian Americans with private or workplace insurance probably have their health care needs adequately met under the existing health care policies of the country. Yet, even for these Asian Americans, adequate health care requires not only the availability of insurance but also the use of the services.

Utilization of Health Care Services

While Asian immigrants may have good health care coverage, and although Asian Americans are as eligible as others for both private and governmental health care programs and services, they may be less knowledgeable about the availability of these programs. They may also be more suspicious of different treatment methods, uncomfortable with interaction patterns with health care providers, and confused by the governmental and other insurance programs and reimbursement procedures. Any or all of these factors discourage them from utilizing the health services that are available to them. U.S. health policy must go beyond a focus on finances to identify and address patient concerns.

It is most important that those who are responsible for providing these services understand culturally based perceptions of medical care and physicians as well as the role of traditional Asian medicine and how it dovetails with modern medicine. For medical personnel working with Asian refugees, knowledge of the refugee experience and its implications becomes particularly important. Finally, when language barriers exacerbate problems of communication, the level of miscommunication and distrust between health care provider and patient can undermine a successful outcome. Although some health care programs have trained bilingual immigrants as translators, the effectiveness of the workers may be reduced unless they also have an understanding of both cultures. They must be able to adequately translate not only the language but also the meanings of events and communication.

A number of phenomena are unique to the Asian experience of illness and treatment and must be understood within the cultural context. The most pervasive of these are the somatization of psychological distress, poor knowledge of preventive health care, and underutilization of services. In the 1990s much was written about the tendency of Asians to somatize distress. Identified primarily among Southeast Asian refugees, somatic ailments such as body aches, headaches, and nausea were recognized as expressions of posttraumatic stress disorder. In Asian cultures, where emotional or mental distress is evidence of weakness, evil, or a variety of socially unacceptable conditions, psychosocial pressures are denied and manifest themselves in physical symptoms.

Although U.S. health care places more emphasis on prevention than ever before, and stresses early detection and treatment, such efforts do not reach many Asian Americans. Cultural, linguistic, and economic barriers can deny Asian Americans opportunities for disease prevention, early diagnosis, prompt treatment, and participation in clinical trials (Sadler et al. 1998). It is essential that those who provide health care services to Asian Americans recognize that most Asian American groups exhibit a bimodal distribution with regard to knowledge of the United States, its customs, and systems. Those who are educated, professional, and can function in the mainstream are better equipped to meet their health care needs. On the other hand, those who have little education, few English-language skills, and remain within ethnic enclaves may be more likely to suffer from physical ailments and less likely to seek professional treatment. The literature suggests that recent immigrants are much less likely than either native-born individuals or those who have been in the United States longer to access medical care or have contact with physicians. Some, in fact, access care as infrequently as those who have no health insurance at all (Leclere, Jensen, and Biddlecom 1994). While it is clear that those who are marginalized are more vulnerable, specific outreach efforts may need to be directed to all Asian American groups because education does not ensure adequate awareness about the range of health needs or health care options.

While advocates call for services that are culturally competent, it is imperative that providers of health care services join others in recognizing the diversity both across and within Asian American groups. This diversity is illustrated by a study of cancer knowledge and screening behaviors of Cambodian and Vietnamese women that revealed that 71 percent did not know what cancer was and 74 percent could not identify a prevention strategy. Those who did have somewhat greater awareness were the ones who were employed outside the home and had more years of education; length of stay in the United States was not correlated with knowledge about cancer (Phipps et al. 1999). Compared to non-Asian Americans, Asian American women are less likely to enroll in breast cancer screening programs; the pattern is similar across Asian groups, with older women participating even less. The removal of financial barriers may not increase participation (Tu et al. 1999). In patriarchal societies and in those in which modesty is paramount, sociocultural barriers prevent the examination of the female body by others, particularly by men. While there is not much literature on South Asian women in the United States, an exploration of general practitioners' perceptions in the United Kingdom suggested that South Asian women may not consult physicians even when suffering severe menorrhagia. A number of women who did consult male doctors for menorrhagia were referred to outpatient hospital services without having internal examinations conducted, but they were reluctant to keep the appointments because of the lack of female gynecologists (Chapple, Ling, and May 1998). In Islamic societies, this hesitation is even more evident (Rajaram and Rashidi 1999), although Islamic tenets such as the importance of cleanliness, prevention, individual responsibility in health promotion, a healthy diet, and exercise should facilitate breast cancer screening.

Among all races and ethnicities, including other Southeast Asians, the H'mong have a very high incidence of several types of cancer: nasopharynx, stomach, liver, pancreas, leukemia, cervical, and non-Hodgkin's lymphoma. Many explanations are offered, among them a combination of cultural factors, the avoidance of Western medical care, and low rates of participation in screening programs (Mills and Yang

1997). While many studies of Asian Americans' health focus on the tendency to avoid Western medical care and preventive measures, it appears that the subjects are typically Asian Americans who evidence the more vulnerable characteristics of the lower-end bimodal curve of personal resources—the marginalized, less educated, blue-collar workers with lower levels of income. Less information is available on the health and the health services utilization of the more educated, professional, acculturated, and higher-income individuals. A study of the latter group of Asian Americans may reveal patterns of prevention, health services use, and compliance with Western treatment that are consistent with those of the majority population.

In 2000 the World Health Organization reported that the Japanese living in Japan led the world in having long and healthy lives; the United States ranked twenty-fourth (Associated Press 2000). However, a face-to-face study of 698 male and 494 female U.S.-born or immigrant Japanese, Caucasian, Filipino, Hawaiian, and Chinese patients diagnosed with colorectal cancer between 1987 and 1991, revealed that a sedentary lifestyle, obesity, smoking, alcohol use, and diabetes increased risk for cancer. Furthermore, the higher rate of colorectal cancer experienced by Asian immigrants to the United States, as compared to Asians in Asia, occurred in the first generation, suggesting that the Western lifestyle played a role in the prevalence of this disease (Lemarchand et al. 1997).

It is also important to note that health beliefs and practices may be evident in one Asian group but not be prevalent in others. The practices of cupping, skin scraping, and moxibustion, used particularly among Southeast Asians in the United States, are specifically Oriental in origin (Look and Look 1997) and are not found among the practices of South Asians. Western practitioners are cautioned not to assume that the marks caused by such treatments are indications of child abuse among Southeast Asians, but similar marks on South Asian children should be suspect. Those who are educated and/or more acculturated may be likely to eschew traditional health care methods in favor of modern medicine, yet they may continue to use traditional methods in conjunction with modern ones. Program planning should be based on a thorough needs assessment, as should intervention (Kline and Huff 1999). The United States highly values self-determination and free choice, but culturally, Asians respond well to structure and direction, and they may be more likely to comply with instructions if Western physicians are cognizant of the importance of projecting medical knowledge through positions of authority.

Traditionally used outreach methods of education and health promotion efforts in the United States, such as seminars at hospitals or public service announcements in the newspaper or on radio or television may not be effective, as many Asian Americans may not feel that such messages apply to them. Sadler et al. (1998) developed innovative strategies of education by training bicultural, bilingual undergraduate students to work as community health educators. Asian grocery stores were selected as the optimal sites. Techniques used in teaching English as a second language were employed, and hands-on teaching aids helped overcome language difficulties. Community-based health education, including information about prevention, health services, and patients' rights, is one way to ensure that Asian Americans, particularly newer immigrants or those who are only marginally comfortable in the United States, are aware of the services available and their right to them. Information about procedures for accessing the health care system and for payment through either public or private insurance can also be disseminated in such community-based educational programs.

Of particular concern for a number of lower-middle-class Asian Americans may be their exclusion from specialized care. The "patients' rights" legislation proposed by former president Bill Clinton on January 27, 2000, would have guaranteed access to specialists and emergency rooms, and the right to challenge the decisions of health plan administrators. In 2001 the House and Senate passed the Patients' Rights Bill, which aims to protect patients and to ensure that health maintenance organizations (HMOs) are held accountable when a patient is denied care. It is unclear whether the measure will allow the specific rights envisioned by President Clinton. For immigrants and those from different ethnic and cultural backgrounds, however, this legislation is not nearly sufficient to ensure that they receive adequate care. Issues in health policy for Asian Americans include not only health coverage but outreach and education, language competence, and cultural awareness and responsiveness to differences. Active outreach and education that allow Asian Americans to understand the practice of medicine in the United States as well as stressing the importance of preventive, maintenance, and therapeutic health care must be built into health care policy. Educational programs for providers must include diversity training, cultural sensitivity, and cultural competence (the ability to tailor interactions and intervention based on knowledge of sociocultural differences). Merely using translators does not always serve the purpose, and translations are always colored by preconceptions and perceptions. If patients do not perceive that health care providers are able to understand their unique concerns, they are less likely to comply with treatment plans and to return for necessary follow-up visits.

Overall, the financial and social costs of poor health care for a nation's citizens are high. In a country that is more likely to subsidize emergency room treatment than preventive medicine and health maintenance programs, the actual financial burden is even greater. Those without insurance are more likely to become ill and to use emergency room facilities. They may also postpone treatment until they are severely ill—and the expense of treatment is very high—or they may overuse emergency room services for routine or minor illnesses. Indirect costs to the nation are also high. Those without adequate health care are likely to be ill for longer periods of time, which affects their productivity at work and, consequently, their employers. If they do go to work while they are ill, their contagious illness can infect others. In the long run, the impact on the economy can only be negative.

Health care providers should be required to be culturally aware and competent in this ever more diverse society, because unless individuals believe that they are understood, many will fail to utilize the available services and health care coverage. The outcome will be the same as if they had no health care coverage at all. They will not seek services unless they are in dire need and will continue to work at lower levels of productivity and higher levels of contagion.

MENTAL HEALTH POLICY

A hundred and fifty years ago, we had to learn to treat people with mental illness as basic human beings. Thirty years ago, we had to learn that people with mental illness had to be treated as individuals, not just a faceless mob. . . . Today, we have to make sure that we actually provide the care all our people need, so they can live full lives and fully participate in our common life.
—CLINTON 1999:1052

Despite a greater level of awareness in the United States that various forms of mental illness strike many people during the course of their lives, and that for a significant number of them it becomes a lifelong burden, the mentally ill still do not truly receive the support and sympathy that physical illness engenders. Perhaps the crux of the problem lies in the absence of physical symptoms, for those who are mentally ill do not look ill. For a large segment of the American population, this situation is compounded by a lack of acknowledgment of mental illness by both the individuals and the people around them. Among Asians, mental illness is not acceptable; it is viewed as reflecting a weakness in the individual and the family. The afflicted individual hides it, insofar as possible. If the illness is serious enough to be apparent to others, the family unites to keep it from public view, as it is an embarrassment that brings shame to the entire group.

Unlike many other policies that are determined at the national level, mental health policy is crafted and articulated by the states and reflects the historical development of mental health services in the United States, which first became prominent in the nineteenth century. During the early part of the century the local poorhouses that had been established during the colonial period were overwhelmed by people suffering from problems associated with the societal changes caused by immigration, urbanization, and industrialization. Instrumental in the construction of institutions to care for the "emotionally deranged" in the 1840s, Dorothea Dix also was able to persuade Congress to pass legislation authorizing federal aid to states. In 1854 the plan was vetoed, however, by President Franklin Pierce, who believed that federal interference in the states' responsibility for social welfare was inappropriate.

State mental hospitals originally were intended to be self-sufficient communities that provided a safe haven for the mentally ill. They also protected the community from those who were violent or unable to control themselves. During the early part of the twentieth century, in the absence of social welfare programs and services and amid increasing unemployment and poverty, mental institutions became overpopulated and moved from providing quality services to warehousing the mentally ill. Furthermore, many who were truly mentally impaired fell victim to the eugenics movement, which believed that mental illness and retardation were the results of hereditary deficiencies and viewed selective breeding as the route to decreasing the burden on state institutions. Legal mandates authorizing involuntary sterilization of the mentally impaired were passed by thirty states in the 1930s, and 20,000 patients had been sterilized by 1935.

Although the National Association for Mental Health, which originated in the early twentieth century, was critical of the care provided by state institutions, the issue of mental health did not command public attention until World War II, when 25 percent of all draftees were rejected because of psychiatric or neurological problems (Trattner 1974). In response to public outcries about mental health problems resulting from the war, Congress passed the Mental Health Act in 1946 (42 USCS §9401), which founded the National Institute of Mental Health (NIMH).

In 1961, as a direct appropriation accompanying the Mental Health Act, the NIMH released an exhaustive examination of the state of the nation's mental health needs and called for a far-reaching national effort to modernize the system of psychiatric care (Joint Commission on Mental Illness and Health 1961). With the support of President John F. Kennedy, the physician Robert Felix, who became director of NIMH, was able to revive Dorothea Dix's assertion that the federal government must play a substantial role in mental health policy. Emerging from this were the Community Mental Health Centers (CMHC) Acts of 1963 and 1965 [P.L. 88–164 (42 USCS §2681)], which sought to eliminate state mental hospitals as they then existed. It was believed that services provided at the community level would be superior to the warehousing approach. Services were emphasized, and they were modeled on the public health system, focusing on primary, secondary, and tertiary prevention.[2]

From Lyndon Johnson's presidency through Jimmy Carter's, a number of circumstances, including waning community support and economic problems, conspired to subvert the CMHC, although funds were still available until 1981. In that year, through the Omnibus Budget and Reconciliation Act, President Ronald Reagan collapsed federal funding into block grants to states, and direct grants to CMHCs ceased. At the same time, states shifted responsibility for the mentally ill to the CMHCs. The process of deinstitutionalizing the mentally ill had been conceptualized in the 1970s and for economic reasons had received widespread support from state officials, who were less concerned about the availability of alternative care for those who were discharged from state hospitals. Only those who were dangerous to themselves or to others could be hospitalized, and the definition of emotional disturbance was interpreted narrowly to limit the numbers who could be admitted to state institutions. Although the states had been absolved of their responsibility to the mentally ill, there was no mechanism in place for the thousands who had been deinstitutionalized.

With no place to go, with negligible resources, and without alternative care, large numbers of the mentally ill joined the ranks of the homeless, and many found their way into the criminal justice system (Freeman and Roesch 1989; Palermo, Gumz, and Liska 1992). With deinstitutionalization and the presence of many severely mentally ill persons in the community, the CMHCs moved from offering the full range of mental health services to providing immediate care to the severely mentally ill. In the absence of any mental health policy, in the 1990s a number of states sought to develop innovative approaches to the delivery of mental health services, particularly the integration of services. Without significant funding, mental health services turned to insurance programs for payment, but mental health expenses were not recognized by insurance companies as health care costs, and reimbursement, if forthcoming at all, was relatively low.

In September 1996 President Bill Clinton passed into law the Mental Health Parity Act, which sought to guarantee that physical ailments and mental illness would receive equal insurance coverage. In response, by mid-1999 twenty-seven states had passed some form of parity coverage, and most of it after 1997 (Manisses Communications Group 1999). In his remarks on June 7, 1999, at the White House conference on mental health, Clinton stated that untreated mental illness costs the nation billions of dollars each year and that the loss of human potential is extreme. However, this Assembly Bill 1000, the Mental Health Parity Act, which requires health insurers to provide coverage for the diagnosis and treatment of serious mental illness (Delevett 1998), does not include coverage of substance abuse (Vatz and Weinberg 1997).

Despite the strides described above, congressional findings (42 USCS §9401) revealed in December 1999 that the problems continue and that

despite the significant progress that has been made in making community mental health services available and in improving residential mental health facilities . . . unserved and underserved populations remain . . . chronically mentally ill individuals, children and youth, elderly individuals, racial and ethnic minorities, women, poor persons and persons in rural areas which often lack access to adequate private and public mental health service and support services. . . . Mentally ill persons are often inadequately served by (A) programs of the Department of Health and Human Services such as Medicare, Medicaid, supplemental security income, and social services, and (B) programs of the Department of Housing and Urban Development, the Department of Labor, and other Federal agencies.

In the last two centuries, policies have progressed from viewing the mentally ill as little better than animals to recognizing them as people with unique treatment needs. It has been a rocky road, with several serious setbacks. Despite increasing professional recognition of the need for strong policies and services to assist the mentally ill, there still reverberates through U.S. society an undercurrent that devalues this population. It is evident not only in the lack of inclusive federal or state policies and adequate funding for services but also in the attitudes and perceptions of the populace at large. The United States ostensibly recognizes the existence of mental illness and the need for services for those afflicted by it, yet there is often evidence of fear and repugnance toward the mentally ill. Among Asians, who do not recognize its existence, there is even greater likelihood of rejecting the mentally ill or failing to seek the services for themselves or their dependents.

Asian American Mental Health

The experience of many Asian Americans has been fraught with turmoil. Whether they are of the immigrant generation or the third, fourth, or fifth generations in the United States, their physique, their cultures, and their values set them apart both from the European American majority and in many ways from the other U.S. minorities as well. Stereotypes about this group range from the negative to the overwhelmingly positive, ascribing to Asian Americans characteristics that they do not possess. Furthermore, those who are political refugees bring with them a burden of horrendous experiences that others cannot begin to fathom. Many have been left with psychosocial problems that are further compounded by the social, economic, and cultural distance between them and U.S. society. This combination of difficulties has not only affected their personal adjustment but has wreaked havoc with long-established family roles and traditional patterns of interaction.

The Southeast Asian refugees, particularly, spent several years in refugee camps, often under deplorable conditions, in other Asian countries such as Hong Kong and Thailand. Before that, many of them suffered the trauma of the Khmer Rouge and the accompanying torture and death of family members. Many still bear the burden of that life of terror, starvation, and relentless stress (Sack et al. 1986), which is evidenced, at the very least, as depression, anxiety, and psychosocial dysfunction (Ying et al. 1997). In an extreme example of the psychological effects of such experiences, some two hundred cases of hysterical blindness reported among Cambodian refugee women in the United States were linked to their having observed the slaughter of those close to them (Cooke 1991).

Among Southeast Asian refugees in a number of U.S. cities a combination of forces, including experiences in their homelands, contributes to family tensions and estrangement, which have been exacerbated by fatigue and depression resulting from economic pressures and cultural alienation. Although many immigrant and refugee groups share similar experiences, each often feels isolated and misunderstood, and thus the probability of mental illness increases. Southeast Asian refugees in particular have evidenced high rates of psychological distress, even after having been in the United States for more than five years. Studies suggest that if Southeast Asian refugees were dependent on welfare at any time in their lives, they were at risk of developing psychological distress (Chung and Bemak 1996). It should not be surprising that refugees experience more challenges to their mental health than any other immigrant group, especially assuming that acculturation in general is stressful and that undesired or unsupported change is even more so (Berry 1986).

Underlying many of the conflicts and concerns that may lead to mental distress are issues of dependency, competition, and loneliness that can emerge from being transplanted, either voluntarily or involuntarily, into an alien environment (Juthani 1992). Despite traditional beliefs that immigrants surmount their difficulties and adjust to U.S. society as they progress through second, third, and subsequent generations, research findings, especially in the areas of immigrant health, mental health, and self-identity, belie these assumptions (Rumbaut 1997b). Even when they have the support of family, friends, ethnic community organizations, and other Asian Americans of the same subgroup, many families experience stress and psychosocial consequences (Ross-Sheriff 1992) that reflect the personality dysfunction most often associated with mental illness. Asians in the United States have also experienced difficulties resulting from discrimination and prejudice at the group, family, and individual levels.

An exploration of various facets of the Asian American experience can point to the mental health issues they face—as a group of immigrants translocated into an alien environment, as descendants of Asians who cannot be assimilated into the dominant culture for a number of reasons (their physical characteristics, for example), as sub-Asian groups with shared experiences of trauma, exodus, and immigration, and as individuals with a variety of life experiences, resources, emotional issues, and personality factors.

While Asians are subject to major psychiatric disorders—depression, bipolar disorder, and schizophrenia—that are believed to be triggered by chemical imbalances, they are also affected by externally caused psychosocial difficulties. The extremely hazardous and degrading experiences of many Southeast Asian refugees increased their risk for developing major depressive and posttraumatic stress disorders,[3] symptomized into nightmares, flashbacks, and unfounded, ongoing fears (Kinzie et al. 1990; Lin and Shen 1991). They are also susceptible to psychologically based somatic ailments such as chronic backaches, headaches, low energy, and weakness (Foulks, Merkel, and Boehnlein 1992). A combination of poverty, isolation, acculturation issues, identity, and poor language proficiency further increases their levels of frustration, stress, and emotional distress (Bemak 1989; Chambon 1989; Vega and Rumbaut 1991). The United Nations reported that well over 40 million of the world's refugees are at a high risk for depression, anxiety, and posttraumatic stress disorder (Mitra 1995), which may further diminish their capacity to adjust to a new country. Studies show that lack of economic resources, minority status, lack of social support, and loss of native language and culture are associated with psychological distress (Hurh and Kim 1988; Rumbaut 1991). In the United States, even for those who are successful eventually, the struggle is usually long and arduous and "its impact is felt for a lifetime" (Nguyen 1994:25). Studies that have been undertaken to examine mental health issues related to refugees have shown that war trauma does affect social functioning, job employment, and adaptation to new conditions, far beyond the cultural adjustment and climatic adaptations that most immigrants encounter (Mayadas and Segal 2000). However, these studies reveal only the tip of the iceberg. First, studies concerned with mental health focus only on clinical populations. Second, because of cultural factors, lack of knowledge, and apprehension, even those with mental health needs are reluctant to utilize services. Last, neither of these groups is necessarily representative of all refugees, many of whom use their own resources to adjust to the changed circumstances.

One characteristic of refugees that should be applauded is their tenacity for survival—they remain resilient despite major losses and stressors (Muecke 1992). Rather than assuming that their lives are fraught with mental health issues, U.S. society may be more helpful in their adjustment if they are credited for their adaptability, and, in turn, it may be useful for society to learn from their perspectives on life. Gerber (1996) suggests that society can learn from these refugee survivors who have flirted with death in the attempt to survive and have been successful, even in the face of disaster.

Clearly, the collective trauma of refugees provides the context for their individual traumas. Even voluntary immigration, though less traumatic, involves loss of the familiar and questions the foundation of tradition. Refugee and immigrant mental health problems can be linked to the larger social and political contexts of our time not only within the United States and its public and private response to immigrant groups, but also based on current foreign relations with their countries of origin (Marsella 1994).

Depending on existing social and political climates, Asian Americans are perceived as either the model minority, who are thus more acceptable than other U.S. minorities, or as the "yellow peril" (or "brown peril"), who are mistrusted and used as scapegoats. These stereotypes and the associated behaviors directed toward Asian Americans may compound the psychological distress that they experience.

Research on rates of mental disorder among Asians provides evidence that the monolithic stereotype of the Asian as successful and well adjusted is a myth. It provides an understanding of the development of mental heath problems among Asians, and it signals to policymakers that a definite need for mental health services exists in the Asian community (Uba 1994). These needs may resemble those of other groups in the United States and may take the form of profound mental illness or of more moderate problems that nevertheless compromise adaptation and functioning.

Research has revealed at least six predictors of mental health problems for all Americans: (1) employment/financial status, (2) gender, (3) old age, (4) social isolation, (5) relatively recent immigration, and

(6) refugee experiences. Although the last two are more applicable to Asians than to the majority group, the nature of the other predictors might differ for Asian Americans, as they also embody cultural factors and varied experiences (Uba 1994). Those with economic stress, women, the elderly, and those who have few social supports are more likely than others to experience psychological distress, but for Asians, recent immigration and refugee experiences also heighten mental health problems. It is important to note, nevertheless, that longevity in the nation does not necessarily mean freedom from mental health problems.

Even the concept of the "model minority," which was coined during the Civil Rights Movement of the 1960s, conspires to disavow the mental health needs of Asian Americans. Now used to describe a group that is successful and well adjusted, it assumes that they have few unmet needs. When first used during the 1960s, however, the term was applied to a group that was believed to be "better behaved" than other minorities, such as the African Americans and the Latinos—it made no waves and brought no attention to itself. It described a group that attempted, despite the numerous differences between it and both the dominant group and other minority groups, to blend in with society's expectations and do all that was "right." The effort merely increased the mental health problems that had their roots in ethnic identity and definition of self in relationship to the majority population. Racism is still pervasive in U.S. society despite rising awareness of diversity. For example, John McCain, a contender for the 2000 Republican nomination for president, while paying lip service to pluralism during his campaign appearances in Texas, referred several times to Asians as "Gooks." The absence of media focus on his statements and the lack of public outcry about them further discounts the sensibilities of the Asian American population. Such a derogatory descriptor of the African American or Latino populations would never have been tolerated. Only after several complaints were voiced over the Internet did McCain issue an apology (National Public Radio 2000).

Membership in a group that is devalued and imbued with negative stereotypes can impede the ability of minority children and immigrant minorities to develop a positive self-identity (Spencer and Markstrom-Adams 1990). Although especially second- and subsequent-generation Asian Americans may not be identifiable by their language or their level of integration into the lifestyle of the dominant European American culture, their phenotype ensures that they continue to be identified as

Asian. Unlike immigrants from Occidental countries, regardless of the number of generations in the United States, individuals of Asian descent are not viewed as "American," but are permanently regarded as "Asian" or "Asian American," as Lee aptly captures in the chapter title "Are You Chinese or What?" (Lee 1999). For many Asian immigrants, this difficulty, along with cultural conflicts and language barriers, can lead to great psychological distress.

Much of the focus in the mental health literature on Asian Americans has been on the identity of immigrants and their American-born offspring. Less has been reported on the mental health of Asian American elders and their use of services, yet it is clear that psychological distress is prevalent among this group (Browne, Fong, and Mokuau 1994), and depression and anxiety among Asian American elders are growing problems and cause for concern (Iwamasa and Hilliard 1999). Adaptation is more difficult for the elderly than for others, and Asian immigrants are often faced with cultural conflicts that they are unable to understand. American-born Asian elders are not exempt from the effects of cross-cultural stresses either, for social segregation in the first two-thirds of the twentieth century prevented them from equal participation in American life. The greatest disadvantage of the elderly Asian American is still racial discrimination (Wong and Ujimoto 1998). Relatively little is known of the problems resulting from the abuse of Asian elders (Rittman, Kuzmeskus, and Flum 1999; Tatara 1999). It is evident, however, that Asian elders also experience a high level of emotional distress that is intensified by acculturative stresses, age-related issues, role relationships in transition, and concerns about dependency. Few services target the Asian population, and even fewer recognize the difficulties faced by the growing elderly population, yet both groups are forces with which the mental health system will increasingly need to contend.

The prevalence of psychopathology among Asian Americans has been a source of debate, and the literature continues to be ambiguous (Sue et al. 1995). It is becoming more widely recognized, however, that when research uses clinical populations as subjects, the findings vary. Because Asians tend to avoid mental health services, and because mental health problems are often somatized, such problems are not believed to be as prevalent among Asians as they are among other U.S. populations. In fact, a number of culturally based syndromes are uniquely Asian, and although several are described in the fourth edition of the *Diagnostic and Statistical Manual of Mental Disorders* (*DSM-IV*) of the American Psychiatric Association, they are rarely recognized or addressed by Western interventions (Herrick and Brown 1999). Particularly frequent are the following syndromes, which have been mentioned in the mental health and psychiatric nursing literature:

Latah among Southeast Asian women and *Ainu* among Japanese women are triggered by something that startles them and results in imitative behaviors, automatic responses, and uttered obscenities. Most often these symptoms are seen among post-menopausal women (Campinha-Bacote 1988).

Hsieh-ping is found among Chinese males, who develop a trance-like state and believe they are possessed by their dead relatives. *Koro*, a panic state, is experienced by Southeast Asian males. In both of these syndromes the male believes he will lose his penis and die (Leveck 1991).

Amok afflicts people from Indonesia, who run through a village or town after a period of depression and threaten murder (Leveck 1991).

Busy-busy syndrome and *anomic syndrome* are found among the Vietnamese and are attributed to depression. The first involves pre-occupation with trivial tasks, while the second reflects lack of motivation and is also associated with bizarre behavior (Aylesworth, Ossorio, and Osaki 1980).

Hwa-Byung is a somatized form of major depression that includes heart palpitations, constriction in the chest, heat sensations, and headaches (Kim 1995).

Shenjing is a Chinese syndrome identified as neurological, with physical and mental fatigue, dizziness, a variety of aches and pains, and difficulty concentrating, difficulty sleeping, and memory loss (American Psychiatric Association 1994).

Shenkui, found among the Chinese, is similar to panic disorder, with somatic symptoms of dizziness, backache, fatigue, weakness, insomnia, and sexual dysfunction (American Psychiatric Association 1994).

With the Asian tendency to somatize psychological distress, and in the absence of sensitization of service providers, this immigrant group is hesitant to seek psychiatric services. Research has shown that even relatively acculturated Asians, such as college students, are less likely to have a positive attitude about seeking psychological help than are Americans. Asians may also have less awareness of their personal need for professional help, less tolerance of the stigma associated with seeking help, less interpersonal openness regarding their problems, and less confidence in the ability of mental health professionals to be of assistance (Atkinson, Ponterotto, and Sanchez 1984). Some additional factors contributing to the underutilization of services are the use of alternative resources such as family or non–mental health services, cost considerations, knowledge and understanding of the services, and responsiveness of the services (Sue and Morishima 1982).

Cultural Competence in Mental Health Delivery

Since the 1980s theoreticians and researchers studying the diversity of peoples in the United States have called for cultural competence. Only since the latter part of the 1990s have guidelines begun to evolve, but they have not yet been systematized. The benefits of advocacy have been evidenced, however, in raising awareness among practitioners that culture *does* affect all aspects of mental health, from mental health issues themselves to (a) perceptions of mental illness, (b) service providers, (c) acknowledgment of need, and (d) compliance with intervention. Practitioners should be knowledgeable about the range of mental health problems that are unique to particular minority groups, and they should also be able to recognize the tendency of many to somatize these problems. They must also be aware that communication between practitioners and Asian American patients is tempered by cultural variables, among them communication patterns, role relationships, and perceptions by and of the larger society. First and foremost, mental health practitioners must be knowledgeable about bicultural issues and issues regarding immigrant, refugee, and minority experiences.

Practitioners must also remain aware that Asian Americans evidence the same mental health problems that are prevalent in the larger society. They experience depression, mania, schizophrenia, and dysfunctional behaviors, including substance abuse, family violence, fear, isolation, low self-esteem, and contemplation of suicide. Extreme cultural sensitivity must not allow practitioners to overlook the obvious, nor must it permit destructive behaviors to be accepted in the name of cultural competence. Thus, although severe corporal punishment of children and spousal violence may be prevalent and accepted in many Asian countries (Segal 1995, 1999, 2000a), it must not be excused in the United States in the name of culture. On the other hand, there must be recognition that directiveness will result in more effective treatment outcomes than will self-determination.

As in the area of health care, the research tends to focus on the more vulnerable section of the bimodal distribution of Asian Americans. Researchers and theoreticians discuss the ideal use of bicultural and bilingual intermediaries if necessary. However, given the increasing rates of family violence, suicide, substance abuse, and other psychosocial problems found among middle-class Asian American families, to focus attention only on the marginalized represents a disservice to a large part of the Asian American population. When a stereotype defines Asian Americans, it camouflages the unique qualities and needs of many. If health and mental health practitioners focus only on the disadvantaged among Asian Americans, those who fit the model minority profile will be excluded from mental health services that they may desperately need. This attitude, along with Asian tendencies to either somatize or deny mental health problems and to eschew professional services, ensures that the more mainstreamed will perpetuate the myth that Asian Americans are emotionally and mentally healthy, and mental health needs will remain unaddressed.

Race, ethnicity, values, beliefs, customs, and socioeconomic status influence not only mental health but also the presentation of mental illness and its symptoms. These variables, especially culture, must be viewed as contextual, contributing to the definition and explanation of psychopathology (Serafica 1997). Feelings are not discussed in the Asian family. Discussion with a therapist or other outsider is unacceptable as well, for in a collectivist culture, the behavior of one individual implicates the entire group. The family and community are disgraced when personal problems are taken outside their boundaries. Personal revelations may also betray expectations of filial piety. It is safer to somatize problems. While younger Asian Americans who become acculturated may be more willing to explore mental health treatment options, the Asian elderly are very reluctant to violate cultural expectations. The size of this generation of the Asian American population is on the rise, because of the aging of the group and the immigration of aging parents. Mental health knowledge about the elderly is scarce, as are services that meet their needs, yet it is evident that the isolation and dependence they experience prompt increasing anxiety and depression (Iwamasa and Hilliard 1999).

Herrick and Brown (1999) suggest that misdiagnosis of mental illness among Asian Americans is common for at least three reasons: (a) the presenting symptoms differ from those of other groups, (b) practitioners lack knowledge of Asian cultures, and (c) practitioners are not really aware of their own low levels of cultural sensitivity. In addition, the religions of Buddhism, Christianity, Hinduism, Islam, and Confucianism have different definitions of self (Almeida 1996). Belief in external forces of control by most Asian cultures can serve as a source of strength, since believers may more readily accept that an event is out of their control. On the other hand, such belief in an external locus of control may be a great source of distress, because believers feel unable to influence the course of their lives.

While cultural factors may hinder the success of treatment of patients with mental illness—and practitioners must address those factors—several Asian traditions can be beneficial to treatment. Religion and spirituality may be used in conjunction with modern treatment methods. Asian cultures are patriarchal and hierarchical, valuing superiors and respecting authority. Therefore the expectation is that the mental health professional will be authoritative and directive. Once a trusting relationship is established with the patient (which is necessary regardless of culture or ethnicity), the service provider is perceived as a caring authority figure whose directions must be followed (Chin et al. 1993). This can ensure treatment compliance. The strength of collectivism can be used, not to focus on the individual but to draw the whole family into treatment (Chang and Yeh 1999). The Asian family is an important resource that heretofore has been untapped in mental health interventions; it can reduce client symptoms and produce change. Medication, individual counseling and psychotherapy, and family therapy are represented in the literature on mental health treatment for Asian Americans, yet the preferred choice for most in this population is medication (Herrick and Brown 1999). This is consistent with the somatization of emotional problems; self-disclosure, necessary in both family therapy and psychotherapy, is inconsistent with Asian tradition.

Based on the literature, Herrick and Brown (1999:288) developed the following fairly comprehensive list of guidelines for the treatment of Asian Americans (figure 7.1).

GUIDELINES FOR THE MENTAL HEALTH CARE PROFESSIONAL

Initially concentrate on establishing rapport.

Use silence and active listening.

Use an indirect gaze, soft voice, and few words.

Refrain from asking too many questions.

Respect the client's reluctance to verbalize thoughts and feelings.

Educate the client about counseling and psychotherapy.

Reassure the client about confidentiality.

Focus on the presenting problem.

Pay attention to somatic symptoms—consider that they may be a reflection of psychological distress.

Be active and directive.

Avoid psychodynamic interpretations.

Do not use psychiatric jargon.

Be flexible.

Negotiate with the client about when and who should participate in the therapeutic process.

Include the interpreter, the indigenous healer, the family, or the community members, as appropriate.

Seek consultation from community leaders, spiritual leaders, or both.

Consider intergenerational conflicts.

Plan care within the context of the culture, community, and family.

Assess strengths and build on them.

Set short-term goals.

Prescribe medications in low doses and monitor medications closely for side effects.

Use storytelling to elicit the expression of feelings.

Coordinate community support: vocational, educational, and other community support systems.

Teach problem-solving techniques.

Conduct research to determine effective interventions to promote bicultural identity and enhance self-esteem.

Conduct outcome studies of culturally sensitive interventions and programs.

Policy Implications

Differences clearly exist in the experiences and needs within and across different Asian groups in the United States, and these variations should be addressed in the delivery of services. Nevertheless, Sue et al. (1995) suggest the importance of aggregate research, in which different Asian American groups are combined, for policy considerations, for broad cultural comparisons, and to establish baseline information. The use, or lack of use, of mainstream mental health services should have implications for resettlement policies for mental health for refugees, immigrants, and native-born Americans of Asian descent (Bemak, Chung, and Bornemann 1996).

The harsh realities involved in refugee policies, services, and interventions specifically, and in immigration services in general, are the practicalities of relocation (Martin 1994). These issues are compounded by cultural differences, traumatic experiences, mistrust of members outside the community, and less-than-welcoming experiences in U.S. society. Immigration and refugee policies provide little recognition of the importance of mental health services and programs, yet there is dire need for biological, psychological, and sociocultural models for recognizing, conceptualizing, and treating the psychiatric problems of refugees (Boehnlein and Kinzie 1995). Mental health policies that really address the needs of Asians necessitate the development of mental health services that improve refugee, immigrant, and minority mental health strategies. Furthermore, policy for training service providers must underscore the importance of integrating trauma education, cross-cultural approaches, interagency collaboration, linkages with Asian refugee, immigrant, and Asian American communities, and traditional methods of mental health intervention.

Mental health policy for Asians—and for minorities in general—must also include sensitization of the U.S. community to the richness of cultural diversity, an investment that will have reciprocal benefits. In the process of exposing the U.S. community to different worldviews, such sensitization can provide an avenue for people to accept those who are dissimilar to themselves. Prejudice, discrimination, and racism are so often the results of fear, ignorance, lack of exposure, and unfounded generalizations rather than of experience. Recognition of Asian contributions to the enrichment of the society can only reduce stress, develop self-sufficiency, involve families, preserve culture, and spark fresh hope among the Asian American population (Steven 1990). Policy interventions could occur not only at the societal level but also at the individual and community levels through the education of children (Brody 1990).

Policy for the development and implementation of mental health services for the Asian population is essential. Resettlement policies for refugees are not sufficient to meet mental health needs; they focus specifically on refugees' reaching economic self-sufficiency within the shortest possible time. Unfortunately, 1999 congressional findings for national mental health (42 USCS §9401) were gloomy, indicating that significant problems persist and large segments of the U.S. population remain unserved or underserved. Among these are the racial and ethnic minorities.

Asians are underserved both because of the lack of sensitivity to their needs and also because of their reticence in using mental health services. Mental health policy for such groups may include recognition of the qualitative differences and similarities in mental health issues and needs between European Americans and Asian immigrants, Asian refugees, and native-born Asian Americans. Cultural and monetary impediments to the utilization of services must be overcome with outreach efforts designed to educate the Asian population in the United States, and intervention services need to be provided by those who are trained for cross-cultural competence. In addition, and perhaps more important, policies must be developed to prevent mental illness and psychological distress. Preventive mental health for immigrants and refugees must include the development of policies that enhance assimilation and/or integration for newcomers to the nation. Lambert and Taylor (1990) raise the question of whether there is a public responsibility in a democracy, such as America, to ensure that the adjustment of newcomers is eased through special attention and resources, or whether it is an issue to be dealt with by the newcomers themselves. In other words, should the nation seek to accommodate them, or should they be responsible for their own assimilation? This is clearly the crux of the immigration concern.

SUBSTANCE ABUSE POLICY

American culture has been accepting of certain substances, ambivalent about some, and phobic about others.
—KARGER AND STOESZ 1998:350

The executive branch of the federal government and Congress became increasingly concerned about the problems of alcoholism and drug abuse during the late 1960s and early 1970s. Since funding to begin new initiatives was limited, traditional mental health professionals were used to launch national efforts of intervention (Mechanic 1999), a strategy that appeared to be logical, since mental health issues often involve the abuse of drugs and alcohol as a mechanism of escape from the stresses of psychosocial difficulties. This interaction is so widely recognized that it has been institutionalized into the Alcohol, Drug Abuse, and Mental Health Administration (ADAMHA) of the Department of Health and Human Services. Since states receive block grants to apportion funds on the basis of state need, they may choose to distribute their monies among mental health and substance abuse services as they wish. Some spend more on mental health services, others on drug abuse programs, and still others on alcoholism treatment programs. A few states choose to combine services into all-encompassing substance abuse programs that address problems of use and abuse of any substance, including alcohol, cigarettes, and legal and illegal drugs. The use and misuse of addictive substances have been associated with a number of societal problems, and also with illness, lost productivity, premature death, and high financial costs to society. To determine the extent of substance abuse and addiction, Congress mandated the National Comorbidity Survey, a structured diagnostic interview of a representative sample of noninstitutionalized individuals between the ages of fifteen and fifty-four; the survey revealed an 11.3 percent rate of substance abuse and addiction (Kessler et al. 1994).

Historically, U.S. society has exhibited a range of responses to the use of addictive substances. Cigarettes, until as recently as the last two decades of the twentieth century, were generally considered acceptable everywhere in the United States. Early smoking was considered acceptable pleasure for the male but not for the female. With the Women's Liberation Movement, large numbers of women began to smoke, as did adolescents of both genders. Regarded as a mark of maturity, cigarette smoking began in younger and younger children, and currently is common at the early age of fifteen. Experts in the field of addiction view cigarettes as a gateway that can lead to the use of illegal drugs. Alcohol, like cigarettes, is legal in this and most other non-Islamic societies, but the nation has responded in various ways to its use, from prohibiting its manufacture and sale from 1919 to 1933 to setting a legal age for drinking. In the first decade of the twentieth century, cocaine was a popular ingredient in medicines, as it remains in Andean cultures, and even in Coca-Cola. It was not until concern about the quality of food production emerged and the 1906 Pure Food and Drug Act was passed, requiring that all ingredients be listed on the labels of foods, that the public became aware of the use of cocaine in a number of products, and local jurisdictions barred their sale.

Increasing concern about mind-altering drugs led the nation to address that issue. As a leader at the Hague Opium Convention of 1912, the United States helped control the international production and sale of opium. The 1914 Harrison Narcotic Act placed restrictions on the manufacture and sale of narcotics, and the 1937 Marijuana Tax Act made marijuana illegal. Despite their illegality, the use of and societal reaction to these drugs have varied over the decades, with the 1960s and 1970s evidencing widespread use of illegal drugs among young adults. The abuse of illegal drugs as well as prescription drugs continues to be a source of significant concern to the nation. The federal government appears to try both to curb the supply of illicit substances and to increase treatment and prevention efforts.

Notwithstanding the problems associated with illegal drug use, a major correlate of social problems in the United States is abuse of the legal drug alcohol, the most widely abused drug. In addition to health problems caused by the misuse of alcohol, which is readily available nationwide to all people over the age of twenty-one, alcohol abusers evidence a range of psychosocial problems, among them criminal activities, highway accidents, family violence, incompetence in the workplace, and loss of personal direction. Among illegal drugs, marijuana is the most popular, but users often combine several drugs; the most common combination is marijuana and alcohol, resulting in impairment of dramatic magnitude.

The National Household Survey on Drug Abuse released national estimates of substance abuse among eleven racial and ethnic groups. The data show that 11.9 percent of all Americans aged twelve and older used illicit drugs between 1991 and 1993 (Associated Press 1998). Rates for Native Americans (20 percent), Puerto Ricans, African Americans, and Mexican Americans (all 13 percent) were higher than the national norm, while those for Asian Americans, at 6.5 percent, fell below the norm. The literature on the epidemiology of substance abuse among Asian Americans is sparse, with most of the available information based on research with clinical populations, most often with adolescents (Zane and Huh-Kim 1998). Other studies have been conducted in Hawaii and on the U.S. West Coast, two areas that have large Asian populations. The findings may not be representative of the Asian populations on the mainland, however, for the groups in Hawaii do not share the same issues of minority status, acculturation, and other experiences as Asians in the continental United States (Kitano and Daniels 1995). In the five-year study of European Americans, Japanese, Chinese, Filipinos, and Native Hawaiians, the Japanese, Chinese, and Filipinos showed a substantially lower rate of alcohol consumption than did the European Americans and Native Hawaiians, and at least 67 percent of the women in each group were either light drinkers or nondrinkers (Marchand, Kolonel, and Yoshizawa 1989).

In the continental United States, abstinence and lower rates of drug use were found more often among Asian groups than among other ethnic groups, but reports are inconclusive. Even among Asians a difference arises based on gender and ancestry, with Chinese men reporting the lowest rate of alcohol use and Japanese men the highest. Immigrant Asians tend to use less alcohol than do their native-born counterparts (Klatsky et al. 1983). Furthermore, Koreans have a low rate of alcohol consumption, perhaps because of a strong Christian background that promotes abstinence. Nevertheless, a relatively recent emic study focusing on immigration patterns, social support networks, and issues surrounding adaptation experienced by Korean immigrant women and Korean American women revealed risks of substance abuse and mental health problems (Kim and Grant 1997). Although most studies suggest that substance abuse is low among Koreans and that Asian women tend to abstain from alcohol and illicit drugs, nonclinical reports by Korean women may indicate a different pattern. Overall, among Asians in the United States, those who tend to drink regularly are men under the age of forty-five, those of higher socioeconomic status, and those living in large cities (Kitano et al. 1992). There are some indications that alcohol use and abuse have been underestimated for the Asian population, particularly among the Filipinos and Japanese males (Zane and Toshiaki 1992), and substance abuse is mentioned as a health problem for Asians (Flaskerud and Kim 1999).

In large-scale surveys of nonclinical populations, it is difficult to determine whether patterns of drinking reveal problems, cultural norms, or addictive behaviors. Patterns of drinking appear to be correlated with economic status, educational attainment, level of acculturation, and genetic factors. Environmental conditions, such as drinking norms and alcohol availability, also influence drinking behaviors. While the study by Kitano et al. (1992) reveals that those individuals who tend to drink are also more likely to be social, participate in sports, and play indoor games than are their more abstemious counterparts, other studies suggest that Asians may cope with the difficulties of adjustment to a foreign culture by turning to mind-altering substances (Varma and Siris 1996; Yee and Thu 1987), with this being particularly true for older Asian Americans, who often become users of tranquilizers and barbiturates (Zane and Toshiaki 1992). Makimoto (1998) reports that while Chinese Americans have the lowest lifetime rate of drinking, particularly heavy drinking, Japanese Americans have the highest. Alcohol abuse and the abuse of other substances is also cause for concern among Filipino groups (Berganio, Tacata, and Jamero 1997), and among Southeast Asians in the United States (O'Hare and Van Tran 1998).

While no prevalence data exist on the Vietnamese, Cambodians, and Laotians in the United States, there are indications that this population uses alcohol, as well as psychoactive drugs and opium, to relieve physical pain or psychological distress (Erickson D'Avanzo 1997). Studies show that the posttraumatic stress disorder evidenced by large segments of the Southeast Asian population and the range of socioeconomic and acculturative difficulties that they experience make them highly vulnerable to substance abuse. It appears that of the Asians in the United States, they are the most likely to have high rates of drug and alcohol use. Patterns of opium use as revealed by Asian addicts show the onset of addiction during the early phase of adult productivity, with a tendency to spread in epidemic fashion to younger people (Westermeyer et al. 1991). Use of opiates has been found particularly among H'mong men who are married and living with family members, with patterns of use marked by periods of abstinence (Westermeyer and Chitasombat 1996).

The few existing studies on the abuse of addictive substances by Asians tend to focus primarily on immigrants of East and Southeast Asian ancestry. Little attention is given to the addictions evidenced by South Asians. But the establishment in New York City of the Nav Nirmaan, a drug and alcohol treatment program developed by South Asian immigrants for immigrants (Sachs 1999) shows substantial substance abuse. Clearly this and the existing number of studies indicate that substance abuse may be more pervasive throughout the Asian community than has heretofore been recognized. Although the literature suggests that Southeast Asians, because of their experience of trauma, may be more susceptible to addictions, and that certain other subgroups, such as Filipino and Japanese men, may be more likely to engage in patterns of heavy drinking because of cultural norms, most studies have tended to suggest that, on the whole, substance abuse by Asians is relatively low.

Other researchers state that inaccurate perceptions and stereotypes of Asians as the model minority mask a true understanding of the prevalence and nature of substance abuse in the population (Nemoto et al. 1999; Ja and Aoki 1993). Although some community-based studies have shown alarmingly high rates of specific substance abuse among different Asian ethnic groups, the heterogeneity of Asians and cultural barriers have contributed to a lack of knowledge regarding prevalence. Drug use and abuse by Asians are often ignored by both Asian and non-Asian health professionals, researchers, and community members, thus perpetuating the perception that substance abuse is not a significant problem among Asians in the United States. This perception is belied, however, by the opening of the Nav Nirmaan and the new American Recovery Services of San Mateo County in California, which address alcohol and drug abuse problems in the Asian community (Peninsula Report 1999). While drug use is evident among Asians, the patterns and correlates are unique to their ethnicity, gender, immigrant status, and age groups (Nemoto et al. 1999).

Although there appears to be general acknowledgment that Southeast Asians are more susceptible to substance abuse, this may merely reflect their greater contact with social service agencies. As refugees, the majority of this population has had some contact with the social welfare system, and hence service providers are more likely to identify difficulties such as substance abuse and mental illness when delivering financial and educational assistance programs. Other Asian immigrants or those of Asian ancestry may not come to the attention of the social welfare system, as they may not identify themselves as having any problems or may not avail themselves of the services for a number of reasons—cultural misgivings, lack of information, poor access—and opportunities to identify areas of psychosocial difficulties are few.

The United States has held a variety of substance abuse policies over time. The perception of alcoholism has moved from regarding it as a moral issue to viewing it as a medical one. It is now recognized as a disease, and the treatment of alcoholics focuses on rehabilitation rather than punishment. However, alcohol consumption is frequently correlated with other behavior that may be either dangerous or illegal, most specifically driving under its influence or consuming alcohol during pregnancy. Such behavior can jeopardize the lives of others, and the former is illegal. Much substance abuse policy focuses on prevention and rehabilitation. Even the federal response to illicit drug use has been two-pronged, attempting to curb the supply by capturing and penalizing the manufacturers, smugglers, and sellers, and to lower the demand by educating the public about the hazards of drug use and by providing rehabilitative treatment to abusers and addicts.

Although several primary prevention programs target children in elementary schools, they are often not sufficient to help high-risk youth. While such programs may be useful for young second-, third-, and fourth-generation Asians, they do not adequately reach adults. Immigrant Asians may arrive in the United States with cultural norms that govern drinking or the use of substances that are illicit in the United States, such as opium and hemp. But marginalization may usher them toward mind-altering drugs to help cope with cross-cultural stresses. Long-term marginalization may also influence native-born Asians who may use psychotropic drugs and alcohol to cope with difficulties.

Finally, cost frequently impedes access to services. Employees with good health insurance policies have the resources to enter drug abuse treatment programs. The poor, by contrast, receive inconsistent treatment. In the late 1970s and early 1980s, drug abuse and alcoholism treatment programs flourished in hospitals as both inpatient and outpatient programs and were part of mental health services; later, however, these programs proved unable to meet the growing needs. Treatment for those who are incarcerated is virtually nonexistent, and changes in insurance laws and guidelines have meant drastic reductions in the allowable and reimbursable length of treatment programs. These developments have slashed the impact of the services that are provided. Furthermore, Assembly Bill 1000, the Mental Health Parity Act, which requires health insurers to provide coverage for the diagnosis and treatment of serious mental illness (Delevett 1998) does not cover substance abuse (Vatz and Weinberg 1997). Hence, although the American Medical Association considers addictions to be illnesses, substance abuse treatment is not necessarily covered by insurance, and it does not receive the same level of coverage that the Parity Act requires for physical and mental illness. For Asians, and for others, the additional financial burden of treatment creates another obstacle. Public policy must recognize substance abuse as an illness or a mental disorder of a type that necessitates treatment and require that it be covered by insurance companies. When financial constraints are not a factor, Asian cultural barriers that prevent the use of available treatment can be more readily confronted.

IDEOLOGY AND PUBLIC POLICY

President Clinton, in his final State of the Union Address, called upon the United States to assume those initiatives that reflect its ideological claims—liberty and justice for all. This includes a call for accountability and responsibility. These ideals are expected to be built into the policies of the country in such a way that they both embody the hopes for the nation and prevent the government from being overly intrusive in the lives of American citizens. An adequate balance of government regulation and individual freedom is difficult to achieve, and in a democratic nation, perceptions of individuals and groups differ substantially, making achievement of that balance ever more remote.

Other industrialized nations provide many more services to citizens at little or no cost. Health care is socialized in most nations, making it accessible to all, regardless of income level. Social security, family leave, child-care services, housing, and even higher education are heavily subsidized in other developed countries. While U.S. government programs do support such initiatives, it is to a significantly smaller degree than in other developed countries, providing fewer and more-limited services to a smaller proportion of the population.

While public programs in other industrialized nations are usually more extensive than in the United States, taxes are also significantly higher, and they are used to subsidize ambitious policies (Steinmo 1993). Most U.S. citizens believe that while government regulation is necessary, it should be limited. This position contrasts with other nations' views; U.S. government institutions are so designed that they ensure that regulations are limited. Kingdon (1999) indicates that the U.S. institutions of government are limited by the separation of powers, the political parties are much weaker than those of other countries, public policies have a much smaller reach, the U.S. tax burden is significantly lower, and the government has a relatively limited role in the general public's collective social and economic life.

U.S. government involvement in citizens' lives is limited by the evolution of the ideas of early settlers to the United States and the collective historical experience of the population (Kingdon 1999). The early settlers (like present-day immigrants) differed from those groups that remained in their homelands, bringing with them distinctive ideas that included suspicion of hierarchy and authority, and, therefore, of government. They also brought values of individualism and equal opportunity, leaving behind beliefs in feudalism and aristocracy that resulted in class distinctions and ascribed privilege. Building values of equality into government institutions implied that the government would reflect the needs of the people, yet limit its involvement in their lives.

This nation, then, had the opportunity of beginning anew two short centuries ago, with unprecedented government guidelines. However, despite the thrust of individualism in American thought that elevates self-interest and self-assertion and that prizes liberty from authoritarian control and the freedom to decide the direction of one's life, there exists a converse value that frustrates the thrust of extreme individualism. Sacrifice, or limitation, of individual interests for the greater good of the whole also formed the basis of the Republic and was built into the concept of a representative government system. This, coupled with Christian injunctions to "love thy neighbor as thyself" and "do unto others as you would have them do unto you," and Judaic traditions of *tzedakah* (charity) adopted into Christianity, ensured that in the process of promoting self-interest, citizens were morally charged with providing for their fellow citizens. Ideologically, then, the American tradition supports the notion of self-determination while recognizing that all individuals must gain access to some level of opportunity. These ideological underpinnings may reflect the centrality of thought and government, yet they are not necessarily either the only values that the government embodies or the values that are held equally, or at all, by all parts of the government and its constituencies.

Policy preferences clearly differ between those who consider themselves liberals and those who consider themselves conservatives. In general, liberals favor more equal distribution of power and advocate greater economic equality. They are likely to accept more government intervention and regulation, particularly in the area of the economy. Meanwhile, conservatives oppose legislative involvement at the economic and personal level and suggest that liberal ideologies threaten the foundation of the American tradition by violating economic freedom.

While both liberals and conservatives are concerned about serving the public good, they differ on how it is best served. The latter believe that it is best served when individuals and families meet their needs through open participation in the marketplace, while the former view the government as the only institution capable of bringing some social justice to a society replete with obstacles such as discrimination and poverty. Conservatives believe also that the growth of government stifles individual initiative and economic incentive; liberals view government programs as mechanisms to help the weak and to redress unequal access to resources and opportunities.

Some believe in the importance of redistributing power and wealth because it helps alleviate discontent among those who face numerous obstacles to the fulfillment of their personal goals. Without this safeguard, those who are unable to avail themselves of the plentiful resources in the richest land in the world may be pressured into engaging in activities that are either antisocial or destructive. Public policy that touches minorities and has specific implications for Asian Americans can benefit from the liberal perspective. While Asians have been perceived as the model minority, it is increasingly clear that some Asian groups are more model than are others, and even within these model groups, a division exists between those who are closer to achieving the American Dream and those who are still far from it. Stress, distress, perceptions of lack of recourse, marginality, and absence of resources all appear to be correlated to some extent with poverty, poor educational attainment, health problems, family violence, criminal activity, and a host of other problems. Public policies that enhance and ensure equal opportunity and equal access may prevent an explosion of discontent that in the long run will rock all levels of society.

8

U.S.–Born Asian Americans

What, then, does it mean to be Asian American? To me, it means living in a place where I don't look much like anyone else but in most respects act like them, knowing all the time that halfway across the globe is a densely populated region full of people who look just like me but don't particularly act like me. It means forever holding the contradiction of belonging and not belonging, of feeling "at home" and wondering where home is.
—CHOW 1998:xii

Who are they, these U.S.-born Asian Americans? Clearly they are individuals born of parents who emigrated to the United States from an Asian country sometime after the middle of the nineteenth century. They may be second-generation Americans[1] or they may be of the third, fourth, or even fifth generation, especially if their ancestors were among the Issei of the early twentieth century. They differ from most second-generation Americans from European countries and from all such fifth-generation Americans in that they are always identifiable, and they must therefore identify themselves as "Asians" or "Asian Americans," not as "Americans." Because of their distinctly different phenotype—whether they are of East, Southeast, or South Asian origin—and the U.S. society's response to them, U.S.-born Asian Americans (USAsians)[2] have not yet been able to completely assimilate into the American culture. This holds true regardless of the extent to which their values, lifestyles, interests, and relationships are assimilated with American ones. They belong to a group that does not have a historical connection to the country of its ancestors and yet is not recognized as an integral part of U.S. history.

Without a direct connection to their families' countries of origin, without acceptance as Americans, and with few role models, USAsians must individually determine the degree to which they acknowledge the heritage of their families or adopt that of American society. What emerges is often a continuum of adaptation between the two cultures, with a few individuals completely assimilating in their beliefs and behaviors and others staying marginalized, but with the majority falling somewhere in between. With third and successive generations, USAsians become increasingly American in their values, thoughts, and behaviors, and the important criterion is no longer assimilation but the establishment of an identity unique to the bicultural experience.

One may propose that the experience of forging a bicultural identity is similar for both more recent USAsians, many of whom are children of immigrants who arrived here after the loosening of immigration laws in 1965, and the Yonsei and Gosei (fifth-generation Japanese) or other USAsians whose families immigrated earlier in the twentieth century. Earlier Asian immigrant generations, whether Chinese, Filipino, Indian, Japanese, or Korean, experienced such xenophobia from the dominant society that they had little choice but to remain ensconced in their own subcultures. Remnants of such exclusion are evident in the still existing Nisei Lounge in Chicago, which was established as a haven for second-generation Japanese Americans when they returned to the United States from fighting in World War II; at least one such veteran still frequents it daily (Hoekstra 2000).

All minorities, including USAsians, can usually identify one specific incident that occurred in their childhood to make them particularly aware of their difference from the majority culture. It is this cognition that begins the process of self-definition as an Asian American. Many may have encountered the experience during the preschool years; others, during the middle school years. However, for all it is clear and distinct. Until that time they accept, with little question or concern, phenotypic differences between their families and the majority society. Throughout their lives, USAsians often have had occasion to doubt their identity in U.S. society, especially when challenging comments are thrown in their direction. In recalling the pain caused by such incidents, they say that "what hurts about these specific memories is not just the remark itself, it is the unexpected and shattering suddenness that wounds" (Chow 1998:169).

In contemporary America, however, because U.S. society is becoming increasingly multicultural, USAsian children are able to see others who do look like them, and therefore they do not feel completely isolated. Euro-American and African American children of contemporary society, particularly in urban and suburban areas, are more likely to be exposed to others of different minority groups on a regular basis, and Asian Americans are no longer the anomaly they were even a generation ago. The adolescent generation of twenty-first-century America is more knowledgeable about and comfortable with accepting diversity than any previous generation. Today's young people are coming of age at a time when interracial marriage, single parenthood, divorce, and homosexuality are not so scandalous as they were a few decades ago. Since this is a generation that is strongly peer-driven and challenges parental attitudes of intolerance, it bodes better for all minority groups. In the experience of a Korean American who grew up in the United States during the 1950s, dramatic advances have been made:

> Young Korean [Asian] Americans today are indeed blessed, living in an era when old ideas about who can be American are giving way to possibilities for new American identities, thanks in part to many people repeatedly challenging race and sex discrimination over the decades. . . . Among the teenagers and 20-somethings I encounter in my albeit very racially diverse environment, I have noticed increased acceptance of multiplicity, hybridity and heterogeneity, and less interest in congealed, mandated identities and communities of taste.
>
> (Kim 2000:6)

USAsians growing up in this environment may not experience as strongly the challenges faced by their Asian immigrant parents or by the USAsian parents of earlier generations. Nevertheless, many still have to respond to the question "Where are you really from?" (Das 2000:25). Despite a much greater degree of tolerance among adolescents, prejudice still exists, sometimes making it impossible for USAsians to establish an appropriate foothold in U.S. society. The results are a suicide rate among adolescent USAsians that surpasses the national average (Wong 1999) and rising rates of depression and mental illness (Wong 1998).

MAINSTREAMING

Since openly xenophobic attitudes are not "politically correct" and are generally not considered acceptable—at least publicly—it is becoming possible for USAsians to move beyond social marginalization. In fact, the majority of USAsians are mainstreaming themselves by participating in all aspects of U.S. society—from the traditional areas of strength (math, science, and engineering) to more recent forays into the fine arts, social sciences, law, and politics. Now Asian Americans in general, and USAsians in particular, are involved in all aspects of U.S. society, because of a combination of dramatic increases in numbers, interests, and range of educational and economic resources and opportunities. Yet little change has been evidenced in the public consciousness as to what it means to be an Asian American in the United States, and Asian Americans, unlike other minority groups, have been slow to articulate the particular issues affecting them (Omatsu 1994).

Media images still tend to portray Asians stereotypically, often as successful scientists or as dangerous underworld criminals, but their involvement across society and their slowly increasing visibility in the political arena show them to be an integral part of the social fabric of the United States. Gordon's (1964) assimilation theory proposes that groups truly become a part of the society with structural assimilation. Tempering this with more recent perceptions of adjustment an a variety of levels of integration, one may suggest that Asian Americans, and more particularly USAsians, are beginning to affect and be affected by the social, economic, and political institutions of this nation. With its increasing size and visibility, the population is now helping to shape all aspects of U.S. society. Former president Bill Clinton designated May 2000 to be Asian Pacific American Heritage Month and stated in a proclamation released by the White House:

> Over the last two centuries, Asian Americans and Pacific Islanders have contributed immeasurably to the richness of our dynamic, multicultural society. . . . The people of this diverse and rapidly-growing community have contributed to every aspect of our national life—from engineering and computer science to government, the arts and sports. . . . [These contri-butions] may be used to reflect on the many gifts Asian Americans and Pacific Islanders have brought to our nation and embrace the contributions that Americans of all backgrounds make to our increasingly multicultural society.
>
> (Haniffa 2000a:12)

A significant proportion of the Asian American population immigrated in the 1960s and 1970s, and their USAsian children are now reaping the benefits of the immigrant generation's move. Most immigrant Asians, as well as previous generations of USAsians, are aware that the many resources and opportunities available to their children at this time in this country are nonexistent in their own lands. The success and economic security of many in the parental generation of Asian Americans allow them to so encourage and nurture their USAsian children that they are able to mainstream into U.S. society to a much greater extent than ever before possible. The result is a cry from USAsian activists, who stress the importance of integrating themselves into the American society by engaging in local welfare and community service activities (Bhowmick 2000). They further call upon USAsians to influence public policy by participating in the political process through voting, lobbying, and running for political office (Haniffa 2000b). It is no longer sufficient to contribute to the nation as a by-product of one's own professional achievements and interests—as is evident as scientists, artists, engineers, and sports figures, for example, contribute to the society's richness through their successes. The time is ripe for Asian Americans to participate in the running of the society by becoming assimilated into the structure of its functioning institutions. This kind of assimilation may have been unimaginable for earlier generations because of discrimination and other societal barriers, but with the gradual lowering of these barriers, it is now conceivable for current generations of young USAsians.

Over the course of the last century, Asian Americans have been involved in U.S. politics from time to time, but their numbers have been small. In 1990, at the state and local levels, a total of 731 Asian Americans held elected or appointed positions in nineteen states, with the largest number being in California, followed by Hawaii, and the remaining states reporting no Asian American governmental officials (Asian Pacific American Municipal Officials 1990). These figures appear to be changing.

Between 1956 and 1992, only eleven Asian Americans were members of the U.S. House of Representatives and the Senate, and all were from either Hawaii or California. In 2000, five Asian Americans served in the 106th U.S. Congress, three in the House and two in the Senate. All are USAsians with profiles similar to the following five:

Daniel K. Akaka—Senate, Hawaii, Democrat, 2nd term
Daniel K. Inouye—Senate, Hawaii, Democrat, 6th term
Robert T. Matsui—House, California, Democrat, 10th term
Patsy Mink—House, Hawaii, Democrat, 6th term
David Wu—House, Oregon, Democrat, 1st term

Of these five, however, none holds a position of leadership. Washington State's Gary Locke is the first USAsian governor, and Oregon's election of David Wu to the House indicates a greater assimilation of Asians in these states with small Asian populations. After taking office in January 2001, President George W. Bush appointed an Asian American woman, Elaine Chao, as secretary of labor, the highest office held by an Asian American woman, and Norman Mineta, as secretary of transportation.

Asian Americans and USAsians are traditionally successful in their chosen careers. They have contributed substantially to the sciences, business, and technology. High-profile professions, such as the arts and sports, however, have not until recently had many Asian American participants, since immigration policies have tended to admit only Asian immigrants with particular credentials. The skills of sports figures or artists have not been particularly sought after, since their contributions have not traditionally been considered necessary for the United States. Physicians, engineers, and businesspeople were more likely to be granted visas. Since Asian children are usually influenced in their choice of profession by their parents, and these Asian immigrant parents have traditionally valued professions such as medicine, engineering, and business, many USAsians abided by their parents' expectations. Only recently have larger numbers of USAsians begun entering the high-profile field of the arts, but fewer enter sports.

USAsians in the media are becoming increasingly prevalent as news reporters and anchors. Their presence is evident in advertising, and they are occasionally employed in the movie and TV industry. On the whole, they are still protrayed stereotypically—men are extremely intelligent, martial arts experts, or a part of the underworld, while women are highly seductive, exotic, and submissive. Asian American males have particularly criticized Lisa Ling, a young Asian American model, for sporting khaki capri pants and cavorting with a group of European American males in current Old Navy advertisements while saying, "Who says you can't buy love?" (Vigoda 2000). Asian American men believe that Asians have not yet crossed the race barrier, and until they do, they should not play roles of individuals with derogatory profiles. While recent reports in the news media (*Newsweek* and the *Wall Street Journal*) have suggested that a new, idyllic image of success, interest, and sex appeal now applies to Asian men, interviews with USAsian men indicate that they do not receive such adulation (Chan 2000).

314

Although the sports world is changing, it still sorely lacks Asian involvement. Among the few high-visibility USAsians are Japanese American Kristi Yamaguchi, the Olympic figure skating champion, and Tiger Woods, the golf champion. As a multiracial child of an Asian American (bi-ethnic Thai and Chinese) mother and a Native American/African American father, Woods often is simply identified as being African American. It was when he went to Thailand and the Thai people greeted him as a native son that the USAsian aspect of his background was recognized by the general U.S. population. He himself has coined a term that includes all his ethnic origins: "Blacaunasian."

Recognition of USAsians as part of the mainstream is growing. The nation has come a long way in the course of one generation. In 1999 a USAsian of Indian origin captured the title of Miss Indiana and was one of the ten finalists in the Miss USA Pageant. In the same year a Vietnamese American woman was named Miss Teenage USA. Selection of these women as representatives of beauty is a substantial change. In 2000 another young USAsian woman of Indian origin, Jhumpa Lahiri, won the Pulitzer prize in fiction for her collection of short stories. The first female Chinese American judge in Arizona, Roxanne Song Ong, received the 1999 Attorney Law Related Education Award from the Arizona Bar Foundation, and Janet Mirikitani, a Sansei, was named San Francisco's poet laureate for 2000. Achievements in science, engineering, and business are practical and unequivocal, and if the opportunity is available, and success is achieved, it cannot be denied. Because the United States provides many more opportunities to Asian Americans now than it did in the 1940s and earlier, they are able to produce much more. However, beauty, success in literature, and contribution to law are abstract, and much lies in the perceptions of the observers, the judges. It is clearly no longer just European American, or even African American beauty, life experiences, and values that capture the attention of the discerning public. It is now apparent that Asian American contributions are valued as well.

THE COMMON ISSUES

Societal issues and marginalization—or at the very least, lack of complete acceptance by the dominant culture—are encumbrances that infiltrate every aspect of USAsians' lives. USAsians must also grapple with other fundamental issues, issues that are affected less by the degree of acceptance and more by the immigrant experience itself. They must contend with differing norms and expectations of behavior between the culture of their ancestors and the culture of the United States, the ability to differentiate between generational and cultural issues, and the very powerful ties that bind them to the land of their families. In her book, *Asian American Dreams: The Emergence of an American People*, award-winning Chinese American journalist Helen Zia (2000) seeks to present the experience of Asian Americans. Her message is founded on her experience of racism, and she begins the book by asking what it takes to become American. In reviewing Zia's book, Nihai adds that despite the desire to fit in, all ethnic groups wish to preserve their own cultures and that "in a diverse, often rootless society such as ours, traditional values are worth keeping" (2000:3). The more pertinent question to ask is, What do we gain, and how much are we willing to lose, in order to become American?

Culture of Ancestors Versus U.S. Culture

USAsians, like children of all immigrants, must cope with the dual expectations of the ancestral culture and their adopted one. While the nature and scope of the conflict that they experience individually may differ, this issue has caused a rift within Asian American families since the time when they began immigrating to the United States. Although the Nisei were significantly more successful than the Issei, they maintained close cultural ties because they were not allowed into European American society. Hence, it is with the Sansei that most of the conflict inherent in the integration of different cultures begins. All USAsians experience conflict between the culture of origin and that of adoption, but because the political and social climates of the country in the first half of the twentieth century prevented assimilation, the conflicts felt by the present-day third and fourth generations of earlier immigrating Asian groups appear to be similar to those experienced by the current second generation.

From an early stage, Asian immigrant parents experience differences in traditional norms and relationships with U.S.-born (second-generation) or U.S.-reared (one-and-a-half-generation, who came to the United States pre-puberty) children. While most USAsians find that the family offers a strong positive tie and a basis for identity (Segal 1998), it also is the source of stress, alienation, and extreme internal struggles (Wolf 1997). Since many Asian immigrants speak very little English, their USAsian children, who rapidly become immersed in the U.S. society through the school system, serve as English-language interpreters, resulting in an immediate role reversal, with the parent becoming dependent upon the child. Even among those who are fluent in the English language, most are strangers to the subtleties of the culture and the functioning of different institutions, and they are taught by their children. Such role reversals dramatically upset the traditional order, creating a situation in which cultural patterns are more readily challenged. In all Asian societies, age, status, and gender are associated with authority and strictly dictate behavior. Role relationships are clearly defined by tradition, expectations are always clear, and challenges to them are neither contemplated nor permitted. Most important, the position of teachers and elders is sacrosanct, and unswerving respect is required.

While roles do dictate U.S. behavior, they are neither as rigid nor as extreme as Asian ones, and they are frequently challenged. In general, children are raised in a relatively democratic atmosphere in which they are allowed some discretion in decision making and may offer their opinions to participate more equally in decisions made about themselves and the family. They are expected to be more independent in their thinking, and this characteristic is fostered not only in the family but also in the schools. In Asian schools, from the elementary level through the college years, the norm is of unidirectional communication, with the teacher imparting knowledge to the student. Students neither question nor ask for clarification. To ask a question or to differ with the teacher is considered challenging and disrespectful. To seek clarification suggests that the teacher has not communicated effectively, and, therefore, it also is disrespectful of the teacher. In the United States, students are encouraged to participate even from the early years. As they bring their knowledge and experience into the classroom, they are encouraged to seek clarification if they do not understand and to critically assess the information they receive, whether it is from a teacher or from the materials they read.

Clearly, the foundation of relationships between those with authority and those with little or none varies between the Occident and the East. These fundamental cultural differences between East and West disrupt USAsians' understanding and acceptance of parental expectations. USAsians commonly perceive their parents to be autocratic and unsympathetic to their needs and the conflicts they experience. First-generation Asian Americans mourn the loss of their cultures as their children become rapidly Americanized. The most immediate indicator of culture loss is a change in language preference. Second-generation children of all nationalities seem to prefer to use English as soon as they begin attending school, especially since it lowers the barrier between them and the children of the dominant society. USAsians who belong to the Christian faith prefer to attend churches or services in English, while their parents attend services in their mother tongues (Rice 1997). As these second-generation children become more proficient than their parents in the English language, the family structure becomes skewed such that the children become the power brokers between the family and U.S. society (Sauerwein 1996). In the process, they become less proficient in their ancestral language.

Concerned about this most apparent indicator of culture loss, first-generation Asian immigrants establish language schools to teach USAsian children their mother tongues. Asian language schools[3] may be found in almost all cities with Asian populations. While some may be formalized, a number are merely tutorials, offered in private homes. Called language schools, with the ostensible objective of teaching the language of the parents (especially to enable children to communicate with grandparents), they do have as a primary goal the transmission of culture and traditions.

USAsian children, even those born in the land of their parents, quickly begin identifying themselves as children of America rather than of Asia (Zuckoff 2000). Parents perceive their children not only as cut off from their roots but as consciously distancing themselves from anything Asian. As different Asian community groups establish themselves and achieve economic security, they turn their attention to institutionalizing the transmission of culture to USAsians. A common means of achieving this goal is through the establishment of an ethnic community center that serves as a place for celebrations, recreation, meetings, education, and other ethnic activities. The aim is to bridge the generation gap and to provide a location in which USAsians can mingle with those of their own backgrounds.

In May 2000 several ceremonies marked the twenty-fifth anniversary of the fall of Saigon, which occurred on April 30, 1975. Contrary to the fears of some Asian immigrants, most USAsians of the late 1990s are bound to, and often proud of, their cultural heritage. Many Vietnamese American teenagers took their Euro- and African American friends to the ceremonies that marked this important occurrence in the recent history of their country. Each year many USAsians join their parents in participating in cultural festivals that commemorate the New Year as marked by their families' homelands, independence days, and other important occasions. In adolescence and young adulthood, they may be more likely to stray from tradition, moving to establish their own identities distinct from those of their parents. For the majority, however, the values of the parents and their traditions make an indelible mark on their attitudes and behaviors.

The literature on adolescence in the West indicates that while adolescents may rebel strongly against their families, unless there is extreme family dysfunction or the child is particularly emotionally disturbed, the rebellions are related to superficial issues, such as clothing, curfews, choice of food, and preferred entertainment. A striking congruence emerges between the basic values of the parents and those of their children; for example, if the family values education and religion, then these issues remain important to the children, even though they may evidence some overt murmurings against them for a time.

This kind of values examination is evident among USAsians also. Despite their preference for the dominant culture, when they leave the home their choices are tempered by the expectations and traditions of their parents (Chow 1998). When they establish their own families, it becomes clear that many of the expectations of the immigrant parents have become so internalized that they color the expectations the second-generation children have of their own children. Whether or not the parents and their children speak the same tongue, their basic values appear to be more similar than different.

Nevertheless, it is difficult for the immigrant generation to recognize its values even when they have become internalized by their Americanized children. The biggest threat to the culture may not be individuals in the dominant society, or even any other minority group, but the members of the culture itself (Gold 2000). Asian immigrants watch with pride as their children adapt to and succeed in the U.S. economy, yet they fear the loss of cultural heritage, identity, and values as the children acclimate themselves to the fast-paced United States. They watch their children stop speaking the language, move away from ethnic communities, and cease to work in the businesses begun by their parents. What parents fail to recognize is the increasing transience of all populations around the world, including those in their lands of origin. The world of the twenty-first century offers individuals more

occasion to move with employment opportunities. The parents fail
to recognize the strength of familial bonds that stretch across borders
and the respect that most USAsians retain for their elders. Traditional
patterns of relationships, though somewhat modified, do persist. The
greater assimilation into the U.S. culture in the third and successive
generations of an immigrant group truly begins when perceptions alter,
traditions are affected, and role relationships change.

Assimilation is often not the prerogative of individuals. *The State of
Asian Pacific America: Transforming Race Relations*, a 507-page study
spearheaded by Paul Ong of UCLA and released in early 2000, includes
contributions from more than a dozen scholars from a variety of disci-
plines whose work reveals that regardless of their citizenship, length of
residence in the United States, number of generations their families
have been in the United States, and levels of assimilation, Asian
Americans are still viewed as foreigners (Kang 2000b). Until they are
recognized as "American," it seems improbable that they can completely
dissociate themselves from the culture of their ancestors and completely
embrace the "American" identity.

To survive, USAsians must come to terms with their dual identities
by forging a new one that is an appropriate blend for their personalities
and experiences. On this Asian-and-American continuum, some may
identify themselves as more American and others may identify themselves as more Asian, but the duality is ever present. As a one-and-a-
half-generation Korean American stated:

> Coming here as a kid, I had a tough time in the beginning, but
> I've found myself. I've learned to assimilate in both cultures
> and to distinguish which parts of me should be Korean and
> which American. I look Korean, but I'm American. When I'm
> with my Korean friends, we speak Korean; when I'm with my
> American friends, we speak English.
>
> (Saslow 2000:16)

Such statements would once have been considered a reflection of a
schizophrenic identity. It is important to realize, however, that in all situations there are different rules of behavior, and one always assumes a
variety of roles and identities in the course of daily routines. A parent
would hardly behave in a parental role at the place of work, nor would
one behave like a senator in the home. Minority ethnicity adds another

dimension to the definition of self and the delineation of rules of behavior as one learns to adapt to the variety of environments one encounters.

The increasing awareness and multiculturalism in society and the presence of other Asians and institutions reinforce the ethnicity and traditions of USAsians and thus diminish pressures to blend in. With recognition that the United States is a mosaic, not a melting pot or even a salad bowl, the hopeful believe that U.S. society is slowly moving toward accepting biculturalism, and even more optimistically, toward cultural pluralism, by accepting and celebrating differences among people, cultures, and traditions.

Generational Versus Cultural Issues

In all societies the parental generation tends to believe that the environment and/or culture in which it was reared was the best—or certainly better than the current one. Every generation bemoans the lifestyle of the younger group, the loss of its own traditions and values, and the movement toward radical and alien ideas, behaviors, and styles. Concern is voiced about the changes in relationships within the family. The 1960s saw a revolution in the United States that so challenged the norms of its society with major upheavals that family relationships have permanently changed. As the 1970s "flower children" sought to express themselves, they violated taboos in behavior, in speech, and in challenges to the establishment. While change is necessary for the evolution of society and occurs with each successive generation, the changes effected by the youth of the sixties were dramatic by any measure. The Vietnam War, the availability of the birth control pill, and the accessibility of illegal drugs served as catalysts in the process of social change. These American "baby boomers," now in their middle years, were vehicles of change then and are now the backbone of U.S. society. Their parents, too, had wondered about the upheaval, the lack of respect, the loss of tradition, and feelings of alienation.

With the shrinking of the world into a global village, the rapid transmission of ideas across nations, the introduction of the electronic information superhighway, and the continuing influence of the United States around the world, traditional patterns of behavior and relationships are altered in every nation. Travel to Asian countries reveals young people whose attire, look, and behavior resemble those of the youth of the United States. Economic opportunities, or obstacles, require that many young people move away from their communities of origin to find jobs, leaving behind the families who have reared them. Interactions with individuals in such Asian countries as Japan, Hong Kong, and India reveal that they, too, are concerned about the diminishing influence of their ancestral traditions and the increasing influence of some universal (or Western) culture. It remains to be seen how this world culture will mold and be molded by traditions of Asian youth in their home countries and what traditions will emerge for their cultures in the early decades of the twenty-first century.

In every society, tradition and culture evolve gradually. Often dramatic experiences or major changes serve to catapult society into patterns that are strange and disturbing. Yet one is always the product of one's culture, and long-ingrained traditions and values temper potential changes. Asian American parents are not unique in wistfully recalling the "good old days" and worrying about the loss of tradition and culture. For them, the catalyst is the influence of Western language, ideas, and patterns of behavior. An additional catalyst is recognizable among adolescents, who are, of course, highly influenced by their peers. It is difficult to predict the extent to which traditional Asian values and customs will be lost among adolescents who are attempting to win the approval of their peers. Kitano and Kitano (1998) found that while the Nisei retained much of their cultural heritage, the ancestral influence barely existed among the Sansei. These data, however, were collected during a time when cultural pluralism was not valued. In the twenty-first-century United States, people of color are on track to outnumber whites in the United States by the year 2025; there may therefore be less pressure for Asians to assimilate into the Euro culture or to completely relinquish their traditions. They, like the baby boomers, will forge a new identity, one that selectively draws on the best of both Western and Asian societies.

Biculturalism

Pluralism may be defined as the society's acceptance of and respect for a variety of cultures and traditions, and biculturalism (or multiculturalism) as the ability of one individual to internalize and integrate one or more cultures into his or her personal definition of self. While the focus of older and immigrant generations is on USAsians and the fear that they will lose long-established traditions and connections with the home culture, even the first-generation immigrants must become bicultural to some extent in order to survive in the new environment. The process of relinquishing some traditions begins long before immigrants arrive in the United States. "Cultural attributes [evident in the United States] cannot be equated with homeland cultures because immigrants tend to select carefully not only what to pack in their trunks to bring to America, but also what to unpack once settled" (Zhou 1997:73). Others are modified, changed, adapted, and negotiated as immigrants work toward adjusting to new environments.

Portes and Zhou (1993) propose that immigrants and second-generation Americans do not relinquish their cultures and assimilate into U.S. society. The majority become segmentally assimilated, accepting norms and expectations in some areas of their lives while maintaining their own traditions and patterns of behavior in others. The most successful second-generation immigrants appear to be those who can do exactly that: assimilate into the dominant culture in some areas of their lives, particularly economically or professionally, yet retain their traditions, social lives, and support systems.

Success depends on the part of U.S. society into which immigrants assimilate and the extent to which they maintain their own traditions. While today's immigrants are integrated into society at higher rates than ever before, the group into which immigrants are assimilated depends upon the human and capital resources that they bring. Becoming American may not always be an advantage for the one-and-a-half and the second generations. Immigrants who enter middle-class communities soon after arriving in the United States may find it to their advantage to acculturate themselves. On the other hand, those who enter at the bottom of the socioeconomic and ethnic hierarchy, which is fraught with poverty and social inequality, are likely to assimilate with the environment and experiences around them, which are viewed as maladaptive. These children would do best to retain a strong identity with their own ethnic communities, which can provide them with the structure and reinforce the behavior necessary for upward mobility (Zhou 1997).

Portes and Zhou (1993) suggest that segmented assimilation may be the ideal route for upward mobility. If, however, USAsian children are surrounded by others of their age and succumb to peer influence, such segmentation may be less possible. It appears that USAsians are more likely to be bicultural, integrating some aspects of both the U.S. culture and their own. To achieve this, they must consciously decide the degree to which they will modify their Asian cultural values and norms, the extent to which they will accept U.S. norms, and how they will temper that acceptance so as not to cause significant dissonance with their Asian traditions. Unlike immigrants, USAsians do not follow patterns of segmented assimilation. They integrate family traditions and the new country's norms, forging fresh patterns that enable them to move between the two worlds with ease. Recognition and acceptance of biculturalism by the family and the society can enhance the healthy adjustment of USAsians.

As they move from adolescence to adulthood, USAsians once more are faced with issues of identity and biculturalism. Especially once they move out of the parental home, a step that is common in the United States, they must decide on the relevance of Asian culture. Some traditions are observable, such as ethnic food preference and observance of cultural rituals, and are easily retained or discarded. Others are abstract, having to do with values such as allocentrism, filial piety, loyalty, and honor, and have indirectly guided most USAsian behavior since childhood. These can be less easy to identify and more difficult from which to distance oneself from.

Decisions regarding cultural retention are major factors in the choice of marriage partner and in the establishment of childrearing patterns. Some individuals choose to raise their children with strongly Asian values, while others encourage Western ones. By this time, however, most USAsians are no longer ABC (American Born and Confused),[4] but have clarified for themselves where they lie on the bicultural continuum in most aspects of their lives. The writings of Asian feminists and women authors, many of whom as children attempted to be "more American than the Americans themselves," reveal that as they mature and establish families of their own, regardless of whether or not their spouses are also Asian, they seek to maintain a strong Asian identity and to impart it to their children (Chow 1998; Hong 1993; Zia 2000). Furthermore, traditional norms and values, as well as parental expectations and patterns of behavior, many of which conflict with U.S. practices of childrearing, insinuate themselves into the USAsian subconscious and emerge when they become parents themselves. Unless conscious decisions are made to the contrary, one tends to parent as one was parented.

Ties that Bind

Frolik (2000) reports the words of Pascal Tran, a Vietnamese refugee, who said, "You can cut down the tree and send the wood away, but the root remains." Regardless of the reason for leaving the country of origin, most immigrants maintain a strong connection with their homelands—perhaps because they still have family there but more often because the roots of their identities lie in the homeland. Throughout their lives, parents talk about it and their heritage, and many maintain contact with people there. The phenomenal changes in communication technologies have meant that relationships are more easily reestablished and maintained.

Both Asian Americans who are immigrants and their U.S.-born children are in frequent contact with their countries of origin. South Asian Americans travel to their homelands and send millions of dollars annually to their families there. Now they are sending money for philanthropic causes as well. Having made a successful living in the United States, having provided well for their children and aging parents, they feel a need to contribute to the development of their countries of origin. East Asians also send money to their family members and frequently visit their relatives. Many who came after the 1965 Immigration and Naturalization Act left their parents and extended families behind. These aging parents are unable to travel to the United States, and many are unwilling to leave their support systems in their own countries to be dependent on their adult children in the United States. Thus the immigrant generation maintains contact through visits back to the homeland, sometimes annually, to ensure that aging parents are comfortable, healthy, and safe.

Though the Vietnamese American community expresses strong opposition to the Communist government in Vietnam, and most of its members say that they would stay in the United States even if that government were to fall, it is believed that hundreds, perhaps even thousands, of Vietnamese refugees and immigrants to the United States will return to Vietnam at the beginning of the twenty-first century (Gold and Tran 2000). While some return to retire, and a few divide their time between the United States and Vietnam, a large number do business there. This kind of bond is not unique to Vietnamese Americans and Vietnam. All Asians (and all immigrants) feel it for their homelands. Chinese Americans and Indian Americans specifically, but also other Asian Americans, are known to engage in "back trade," making investments in Asia (Collier 2000). They also follow the social, economic, and political activities of these nations closely and react to them by demonstrating, writing letters, and eliciting media attention when they support or disagree with some action by the country or by the United States and other nations toward that country.

It appears that after about ten years, members of the immigrant generation acquire sufficient resources to travel to their lands of origin, often for the first time. When they do, whether they go with their parents or on their own, seeking a better understanding of their heritage, and thus of themselves, the ties they have to the homeland become concrete. Time and again, these USAsians, who feel they do not truly belong in the United States, confront the reality that they do not really belong in the land of their ancestors either. When USAsians contemplate returning to their ancestral countries, they often say that if they were to go back to Korea/India/China, they would not fit in there either, for their ways of thinking and behaving now are neither entirely American nor entirely Asian (Saslow 2000). They are faced with the question posed to writer Amy Wu (2000:9) by her aunt: "What kind of Chinese are you?" Another USAsian author, Claire Chow (1998:xii), states: "That trip to Beijing was an important step in my journey to integrate ethnicity and identity. I am still traveling that path." Asians, particularly women, who are born in the United States usually feel they are not fully American, yet when they travel to the land of their parents, they find that they are definitely not like the women there (Chow 1998).

Thus the bonds to the ancestral homeland are enigmatic. They give meaning to identity and draw USAsians to the borders of the homeland, where they look like natives and experience familiar traditions in context. Welcomed with warmth and pride by members of their extended family, they find the meaning of family love, respect, and interdependence reinforced. Many, however, who have grown too accustomed to the United States, its freedoms, its respect for privacy, its host of other intangible values that allow the expression of individuality, find that they do not belong in the land of their parents' origin. The realization for most is that despite the difficulties that they experience in the United States, they belong in this land. Their ties to their homelands are so great and unseverable, however, that they probably will travel there in the future and they will retain an interest in them, even if from afar. Depending upon the rate at which the United States truly becomes multicultural and accepts pluralism, subsequent generations of USAsians may not feel so strong a need to return to the countries of their parents in order to complete their definitions of self. On the other hand, with the internationalization of the world and the ease of transnational travel and communication, they may so develop their bicultural natures that they become world citizens, bringing both the cultures and the countries closer in their understanding of each other.

Marriage and Twenty-first-Century USAsian Children

Perpetuation of the race and the culture are concerns of any minority group outside its own country. With successive generations, the most ready mechanism for the transmission of culture and tradition is marriage to people of the same race and background. Asian Americans prefer that their children marry not only other Asians but Asians from the same ethnic group. Within the Asian framework, marriage does not mark the creation of a new family; it is rather a continuation of the husband's family line (Ho 1987). Therefore, the family has a vested interest in the choice of marriage partner. Asian males are charged with the responsibility of maintaining the lineage, and so the eldest male is encouraged to marry within the cultural group. Asian females do not hold such responsibility (Yee et al. 1998) and thus may not feel such pressure. Values of Confucianism and filial piety, while not so labeled in all Asian cultures, nevertheless affect all aspects of the marital and parent-child relationships.

Marriage. In traditional Asian style, families ensure that their children marry partners who are well matched in terms of background, such as social class, education, and ethnicity, and also in religion, beliefs, and values (Yee et al. 1998). While the arranged-marriage system is formalized in Asian cultures, it is not absent in Western ones. Members of the Occidental family often introduce people of matched backgrounds to each other, hoping that a marriage will ensue, and conversely, when the family feels that a planned marriage is unsuitable, they may pressure the couple to dissolve the relationship. Even among European Americans or African Americans, family approval is generally considered important. In Asian American communities, which continue to stress filial piety, there has been a move away from the arranged-marriage system. Among East Asian Americans it is now virtually absent, perhaps because it is rarely practiced in its traditional form in East Asia. Among Southeast Asians, however, there is still some tendency to acquiesce to parental preferences.

Among South Asians, in whose countries of origin arranged marriages are still prevalent, the practice also continues in the United States. While greater numbers of individuals find their own partners, the practice of arranged marriages with other South USAsians or with someone from South Asia is still commonplace. Potential candidates are identified through advertisements and referrals from family and friends, and they are screened by parents and other relatives, who also oversee the engagement process. Furthermore, among Indian Asian Americans, caste and dowry are still matters of concern and often cause intergenerational conflict.

Unlike other Asians, Filipino Americans reflect patterns of familial interaction similar to those of their Euro counterparts. Relationships are based on egalitarianism rather than on patrilineal principles, and ancestry is traced through both the maternal and the paternal lines. The Catholic and Spanish traditions that underlie the Filipino culture differ significantly from Confucian, Hindu, and Muslim traditions and are more likely to reinforce equality between the genders, which has implications for mate selection and personal choice.

USAsians must consciously decide the extent to which they will accept parental authority in decisions about mate selection. With the influence of American culture, USAsians are more often choosing to marry for love, which until recently was not considered acceptable. They find themselves torn between the expectation that they will select a partner who suits the parents and their own desire to find one who offers the love that is so accepted and glamorized in Western society. Many USAsians are now marrying of their own volition, but they find that if they go against their parents' wishes, great heartache can ensue.

Children and parenting. Childrearing practices and parent-child relationships in the United States are very different from those in Asia, where patterns of interaction are prescribed based on age, gender, and socioeconomic status. The relationship between parent and child is well defined, and children are expected to be obedient and dutiful, bringing honor to the family and in general causing no conflict. In the United States, however, particularly in contemporary society, children are outspoken and expect their opinions to be considered in all decisions. They make their choices at an early age, and parents encourage independence.

USAsians, growing up as they do in a bicultural environment, though still influenced strongly by parental expectations, are nevertheless not so bound by traditional role relationships. Taught in schools to be assertive and involved, they take a more active role in their families.

They are not as outspoken as their American counterparts, but they are not as reticent as their parents were as children. Since Asian American parents are also affected by U.S. culture, they are less likely to maintain the same kind of parent-child relationship as that found in their families of origin.

The literature suggests that by the third generation, immigrant families, even those of color, are well integrated and often assimilated into the norms of U.S. society. Although the parents of second-generation USAsians may teach them about their culture, their experience already differs from the usual one in Asian countries. Patterns of childrearing are strongly influenced not only by the family but also by the larger community and the society. So while USAsians must consciously decide what traditions—such as foods, holiday festivities, clothes, dance, music, and religion—they will transmit to their children, patterns of parent-child interaction are not as readily controlled. Despite tradition, then, third-generation USAsian children of the twenty-first century will behave more like their American counterparts than like either their USAsian parents or their Asian immigrant grandparents. Sometimes USAsians make conscious decisions about how they will or will not repeat their upbringing with their children; at other times ingrained beliefs die hard. Chow (1998) reports that both she and many of the women she interviewed, like their Asian American parents, found that they were placing a great deal of focus on the academic performance of their children. While Chow as a psychotherapist knows that such pressure may not be in the best interests of the child, she is still unable to find a lowered commitment to education acceptable. Because of her awareness of the U.S. culture, though, she may be more willing to make allowances in other areas. USAsians have to decide to what extent their childrearing practices will reflect their culture of origin and to what extent they will reflect their culture of destination. They will also need to note that childrearing, even in a USAsian family in the twenty-first century, is vastly different now than in earlier times. As USAsians raise children in an increasingly diverse society, the influence of other cultures will infiltrate the home, making USAsian children of the twenty-first century ever more like other children in the United States.

Interracial, Biracial, and Transracial

Most societies of the world have traditionally frowned upon marriages or intimate extramarital relationships between people of different socioeconomic backgrounds. Prohibition against marriages and extramarital relationships between two people of different races has been even more common. Prejudice, lack of trust, fear, concern about contamination of bloodlines, and a variety of other economic and psychosocial factors, endemic in U.S. history and transmitted through generations, have worked in concert to prevent intermarriage between races or ethnic groups. Prohibitions against intermarriage and severe social ostracism have not only affected the marital relationships of people who, against all odds, marry outside their race but have had immeasurable effects on the lives of their offspring, whether biological or adopted. Although miscegenation[5] is becoming somewhat more acceptable, it still raises concerns in U.S. society and has significant implications for mixed-race families.

Interracial marriage. Antimiscegenation laws in the United States appeared as early as 1661. Passed during colonial times and the early years of slavery, they were designed to protect the rights of white slaveholders from claims on their property by children born of relationships with slaves. Penalties for disobedience were harsh. Subsequently, the majority of the states passed antimiscegenation laws as a means to prevent marriages that would contaminate the white bloodline. By 1920 thirty of the forty-eight states had such laws, and marriages that took place in the remaining eighteen states were not recognized in the thirty that did have them. Punishment carried high fines and long prison sentences. In 1883 the U.S. Supreme Court upheld an Alabama statute against sexual relations even outside marriage between people of different races. While these laws did not entirely erase the occurrence of interracial relationships, they greatly curtailed them.

Established to prevent marriage between blacks and whites, antimiscegenation laws soon were generalized to prevent marriages between whites and other races, and then were further broadened to encompass all intermarriage. While the antimiscegenation laws affected all Asians in the United States, those who were most severely affected were the Chinese who arrived as laborers in the United States in the latter half of the nineteenth century. Most were either unmarried or came without their wives, hoping to become wealthy and return to China. Not only were they unable to accumulate any wealth because of exploitation and difficulty in saving, but most did not have the means to return to China. Immigration laws prevented the immigration of women, and except for a few prostitutes no Chinese women entered the country. Thus the immigration and antimiscegenation laws worked together to force these early Chinese immigrants into solitary lives. Many of them turned to alcohol, gambling, and dance halls to fill their lonely hours, behavior that resulted in extremely negative stereotypes about the Chinese male during that period.

Early male immigration from Japan was followed by female immigration, since women were able to enter the United States to be reunited with their spouses under the Gentlemen's Agreement with Japan. Since the men were required to show that they had the means to support their wives, they developed a system in which several men pooled their resources into one account, then one man at a time presented it as evidence that he had sufficient assets to support a wife. The long-standing Asian tradition of arranged marriages was transformed into the picture bride system, and the Japanese man in the United States married his bride in absentia. She was then able to immigrate to the United States. Thus the Japanese were not as greatly affected as were the Chinese. However, early Indian immigrants, like the Chinese, did not have a means of bringing in women from India. The majority returned to their homeland when they found that they could not become citizens, could not own property, could not bring in women from India, and could not marry someone of a different race.

Miscegenation laws persisted in many U.S. states until as recently as 1967, when the landmark case of *Loving v. Virginia* brought an end to them. In 1958 a white bricklayer, Richard Loving, married a black woman, Mildred Jeter, in Washington, D.C., since interracial marriages were illegal in their home state of Virginia. When they returned, they were indicted for having violated Virginia's Racial Integrity Act of 1924. The trial judge suspended their one-year jail sentence but required that they leave the state for a period of twenty-five years for the crime of violating the 1924 act, saying:

> Almighty God created the race's [*sic*] white, black, yellow, malay and red, and he placed them on separate continents. And, but for the interference with his arrangement, there would be no cause for such marriage. The fact that he separated the races shows that he did not intend for the races to mix.

After having gone through a number of appeals, the case was finally heard by the U.S. Supreme Court as Case No. 395 on April 10, 1967. On June 12, 1967, the court decided, with the guidance of Chief Justice Warren, that under the Constitution, the rights of individuals to marry cannot be infringed upon by the state. Sixteen states in 1967 still upheld antimiscegenation laws; they were forced to erase them. As recently as March 2000, Bob Jones University, a Christian college in Greenville, South Carolina, upheld its ban on interracial dating, and even when the ban was lifted, students were informed that they would have to receive written permission from their parents if they wished to date someone of a different race. The ban had been established in the 1950s to prevent relationships between whites and Asians; African American students were not admitted to the university until 1970 (Hebel and Schmidt 2000).

Although intermarriage was illegal in many states in the first six and a half decades of the twentieth century, several individuals challenged the constitutionality of the laws, and Asian Americans occasionally were among them. Filipino Salvador Roldan, for example, challenged the antimiscegenation law in California that prevented his marriage to a white woman (Ethnic News Watch 1996). Interracial marriages, however, did occur with Asians, particularly between the Japanese and European Americans, and they began in earnest during World War II. After the Korean War (1950–1953), war brides from Korea contributed to the next large wave of interracial marriages.

Asian American attitudes toward interracial marriage. It is not only Americans and Europeans who are skeptical about interracial relationships. All societies evidence concern about a number of effects of such unions, both real and imagined, that they believe are not in the best interests of their members. Even in their own countries Asians have hesitated to sanction marriages between people of different backgrounds (Kitano and Kitano 1998; Min 1998; Segal 1998; Tran 1998). Concerns about interracial marriage in the United States between Asian Americans and non-Asians have carried these taboos and also have included highly xenophobic concerns.

Traditional issues about exogamous marriage have focused on contamination of the purity of the bloodline. The concern is that someone who is not of the same racial and ethnic background dilutes the purity of the race. Asian Americans, particularly immigrants, fear the loss of their cultural identity, heritage, and values. As it is, USAsians tend to assimilate to a large degree with the dominant U.S. culture and identify with their Asian roots a great deal less than do their immigrant parents, and such behavior alarms the latter. An exogamous marriage can only exacerbate the situation. That marriages in the United States evidence such a high rate of divorce, 50 percent within the first two years, is particularly troublesome to Asian Americans. Divorce in most Asian cultures carries a substantially greater stigma than it does in the United States, including ostracism, particularly of women, in their countries of origin. Asian American parents worry about the futures of their children whose marriages may not last.

In traditional Asian families, arranged marriages were the norm. The spouse was chosen for the adult child by the parents, who evaluated the family, the personal background, and the qualities of the potential spouse. Matches were sought between people of similar backgrounds so that there would be status, economic, educational, and cultural compatibility. The personal wishes and concerns of the individuals to be married were less important, as marriage represented the uniting of two families to perpetuate them, the culture, and the society. While arranged marriages are still fairly common in many Asian countries, and even among South Asians in the United States, most are now modified to take into consideration the wishes of the couples involved. Arranged marriages never involve exogamy, however, and most Asian American parents do not prefer interracial marriages.

Despite concerns about interracial marriages, a poll conducted by the National Opinion Research Center of the University of Chicago in 1990 (Smith 1991) revealed that Asians and Hispanics are more tolerant of the idea of interracial marriage than are African Americans. While 65.3 percent of African Americans stated that they would be opposed to their relatives marrying a non-black, a far lower 41.2 percent of Hispanics and 41.7 percent of Asian Americans indicated such opposition. Similarly, white opposition to marriage to an Asian American (42.4 percent) was slightly higher than that to a Hispanic (41.5 percent) but substantially lower than to African Americans (57.5 percent). Although it is clear that many Americans are opposed to the intermarriage of racial and ethnic groups, there are a number of marriages in the United States between USAsians and non-Asian Americans. The 2000 census reports that more than 1.6 million individuals identified themselves as being of mixed race (Asian and other), indicating a high frequency of such interracial relationships.

Exogamy among Asian Americans. The first wave of interracial couples in the United States consisted of about 30,000 American soldiers and their Japanese brides who married in Japan during World War II and moved to the United States during the 1940s and 1950s after immigration laws were changed to allow their entry. These couples received little attention when they arrived, and more than half a century later, a number of the women who are still alive are unassimilated, with some unable to speak English with comfort.

When they left Japan for the United States, many women were disowned by family members. Perceived by their families and Japanese society as opportunists who chose to escape the destruction of war, they arrived in the United States at a time when discrimination against those who looked non-European continued to be high. Reports abound of threats made to Japanese women and their American husbands. Not only were these couples not accepted by the dominant American society, they were further isolated by the rejection of most Japanese Americans (Noriyuki 2000). The second wave of war brides, close to 80,000 in number, came from Korea in the 1970s and 1980s, since many U.S. servicemen were stationed there. Many of them fared as poorly as did the Japanese war brides (Min 1998). Asian women who had married African American soldiers experienced much more severe rejection, even from their own families.

Times are changing, however. In the 1960s, when Thurgood Marshall was only months away from an appointment to the Supreme Court, he could not lawfully live with his wife in Virginia because he was African American and she was Asian, but in the 1990s another well-known African American and Asian American couple has not faced such discrimination. Eldrick Woods Sr. and his Thai wife, Kultida, have been widely praised for rearing their now famous son, golf champion Tiger Woods, whom many people envision as a symbol of a postracial age (Sailer 1997).

Kim (2000) applauds the present society and current generation of USAsians, when old ideas about who is an American are being replaced with possibilities for new American identities. Much of this progress has resulted from the efforts of numerous people who in the second half of the twentieth century challenged race and gender discrimination. Now, not only do antimiscegenation laws no longer prevent marriage between the races, but especially among the current adolescent generation, a much greater acceptance of multiracial people and less-stereotypical definitions of identity are evident.

Researchers and demographers, including census takers, agree that interracial marriage is on the rise, and they view such unions as an advance in race relations and a decline in racism (Besharow and Sullivan 1996). That almost half of all third-generation USAsians marry non-Asians also suggests an increasing rate of assimilation, for in order to inter-marry, one must accommodate and internalize cross-cultural values and patterns of behavior. For intermarriage to occur, opportunity for social contact must exist. Such contacts are influenced by the size of the group, however. The smaller the minority group, the fewer opportunities there are for its members to interact and the greater likelihood there is for them to marry exogamously (Qian 1999); Hispanics and USAsians are more likely to marry outside their groups than are African Americans, whose rate of outmarriage is one-third that of Hispanics or Asian Americans.

Through an analysis of the U.S. Census Bureau's 1998 Current Population Survey, researcher William H. Frey found that one-fifth of all married Asian American women have married someone of a different race twice as often as Asian American males have (Suro 1999). The discrepancy in the rate of intermarriage among USAsian women and USAsian men has been reflected in a number of demographic studies. Fujino, however, (1997) found that patterns of interracial dating were similar for the genders. Among USAsians of Indian origin, many males date European American women yet marry Indian Americans whom they have met and courted in the United States or women with whom marriages have been arranged either in the United States or in India. However, Indian USAsian women who date European American men tend to marry them (Segal 1998). This pattern provides explanation for the results of both Fujino's (1997) study and the findings of the U.S. Census Bureau, perhaps reflecting the patriarchal need to maintain bloodline, tradition, and culture through the male.

The Asian Americans who are most likely to marry non-Asians are usually those living in areas with relatively small Asian populations. In avant-garde California, however, where the Asian and Latino populations are high, close to one of every twelve European Americans marries either an Asian American or a Hispanic. Thus the absence of other Asians encourages Asian intermarriage, and the presence of a large Asian population increases the frequency of contact between the dominant society and Asian Americans, lowering barriers, minimizing stereotypes, and therefore increasing the opportunity for members of both communities to meet and establish personal relationships.

Interracial marriage is even higher among young people. Thirty percent of married USAsians between the ages of fifteen and twenty-four
are married to someone outside their race, and among third-generation
USAsians, the percentage rises to fifty. Furthermore, when Asians marry
outside their group, they overwhelmingly select white spouses. In addition to the greater availability of whites as potential mates, much has
been written about "Eurogamy," Asian Americans' preference for white
spouses (Hall 1997). Both East Asians and South Asians have long
valued fair skin and Occidental features, reflections of well-ingrained
beliefs of white superiority and the experience of white colonialism.
One indicator of the desire to feel "white" is the common practice of
eyelid surgery among East Asians (Jeong 1999). Immigrants to the
United States from South Asia have constantly sought ways to prove
themselves as "white" (Mazumdar 1989) and to dissociate themselves
from people of color, particularly African Americans. In the 1990s
the movie *Mississippi Masala* portrayed a sensual romance between a
one-and-a-half-generation USAsian of Indian origin and an African
American male; the Indian family's dismay stemmed not so much from
the sensuality but more from the relationship with a black man. The
reaction among Indian Americans reflected the fictional family's
response, and the community overwhelmingly believed that such a
liaison was far-fetched. A subplot of a movie released in 2000, *Romeo
Must Die*, has to do with a romance between a Chinese man and an
African American woman. While not the focus of the movie, it portrays
a relationship that has never before been reflected in the American
movie industry. Interracial movie relationships with Asians have always
involved European Americans.

    Besides the long-established preference for "whiteness," Asian Amer-
icans recognize that marriage to an African American can present barriers to assimilation and access to a better quality of life (Keown 1986).
For Asian Americans, particularly women, marriage to a European
American with light skin is regarded as an invaluable asset in the quest
for assimilation (Hall 1997). Since the offspring of such a marriage are
almost always children of lighter skin and more-Western features, the
process of adjustment and assimilation for them is easier (Hall 1997).

    In general, and across cultures, women have tended to marry men
who are their social and economic superiors. A comparison of characteristics of those who intermarry indicates that intermarriage is more
likely among those who are more educated than among those who have

little education. In exogamous marriages, it is more common for white males to marry Hispanic and African American women who are less educated than themselves, but they marry USAsian women who are better educated (Qian 1999). Consistent with traditional patterns, white women marry men of color who have more education than themselves. Asian Americans who marry exogamously tend to be USAsians, female, older, better educated, with higher occupational status and with higher incomes (Sung 1990). These USAsian women may exchange educational and occupational status for the status of being accepted by the dominant society through intermarriage to men who are their social and economic inferiors. USAsian women frequently mention their dislike of the traditional patriarchal relationships that they observed in their families of origin and state that they hope to avoid such outcomes by marrying a European American (Kitano et al. 1998). Nevertheless, USAsians who are very highly educated appear to prefer endogamous[6] marriages (Qian 1999).

Intramarital issues. Individuals in an exogamous[7] marriage must contend with a number of familial and societal pressures. Despite the increasing acceptance of such unions (Smith 1991), marriage between Asian Americans and non-Asians still raises concerns, at the very least among the members of the couple's respective families. From early childhood, most USAsian children learn that although a non-USAsian might be acceptable, the family would prefer a marriage within the community. This attitude means that USAsians seeking to marry exogamously must struggle with their own families' responses as well as those of the (usually) European American families, who may not approve of intermarriage with minorities.

Even after mollifying their own families, interracial couples must go through life facing society's stereotypes of exogamous relationships and the perceived reasons that people marry outside their own groups. For many outside the marital dyad, it is difficult to accept that most people intermarry for the same reasons that others marry endogamously (Root 1998b). They marry for love, companionship, security, and the range of other acceptable and sometimes less than admirable reasons. The experience of discrimination or, at the very least, the recognition that they are "different" is common for the USAsian. In an interracial marriage, however, European American partners are for the first time dramatically exposed to prejudice through their intimate association with USAsians, causing additional stress in the relationship. Most mixed-race couples must therefore face both familial and societal barriers that threaten their relationship.

As interracial couples establish a life together, they may prove to be more apt to develop strong bonds and an ability to adapt and adjust to each other than those who encounter fewer obstacles. And because they must cope with racism and other conflicts, they may be able to view the daily difficulties of marriage from a different perspective, rendering them less threatening to the relationship. On the other hand, cultural differences that have a significant influence upon daily living affect the stability of interracial relationships. Real differences may exist in gender roles, patterns of communication, methods of childrearing, relationships with members of the extended families, religious beliefs, values, and expectations. Differences may also exist because of perceptions based on long-established stereotypes—for example, if the European American male expects a submissive and sensual USAsian female, and the latter expects an equal-partner relationship, the very foundation of the relationship can crumble.

Responsibilities that USAsians may feel toward members of the extended family and aging parents could also cause difficulties in the marriage if non-Asian partners do not recognize the significant hold of filial piety. Despite the exposure to American traditions, USAsians, like all individuals, are greatly shaped by their families of origin, many of whom adhere strongly to Asian beliefs and traditions. Many USAsians in interracial marriages, even those who are highly Americanized, find that their Asian backgrounds emerge dramatically with the birth of children, and they experience the need to perpetuate their traditions and share their culture with their offspring (Chow 1998).

These and other differences that are a basic part of one's identity and that color one's worldview must be communicated, understood, negotiated, and compromised in interracial marriages. Marriage to someone of the same background is itself a process of communication, negotiation, compromise, and adaptation. In interracial marriages, the concerns common to all marriages are multiplied by cultural differences and extramarital pressures. Those who commit to these relationships must be commended for their ability to persevere in the face of such obstacles.

Biracial/Multiracial Heritage

Approximately 310,000 interracial marriages were reported to the U.S. Census Bureau in 1970. By 1998 the number had soared to more than 1.5 million, with the number of biracial and multiracial children quadrupling to an estimated 2 million. The 2000 Census shows a significantly larger number, as 6,828,228 people reported bi- or multiracial heritage. Since the abolition of the antimiscegenation laws, and the increases in interracial marriages, the United States has become the breeding ground of a "biracial baby boom" (Root 1992), but society has only just begun to develop an awareness that when two races unite, the offspring belongs to neither one nor the other but to a third category of "race" that has been created by the union. As the mixed-race population increases in size and begins to research and understand the experience of integrating different cultures in its definition of self, the awareness of its unique position and needs will be raised in the nation.

For too long, society has forced biracial[8] individuals to identify with one race. During slavery in the United States, miscegenation resulted in dilemmas about how to classify children who were half-white and half-black, or those who were one-quarter black, or one-eighth black. The outcome was the infamous one-drop rule, which required anyone with even a trace of black blood to be classified as black. This rigid categorization was upheld by the U.S. Supreme Court in 1896 in the case of *Plessey v. Ferguson*, when Homer Plessey, who was one-eighth black, was not permitted to ride in a railroad car reserved for whites. For the first time, in the 2000 U.S. Census, people of mixed heritage had the option of identifying themselves as belonging to more than one racial category. They were not, however, permitted to identify themselves as multiracial; they were required to identify themselves as belonging to multiple races, which advocates for mixed-race people believe is different from being multiracial.

Until the end of the twentieth century, however, regardless of their burgeoning numbers, biracial people were still identified with one race. In European-minority marriages, children are usually phenotypically more similar to the parent of color, and in mixed-minority marriages one parent's racial traits tend to dominate. Children were always identified with the race whose physical characteristics were dominant. Even with greater awareness of biculturalism, individuals must still respond to the question "But what are you really?" Biracial children growing up in the 1960s through much of the 1990s had to choose to which group they belonged (Robertson 2000). Especially in the earlier decades, the issue did not arise, as it was decided for them. When biracial individuals are forced to select a racial identification, they are expected to deny a part of themselves and a segment of their families. Mura (1998) suggests that although skin (or phenotype) may not be the most accurate reflection of one's identity, it often defines one's perceptions and allegiances.

Even with growing awareness of biracial identities, biracial children may still select a minority classification because they constantly struggle with the belief that their appearance identifies them (Ryckman 1998). They often echo a teenager from Houston who says, "Biracial people have a harder time being accepted by others. . . . I have always hung out with Asian people, simply because I look more Asian than Jewish" (Wang 1999). And when an individual's appearance does not reflect the minority lineage, the person might feel barred from that heritage (See 1998).

Just as American society has been less than welcoming to biracial individuals, the ethnocentrism of most Asian cultures has operated to ensure their xenophobia toward biracial Asian Americans. Asian communities in their homelands have traditionally rejected the offspring of interracial liaisons. The increase in numbers of biracial children often occurs during and after wars; many, born of American fathers, were found in Japan after World War II; in Korea, Japan, and the Philippines after the Korean War; and in Vietnam and the Philippines after the Vietnam War. Some military personnel who had been stationed in Asian countries brought back their war brides and raised biracial children in the United States. Most of these mixed-heritage children were ostracized to a great degree, even if they were born within wedlock, and found that they were unacceptable to the society of either parent. Particularly in the homelands of their Asian parents, many were abused and subjected to cruel social conditions. The Amerasian Homecoming Act of 1987 sought to provide refuge for some of the 40,000 to 50,000 Vietnamese children born of American fathers. These young people experienced extreme distress, maltreatment, and degradation, often because they were fatherless and nearly always because they were of mixed blood.

Biracial children born of Asian women and the American men stationed in the Pacific Rim for more than half a century accounted for the initial surge in their numbers in the United States. The children were often known as war babies and carried associations of illicit sex, though many were the offspring of committed, long-term unions (Felsman et al. 1989). Beginning in the last quarter of the twentieth century, a dramatic increase in exogamous marriages of Asian Americans occurred, which has resulted in a rapid rise in the number of biracial USAsian children. For the first time the U.S. census has responded to the cry of biracial and multiracial people to be allowed to identify themselves as such. Not only do interracial marriages embody the xenophobia culturally ingrained into most Asians, but they also reflect concerns about loss of heritage, cultural identity, and values—and the mistrust of interracial marriages extends to the biracial products of such marriages. With the continuing growth of interracial marriages in the United States, and with the disproportionate numbers of marriages between Europeans and Asians, both the dominant community and the Asian American communities will have to contend with the baby boom of biracial USAsian children. "The various social and political contexts within which the Amerasian[9] has emerged have very different implications for identity, adjustment, and cultural transmission" (Root 1998b:264).

The 2000 U.S. Census reports that 1,655,830 individuals identified themselves as being of mixed Asian/non-Asian heritage. Of these, 868,395 (0.3 percent of the total population) were of mixed Asian-white heritage; another 138,802 (<0.1 percent of the population) were of mixed Asian–African American heritage; 106,782 (<0.1 percent of the population) were of Asian–Hawaiian/Pacific Islander heritage; and 249,108 (0.1 percent of the population) were of Asian–some other race heritage. The most significant of the changes for biracial Asian Americans of the twenty-first century is that the majority of them are USAsian, neither Asian immigrants nor the one-and-a-half generation of Asian Americans. Unlike Amerasians of earlier decades since World War II, when many were conceived in their mothers' homelands or their mothers came as young brides to the United States, the biracial Asian Americans of the twenty-first century are the offspring of USAsians who were born and reared with their non-Asian American counterparts. Most have no binational experience (Root 1998b) and are growing up in an age when exogamous marriage does not elicit the same degree of xenophobia it did in the 1960s and before. These children are not the progeny of U.S. political excursions into foreign lands, and the rise in the Asian American population ensures that their Asian features are not quite the anomaly that they were in earlier decades.

What, then, of O'Hearn's (1998) anthology of writings by authors concerned about individuals who are "half and half," writings that contribute to the understanding of the intricacies of being biracial? They challenge the existing frameworks of society that are unable to accommodate multiracial and multicultural affiliations. They discuss the modicum of schizophrenia that is necessary to survive in cultures that have contradictory norms (Ganesan 1998). While many biracial USAsians feel they do not fit into either of the racial categories of their heritage, research has found that most do not differ from monoracial USAsians in the amount of psychological distress they experience, in their psychological adjustment, in their sense of competence, or in their level of self-esteem (Cauce et al. 1992; Mass 1992).

Researchers and scholars have only recently begun to address the identification dilemma for biracial individuals. Because many from this population who are now in positions to conduct research grew up during a period when intermarriage was less prevalent, the issues they explore may reflect the ones that they themselves faced. In this multiracial America, the extent and depth of struggles depicted in anthologies such as Maria Root's *Racially Mixed People in America* (1992) or Claudine O'Hearn's *Half and Half* (1998) may not reflect the changing experience of the biracial youth of the twenty-first century. While some undoubtedly experience difficulties in discovering their niche in society, perhaps just as many are comfortable identifying themselves with more than one race. U.S. society may not yet be ready for these outspoken bicultural youth, many of whom challenge social, political, and economic decisions made on the basis of race.

As researchers struggle with theory, issues of validity and reliability, and control groups, biracial youth are speaking to the media about the increase in their numbers and their ability to mainstream as they find a population like themselves. Although they must still counter societal preconceptions, decide who they are, and assess the extent to which their mixed heritages affect them, they no longer feel quite the need to identify themselves with only one race. This development provides a level of comfort for the present generation of biracial youth that was previously nonexistent. As indicated in the Root (1992) and O'Hearn (1998) anthologies, many biracial writers and scholars of biracial issues belong to the middle-adult and older stages of life. Their struggles to find a voice and establish an identity may have been more difficult, since they lacked biracial cohort support of sufficient magnitude and their interracial parents were so divorced from tradition and isolated from their respective communities that they had little to offer their children in the quest for self-understanding. Author Pearl Fuyo Gaskins, a forty-two-year-old biracial USAsian, says of her childhood, "Back then there was more of a sense of isolation, of being ignored. . . . There wasn't a consciousness that being mixed was, in and of itself, an identity. It was lonely" (Clemetson 2000a:72). For many of today's biracial adolescents, their parents serve as the advocates for their multiethnicity, helping them respond to the barbs of the prejudiced and making them aware of potential stereotypes that they may encounter. In this positive context, many twenty-first-century biracial individuals do not experience the same feelings of alienation that their parents endured a mere two and a half decades ago. To present-day biracial youth, the lines of race are blurred, faded, and antiquated (Robertson 2000), since they choose to consider themselves multiracial. Many children are being raised not identifying with any single part of their heritage but honoring all its facets, and although they may evidence some confusion they need not deny any part of themselves, as earlier biracial generations were forced to do. While such confusion may appear to touch the very core of one's being, it may help to acknowledge that there are always different rules for different environments, regardless of whether one is biracial or monoracial, and many of them conflict with each other. The successful individual is one who can accommodate the varying expectations of the situation and the time. If situations require behaviors that reflect alternative cultural traditions, adapting to them may not be as stressful as it has heretofore been. Much depends on society's acceptance as well as on the particular races in the biracial person's heritage. Since biracial Asians have a "flexible look," their identification may reflect situational ethnicity that is an adaptive strategy to situational demands and changes in the meaning of ethnicity and acceptance (Root 1998b). On the other hand, those who do not look Asian but identify themselves as such may experience distress and disqualification when society registers its disbelief of their Asian heritage (Chao 1995).

None of this provides a niche in the United States for those who are biracial USAsians. A number of questions emerge regarding this population: (1) Who is a biracial Asian American? Inextricably interwoven in this question is whether a biracial Asian American is an Asian American; (2) How does U.S. society perceive the biracial Asian American? Is this person seen as an Asian American, a white (if one parent is white), or an African American (if one parent is African American), and so on? (3) How does the Asian American community accept biracial individuals? Are they viewed as inferior, equal, or superior? (4) How do these biracial individuals identify themselves?

While still looking somewhat Asian, biracial USAsians (whether they have either East or South Asian parentage) tend to look more like a blend of their Asian and Euro- or African American parents. The biracial children of African American and Euro-American parents, whose physical characteristics more often primarily reflect their African heritage, are frequently forced by society to identify themselves as African American. Asian–African American children may have the option of more comfortably moving between their parental cultures. Asians themselves, however, often indicate a desire to look more European, and most Asian parents agree that if their children must marry a non-Asian, they would prefer a European American to someone of another minority group. Thus, with increasing societal openness toward mixed heritage, the USAsian tendency to Eurogamy may be reinforced. Since biracial USAsians born of a European American parent look more European, they may more readily be accepted by the dominant culture. With the advent of exogamy unrelated to political strife, although Asian American parents may still express concern about intermarriage and the loss of racial purity, culture, and tradition, the implications of interracial relationships during times of war are not applicable anymore. With greater general acceptance of exogamy, Asian American parents may be moving toward more tolerance of such liaisons and more acceptance of biracial grandchildren. Research suggests that the racial identification of biracial children with one Asian parent as Asian is an arbitrary option within the current racial classification system. It takes into account a number of factors, including the child's characteristics, the parents' characteristics, and the geographic community's racial composition (Xie and Goyette 1998). Other studies suggest that Asian ethnic identity also evolves from other variables, such as interdependence with family, a sense of connectedness to heritage and tradition, and a belief that achievement is a reflection upon the family and group. For one to truly identify with a specific group, however, three aspects of ethnic identity must be present:. There must be a consciousness of the ethnic identity, the individual must adopt that ethnic identity, and he or she must behave in a way that reflects the ethnic identity, through adherence to norms, values, and traditions.

Clearly, these three aspects, in addition to environmental factors and societal acceptance of biracial individuals, must be evidenced among biracial USAsians who successfully identify with their group. Because of their flexible features, biracial USAsians, more than any other ethnic group, may need to make these decisions consciously, while those of other ethnic groups may have their identity thrust upon them by society. As the size of the biracial and multiracial USAsian population grows, and as it continues to intermarry, color lines will continue to blur. Instead of categories of color, the United States will display a color continuum. Asian Americans, like other ethnic groups, worry that the intermingling of genes and traditions will result in the termination of the Asian American community as it becomes absorbed into the dominant culture. Others do not fear such absorption, instead predicting the development of such a modified mainstream that Americans will have to define themselves along lines other than those founded on racial and ethnic identities (Belsie 1999).

Transracial Adoption

The literature on Asian Americans and USAsians is growing rapidly, as is the size of the population. A glaring gap in both theoretical and empirical publications, however, is the phenomenon of international adoption of children from Asian countries. Collected volumes such as Root's *The Multiracial Experience* (1996), which includes a chapter on interracial adoptions, and Lee and Zane's *Handbook of Asian American Psychology* (1998), exclude the adoption of Asian children by Americans (or even by Asians). The available information comes most often from the medical field and focuses on the health conditions of children adopted outside the United States. While there is a small body of extant literature on transracial adoptions of African American children by European American parents, issues of psychosocial adjustment, raising children from other cultures, and perceptions of transnational adoption have received little attention. These areas of inquiry are only now beginning to be discussed and are explored primarily in the news media, which often focus on personal stories of the adoptees or the adoptive parents. International adoptions are continuing to rise, however, and when children are adopted from non-European countries, transracial and transcultural issues must be addressed.

Who adopts, why, and why internationally. In the United States people who adopt children are usually married, white, childless, experiencing problems with fertility, and with higher levels of education and income (Moorman and Hernandez 1989; Mosher and Bachrach 1996). While the actual number of adopted children is not known, it is estimated to be as high as five million (Hollinger 1998), with between 2 percent and 4 percent of all American families having adopted children (Mosher and Bachrach 1996). In 1995 approximately 232,000 couples in the United States had taken steps toward adopting children (National Center for Health Statistics 1997), and between 11 percent and 24 percent of couples with infertility problems seek adoption (Mosher and Bachrach 1996). While transracial adoption is controversial, it accounts for almost 14 percent of all adoptions in the United States (Smith 1994); of these, the majority are from countries outside the United States (Vonk, Simms, and Nackerud 1999). The U.S. Immigration and Naturalization Service reported that the number of children adopted from abroad more than doubled (Lang 2000) from 1990 (7,093) to 1999 (16,396), with the primary sending countries in 1999 being Russia (4,348), China (4,101), Korea (2,008), and Guatemala (1,002). Since 1986, families in the United States have adopted more than 125,000 children from other countries (Miller 1999).

A number of conditions have directly influenced the availability of infants for adoption in the United States and the increase in international adoptions, among them readily available and effective methods of birth control, legalization of abortion, and relaxation of taboos against single motherhood. With the decrease of available healthy babies in this country (particularly those of European American descent), the high rate of infertility, the profile of those who are interested in adoptions, the controversy surrounding domestic transracial adoptions (Lefferman 1998), long waiting periods, and fears that birth parents may try to regain custody (Scrivo 2000), many European Americans are seeking adoption outside the borders of the United States. It is abundantly clear that many children in war-torn, Third World, and other disadvantaged countries benefit from adoption by a couple in the United States. Through adoption, children who have been abandoned, who are in orphanages, and who have been rejected by their own societies can be given an opportunity to survive, develop, and often experience good fortune to a degree unimaginable to the parents who had to leave them.

Many in the academic community are nevertheless critical of the ethics of transnational adoptions, taking the view that economic conditions place increased pressures on families and their governments to participate in international adoption (Vonk et al. 1999). Some believe that such adoptions are exploitative and victimize poorer countries (Trolley 1994) and suggest that since international adoptions involve large sums of money (up to $15,000 each), there ought to be concern about baby buying, as well as about abduction, trafficking, and the sale of infants (Freundlich 1999). Many believe that international adoption of Third World children by adults in developed countries exploits the women and children in the developing countries (Herrmann and Kasper 1992). Despite the concerns surrounding international adoptions, the increasing frequency of such adoptions indicates that a match exists between the supply of unwanted children in other countries and the demand for babies among European American parents in the United States.

Issues facing multinational families. In the first half of the twentieth century, and into the 1960s, adoption was a secret that was kept hidden. Parents adopted infants of the same race, often not informing them that they were adopted. When international adoptions occur with white babies from countries such as Rumania or Russia, it is possible to overlook cultural differences. With the adoption of children of color by European Americans, total assimilation into the mainstream or into the adoptive family is not truly possible. Given the number of adoptions of Asian children by Euro parents, it becomes especially important that theoreticians, researchers, and practitioners interested in the adjustment and welfare of Asian Americans include in their discourse the adoption of these children. It is clear that advocates for the Asian American population have not yet thought to include transracially adopted Asian Americans in their inquiries. Empirical information regarding the outcome of intercountry adoption is scarce, and professional human service communities give little attention to the adjustment of children from other nations.

American medical professionals share concerns about the health of babies now being adopted from Asia, since most of them are diagnosed with at least one major medical condition, including tuberculosis, intestinal parasites, or other infectious diseases (Hostetter et al. 1991; Miller 1999). Children from China are exhibiting disproportionately high levels of lead poisoning, with very elevated blood lead levels (Aronson et al. 2000). Most prospective parents receive little or no information about a child's health and are unprepared for the severe health and behavioral problems of children who have spent several years in orphanages or other institutions in countries such as Korea, China, and India (Scrivo 2000). Physicians are advising adoptive parents of the importance of recognizing the health care needs of children from other countries and encouraging them to provide primary and remedial care early (Quarles and Brodie 1998).

This concern about adoptees at the time of entry into the United States has not generalized to the social services. Adoptive parents still receive relatively little guidance as they attempt to integrate these foreign children into their European American families. Besides health concerns, adoptive parents of children from Asian countries (or any countries with people of color) must scrutinize their ideas about race. After all, Asian children have physiological characteristics that are decidedly different from their own. The parents must explore how they feel about being an interracial family and how they and their foreign-looking children are perceived by society. They must assess whether, as part of the majority, they can understand the experience of a minority child. They must decide whether they will raise their children as Euro-Americans or Asian Americans and if they will expose the children to their native cultures. The processes of growth and development are replete with difficulties for all. Adopted children struggle with concerns about who their birth parents were and why they were given up for adoption. For adoptees of Asian origin, learning of their heritage and establishing an identity in the midst of family members they do not resemble greatly magnifies the complexities of the situation (Chinn 1997).

Researchers of transracial adoptions find that parents tend to assume one of three distinct approaches to raising children of a different race (McRoy et al. 1984). The first is an approach of color blindness, the second is the acknowledgment of the adoptees' race and the need for same-race role models, and the third is identification of the family as an interracial family. The color-blind approach tends to produce children who deemphasize their minority heritage, believing that human identity is more important than racial identity. The second group acknowledges its mixed heritage, and while the children have friends of their ethnicity in the schools, they live in white communities. Among families that identify themselves as being multiracial in terms of friends, experiences, and residential community, the children reflect a high degree of comfort and allegiance to their minority identity. Most of the research in transracial adoptions has been conducted with African American children who are placed with European American families and has focused on self-esteem, racial awareness, and racial classification choice (McRoy and Hall 1996). Some concern exists that while

European American parents may be able to instill high self-esteem and pride in culture, they may not have the resources to provide minority children with necessary coping and survival skills (Miller and Miller 1990). However, a radical change has occurred in the half century since transracial adoptions from Asian countries began. The philosophy that the dissociation of children from their heritage and assimilation into the American society is best has been replaced by the conviction that children's background and heritage should be embraced and incorporated into their lives (Pertman 1999).

History of transracial Asian adoptions. The first wave of adoptions from Asia began in the 1950s, following the Korean War, and lasted until 1978. Harry Holt, an Oregon farmer and lumberman, is credited with the widespread acceptance of international adoption. In the mid-1950s, he used his savings to adopt eight Korean War orphans, and he launched a crusade to house the thousands who needed homes because of the war. Many of these children were the biracial offspring of American soldiers (Enrico 1999). Adoption across races had little precedent, and during the 1950s adoption practices were secretive, judgmental, and obscure. Early Korean adoptions had to be acknowledged, however, since the children did not look like their adoptive parents. Despite the difficulties and the discrimination encountered, practitioners, adoptive parents, and adoptees by and large agree that the international adoption of the children of the Korean War was a success. Since the 1950s, nearly 100,000 Koreans have been adopted by Americans and are living in the United States (Teicher 1999). This success has paved the way for other transracial and transnational adoptions.

One of the most significant difficulties experienced by Korean adoptees of this wave was the lack of recognition of their cultural heritage. Parents and social workers believed that the interests of these children would be best served if they severed their ties to the past, their culture, and their language and became integrated into their new situations as rapidly as possible (Teicher 1999). Adoptive Euro parents, concerned about not treating their adopted children differently, went to great lengths to convince them that they were no different from their biological children. In September 1999, approximately four hundred of the first generation of Koreans, adopted before 1978, met at the first International Gathering of Korean Adoptees in Washington, D.C. Reflecting on their childhoods, many said that their adoptive parents made them feel so assimilated that they thought of themselves as Caucasian and were surprised when people treated them as Asian. Some voiced frustrations about being Caucasians trapped in Korean bodies (Pertman 1999). In this process of adoption integration, many feel the loss of their birth parents and family, as do a number of adopted individuals who are placed in same-race families. They also experience the loss of a nation, a culture, and "the comfortable anonymity of growing up among people of the same race" (Enrico 1999). Almost all the Koreans interviewed at the gathering said they had encountered racial bias, but all insisted they were not scarred by it (Pertman 1999). The vast majority described life with their adoptive families as being positive and were grateful for them.

The next large wave of Asian adoptees came to the United States from Vietnam, most of them the children of U.S. servicemen stationed there. Like the biracial children of the Korean War, these Amerasian children were rejected and abused by the Vietnamese, and large numbers were adopted by European American parents beginning in the mid-1970s. Also like the Korean children, most were not infants when they arrived in the United States. Many were between the ages of three and five years and had already spent a large part of their short lives in orphanages, where they were victims of abuse and disease. In 1975, two years after the United States had withdrawn its forces from Vietnam, when Saigon fell under attack from the North Vietnamese, President Gerald Ford ordered the "Babylift" evacuation. More than four thousand Vietnamese babies were airlifted out of the country and flown to the United States for adoption, and about a hundred of these young adults met at the Vietnam War Memorial in April 2000 on the twenty-fifth anniversary of the fall of Saigon.

Unlike the adoptive parents of the first wave of Korean children, the adoptive European American parents of these Vietnamese children encouraged them to learn about their culture. And many, in the last twenty-five years, have taken the adoptees back for visits to Vietnam. They also attempted to integrate the children into their own lives, giving them American names to minimize the differences between them and the children of the majority culture (Thompson 2000). Many of these children were the only Asians in European American communities, and they experienced a sense of disconnectedness despite increased parental sympathy to their cultural dilemmas. The reunion in 2000 made several aware of what they had missed. One twenty-eight-year-old woman stated, "Here, maybe for the first time, I really feel like I fit in" (Pertman 2000). Not all of these children experienced a longing for others of Vietnamese descent. Nevertheless, meeting a group of young people like themselves made them aware of their isolation. The sentiment is captured in the words of a twenty-five-year-old man who attended: "I just came because I was curious, to be honest. But I discovered all these people who I have a common bond with, who have a story similar to mine. . . . It's a first for me, definitely; it's a feeling of connection that's different from any I've had before" (Pertman 2000). Despite the encouragement of adoptive parents, many Vietnamese adoptees chose to separate themselves from their Vietnamese identity rather than learning about their Vietnamese culture or their biological families. As they have grown into adulthood, some have become more willing to explore their backgrounds (Hudson 2000). Others, like other USAsians, find that when they return to their land of origin, they do not fit in, because although they look Vietnamese, their behavior is American (Pertman 2000). These young adoptees, like the majority of the Korean adoptees, feel closer to their adoptive families than to the biological ones with whom they may make contact (Hudson 2000).

The third wave of Asian adoptions began in the latter part of the 1990s, when large numbers of children came from China (first-wave Chinese adoptions) and South Korea (second-wave Korean adoptions). Smaller numbers have come from India and Sri Lanka. The majority of these children arrive with health and behavioral problems, but now, unlike the transnational adoptees of earlier decades, most have much more complete health records. The U.S. medical profession is also much more aware of their unique needs, and doctors urge adoption agencies to encourage adoptive parents to provide remedial and preventive care for the children as early as possible (McKenna 2000). Today's adoptive parents are much more knowledgeable about the ramifications of having a child who does not look like them. They also realize that they cannot raise the child without the support of other multiracial families like their own or without the support of the community in the United States that shares an ancestry with their children. The environment into which these new adoptees are brought is decidedly different from what earlier adoptees encountered. The United States, with its large numbers of Asians and other ethnic groups, no longer exhibits the profile of the 1950s, 1960s, or 1970s. The increasingly multicultural and multiracial environment and a heightened awareness of pluralism

ensure that transnationally adopted Asian children no longer feel the
extreme sense of isolation that once was commonplace. While these
young Asian adoptees must still struggle with issues of identity, adoption,
and diversity within their families, they are now likely to see other children who look like them, and non-Asian children are more likely to
have had contact with other Asian children. Furthermore, the slowly
growing acceptance of multiracial families bodes well for interracial and
international adoptions.

Adoptees adopt. A number of issues are involved in transracial adoptions. In addition to the normal difficulties of childrearing and family
life, transracially adopted children and their adoptive parents must constantly address issues of adoption and of race, culture, and health. They
must carve a niche for themselves is society and must cope with the
numerous stereotypical inclinations of society. Often, both intrafamilial
and extrafamilial concerns create stressful situations for these families.
To adopt a child of a different culture is not only a lifelong commitment, it is a commitment that continues through the generations, as
these minority children marry other minorities or European Americans
but produce offspring who will likely appear to be of minority heritage.
Not only the children but also the grandchildren of adoptive parents
will not look like them. Despite all of this and the difficulties of isolation that many adult Asian adoptees have voiced, most feel that they
truly belong in their adoptive families. One young Korean woman,
Laura Taylor, a college newspaper columnist, writes:

> Like most women, I find that I am more and more like my
> mother every day. People constantly confuse us on the phone
> and my mannerisms mimic hers. . . . I'm a lot like other mem-
> bers of my family, too. . . . My bull-headedness is reminiscent
> of my paternal heritage. . . . Nothing is really spectacular about
> a child inheriting certain characteristics from her parents and
> relatives. It happens all the time. But I was adopted . . . from
> Korea. . . . A lot of people ask me if I would like to seek out my
> "real" parents someday. . . . There was a good reason I was given
> up for adoption. . . . I know that I was definitely wanted by my
> parents. I've never heard of a surprise or unwanted adoption! . . .
> I may have inherited some things from my birth parents, but I
> am pretty sure that my family has made me who I am.

Attesting to the experience of adoption, many Asian adoptees are returning to their birthplaces to adopt children themselves (Enrico 1999; Teicher 1999; Wood 1998).

RETURN MIGRATION

Literature on early migration from Asia, particularly in the latter half of the nineteenth century, called the Chinese especially, but also later migrating groups such as the Japanese and the Indians, "sojourners." Although some expected to settle abroad permanently, the initial intent of most was to spend a few years working in the United States, accumulating sufficient wealth to support their families in Asia, and then to return to their homelands. A large number were not able to return, however, and those who did had few assets to take home with them.

Little has been written about the return migration of Asians from the United States to their homelands. Occasional articles have discussed the return of Japanese immigrants from South American countries such as Brazil (Tsuda 1999) and Peru (Takenaka 1999). Other articles have explored the return of Filipinos from other Asian countries (Aguilar 1999), but there appears to be no empirical literature that covers this phenomenon in the United States. Asian immigrants in the United States do, however, report that their friends and relatives have returned, particularly to Japan and India. There are media reports of Vietnamese who came to the United States in the 1970s returning to Vietnam to retire (Sevrens 2000). Community activists believe that in the twenty-first century, hundreds, if not thousands, of Vietnamese Americans will return to their homeland (Gold and Tran 2000). Among Asian immigrants, a fair number have retired from their occupations in the United States and quietly sought the environment of their own countries. Others report that upon returning to their Asian homelands they found that they could no longer adjust to the style or quality of life there, and so they came back to the United States. Still others find that returning to Asian countries on their American pensions and Social Security monies allows them to live more comfortably than they would be able to do in the United States.

Even less is known about the USAsians who are returning to the lands of their ancestors. Recent news reports indicate that a combination of factors, including the opening of economic opportunities, is attracting young USAsian entrepreneurs. Many voice the need to give back to the countries of their parents, while others say their motivation is to reclaim their heritage (Lamb 1997). But a large number of these USAsians do not return permanently to their homelands. Rather, they make their homes in both the United States and Asia, spending half the year in the United States and the other half in Asia (Dugger 2000; Gold and Tran 2000), moving comfortably between the two cultures that define them.

With the opening of borders and trade, the ease of international travel, the richness of telecommunications, and the unimaginable capacity of the information superhighway, the world is truly becoming a global village. In this village, multiculturalism will be the norm, and even as Asian Americans become more comfortable in the United States, European and African Americans will have more opportunity to be exposed to Asians and their cultures. The phenomenon of Asian migration to the United States over a century and a half may have come full circle, with USAsians now fulfilling the hopes of their immigrant parents, grandparents, and great-grandparents by returning to their homelands with enough wealth to live in comfort. Perhaps they are the ones who constitute the group that is truly bicultural, maintaining close contacts with the United States and enriching both countries while reaping the benefits of both.

9

Implications, Directions, and Action Guidelines

We forget that what makes us great comes not from the loud and flashy things we use to impress visitors, but from quiet abstracts that lie hidden most of the time in books. For instance, in this country—in theory and, sometimes, in fact—all of us are equal before the law, no one above it and no one below. In this country—in theory and, sometimes, in fact—a man is free to rule his own life, to seize his own fate, to make decisions for himself. And his children.

—Pitts 2000

As one looks at the immigrant experience in the United States, one is struck by the realization that for some this is the "land of opportunity" and endless possibilities, but for others it is a "field of dreams" where goals are unattainable. Many immigrants in the latter half of the twentieth century were highly successful, while others continued to struggle. A closer inspection reveals why people come, why most stay, and what that means for both them and native-born Americans. The nation is not without discrimination and prejudice, and historical and current experiences with immigrants and those who look different from the majority affect behavior toward "outsiders." Asian Americans, who have always looked like "outsiders," must cope with the perception of being alien, even if they are U.S.-born. This has most recently been evidenced in the fallout on those of South Asian descent who have been targeted for both physical and verbal violence after the terrorist attacks of September 11, 2001, on the World Trade Center in New York and the Pentagon in Washington, D.C. Such perceptions of Asian Americans as non-American have implications for the definition of self, affecting behavior and the ability to become an integral part of U.S. society. U.S. policymakers, service providers, and researchers, along with the Asian American community, need to work toward the inclusion of Asian Americans, recognizing commonalities and differences among and between the Asian groups and the implications for the United States. This growing population brings with it a number of advantages, as is evident in the contributions Asian Americans have made to the society in science and technology, as well as in a variety of other areas. They also contribute substantially to the economic base of the country and pay taxes. With the bimodal distribution of the population, however, Asian Americans also struggle with unmet health, education, and welfare needs, which can be a social, if not an economic, drain on the country. Lack of focus on the Asian American community, furthermore, suggests a lack of awareness of political, social, and cultural resources that can be tapped in a community that has much to offer besides its economic contributions.

WHY THEY COME, WHY THEY STAY

Individuals and families from around the globe form a continuous stream of immigrants to the United States. The backlog of visa applications and waiting lists stretches to several years. Undocumented immigrants, both those who enter without legal papers and those who overstay their visits, abound. Refugees and asylees from countries in political turmoil continue to enter in record numbers. Disproportionately large numbers of those who have entered the United States in recent years have been people of color from Asia, Africa, and South America, and despite encountering barriers in this country, an overwhelming majority remain, making this nation their permanent residence. Reasons for this ongoing influx are readily apparent, for in spite of the problems prevalent in the United States, it continues to be the most attractive nation on earth.

The United States offers much that is not available in other countries. "In theory, and, sometimes, in fact," this is a land of freedom, of equality, of opportunity, of a superior quality of life, of easy access to education, and of few human rights violations. It is a land that is struggling toward multiculturalism and pluralism in its institutions and social outlook. It is a land that, compared with others, offers newcomers a relatively easy path to becoming integrated into its largesse. While the debate over the value of immigration persists, the fact is that it is a debate, and while immigration policies are not without discrimination and selectivity, they are more open now than they have ever been here and they are more open than those of other nations.

Many U.S.-born Americans take for granted the numerous freedoms bestowed on them through their Constitution. The freedom of speech, the freedom of religion, the freedom to choose, the freedom of the press, the freedom to gather in public places, and the range of other freedoms that affect everyday life are not commonplace in all countries. Besides politically guaranteed freedom, other types of "freedoms" are intrinsic to the social fabric of the society. Individuals and families can make decisions that are less constrained by tradition and norms than in other countries. Rules of behavior are not as strictly regulated in the United States as they are elsewhere, and deviations from existing patterns do not usually result in social ostracism. An integral part of the value of freedom is the possibility of an existence relatively free of the many human rights violations found in a number of other nations. News reports do reveal that even in the United States, the rights of individuals and groups are occasionally violated, but perhaps because of society's penchant for sensational news, less is written about the many rights that human beings enjoy in the United States. While these rights may certainly be taken for granted because they are intrinsic to the culture, many do not value them until they find them violated in the United States or nonexistent in other nations.

At least in theory, in the United States all people are created equal, and therefore laws exist that protect those who may experience discrimination. While other nations may move toward such protections, no similar body of laws protects those who are different and those who are vulnerable from exploitation and harm. These laws aim to allow all individuals equal access to all the opportunities and services available in the country, and while they are not infallible, equality is more possible in this nation than in most others. Therefore, all individuals potentially have access to the wealth of opportunities that are available.

While many are attracted to the United States because of the freedom they may experience here and the release from political constraints, the majority enter because of the opportunities offered. In the United States one can be "anything one wants to be." Dedication, hard work, and competence are so valued that all people have the potential to maximize their abilities. Individuals are encouraged to seize success from among the myriad opportunities available. Theoretically, class or caste, gender, economic status, race, age, disability, or any other factor does not limit individuals in the United States. If they effectively use the available resources, it is possible for even penniless and uneducated

immigrants to become senators, astronauts, artists, sports figures, educators, business tycoons, or whatever else they choose to be. While they
may encounter obstacles along the way, most are not insurmountable.

Ready access to quality education, the availability of material comforts, and a lifestyle relatively free of societally imposed sanctions such
as those found in Asian nations ensure that most residents of the United
States experience a quality of life that is available to only a wealthy few
in Asia. The opportunities and amenities that the average U.S. resident
takes for granted—relatively inexpensive and good-quality higher education, hot and cold running water, uninterrupted electricity, a good
infrastructure of roads, buildings, and utilities—are not available even
to the wealthy in some nations, simply because they do not exist or are
inconsistent in quality. Thus, a number of factors, some tangible and
some intangible, attract immigrants to the United States, but almost
all of those who immigrate do so with the expectation of a quality of
life and experience that are superior to what they had access to in their
countries of origin.

Most remain for the same reasons they came. Having experienced
the quality of life and the freedom of the United States, they find little
reason to return to their countries of origin. While the ease of international transport has escalated the frequency with which immigrants
return to their homelands as visitors, only a few return permanently. Of
those few, some find that they no longer belong in the lands of their
birth. Years of living in the United States not only allow immigrants to
grow accustomed to the American lifestyle, but acculturation colors
perceptions, thinking, behavior, and other intangible aspects of their
lives in so profound a manner that many find they no longer hold the
same worldview with which they left their homelands.

The dilemma of being American arises for people of color, such as
Asians, who find that their physical characteristics so set them apart from
the dominant Euro-American population that even into the third and
fourth generations they are perceived as foreigners. Asian Americans,
even more than African Americans or Hispanic Americans, are viewed as
aliens. Since the United States has so long had populations from Latin
American countries and U.S.-born African Americans, first-generation
immigrants of color from African nations and Spanish-speaking
countries often find that they are grouped with and treated as Americans. While African Americans and Hispanic Americans are viewed as
minorities, Asian Americans are regarded as foreigners. Consequently,

and ironically, a large number of Asian Americans find that they are not an integral part of U.S. society and culture, but, at the same time, they no longer belong in their countries of origin.

CARVING AN IDENTITY

The receptiveness of the United States to Asians can go a long way in helping them to establish a healthy identity. The experience of most Asian Americans, however, is that they can never completely blend in with the dominant U.S. society and yet do not feel quite at home in their countries of origin. They must therefore carve a niche for themselves. Regardless of how "American" they feel, they still look Asian. If they ask themselves the question "When do I become an American?" in the United States at the beginning of the twenty-first century, the answer is "Never!" Although they may become (or be) Americans under the law by virtue of having attained U.S. citizenship, the general U.S. society does not yet see itself as sufficiently pluralistic to embrace the variety of peoples who have committed themselves to this country. While the immediate circle of friends of Asian Americans may be able to transcend perceptions based on physical characteristics, many individuals in the society will continue to reinforce the differences, responding to them only as Asians and aliens. Thus Asian Americans must always deal with issues of bicultural identity.

That identity is not merely the sum of their Asian and American identities, nor does it merely involve the inclusion of certain American characteristics and the rejection of others or the retention of only some Asian characteristics. What emerges is a synthesis of both American and Asian identities, in fact neither Asian nor American but a unique amalgam of both. This synthesis, moreover, differs between Asian American groups and among individuals within each group as they integrate those aspects of both cultures that help them most satisfactorily address the cognitive dissonance that arises in the face of conflicting values and beliefs. First-generation immigrants must decide the degree to which they will become American and embrace American values, beliefs, and behaviors and the extent to which they will remain Asian and retain Asian characteristics and values. Even as they consciously or unconsciously make these decisions, the American behaviors and attitudes that are internalized are flavored with Asian ingredients and their "Asianness" is touched with an American brush. For the second and subsequent generations, identity formation becomes even more perplexing, for they must decide the level at which they will become *Asian*. Developing in a society that predominantly looks different from them and being surrounded by non-Asian media that infiltrate even the sanctuary of the home, second-generation Asian Americans grow up being more American than Asian. They must consciously choose the degree to which they will adopt Asian values, tradition, culture, and lifestyle. The Asian characteristics that they do accept will be modified to fit in with their American personae and may not appear at all Asian to their parents. So second-generation Asian Americans find they look dramatically different from most of their peers, yet they feel and think differently from their parents and the older Asian American generation. The dilemma in establishing their identities revolves, then, around bridging differences in culture as well as differences between generations. First-generation immigrants from Asia must also deal with disparities between generations and cultures when their aging parents join them in this country and find that their children's styles of life and views of parental-child relationships have not remained quite as Asian as they had expected.

Asian Americans are also marrying outside their ethnic group, and more than any other ethnic group, they are marrying outside their race. The result is an ever-growing biracial population, usually with one Asian American parent and one Euro-American parent. This group, which tends to look more like its Asian American parent, faces an even greater challenge in establishing its identity. If its members define themselves as Asian, they are rejecting half of their being and not acknowledging the race of one parent, yet their phenotype causes others to categorize them and relate to them as Asians. As children, these individuals often find themselves in limbo. If they look more Euro-American than Asian, they may have the choice of "passing" as Euro-American and thereby can experience greater acceptance and integration into U.S. society—yet they also have to deal with being distanced from their Asian half. What they might experience is biracial identity confusion, which may be even more difficult to sort through than are the identity issues faced by those Americans whose parents are both Asian.

Belonging to an Ethnic Minority

Ethnic minority groups are often compared with the majority society, but people of color in the United States, while differing from each other substantially in their historical experience, have many experiences, and sometimes values, in common. The United States, land of immigrants, is composed of many peoples from different cultures, with differing values, so much so that it is almost impossible to truly identify that which is now "American." American values, attitudes, and perceptions have changed dramatically since the middle of the twentieth century. Currently, a significant part of the American population tends to hyphenate its ethnicity. One is no longer merely an American; one is an African American, a Mexican American, a Native American, an Asian American (further subdivided into Chinese American, Japanese American, Indian American, and so on), a Jewish American, an Italian American, or an Irish American. It is not only people of color who seek to establish their identities in connection with another country and culture. The difference between the last three ethnic groups and the former ones is merely the choice of the hyphenation. The last three groups have this alternative, or they may just call themselves American. People of color, on the other hand, are first identified by their nonwhite ethnicity, whether or not they wish to identify themselves with their ethnic group.

What do Asian Americans share with other Americans of color? Most obviously they share the experience of personal, social, and institutionalized discrimination. While the type and degree of discrimination and prejudice have varied, Americans of color have generally been treated as second-class citizens. While this experience binds them together, Asians are viewed with suspicion by other minorities of color because they have been successful in recent decades and are not perceived as "oppressed."

In addition to the lack of acceptance, all minorities of color stress a group commitment, strong family ties, and responsibility to their elders. Parental authority and control are greater in the minority family than in the Euro-American family, and discipline is more stringent. The egalitarian relationship that develops in the Euro-American family, even when children are very young, and that results in a high level of independence as children reach maturity, is noticeably absent in minority families, in which role relationships are much more clearly defined and maintained through the lifetimes of the family members.

While African Americans may be more American than African and have developed a culture that is also distinct from the majority culture, they are more similar to the Westerners portrayed in the list developed by the Vietnamese than to the Easterners. Even the overall Latino-Americans' perception of the world and their ability to control their universe appear more consistent with Euro-American than with Asian views. Yet most values, attitudes, and behaviors, whether seen as Eastern or Western, are human and can be placed on a continuum stretching from the singular to the multidimensional. Where on that continuum an ethnic group in the United States falls depends on its culture of origin and the impact of Americanization. Suffice it to say that with the globalization of the world, the West is becoming affected by the East, but Easterners, even those who have never traveled outside their home-lands, are heavily influenced by American values and style of life.

With increased interaction between countries, cultures, and lifestyles, a clearly recognizable American identity may have been evidenced only in the past. Reciprocal influences have shaped identi-ties, and in a multicultural world and a multicultural nation, Asian Americans are able to make individual choices about who they are, how American they are, and how Asian they choose to be. In carving an identity for themselves, Asian Americans have greater opportunity now than ever before to both consciously and subconsciously embrace those characteristics of both East and West that most suit their dispositions. The increasing acceptance of diversity in the United States and the loos-ening of Asian tradition in the homeland and in the United States allow a more independent definition of the Asian American self.

IMPLICATIONS FOR HUMAN SERVICES

Asian Americans in all walks of life may need human service interven-tion at some time. That social service programs are underutilized is clear, but the evidence suggests also that this group underutilizes health and legal services. When Asians have difficulty in housing or employ-ment, they usually fail to seek assistance from professionals trained to provide guidance or advocacy in these areas. A tendency exists among Asians to rely on themselves and not to avail themselves of the support-ive services provided by the society. Because of the extreme value placed on privacy and the tremendous sense of family loyalty, group sense, and issues of shame, Asians are disinclined to reach out even to the Asian American community for aid. Hence needs are not met by mainstream social services because Asian Americans do not believe that the society understands their needs, nor do they trust the dominant society because of the history of discrimination against them and the tendency of that society to adopt a patronizing attitude toward them. However, they do not go even to the Asian American community because it is shameful to reveal that there are problems within the family and the family must be protected at all costs. The result of these attitudes is that individuals within the Asian American family, or the entire family, may be highly dysfunctional yet seek little external support. In Asian countries, the guidance of the extended family is fundamental, and external intervention is usually not needed. Within the nuclear family structure, or the attenuated extended family of Asian Americans in the United States, however, few options for support exist.

Asian Americans are more likely to use health care services than social services, but not always effectively. The literature reveals that Asian Americans often deal with emotional distress by somatizing it. Chronic illness, such as high blood pressure, fatigue, backaches, and headaches, are frequently present among this population. Treatment of these may be helpful, but the insightful practitioner will need to explore the source of the somatization. On the other hand, Asian Americans are less likely to seek preventive services and they also do not seek health care services during the early stages of an illness, believing they can treat many illnesses with home remedies. Even when they do seek medical attention they may not comply with the physician's directions, either because they do not understand them, do not trust the physician, or begin to feel better.

Concomitant with this underutilization of services is the dominant society's misinterpretation of the lack of use as an indication of a lack of need and evidence of the social, emotional, and physical well-being of the Asian American. Since many Asian Americans live and work in ethnic enclaves and correspondingly large groups choose to be assimilated in the work arena, though not in their social lives, the personal needs of the community are not readily apparent to the dominant society. It is imperative that service providers avoid viewing this low level of service use as an absence of need, for the needs are in fact substantial, and if not addressed, in the long term they will be detrimental to the Asian American community and to U.S. society.

Public policies, particularly those that have implications for the largest number of Asian Americans are those in the areas of (a) social and family welfare, (b) housing, (c) education, (d) health, (e) mental health and substance abuse, and (f) criminal justice. Clearly immigration policy continues to influence the lives of Asian Americans, since it determines the profile of Asians entering the United States and limits the flow from Asia of family members of Asian Americans, but the effects of the public policies named above on the lives of Asian Americans who are already residing in the United States are significant.

Social and Family Welfare

Social and family welfare policies can greatly improve the lives of those in the population who have limited personal resources. As in most areas of life, in this area also, the focus tends to be on remediation; little effort or expense is directed toward the prevention of problems. This approach is consistent with the inclination of Asians to deal with problems once they arise. Despite the evidence from Asian American scholars illustrating the bimodal distribution of the success of Asian Americans, the image of them as people of superior abilities who do not need help persists. While policy may be changed to better meet the needs of Asian Americans, it is more important that service providers recognize that this population requires more attention than it seems to and can benefit from existing programs. The evidence shows, for example, that although elderly Asian Americans do seek Social Security benefits and Supplemental Security Income, the majority of needy Asian Americans lack information about public assistance. Even if they are aware of its availability, the cultural barriers to seeking help as well as the complexity of the application process are deterrents to access for those who most need assistance. When low English proficiency compounds the difficulties, the hurdles may seem insurmountable. Community workers and advocates must take an active role in explaining the process to Asian Americans and helping them cope with the dissonance of accepting aid from "outsiders." Welfare workers can offer more assistance through the application process. Connecting Asian Americans to assistance for which they are eligible and which they desperately need can be facilitated if workers and potential recipients understand both the cultural and the practical nature of the obstacles.

Even before the enactment of Welfare Reform in 1996 and the limits on the length of time individuals can receive welfare assistance, the majority of beneficiaries of public aid who were under the age of sixty-five remained on welfare for only an average of two years. This relatively short time can be enough to help people out of poverty by providing them some economic help and health care insurance as a boost.

Social welfare policy seeks also to address the nonfinancial problems that individuals and families face. Particularly vulnerable to abuse and neglect are children, women, and the elderly. Recent research on the lives of Asian Americans suggests that contrary to the long-standing beliefs that Asians always protect and support their family members, family violence is higher than has heretofore been recognized or admitted. While less is known about children and the elderly—who are truly dependent, vulnerable, and have few options—much more is known about the abuse of Asian American women. The increasing use of shelters established for them reveals that in the Asian patriarchal cultures, men have long had the social right to control their women through physical and emotional force. Once again, awareness is the key to effective interpretation of policy and services. Policymakers and providers, as well as the Asian American population, need to become aware of the existence of family problems, which are of such magnitude that over time they can cause a great drain on society through absenteeism from work and mental health problems. Providers must take into account the culture of silence and family loyalty that prevents Asian Americans from seeking social and emotional assistance. Outreach to affected individuals can help them realize that they have alternatives. The education of the perpetrators and intervention when other problems are actually the impetus for maltreatment is one direction that welfare workers can take. Finally, prevention programs that target Asian American children can be most important in teaching them how to avoid the cycle of violence. The literature on family violence emphasizes that it is prevalent among all people, in all cultures, and across all socioeconomic groups. However, in patriarchal societies it may be even more prevalent, and a person's ability to function outside the family may mask the emotional and behavioral problems that beset the family. Unless and until policy integrates prevention as an essential element of family welfare, violence within the family will continue unabated.

Housing

Housing policies seek to provide safe and sanitary shelter to low-income families. While data show that relatively few Asian Americans are homeless and living in shelters (one percent) despite a poverty rate of 14 percent, less is known about the degree of overcrowding in Asian American households. At one end of the bimodal distribution is a group that lives in superior housing, but at the other end are those who live in ethnic neighborhoods in low-quality housing. Many pool their resources to live in crowded facilities, usually in urban areas. Census figures reveal that Asian Americans have larger numbers of individuals belonging to one household than do other ethnic groups. While there is a tendency to believe that this population has more children than do average Americans, the high numbers actually reflect the extended family structure, which includes grandparents, aunts, uncles, and cousins, as well as unrelated individuals who feel a strong bond for each other. Improved housing of lower cost would certainly help alleviate problems of overcrowding, but education and other forms of support would be even more useful.

Borrowing substantial amounts of money for the purchase of a home is a Western trait. Until recently, Asians did not purchase anything on credit. To buy a home, one was expected to have sufficient savings to pay for the house at the time of purchase. Although Asian Americans in the United States are made aware of the process of purchasing a home with borrowed money, there may be cultural barriers against the practice. What may help many Asian Americans in this area is education about the existing financial avenues for home purchase as well as usable information about the credit system. Cultural gaps, misunderstandings, and biases often interfere with the lender's and the potential Asian American homeowner's arrival at an agreement. The lack of understanding of the complexities of loan acquisition and the home purchase process, on the one hand, and cultural and language barriers perceived by the lending institutions, on the other, often reinforce stereotypes and mistrust.

Housing policies attempt to address issues of discrimination in both housing and lending policies. On November 2, 2000, U.S. Housing and Urban Development Secretary Andrew Cuomo said, "Housing discrimination is outrageous, intolerable, and illegal, and it takes courage for people to fight back if they become victims." Housing advocates, however, have little awareness of the discrimination experienced by Asian Americans—most Asians will not pursue the matter. When they do, it becomes obvious that the discrimination they experienced in the early twentieth century persists still. For example, an Indian American family attempted to rent a condominium at the Lake of the Ozarks but was repeatedly informed over a period of several months that no apartments were available. When they finally recruited a Euro-American colleague to apply for housing at the same complex, she was shown an apartment ready for immediate occupancy. On November 2, 2000, HUD charged the apartment complex with housing discrimination (Dutt 2000). Cases that pursue the exposure of injustice are rare, however, for Asians fear the physical, social, and emotional repercussions on their families.

Sanctions against discrimination in housing and lending can be made effectively only if Asian Americans voice their experiences. Victims of all cultures tend to avoid reporting, for they fear revictimization through repercussions on themselves, their families, and communities. Asian Americans are socialized to keep silent about difficulties, partly because of norms of silence but also because of a fatalistic outlook and a belief in an external locus of control, which belies their own ability to have any effect. They must be encouraged to share information so that both they and other Asian Americans realize that the U.S. system does provide them rights, protections, and options. If they do speak up, the housing authority and social service advocates will become aware that they belong to a population that faces discrimination based on race. Perhaps in working with Asian Americans who have experienced discrimination in housing or elsewhere, service providers need to address the issues that prevent the exposure of these practices, encouraging Asian Americans to help the country deal with behaviors they encounter that are illegal and unethical.

Education

Asian Americans are viewed as high academic achievers, but data from both the Census Bureau and the Educational Testing Service show the bimodal characteristics that have been discussed previously: While one group clusters around the high end of achievement, another clusters at the low end. Given the reality of Asian American academic achievement and the implications for success in a world that increasingly requires academic competence and sophisticated literacy skills, the misinformed perception that this entire group enjoys universally excellent scholastic ability has acted as a disservice to many in the Asian American population. Data indicate that the Japanese, Chinese, Koreans, and South Asians reach the high end of achievement, while the Filipinos and Southeast Asians fall to the lower end throughout their school years. As with any assessment, the data reveal averages, and even within the high-achieving groups, some individuals are not so successful. While the high achievers may bring with them the resources for academic success, the needs of the low achievers are often overlooked.

U.S. educational policies hold sacred the right of every child, including those with special needs, to an education. Recognizing the growing immigrant constituency in the population, policies also address the special needs that immigrant and minority children may have. Yet when these policies are translated into services, the needs of many immigrant and particularly Asian and second-generation Asian American children who are struggling academically are not adequately met. If programs do exist, these children may not be able to take advantage of them because their parents are unaware of them or hesitant to advocate for their children. Remedial programs should not only be sure to include Asian American children but should also make a concerted outreach effort to ensure that parents are aware of them and encourage their children to utilize them. It is especially important for the children to have access to such programs if the parents are of either low literacy or low English-language proficiency.

Asian American children who are low academic achievers may be disregarded in the educational system because of the stereotype that all Asian Americans are successful students. The stereotype is actually detrimental also to the successful Asian Americans, who must compete against each other for quota limits set for Asian Americans at universities. Even if the group as a whole is viewed as advantaged and taken out of the minority quota, individuals from the group ought to be able to compete in the general Euro-American applicant pool rather than facing limitations on the number of Asian Americans. The practice appears to be inconsistent with educational and antidiscrimination policies that aim to be inclusive. Rejecting individuals solely on the basis of race is discriminatory, and while most universities that limit Asian American admissions will not openly acknowledge it, college counselors working with high school students are well aware of the practice.

Implementation of educational policies that ensure opportunity for all children should include a recognition that not all Asian American students are academic successes and many do not have either the family support or the knowledge to utilize the resources available in the school system. Ongoing outreach efforts must be an integral part of school educational programs and must target Asian American children and their families as much as they do other minority groups. Furthermore, almost all universities receive some federal funding, for most are tax-exempt by virtue of their nonprofit status. They should not be permitted to discriminate against qualified Asian American students on the basis of race. The Asian American community ought not to be fatalistic and passively accept decisions of exclusion, and advocates for the community should actively explore the reasons for the rejection of Asian American applicants who are superior (academically, in extracurricular and community service involvement, with strong references and application essays) in favor of less qualified students. Despite the U.S. recognition of education of children as a sacred responsibility, the stereotype of the model minority works against many achieving and failing Asian American students. It is time to challenge this discrepancy.

Health Care

The absence of universal health care coverage in the United States is both surprising and disturbing. The universal right of education, which is believed to have a direct effect upon the success of the nation, is seen as a national responsibility. Adequate health care lowers absenteeism from school and work, but the nation does not accept accountability in this area. Although low literacy and poor health can be detrimental to the functioning and the competitiveness of the country, health care services, particularly quality services, are not considered a fundamental American right. The nation must realize that not only is access to basic preventive, curative, and rehabilitative care in its best interest, but the government must assume some responsibility for ensuring that all individuals have access to such a level of care. Many Asian Americans are among those who are uninsured and underinsured, yet in discussions of noncoverage rates based on ethnicity, authorities in the field fail to mention the lack of coverage among Asian Americans, which in 1997 was 18.8 percent (Centers for Disease Control 2000). Again, the image of the model minority works against the Asian American community, in that the assumption is that since it is not mentioned, the coverage for the whole group is satisfactory.

While the provision of health insurance for this population is very important, just as important is the recognition that Asian Americans' knowledge of the private and the government health care programs may be limited and their perceptions of health care may differ dramatically from those of Euro-Americans. Another important factor is that the various groups of Asian Americans differ in their use and understanding of Western medical practices. In order to provide effective health care to all Asian American groups, it is essential that Western practitioners understand cultural biases against Western medicine within each ethnic Asian group and realize that instructions and information provided to patients are often colored by differing perceptual lens. Health care providers must be willing to educate patients about the significance of prevention, the nature of the illness for which they are seeking remedies, the benefits and side effects of treatments, and the importance of compliance with directions. Most important, health care practitioners must understand how, when, and why Asian Americans, particularly first-generation Asian Americans, and their children use health care services.

Asian Americans place little emphasis on preventive care and postpone seeking professional treatment until the illness has progressed to a point that they find unmanageable or until home remedies have proved unsuccessful. Not always confident about Western medicine, many Asian Americans may not comply with treatment guidelines, or they may discontinue treatment when symptoms disappear, a particularly troubling practice if they cease taking antibiotics for bacterial infections or medications used to control high blood pressure. The absence of symptoms does not mean that the problem is cured, but not all individuals truly understand that. Furthermore, the explanation of side effects must be carefully worded so that they do not appear to be more harmful than the illness itself.

Health care practitioners, particularly physicians and nurses, are perceived as being knowledgeable about illness. Once Asian Americans grant these professionals the authority to treat them and trust the knowledge and skill of the practitioners, they expect to be directed to the correct choices. After all, they assume that if it were the patients who were acquainted with the options and their consequences, they could merely specify the preferred treatment to practitioners. While it is important to provide choices to the patients, it is more crucial that physicians and nurses provide very clear guidelines for action. Unless the patient and the family are well versed in Western medicine, as are many Filipino Americans and Indian Americans, a more directive approach works better. Even the Filipinos and Indians prefer greater direction than does the general U.S. population. At the very least, health care practitioners need to be cognizant of Asian American perceptions of Western medicine and physicians and the implications for compliance. Particularly astute physicians will seek to synthesize Eastern and Western interventions in such a manner that patients feel comfortable in accepting the latter while continuing to practice Eastern treatments that can supplement Western methods without conflict. In order to assess this, Western practitioners must keep an open mind in exploring and understanding Eastern medicine, much of which has had application for centuries in Asian countries.

Mental Health and Substance Abuse

Contrary to the prevalent perception of the mental health of Asian Americans, this group does show evidence of mental illness and substance abuse. Both public data and research information confirm psychosocial and emotional distress among Southeast Asians, particularly as a consequence of their refugee experiences and the traumas associated with relocation and adjustment. Yet the model minority image persists for the rest of the Asian American community, reinforcing the notion that the majority has few mental health or substance abuse difficulties. Mental illness does not have parity with illness in Asian countries. Although mental illness is now more often recognized and accepted in the United States as a condition that requires professional intervention and the public is becoming better informed about the difficulties faced by those who are mentally ill and by their families, many Asian Americans still hold the belief that this illness is caused in some way by the individual.

Mental illness, the inability to cope with stress, and emotional distress are generally not acceptable in most Asian countries. Asian cultures regard such problems as signs of weakness, the results of bad behavior, or punishments for misdeeds in a previous existence. Since they reflect poorly not only on the individual but also on the family, causing shame and blame, most mental health problems are not acknowledged by either the community or the individual who experiences them. Instead, they are somatized into chronic ailments such as headaches, backaches, and fatigue. Health care professionals must be aware of the strong connection between the psyche and the soma in order to respond appropriately when Asian Americans bring complaints of chronic physical problems. These somatic illnesses are perceived as "real" ailments that necessitate treatment and rest, yet since treatment focuses on the symptoms and not on the underlying cause, the problems that resulted in the illness may never be addressed. Sometimes, however, resting or receiving emotional attention does offer some relief, at least from the symptoms.

While researchers continue to indicate that substance abuse is a greater problem in the Asian American community than is generally accepted, the issue does not come to the attention of service providers, as those in need do not seek intervention. The family and the ethnic community are more likely to provide assistance privately. Many substance abuse problems go untreated but often are concomitant with other difficulties, such as unemployment, family violence, and physical illness.

Intervention in the areas of mental health and substance abuse can be the most difficult for service providers. Not only are these problems not admissible in the Asian American community, but even if they are admitted, there is little confidence that solutions will be forthcoming. Given the community's strong constraints against airing problems to outsiders, Asian Americans will probably not be able to honestly explore mental illness and substance abuse with a counselor. Since most interventions are therapeutic and psychosocial in nature, and since most Asians are socialized to "save face" and not share their difficulties, interventions based on "talk therapies" are likely to be ineffective. Service providers must instead expend considerable effort in (a) establishing rapport with patients, (b) establishing credibility and authority, and (c) directing individuals to appropriate solutions. Establishing rapport requires that the practitioner evidence empathy and understanding of both the culture and the individual, as well as of the immigrant, refugee, or second-generation experience. The age, expertise, and authority of the provider are inextricably linked to the chances for success. It is essential to establish credibility and authority by explaining training and experience garnered by working with specific problems with people of similar background. "Nondirective" and "nonjudgmental" approaches to therapy will be less effective with Asian Americans, who, if they seek mental health or substance abuse intervention at all, are often looking for clear direction and guidance. Effective services for this group must be highly directive. Asians go to professionals for assistance because they do not have the answers, and most seek help only after they have exhausted their personal resources. When they finally reach out to a professional, they expect concrete direction. Practitioners who merely provide options and their consequences and expect Asian American patients to decide what route to take are perceived as abdicating their responsibilities or as being incompetent.

It is essential that practitioners truly understand the particular Asian culture of the person seeking treatment and that they be able to communicate that understanding. As in any worker-client relationship, the importance of rapport and empathy cannot be overstated. Only when clients are convinced of practitioners' expertise and perceive that they are also sensitive to their unique needs and situations will they consider sharing their difficulties honestly enough that they can benefit from treatment.

Criminal Justice

Most offenses for which Asian Americans have come to the attention of the criminal justice system have been related to (a) public disorder, (b) gang behavior, or (c) international organized crime. In general, the Asian American population in federal and state prisons has come from the group that engages in organized crime. Unlike other ethnic minorities, Asian Americans are underrepresented in the criminal justice system. Although the system is becoming more vigilant about organized crime, reports of prostitution and drug smuggling continue to increase. It is imperative that the system find means to break these smuggling rings, not only because they engage in illegal criminal activity but also because they victimize the vulnerable. The sale of drugs increases dependency and exploits those who are addicted. The sale of prostitutes victimizes them twice—once when they agree to pay as much as $40,000 to be smuggled into the United States to escape the exploitative environment of their own country, committing themselves to bonded prostitution because they cannot afford to pay for the passage at the beginning of their journey, and again when they are repeatedly used and abused as prostitutes.

Though the criminal justice system is now much more alert and knowledgeable about Asian organized crime and gang behavior, it still fails to acknowledge the prevalence of family violence in the Asian American community. Domestic violence crimes have been relegated to social welfare, and shelters provide some safe harbor, support, and counseling to battered Asian American women who find the courage to leave their spouses. Little is done to prosecute the perpetrators, however. In addition, neither the criminal justice system nor most social services know much about the extent of child abuse or elder abuse in this community. Once again, in this immigrant community that is shrouded in the myth of the model minority, intervention for these abuses is rare. The community's tendency to place little confidence in the law—since large parts of the criminal justice system in Asian countries are known to be corrupt—plays out in their attempts to resolve disputes themselves without the assistance of the legal system. Language barriers also increase problems, since communication of sensitive issues becomes more tedious and painful if one does not have the tools with which to express them. Police awareness of the existence of domestic violence among Asian Americans can go a long way in providing assistance to families in distress. Education programs for police officers that include issues of diversity must also include information about Asian American populations and the culture that prohibits the discussion of problems outside the family.

Linkages between the criminal justice system and the Asian American community are essential in addressing criminal activity among this group. Communities with large Asian American populations are now more often recruiting Asian Americans for service on the police force, and community-based police stations increase the visibility of the police officers and enhance their interaction with the community. Civilian groups who serve as liaisons between the police and the community can help minimize distrust. Such links need not be limited to adults; they may also include adolescents who will carry the concerns of their peers to the police and who provide an entrée for the police into the adolescent population. Such methods of proactive intervention serve a preventive function that may minimize the attraction of gangs and illegal activities.

Although criminal behavior among Asian Americans is believed to be relatively low, it is necessary that law enforcement officers who work with individuals from this population be aware of the impact of culture, including similarities and differences among and between the various Asian groups. The officers' training must focus not only on the disparate experiences of the Asian American populations but also on the differences in patterns of verbal and nonverbal communication, cultural norms and taboos, and family structures and relationships. And it is not sufficient to train only law enforcement personnel. It is essential that communities of Asian Americans recognize the role of the criminal justice system in providing protection through law enforcement. The Asian American community's perception of the police force must be addressed in order to minimize stereotyping and mistrust. It is imperative that the criminal justice system recognize the need to develop training programs to increase mutual understanding between the Asian American community and law enforcement. Only when both groups resolve their feelings of anxiety, uncertainty, distrust, and discomfort can the services of the police force be effectively applied in the protection of the community.

Services for the Community

Among Asian Americans a tendency exists to rely only on themselves and to minimize the use of supportive services that are available in U.S. society. Because of the devotion to privacy and the tremendous sense of family loyalty, group sense, and issues of shame, Asian Americans evidence an aversion to reaching out even to their own community for assistance. Thus, needs are not met by the dominant society's social services because Asian Americans do not believe that the society understands their needs, nor are they sure that they trust the larger society, given the history of discrimination and paternalism. They will not go to their own community members either, because it is shameful to reveal that there are problems within the family and the family must be protected at all costs. These ingrained cultural attitudes mean that individuals within the family, and the family itself, may be extremely needy, unhealthy, or dysfunctional, yet seek little external support.

Outreach efforts must encourage Asian Americans to use services that act as surrogates for the extended family in providing support and guidance. Ongoing debates about who should be the service providers for ethnic minorities achieve only disagreement: Do ethnic services best meet the needs of their own community or are the services provided by more inclusive organizations more effective? Whether programs and services should be culture-specific is another unresolved issue. A number of controversial questions about multiculturalism have been raised, with disagreements about whether similarities or differences should establish the foundation in the delivery of services (de Anda 1997). There are opposing viewpoints on whether the theory that drives intervention, the intervention itself, methods of evaluating effectiveness, or research methods should be modified based on the culture of the target population.

In large urban areas with substantial Asian American populations—such as San Francisco, Chicago, New York, and Houston—a number of services, from health care and social services to financial planning and legal assistance, have sprouted specifically to address the needs of the Asian American community. Not always managed by Asian Americans, they are staffed mostly by Asian Americans, many of whom are responsible for consumer contact. These organizations are heavily utilized by Asian Americans, while organizations that do not target this population evidence a disproportionately lower representation of Asian American clientele. It may be argued that the lower representation occurs because the ethnic organizations divert the Asian American population. It is also clear, however, that in geographical areas where there are large numbers of Asian Americans but no services specifically for this population, several needs in the community remain unmet. In the absence of cultural sensitivity on the part of service providers, especially in sensitive areas such as money management, family discord, or limited English proficiency, Asian Americans are more likely to forgo accessing existing services. In that case, whether or not a qualitative difference exists between Asian American service organizations and organizations that provide services to Asian Americans, perceptions of them differ in the community. While Asian Americans may even agree that both types of organizations are equally competent, they report a higher level of comfort for Asian American service organizations.

Model for Practitioners (and Researchers)[1]

Practice and research in the human services are intrinsically fraught with a variety of difficulties. As clients and subjects in the United States become more ethnically and culturally diverse, it becomes important to recognize that a variety of additional factors can complicate service provision and data collection. While provision of services to ethnic minorities has become more of a priority, the focus on Asian Americans continues to be relatively limited, and the knowledge about them is scattered. Despite disagreements about the transferability of interventions and research methods, experience shows that even cross-culturally validated methods and instruments are not readily applicable across cultures and communities (Segal 2000a, 2000b).

First generation. In practice with minorities, several issues confound effective service delivery and intervention related to the client system. Resistance, communication barriers, personal and family background, and ethnic community identity (Lum 1992) are complicated by the experiences of many immigrants and refugees, who closely guard information because of fear (perhaps unfounded) of exposure, past experience with oppression, and mistrust of authority. A number of Asian Americans arrive from nations in which they do not have freedom of speech or of choice. Fears about authority, including the possibility of deportation from the United States, can erect formidable barriers when service providers probe into the lives of immigrants and refugees from

Figure 9.1 Working with Asian Americans

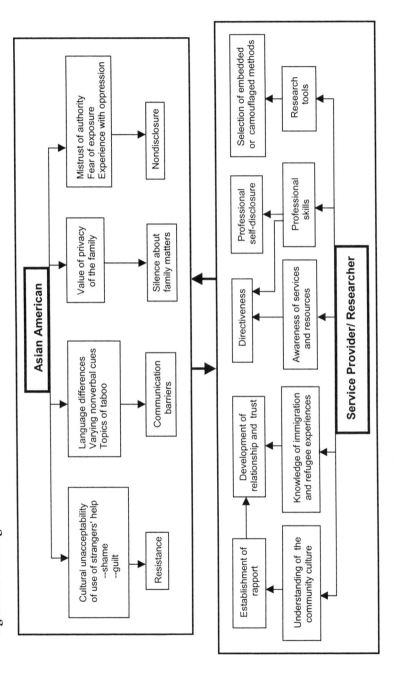

Asian nations. In order to alleviate such concerns, service providers must establish good rapport, credibility, and expert authority, through directiveness and appropriate self-disclosure.

The model shown in figure 9.1 delineates the barriers that those who work with Asian Americans may confront. Though these difficulties may be more evident among first-generation immigrants who have been in the United States a fairly short time, the culture of privacy and silence is pervasive throughout Asian American groups, as is the tendency to avoid sharing information of a personal nature with outsiders.

Service providers, whether they are health care professionals, social service workers, or professionals in the worlds of law and finance, must become aware of the conditions that can hinder the development of an adequate working relationship with Asian Americans and of the implications of interventions, services, and resources for those from Eastern cultures. Service providers must establish credibility, rapport, and sensitivity with their Asian American clients in order for them to be comfortable enough to provide crucial information or to comply with the guidelines of the necessary intervention. While many Asian Americans may fear authority and seek to avoid it, they are socialized to respect (and obey) it. Practitioner directiveness can be effective with this population. Researchers interested in exploring sensitive and personal issues may find that the culture and experience of the Asian American prevents disclosure. Unlike practitioners, researchers will be more successful if they avoid a direct approach. Research tools that employ embedded methods (such as psychological tests) may yield results that more adequately capture reality than will direct questioning through interviews or questionnaires.

Discussions about the need to link theory and practice are ongoing. Educators and theoreticians have written much about cultural diversity, the need to be ethnically sensitive, and the aim to provide services consistent with the sociocultural framework of the clients. With this kind of approach, clients experience less cultural dissonance, and the likelihood that they will utilize the services to their benefit is increased. Practice models provide guidelines for integrating cultural awareness with Western interventions to synthesize approaches that are of the greatest relevance for the client and yet are consistent with the guidelines of the practitioner's profession.

Second generation. The tendency to treat Asian Americans across generations as being similar needs to be examined more closely. The second, third, and fourth generations of Asian Americans in the latter part of the twentieth century were indeed much like the first generation in terms of values, attitudes, and behaviors. The second and subsequent generations of Asian Americans of the twenty-first century, on the other hand, are more similar to their Euro-American counterparts than to any previous Asian American group. In earlier years, despite their desires to become integrated into the American community, most Asians were kept segregated and isolated. The most often cited examples are those of the Nisei, who caused their parents much distress as they rejected all that was Japanese, yet were not allowed by the Euro-Americans to become a part of their society. Since that time, U.S. society has changed. Despite some continuing prejudice and discrimination against people of color, the opportunity to be an integral part of the U.S. society is now not only possible, it is a reality. A greater commitment to cultural pluralism exists, as well as the recognition that differences need not only be tolerated but celebrated. Second-generation Asian Americans find it less necessary to behave in a manner that reflects only the heritage that is obvious by their physical characteristics and to deny the bicultural one they inherited with their birth into American society. It is no longer necessary for them to hide themselves and their feelings from those who can assist them; the shroud of secrecy that traditionally keeps Asians from discussing their feelings, attitudes, and experiences can be lifted for this group of U.S.-born Asians. It is clear that second-generation Asian Americans of the twenty-first century feel that they are Americans and are just as entitled to the rights and privileges of the nation as is any other citizen. The fears resulting from experience or from cultural taboos that inhibit many first-generation Asian Americans are less apparent among this second generation.

While service providers must still be culturally sensitive in delivering services, the emphasis with second-generation clients can be focused on understanding the experience of being USAsian and bicultural and any associated problems. Often such difficulties spring from looking Asian, like their parents, but feeling American, like their peers. Second-generation Asian Americans are more likely to respond well to services and interventions from the human service professions, and the model presented in figure 9.1 may not be as applicable to this group of Asian Americans as it is to first-generation immigrants from Asian countries. Practitioners will find that the second generation is very knowledgeable about and receptive to Western medicine, financial management, business opportunities, legal matters, the U.S. political system, social services, and citizens' rights and privileges. Barriers that are erected by the individual will more often reflect personal characteristics and history than an Asian culture or immigration experience. While service providers must also establish rapport and develop a relationship of trust with second-generation clients, they will likely find that this group is more open about its needs, expects to have greater input into decisions about itself, and shies away from undue directiveness.

SOCIETY AND IMMIGRANTS MUST
ACTIVELY ENGAGE IN THE ADJUSTMENT PROCESS

In many respects the United States presents a series of dichotomies. Many embrace the diversity brought by immigrant peoples, but just as many abhor it. This variance is evident at the informal and personal levels as well as at the formal and institutional levels. Many individuals and groups of different backgrounds are integrated in the workforce, yet social integration at the personal level in friendships and residential communities is less common. While selective integration may be a preference of minority community members, as in the segmented assimilation process, it may also be the choice of the dominant society, as those who are similar still feel more comfortable with each other. U.S. society of the twenty-first century, based on the civil rights legislation of the 1960s and 1970s, clearly mandates equal opportunity for all and prohibits discrimination, but these rights are difficult to enforce, and the most subtle forms of discrimination are impossible to prove.

What, then, are the responsibilities of the immigrant individual and of the U.S. society in the process of adjustment to the United States? Much depends on the resources that immigrants bring with them as well as the readiness of the receiving country to accept them. Most Asian immigrants to the United States, whether they are voluntary immigrants or refugees, have brought with them a tremendous range of psychological strengths. They have varied greatly in their language competence, their professional and vocational skills, their economic resources, and their social supports, all of which are necessary for successful adjustment to a new environment. While assimilation may no longer be the preferred goal for Asian immigrants, they, like any other member of the society, must have the competencies that will allow them to work and support themselves in the country.

A nation that has immigration policies that allows the entry of people who do not have the necessary survival tools must then take responsibility for providing the services, training, financial assistance, and other supportive programs to ensure that opportunities are available through the adjustment process. These programs must also be sensitive to the fact that adjustment occurs over a period of time, often several years. Needs, issues, and problems may emerge at different points in an individual's life and be related to physical and psychological health, to financial and business security, to the bicultural experience and the raising of children, or to a variety of other areas. While federal and private-sector programs such as the Refugee Resettlement Program must be lauded for their aims in assisting refugees, they also provide too little for too short a time. Such assistance programs must be supplemented on a consistent basis, and ongoing outreach efforts must make immigrants aware of their existence.

While opportunities must be made available to immigrants and they must be made aware of the resources and services available to all residents of the nation, it is their responsibility to avail themselves of these opportunities. The nation must be welcoming and try to increase opportunities and minimize obstacles to a successful adjustment to the United States, regardless of whether the immigrants' goals of adjustment are acculturation and assimilation, segmented assimilation, integration, or accommodation, but it is also necessary for immigrants to learn the society, its functioning, and its culture, because successful adjustment involves a certain degree of acceptance by the immigrant and a willingness to adapt to the new environment. While some may find it easier than others, they must share the responsibility for easing their own adjustment and that of their family members and must have or develop the resources to function both in their ethnic communities and in the dominant society.

Most first-generation Asian Americans come from cultures where their options were limited, their socioeconomic status in life was fixed, or personal freedom was controlled either politically or socially. Besides the language, cultural, and social differences that they experience in the United States, they encounter variations in interaction patterns of social groups. Among Asians, relationships are closely regulated by age, gender, and generational status, but these are not the predominant criteria that define relationships in the United States. Social status in the

United States is related more to education, occupation, and income level. Asian Americans' spiritual beliefs and practices greatly influence their understanding of the world, and their fatalistic worldview permits them to accept their circumstances (sometimes more so than Americans), but it also makes them passive and allows them to be victimized by circumstances that they might be able to control. Their beliefs and attitudes about health and healing also influence their attitudes about available assistance. If they believe that illness is punishment for some behavior, either in this life or a previous one, they are less likely to either access or comply with Western medical interventions, particularly if those interventions are inconsistent with Eastern methods.

Bicultural services that truly understand not only the language but also the experience of both cultures can be the most effective in facilitating the adjustment of first-generation Asian Americans, soon after they enter the United States and also later, as they begin to deal with issues of managing businesses, raising families, and coping with old age. In the process of translation, bicultural services can interpret U.S. culture for immigrant Asian Americans and also ensure that the continuing prejudice and discrimination in U.S. society are identified, and that, through advocacy, policies and programs are developed to address such attitudes.

"GIVING BACK" TO THE UNITED STATES

The Asian American population is no longer young. It has been in the United States in significant numbers since the mid-1960s, and it is well past the adolescence of carving an identity—it has carved one in the image of the model minority. It is now in its middle years and has established itself as a contributing segment of society, adding to the nation's success both locally and internationally. The time has come for this group to awaken and realize that it is truly a part of this country and this multicultural society. It must begin contributing to the country's maintenance, sustenance, and well-being. The Asian American community, though successful as a whole, still has such strong allegiances to its homeland that it often is not aware of the need for more participation in the United States. While allegiance to the homeland is important, it is equally important that the community make a commitment to the welfare of the land in which it has chosen to reside and to raise its children.

Asian Americans have consistently contributed to U.S. society. Literature and news reports abound with the successes of Asians in the sciences, business, and the fine arts (particularly music). These contributions, however, are the by-products of these specific individuals' abilities, what they enjoy doing, and their careers. That the United States benefits is significant, but benefit to this country is not the primary reason that Asian Americans engage in these activities. The time has now come for Asian Americans to become immersed in all areas of U.S. society and to contribute to it by becoming involved in running it. Except for a handful of individuals, Asian Americans have been noticeably absent from public life, particularly in the political arena and to a large extent in the social services and the voluntary sector. To show their commitment to the country, both for themselves and for others, they must now demonstrate their concern for its welfare and its maintenance and be proactive in assuming responsibility for directing its course. Only then will they truly feel an integral part of it and also truly be able to influence the future of Asian Americans in the United States. They must not only be the lobbyists; they must also be the decision makers.

The collective is of significance in the Asian value system, and responsibility to the group is paramount, but differences exist between the in-group and the out-group, and one's obligations are primarily to the in-group—out-group obligations are perfunctory. While Asians are expected to suppress individual needs for the good of the group, they are not socialized to feel responsibility for those outside the group. Even in the Asian American community, there is a tendency to face inward toward the family and place emphasis on meeting its needs. In the United States, some Asian Americans may generalize this responsibility for the in-group to caring for the Asian community to which they belong. There is much less of a sense of civic duty toward political and social involvement on a broader level, and the Asian value of privacy and a tendency to avoid "rocking the boat" or challenging the status quo works to foster detachment from the society rather than involvement.

Many Asians or their parents and grandparents came to the United States from nondemocratic societies, where the emphasis was placed primarily on caring for the family; political barriers and social constraints allowed little opportunity to affect the larger society. Even in democratic nations such as India, additional problems in the social infrastructure allow little time or opportunity for the average person to become involved outside the family. Although Asian cultures stress the importance of the group and support of the group, that concern does not extend to civic responsibility. Perhaps there is an underlying belief that if all people take care of their in-group members, there will be no isolated or needy individuals.

The commitment of Asian Americans to the United States will be clear when they give of their time, their services, and their financial and personal resources to help maintain and improve society. Not only do Asian Americans typically avoid political life, but they shy away from volunteering their time for community service activities and they are not known for making contributions to help the needy, mentoring young people, or serving on the boards of organizations. If they do contribute, they tend to focus on Asian American causes and services. While it is important that Asian American needs be met through the assistance of successful Asian Americans, it is also time for this group to move away from the traditional "in-group" and "out-group" distinction and begin to contribute in all areas of society.

A handful of Asian Americans, notably those who are in the prosperous information technologies sector, however, blazed a trail beginning in the year 2000 for other Asian Americans. Recognizing the importance of sharing their success and providing opportunities for others, some Asian Americans who were particularly fortunate in seeing their visions come to fruition established funds to provide seed money to others with unique ideas, whether they were from the Asian American community or not. Despite the bimodal socioeconomic distribution among Asian Americans, the fact remains that as a whole they are highly successful, and the higher-end mode is larger than the lower-end one. On average, they have more resources than other ethnic minorities in the United States.

The United States relies heavily on the involvement of its constituents in the public and volunteer sectors. Civic responsibility is highly valued, and citizens of the United States in the twenty-first century champion causes that have little to do with their immediate family members. Companies evidence social responsibility and support the causes of vulnerable populations and of endangered U.S. assets. Schoolchildren are encouraged to participate in community service activities that benefit others. Children are taught that public service is a noble calling and that political involvement is necessary to bring about change that will benefit the society. Asian Americans continue to steer away from public service, and parents persist in encouraging their children to pursue careers in medicine, the sciences, and business so that they may live comfortable lives and support their families well. Change is under way, however, for some Asian American youth of the twenty-first century are beginning to challenge parental direction and find their own way into politics, social services, school education, sports, and entertainment. As their numbers increase and they become a visible and successful presence in all areas of U.S. life, they will blaze a path for other Asian Americans, convincing them that these are fields in which individuals can prosper, through which they can bring honor to their families, by which they can contribute to the United States, and in which they are sorely needed.

The time is ripe for the community to look outside itself and complete the cycle of success by contributing to the sustenance of the country and also "giving back" in such a way that others, both Asian Americans and non-Asian Americans, may benefit from its success. Only when the community can be committed to the well-being of the nation as a whole will it perceive itself as an integral part of this multicultural nation.

Any immigrant community faces a long road from its country of origin. The physical distance may be great, but the social, psychological, and emotional distance is always greater. Nevertheless, the human condition and its similarities bind peoples together to a much greater extent that one tends to realize. Regardless of social norms, culture, religion, or language, all people at the very least have the same desires for health and the ability to provide for their families. All people experience joy, fear, pain, hope, and despair. All are vulnerable, need other human beings, and are influenced by environmental factors.

For immigrants, as for all people, much depends on the personal resources that they possess. Even more important, however, is the readiness of the receiving country to accept immigrants and their American-born descendents. Immigration policies may reflect the interests of the nation in allowing entry to certain groups of people, but the opportunities and obstacles that immigrants and their offspring, particularly those of color, encounter on a daily basis are what affects their ease of adjustment and mutual acceptance. Immigrants and the host nation must make a conscious decision to adapt to each other—it is the exclusive responsibility of neither the host nation nor the immigrant. If the nation is to be truly multicultural it must embrace pluralism, recognizing, accepting, and lauding the differences among peoples, and celebrating them as a national asset.

EPILOGUE

Author's Immigration Experience

As a thirteen year old in 1965, I did not understand that I was coming to the U.S. at the very time of the liberalization of its immigration policies. Much to my delight, my parents had made arrangements for me to join ninth grade at a boarding school in New England. For me the process began when in the summer of 1964, I traveled to the Indian capital of Delhi to take the Secondary School Admission Test in order to get into Northfield School in Massachusetts; it was also necessary for me to qualify for a scholarship, for without it the school would have been unaffordable for us. I was admitted for the fall 1965 and arrived in September in New York, was met by my brother and his friend, and taken the next day to Northfield, where I spent the next four academic years. After graduation I decided to attend Barnard College in Manhattan to be closer to my parents, who by this time had immigrated and lived in New Jersey, and at Barnard I majored in anthropology. I went on to get master's and doctoral degrees in social work at the University of Texas at Arlington and Washington University in St. Louis, respectively. I married in 1978, had two children, and during the time, and into the present, have been involved in practicing, teaching, and researching in the field of social work.

The trip to the United States, for me, began traumatically. It was at the peak of the 1965 India-Pakistan War, and I was unable to leave from Delhi as all flights had been canceled. My father finally put me on a plane in Bombay, and I left during a blackout. This was my second plane ride (my first was an hour-long trip when I was five years old). I was afraid, sure I would never see my father again (and I didn't until 1968), and alone. I had eight dollars in my pocket, as that was all emigrants were allowed to take out of India at that time. Seeing my brother again, after three years, was both pleasant and awkward—he seemed so different, and sounded so American.

As I look back at my entry into the United States and my process of adjustment, particularly in light of the model presented in chapter 1, I find it was relatively easy. My experience in India was good, and growing up was simple, as I belonged to a middle-class family of modest but comfortable means. My reasons for leaving were based on a parental decision to move the family to the U.S., for personal reasons, but primarily for the increased opportunities that would be available. Both emigration and immigration processes were planned in detail, were voluntary, safe, and legal. Furthermore, I came with the resources that would make my transition and adjustment as easy as possible and at a time when U.S. immigration had just opened to the Eastern Hemisphere. I arrived to attend a school that desired my presence and that provided the opportunities that my family sought for me. Thus, adjustment had little to do with physical or practical adaptation; nevertheless, there were a number of other issues that did not fall into place as easily.

The initial culture shock came when I found that although I spoke English (and rather well, I thought), I could not understand the Americans, nor was I understood, and that norms of behavior often differed. For the first two weeks I spoke little and responded with a "yes" or "no" to almost every question, reinforcing the belief of my classmates and teachers that I spoke no English. When I was referred to as an "alien" and told I would have to register with the Immigration and Naturalization Service (which had to be done annually in those days), I was further shocked, as I had always believed an alien was a creature from another planet!

In addition, two other lessons that stand out in my mind about my first month in the U.S. are (1) behavior that is appropriate in one culture is impolite in another, and (2) in the U.S. one must be direct about one's wishes. In the former instance the senior student assigned to the dining table at which I sat, watched me eat my food with knife and fork in good colonial fashion—holding the food speared by a fork in the left hand, cutting food with a knife in the right, and then transferring the food from the plate to my mouth with the fork still in my left hand, without relinquishing the knife. After a couple of days, all the students at the table were informed of the "polite" way of eating, which was to cut the food, place the knife across the top of the plate, transfer the fork to the right hand to put the food in the mouth, and then repeat the process for each bite. The second instance occurred when I accompanied a student home for the weekend (after all, I was exotic). In India one does not take a large helping of food or subsequent ones without the repeated urging of the host. Declining the food until the host has insisted sufficiently is both polite and expected. Therefore, when my American friend's mother asked me if I would like a second helping (and I did), and I said "No," the food was put away, and that was the end of the meal. Never again have I said "no" when I meant "yes" or vice versa!

Such differences in social norms continue to crop up periodically, or an awareness of variations in patterns of behavior become evident, especially when they are identified by our U.S. born children. However, what I had to negotiate in my early years in the U.S., both for myself and for those around me, was the reformulation of my identity. This continues, to some extent, into the present—over thirty-five years later! All Asians in the U.S., on a fairly consistent basis, experience the process of redefining the identity, as they are almost always asked of their origins by new acquaintances.

In the first year of my high school education, I was frequently asked about India and Indians, and, in fact, I perceived myself to be a representative of the nation and always very different from those around me. The girls at the school (at the time Northfield was a girls' school) and the teachers found me a curiosity, and the boys at the brother school (with whom we mingled on weekends) shied away from me. My questioning of my identity, however, truly began when I was spending the summer after my freshman year in Vancouver, Canada with my mother and aunt (both of whom always wore saris). As we were shopping, I overheard a conversation between two Canadians who said, "If they want to live here, why don't they dress properly?" Chow (1998) states that in each minority individual's life there is one traumatic and identifiable incident that awakens the realization that there is a deep and permanent difference between the individual and the majority society and raises questions about identity that were never before evident. For me, this was the incident. For a couple of years, I developed a tremendous sense of embarrassment in being in public with my mother, and always walked far ahead of her or far behind. Yet I knew of her pride in her heritage. A professor of English literature, she was denied several university positions in both Canada and the U.S. because she refused to discard her sari. At that time her adamant refusal was not understandable to me.

In my second and subsequent years in high school, I felt, at least on
the surface, I had become very much like my peers, and found that I
was not treated very differently by the girls around me, and the boys
had begun talking to me because my "exotic" looks were now interesting rather than intimidating. However, when I looked in the mirror I
knew I was not American, and was not always comfortable with my
appearance or my difference. This was exacerbated by the fact that I was
very shy and did not like to stand out, and I did, because I was neither
white nor black. Nevertheless, I think I began thinking like an American,
feeling American, assuming American norms of behavior, and identifying myself with my American peers. Despite the liberation of
immigration laws, and the influx of Indians in 1965, there were few
Indians who were in the U.S. who were of my age. They were all either
graduate students (because India has quality undergraduate programs
around the country), or they were young professionals, or they were the
very young children of the professionals. Few, if any, teenaged children
or middle-aged immigrants came to this country at that time, and I
lived away from my parents. Thus it was inevitable that I would begin
to identify myself with the American peers with whom I studied.
Nevertheless, my first thirteen years of socialization in India provided a
strong foundation, and, despite observable indicators, my Indian values,
cultural consciousness, and basic identity always tempered my perceptions and understanding of my environment.

While some cultural and social variations made adjustment difficult, others were welcomed. The freedom I experienced, of movement,
of selecting courses, of coming and going from the dormitory, and of
walking to the town without supervision was very liberating. My perception of the rules and monitoring was that they were minimal, as I
had always attended very strict boarding schools in India—other girls
who had come to Northfield from living at home and attending public
schools felt constrained. The sense of independence added tremendously to my growth and development as had the experiences of
traveling alone and adjusting to another land and culture.

My parents' westernization and their several experiences in England
and the U.S. made them tolerant of my Americanization and that of
my brother. I experienced few of the intergenerational difficulties most
1.5 generation (which I was) or U.S.-born Asian Americans report.
However, struggles with identity persisted. Although I felt increasingly
American, of course I continued to look Indian. When I arrived in

cosmopolitan New York and Barnard College, I found I was one of two Indian undergraduates (the other was also a freshman woman). As far as we knew, there were no Indian undergraduate males at Columbia College. At that point, although I felt I was American, as a college freshman I decided to reclaim my Indian identity. I began wearing saris, which I continued to do professionally until I was in my early thirties. On introspection, I think it was then, when I gave up wearing the sari professionally, that I finally became comfortable with both my integrated bicultural identity of Indian and American and the extent of that integration. The sari no longer needed to be worn as a statement.

Growing through my adolescent and college years surrounded by Americans, my exposure to Indian society and culture in the U.S. was minimal. The only other Indian woman at Barnard and I eventually became friends in our junior year. Her father was with the United Nations, and she had spent very little time in India and also probably struggled with identity issues, although we never discussed them. Through my master's and doctoral education, I continued to be surrounded by Americans, but in the second year of my graduate education I met an Indian business student who had been in the U.S. for three years and who was to become my husband four years later. Following our marriage, since most of my husband's family was in the U.S., I gradually got reintroduced to the Indian culture and to the Indian community in the U.S. Much of my Indian identity and values that had either been suppressed or become dormant reemerged, and over the course of the next twenty or so years, another, more bicultural identity became shaped when I began drawing more equitably and, hopefully, from the best, of both the cultures to which I now feel I belong.

Coming from similar, though somewhat different backgrounds, as any young couple, my husband and I sometimes consciously and sometimes subconsciously negotiated roles, responsibilities, and expectations and tried to forge a relationship that would be acceptable to both of us in light of our dual Indian and American influences. As we had both come as students and interacted fairly closely with Americans both professionally and socially, our experiences may have been more similar to that of each other than if one of us had completed all education in India. The adjustment experience of the Indian who emigrated as a professional to begin work here is somewhat different from that of the student who has the opportunity for greater exposure to the American social life. During our student days both my husband and I socialized more closely with Americans than after we got married and began working. Along with our marriage we appeared to move into the form of assimilation that Portes and Zhou (1993) have termed *segmented assimilation*, for, as educators, we are fairly well assimilated into the dominant Euro-American society professionally, yet have chosen to socialize primarily with other Indian Americans. This pattern of socializing was partially happenstance and partially planned, resulting from a level of comfort with familiarity and the need to preserve the Indian culture, to enable the transmission of that culture to the children, and because of a limited amount of time and various demands on it.

Since I came to the U.S. with most of the requisite resources for adjustment, and because I came in the early stages of the liberalization of U.S. immigration laws, there were few Indian immigrants in my age group or in my environment. As such, barring some initial xenophobic reactions from my peers, the U.S. society was ready to accept me and made available resources, such as scholarships and host families, very readily. Application to colleges generated no anxiety, for I was justifiably confident that I would be accepted wherever I applied, because I was "different." I was not disappointed—I applied only to Barnard College and the University of Pennsylvania, and was accepted at both. Furthermore, the increasing size of the Indian population in the U.S. by the time I began exploring job opportunities ensured that more individuals had been exposed to Indians, yet the size of the population was still not so large that it had begun experiencing discrimination. Hence, I was able to find jobs without the sari being an obstacle (as it had been for my mother). Now, with the burgeoning Asian population in the U.S., Asian American children find they face an "Asian" quota in prestigious universities, and often compete with each other, rather than with the general applicant pool, for limited seats.

Raising the second generation is always a challenge for immigrants. Ideally, one seeks to instill in them the parental values and cultural heritage but with the skills of survival in the host country. However, parental influence is only a small fraction of the many effects on children. We have consciously attempted to expose our children to the Indian culture, its values, and norm of behavior and have taken them several times to India to allow them an understanding of the foundations of their background. Raising bicultural children is rarely easy, especially when we think that expectations, norms, and values of the two societies differ. While we have tried to offer our children more freedom than does the traditional Indian family, we are also aware that we may more closely monitor and control them than do American parents. On the other hand, often our children misinterpret intergenerational conflicts as cultural conflicts, and it is only when they find that their American counterparts have similar experiences that they acknowledge the difference. Furthermore, as our eldest child claims, as does the first-born of any culture, the boundaries placed on him are significantly greater than are those placed on his younger sibling.

As our sons, born in 1981 and 1986 respectively, have begun spreading their wings, we are again faced with issues concerning our values and expectations, the extent to which our sons follow patterns of Indian versus American norms, and the degree to which we, as parents, adapt and adjust to their independence. Traditional Indian parent-child relationships were long ago questioned, but they are daily under negotiation. Both in India and in the U.S., neither my husband nor I had the close daily physical proximity to our parents that our children have experienced—which can be an advantage in some instances and a disadvantage in others. On the other hand, once they begin driving, these U.S.-born children are able to have much more independence than did either my husband or I. As they chart their way, we struggle to determine the appropriate amount of guidance, for allowing complete freedom would be the abdication of parental responsibility, yet tight controls and strong directives, though consistent with traditional Indian norms, are neither in the best interest of children growing up in this society nor acceptable to them. While all parents must grapple with issues of independence, Asian American parents and children often face cultural conflicts that further confound the situation.

Thus, even when I feel I have adjusted to this country and the society and am comfortable with my identity, my definition of self and my position as Indian American is forced to further evolution. When I am still asked about my home (and the reference is India), when we have to adjust our thinking as our children challenge our perceptions, or when our awareness increases about alternative ways of handling things, I find that the adaptation and adjustment process for an immigrant is ongoing and may never be complete. On the other hand, after September 11, 2001, I have also come to the sad realization, that perhaps not for a long time, and perhaps never, will our sons experience the extent of freedom and absence of suspicion to which Indians were privy during the latter third of the twentieth century. Even before this tragic incident I often wondered about the intercultural and intergenerational conflicts our USAsian sons encounter and how they are perceived by, and perceive, their peers of non-Indian origin. It is also interesting to note that both our sons identify themselves as "Indians" or "Indian Americans" rather than "Americans," nevertheless, while they have traveled often to India and are interested in it, their allegiance is clearly to the United States. And, while we continue to have great pride in, and affection for, our Indian heritage, we are doubly blessed—we hail from a nation of rich culture and beauty and have settled in a wonderful land of opportunity and largesse—and my husband and I, too, are Americans.

NOTES

Prologue: "Racism"

1. Quoted in J. Grieve, "The Evidence Against Me Is Compelling. I Am a Policeman Guilty of Racism," *Daily Telegraph*, May 10, 2000, p. 15.

2. December 22, 1991, from "How to Tell Your Friends from the Japs," discussed in *Time*, March 9, 1998. "Regrets, We Have a Few," p. 100.

Chapter 1. Introduction: A Framework for the Immigration Experience

1. See the Amnesty International Web site: http://www.amnesty.org.

2. See the United Nations High Commissioner for Refugees Web site: http://www.unhcr.org.

3. See the Amnesty International Web site: http://www.amnesty.org.

4. Class is defined by economic and social status and sometimes level of affluence, while caste is determined by birth and restricts people to specific professions in the hierarchy of society.

5. See the Amnesty International Web site: http://www.amnesty.org.

6. See the United Nations High Commissioner for Refugees Web site: http://www.unhcr.org.

Chapter 2. Pre-1965 Immigration: Leaving the Homeland for the United States

1. The focus is on South Korea, as immigration to the United States from North Korea was nonexistent.

Chapter 3. Post-1965 Emigration: Changes in U.S. Immigration Policy

1. See the U.S. Department of Justice Web site: http://www.ins.usdoj.gov/graphics/aboutins/statistics/legishist/526.htm.

2. See Web site http://www.ins.usdoj.gov/graphics/aboutins/statistics/legishist/511.htm.

3. Most references to Korea and Koreans address citizens of South Korea. From the Korean War to the year 2000, U.S. relationships with North Korea were virtually nonexistent. At the beginning of the twenty-first century, glimmers of opening became evident.

4. The Amerasian Homecoming Act of December 22, 1987 (101 Statutes-at-Large 1329), is "an appropriations law providing for admission of children born in Vietnam

between specified dates to Vietnamese mothers and American fathers, together with their immediate relatives. They are admitted as nonquota immigrants but receive refugee benefits."

5. In 1986 the Laotian government adopted a package of reforms to move its economy from a centralized command system to a decentralized one, with the private sector being a key player in decision making. The economic management system that emerged is referred to as the New Economic Mechanism (NEM).

Chapter 4. Entry Into the United States and the Nation's Response to Asian Immigration

1. Asian immigration to the United States 1993–1998: 1993—358,047 (39.6%); 1994—292,589 (36.4%); 1995—267,931 (37.2%); 1996—307,807 (33.6%); 1997—265,786 (33.3%); 1998—219,696 (33.3%).

2. Discussed in chapter 2.

3. Formed by a group of white workers, its constitution stated that the Caucasian and Asiatic races are unassimilable and that the preservation of Caucasians in America necessitates the prevention of Asians' entering the country.

4. Census 2000 data that present the breakdown of educational and income levels by ethnicity will not be available until late 2002.

5. Census 2000 data will be available in late 2002.

6. Barred legal immigrants from receiving food stamps and Supplementary Security Income (SSI) and established screening procedures for current recipients; barred them from most federal means-tested programs for five years after entry; provided states with flexibility in setting eligibility rules for access to federal and state programs; increased responsibility of immigrants' sponsors.

7. Barred nondocumented or nonimmigrants from most federal, state, and local public benefits. Required the INS to verify immigration status in order for aliens to receive most federal public benefits.

8. The September 11, 2001, attacks on New York and Washington, D.C., and the aborted one in Pennsylvania are believed to have been perpetrated by Middle Eastern terrorists. Part of the fallout from these attacks has been an increasing suspicion of and violence directed toward Middle Easterners as well as those of South Asian ancestry.

Chapter 5. Asian Adjustment

1. Second-generation Japanese.

2. First-generation Japanese immigrants.

3. Vulnerability—biopsychosocial considerations that increase or decrease risk; Experience—cognitive and emotional organization; Manifestation—symptom expression; Prevalence—in population (p. 457).

4. Most countries do not permit individuals to retain dual citizenship. Hence, to become a U.S. citizen, one must renounce one's original citizenship. A few nations, such as Great Britain and Israel, which have unique relationships and agreements with the United States, permit dual citizenship.

5. Foreign-born persons over the age of eighteen can become naturalized citizens of the United States after they have lived in the country for a minimum of five years and have passed a citizenship examination. Spouses of citizens, and other select people, can

become naturalized after three years. If children are under the age of eighteen, they generally become naturalized along with their parents (U.S. Bureau of the Census 1998).

Chapter 7. Public Policies: Health, Mental Health, and Substance Abuse

1. Assets and monthly income cannot be above a governmentally predetermined level for eligibility.

2. Primary prevention targets the entire population to prevent problems; secondary prevention targets high-risk populations; tertiary prevention focuses on preventing relapse.

3. Posttraumatic stress disorder (PTSD) is defined by the American Psychiatric Association as a mental illness resulting from an individual's exposure to a traumatic event, which causes the individual to evidence symptoms from each of three symptom clusters—intrusive recollections, avoidant/numbing symptoms, and hyperarousal symptoms (American Psychiatric Association 1987).

Chapter 8. U.S.-Born Asian Americans

1. If one or both of their parents arrived in the United States before their births, or when they were prepubescent (sometimes known as the one-and-a-half generation), they are known as the second generation.

2. Since "Asian American" refers to all Americans of Asian origin, whether they are immigrants (particularly those who have assumed U.S. citizenship) or are born in the United States, for purposes of this chapter only, U.S.-born Asian Americans will be identified as USAsians.

3. There are discrete Chinese language schools, Japanese language schools, Hindi language schools, Korean language schools, Vietnamese language schools, and so on.

4. Many second-generation Asian Americans refer to themselves (and each other) in humor as being American-born and confused as they learn to balance the expectations and lifestyles of two disparate societies.

5. Marriages between people of different races.

6. Marriages between people of the same group or background.

7. Marriages between people of different groups or backgrounds.

8. The term "biracial" will be used to apply to both biracial and multiracial individuals.

9. "Amerasian" refers to all children of mixed Asian and American heritage, although most recently it has been used specifically to identify children born in Vietnam of Vietnamese mothers and American fathers.

Chapter 9. Implications, Directions, and Action Guidelines

1. A variation of this model is presented in U. A. Segal, "Exploring Child Abuse Among Vietnamese Refugees," in D. de Anda and R. M. Becerra, eds., *Violence: Diverse Populations and Communities*, 159–191 (Binghamton, N.Y.: Haworth Press).

REFERENCES

ABCNEWS.com. (1998). Cambodia's troubled history. http://archive.abcnews. go.com/sections/world/cambodiatimeline709.

Abraham, M. (1999). Sexual abuse in South Asian marriages. *Violence Against Women,* 5 (6): 591–618.

Ackerman, L. (1997). Health problems of refugees. *Journal of the American Board of Family Practice,* 19 (5): 1005–1020.

Agbayani-Siewert, P. (1994). Filipino American culture and family: Guidelines for practitioners. *Families in Society: The Journal of Contemporary Human Services,* 75: 429–438.

Agbayani-Siewert, P., and L. Revilla. (1995). Filipino Americans. In P. G. Min (ed.), *Asian Americans: Contemporary Issues and Trends,* 134–169. Thousand Oaks, Calif.: Sage.

Agoncillo, T. A. (1975). *A Short History of the Philippines.* New York: New American Library.

Aguilar, Jr., F. (1999). Ritual passage and the reconstruction of selfhood in international labour migration. *Journal of Social Issues in Southeast Asia,* 14 (1): 98–131.

Ahn, H. N. (1994). Cultural diversity and the definition of child abuse. In R. P. Barth and J. D. Berrick (eds.), *Child Welfare Research Review,* 1: 28–55. New York: Columbia University Press.

Alba, R. D., and V. Nee. (1997). Rethinking assimilation theory for a new era of immigration. *International Migration Review,* 31 (4): 826–975.

Almeida, R. (1996). Hindu, Christian, and Muslim families. In M. McGoldrick, J. Giordano, and J. K. Pearce (eds.), *Ethnicity and Family Therapy,* 395–423. New York: Guilford Press.

Altman, I. (1995). Spanish migration to the Americas. In R. Cohen (ed.), *The Cambridge Survey of World Migration,* 28–32. Cambridge, U.K.: Cambridge University Press.

American Psychiatric Association. (1987). *Diagnostic and Statistical Manual of Mental Disorders.* 3d ed. Washington, D.C.: American Psychiatric Association.

——. (1994). *Diagnostic and Statistical Manual of Mental Disorders.* 4th ed. Washington, D.C.: American Psychiatric Association.

Amnesty International. (2000). *Torture Worldwide: An Affront to Human Dignity.* New York: Amnesty International.

Amott, T. L., and J. A. Matthaei. (1991). *Race, Gender, and Work.* Boston: South End Press.

Aronson, J. E., A. M. Smith, V. Kothari, M. Alonso, J. Bledsoe, N. Hendrie, M. Hostetter, D. Johnson, A. Mandalakas, K. Olness, L. Miller, T. Ochs, and M. Traister. (2000). Elevated blood lead levels among internationally adopted children—United States, 1998. *JAMA, the Journal of the American Medical Association,* 283 (11): 1416–1418.

Asian Americans and Pacific Islanders in Philanthropy. (1992, December). *Invisible and in Need: Philanthropic Giving to Asian Americans and Pacific Islanders.* San Francisco: AAPIP.

Associated Press. (1998, July 7). Substance abuse: Study reveals disparity among races. *Macon Telegraph,* National Journal Group, American Health Line.

——. (2000a, March 9). Women's Day highlights problems of injustice, poverty and violence. *St. Louis Post-Dispatch,* A8.

——. (2000b, June 5). Japanese lead world in prospect of having long, ailment-free lives. *St. Louis Post-Dispatch,* A1, A6.

——. (2000c, July 9). Koreans arrested after being smuggled into U.S. *Korea Times,* 5.

Atkinson, D. R., J. G. Ponterotto, and A. R. Sanchez. (1984). Attitudes of Vietnamese and Anglo-American students toward counseling. *Journal of College Student Personnel,* 25 (5): 448–452.

Ayers, S. M. (1996). *Health Care in the United States: The Facts and the Choices.* Chicago: American Library Association.

Aylesworth, L. S., P. G. Ossorio, and L. T. Osaki. (1980). Stress and mental health among Vietnamese in the United States. In R. Endo, S. Sue, and N. N. Wagner (eds.), *Asian-Americans: Social and Psychological Perspectives,* 2:64–79. New York: Science and Behavior Books.

Bach, R. L. (1988). State intervention in Southeast Asian Refugee resettlement in the United States. *Journal of Refugee Studies,* 1: 38–56.

Bach, R. L., and R. Argiros. (1991). Economic progress among Southeast Asian refugees in the United States. In H. Adelman (ed.), *Refugee Policy: Canada and the United States,* 322–343. Toronto: York Lanes.

Balgopal, P. R. (1995). Asian Indians. In R. Edwards (ed.), *Encyclopedia of Social Work,* 256–260. 19th ed. Washington, D.C.: NASW Press.

Bankston, C. L., and M. Zhou. (1997). The social adjustment of Vietnamese American adolescents: Evidence for a segmented-assimilation approach. *Social Science Quarterly,* 78 (2): 508–523.

Bartholet, E. (1993). International adoption: Current status and future prospects. *The Future of Children,* 3 (1): 89–103.

Barton, J. J. (1975). *Peasants and Strangers.* Cambridge: Harvard University Press.

Bean, F. D., B. L. Lowell, and L. J. Taylor. (1988). Undocumented Mexican immigrants and the earnings of other workers in the United States. *Demography,* 25 (1): 35–52.

Beasley, W. G. (1995). *The Rise of Modern Japan.* New York: St. Martin's.

Bello, W. F., F. Lynch, and P. Q. Makil. (1969). Brain drain in the Philippines. In W. F. Bello and A. de Guzman II (eds.), *Modernization: Its Impact in the Philippines,* 4:93–146. Quezon City, Philippines: Ateneo de Manila University Press.

Belsie, L. (1999, July 28). Census nods to new views of ethnicity. *Christian Science Monitor*, 1.

Bemak, F. (1989). Cross-cultural family therapy with Southeast Asian (SEA) refugees. *Journal of Strategic and Systemic Therapies*, 8: 22–27.

Bemak, F., R.C-Y. Chung, and T. H. Bornemann. (1996). Counseling and psychotherapy with refugees. In P. B. Pedersen, J. G. Draguns, W. J. Lonner, and J. E. Trimble (eds.), *Counseling Across Cultures*, 243–265. 4th ed. Thousand Oaks, Calif.: Sage.

Bennett, Jr., A. B. (1971). Managers and entrepreneurs: A comparison of social backgrounds in Philippine manufacturing. In F. Lynch and A. de Guzman II (eds.), *Modernization: Its Impact in the Philippines*, 5:101–140. Quezon City, Philippines: Ateneo de Manila University Press.

Bennett, C. E. (1992). Asian and Pacific Islander population in the United States: March 1991. *Current Population Reports, Population Characteristics*. P20–459. U.S. Bureau of the Census. Washington, D.C.: Government Printing Office.

Berg, J. A. (1999). The perimenopausal transition of Filipino American midlife women: Biopsychosociocultural dimensions. *Nursing Research*, 49 (2): 71–77.

Berganio, J. T. J., L. A. Tacata Jr., and P. M. Jamero. (1997). The prevalence and impact of alcohol, tobacco, and other drugs on Filipino American communities. In M. P. P. Root (ed.), *Filipino Americans: Transformation and Identity*, 272–286. Thousand Oaks, Calif.: Sage.

Bernard, E. (1994). The United States should adopt a system similar to Canada's. In C. Wekesser (ed.), *Health Care in America: Opposing Viewpoints*, 151–159. San Diego: Greenhaven Press.

Berry, J. W. (1986). The acculturation process and refugee behavior. In C. J. Williams and J. Westermeyer (eds.), *Refugee Mental Health in Resettlement Countries*, 25–37. The Series in Clinical and Community Psychology. Washington, D.C.: Hemisphere Publishing.

Besharow, D. J., and T. S. Sullivan. (1996, July 21). The interracial generation: From mixed marriages, the offspring of hope. *Washington Post*, 14.

Bhattacharya, G. (1998). Drug use among Asian-Indian adolescents: Identifying protective/risk factors. *Adolescence*, 33 (129): 169–184.

Bhowmick, A. S. (2000, May 12). Community urged to integrate into American society. *India Abroad*, 2, 4.

Birman, D. (1998). Biculturalism and perceived competence of Latino immigrant adolescents. *American Journal of Community Psychology*, 26 (3): 335–354.

Black, C. E., M. B. Jansen, H. S. Levine, M. J. Levy Jr., H. Rosovsky, G. Rozman, H. D. Smith II, and S. F. Starr. (1975). *The Modernization of Japan and Russia*. New York: Free Press.

Blau, P. M. (1977). *Inequality and Heterogeneity*. New York: Free Press.

Boehnlein, J. K., and J. D. Kinzie. (1995). Refugee trauma. *Transcultural Psychiatric Research Review*, 32 (3): 233–252.

Bonacich, E. (1984). Some basic facts: Patterns of Asian immigration and exclusion. In L. Cheng, L., and E. Bonacich (eds.), *Labor Immigration Under Capitalism: Asian Workers in the United States Before World War II*, 60–78. Berkeley: University of California Press.

Booth, W. (1999, August 20). 13 charged in gang importing prostitutes. *Washington Post*, A3.

Borjas, G. J. (1990). *Friends or Strangers: The Impact of Immigrants on the U.S. Economy.* New York: Basic Books.

Borjas, G. J., and S. Trejo. (1991). Immigrant participation in the welfare system. *Industrial and Labor Relations Review*, 44 (2): 195–211.

Bowers, J. Z. (1965). Medical students in the Philippines. *Journal of the American Medical Association*, 191 (2).

Boyne, W. J. (1999). The Plain of Jars. *Air Force Magazine*, 82 (6): 78–83.

Branigin, W. (1997, April 9). Nearly 1 in 10 in U.S. is foreign-born, Census says. *Washington Post*, 18A.

Briggs, J. W. (1978). *An Italian Passage.* New Haven: Yale University Press.

Brody, E. B. (1990). Mental health and world citizenship: Sociocultural bases for advocacy. In W. H. Holtzman and T. Bornemann (eds.), *Mental Health of Immigrants and Refugees*, 299–328. Austin: Hogg Foundation for Mental Health.

Brown, A. J. (1912). *The Chinese Revolution.* New York: Student Volunteer Movement for Foreign Missions.

Brown, F. (1987). Counseling Vietnamese refugees: The new challenge. *International Journal for the Advancement of Counseling*, 10 (4): 259–268.

Browne, C., R. Fong, and N. Mokuau. (1994). The mental health of Asian and Pacific Island elders: Implications for research and mental health administration. *Journal of Mental Health Administration*, 21 (1): 52–59.

Bruner, R. W. (1997, November 3). Execs burn over proposed limits on foreign hires. *Electronic News*, 43 (2192): 30–31.

Buckley, J. (1998, September). Minority optimism. *Mortgage Banking*, 58 (12): 54–62.

Bui, H. N., and M. Morash. (1999). Domestic violence in the Vietnamese immigrant community. *Violence Against Women*, 5 (7): 769–795.

Bun, C. K. (1995). The Vietnamese boat people in Hong Kong. In R. Cohen (ed.), *The Cambridge Survey of World Migration*, 380–385. Cambridge, U.K.: Cambridge University Press.

Bureau of Justice Statistics. (1996). *Non-Citizens in the Federal Criminal Justice System, 1984–1994.* Washington, D.C.: Government Printing Office.

——. (1998). *Sourcebook of Criminal Justice Statistics.* Washington, D.C.: Government Printing Office.

Butcher, K. F., and D. Card. (1991). Immigration and wages: Evidence from the 1980s. *American Economic Review*, 81 (2): 292–296.

Cain, B. E., and D. R. Kiewitt. (1986). *Minorities in California.* Pasadena: California Institute of Technology.

Cain, B. E., D. R. Kiewitt, and C. J. Uhlaner. (1991). Acquisition of partnership by Latinos and Asian Americans. *American Journal of Political Science*, 35 (2): 390–422.

Campinha-Bacote, J. (1988). Cultural assessment: An important factor in psychiatric consultation-liaison nursing. *Archives of Psychiatric Nursing*, 7: 311–316.

Caplan, N., J. K. Whitmore, and M. H. Choy. (1989). *The Boat People and Achievement in America: A Study of Family Life, Hard Work, and Cultural Values.* Ann Arbor: University of Michigan Press.

Cariño, B. V. (1996). Filipino Americans: Many and varied. In S. Pedraza and R. G. Rumbaut (eds.), *Origins and Destinies: Immigration, Race, and Ethnicity in America*, 293–301. New York: Wadsworth.

Carrillo, R. (1992). *Battered Dreams*. New York: UNIFEM.

Cassidy, W. (1995). *Self-fulfilling Prophesy: Color of Authority and the Rise of Vietnamese Street Gangs in Orange County, California*. http://www.users.deltanet.com/~wcassidy/wlrc/vietoc.html.

Castles, F. G. (1998). *Comparative Public Policy: Patterns of Post-war Transformation*. Northampton, Mass.: Edward Elgar Publishing.

Cauce, A. M., Y. Hiraga, C. Mason, T. Aguilar, N. Ordonez, and N. Gonzales. (1992). Between a rock and a hard place: Social adjustment of biracial youth. In M. P. P. Root (ed.), *Racially Mixed People in America*, 207–223. Newbury Park, Calif.: Sage.

Centers for Disease Control. (1999a). *Health Care Coverage for Persons Under 65 Years of Age*. National Center for Health Statistics. Data computed by the Division of Health and Utilization Analysis from the National Health Interview Survey. http://www.cdc.gov/nchs/products/pubs/pubd/hus/tables/99hus129.pdf.

——. (1999b). *Health Care Coverage for Persons 65 Years of Age and Over*. National Center for Health Statistics. Data computed by the Division of Health and Utilization Analysis from the National Health Interview Survey. http://www.cdc.gov/nchs/products/pubs/pubd/hus/tables/99hus130.pdf.

——. (2000). *Health Care Coverage and Major Federal Program*. National Center for Health Statistics. Data computed by the Division of Health and Utilization Analysis from the National Health Interview Survey. http://www.cdc.gov/nchs/products/pubshus/99hccmfp.htm.

Chambon, A. (1989). Refugee families' experiences: Three family themes—family disruption, violent trauma, and acculturation. *Journal of Strategic and Systematic Therapies*, 8 (3): 3–13.

Champagne, A., and E. Harpham. (1984). *The Attack on the Welfare State*. Prospect Heights, Ill.: Waveland Press.

Chan, C. S. (1997a). Attitudes toward sexuality and sexual behaviors of Asian-American adolescents: Implications for risk of HIV infection. In R. D. Taylor and M. C. Wang (eds.), *Social and Emotional Adjustment and Family Relations in Ethnic Minority Families*, 133–144. Mahwah, N.J.: Lawrence Erlbaum Associates.

——. (1997b). Don't ask, don't tell, don't know: The formation of a homosexual identity and sexual expression among Asian American lesbians. In B. Greene (ed.), *Ethnic and Cultural Diversity Among Lesbians and Gay Men*. Vol. 3 of *Psychological Perspectives on Lesbian and Gay Issues*, 240–248. Thousand Oaks, Calif.: Sage.

Chan, K. B., and D. Loveridge. (1987). Refugees in transit: Vietnamese in a refugee camp in Hong Kong. *International Migration Review*, 21 (3): 745–759.

Chan, K. S., and S. Hune. (1995). Racialization and panethnicity: From Asians in America to Asian Americans. In W. D. Hawley and A. W. Jackson (eds.), *Toward a Common Destiny: Improving Race and Ethnic Relations in America*, 205–233. San Francisco: Jossey-Bass.

Chan, S. (1991). The exclusion of Chinese women. In S. Chan, D. H. Daniels, M. T. Garcia, and T. P. Wilson (eds.), *Entry Denied: Exclusion and the Chinese Community in America, 1882–1943*, 94–146. Philadelphia:: Temple University Press.

———. (1994). *Hmong Means Free: Life in Laos and America.* Philadelphia: Temple University Press.

Chan, S. P. (2000, May 7). Six bachelors wonder where the action is. *Seattle Times,* L1.

Chandrashekhar, S. (1982). A history of United States legislation with respect to immigration from India: Some statistics on Asian Indian immigration to the United States of America. In S. Chandrashekhar (ed.), *From India to America: A Brief History of Immigration, Problems of Discrimination, Admission, and Assimilation,* 11–29. La Jolla, Calif.: Population Review.

Chang, T. H-H., and R. L. Yeh. (1999). Theoretical framework for therapy with Asian families. In K. S. Ng (ed.), *Counseling Asian Families from a Systems Perspective,* 3–13. Alexandria, Va.: American Counseling Association.

Chao, C. M. (1995). A bridge over troubled waters: Being Eurasian in the U.S. of A. In J. Adleman and G. Equinados (eds.), *The Significance of Racism in the Psychology of Women: Building Consciously Anti-Racist Models of Feminist Therapy,* 33–44. New York: Haworth.

Chao, K. (1986). *Man and Land in Chinese History: An Economic Analysis.* Stanford: Stanford University Press.

Chapin, R. K. (1999). It is expected by the year 2000: Using lessons from the past to plan for the elder boom. *Journal of Gerontological Social Work,* 32 (2): 21–40.

Chapple, A., M. Ling, and C. May. (1998). General practitioners' perceptions of the illness behavior and health needs of South Asian women with menorrhagia. *Ethnicity and Health,* 3 (1/2): 81–83.

Chen, H-S. (1992). *Chinatown No More: Taiwan Immigrants in Contemporary New York.* Ithaca: Cornell University Press.

Chen, P. N. (1979). A study of Chinese-American elderly residing in hotel rooms. *Social Casework,* 60 (2): 89–95.

Chen, S. A., and R. H. True. (1994). Asian/Pacific Island Americans. In L. D. Eron and J. H. Gentry (eds.), *Reason to Hope: A Psychosocial Perspective on Violence and Youth,* 145–162. Washington, D.C.: American Psychological Association.

Chen, X., J. B. Unger, T. B. Cruz, and C. A. Johnson. (1999). Smoking patterns of Asian-American youth in California and their relationship with acculturation. *Journal of Adolescent Health,* 24 (5): 321–328.

Cheong Wa Dae. (2001). President Kim Dae-jung. Web site: http://www.cwd.go.kr/english/president/index.php.

Cheung, F. M., B. W. Lau, and E. Waldmann. (1981). Somatization among Chinese depressives in general practice. *International Journal of Psychiatry in Medicine,* 10 (4): 361–374.

Cheung, M. (1989). Elderly Chinese living in the United States: Assimilation or adjustment. *Social Work,* 34 (5): 457–461.

Chin, J. L., J. H. Liem, M. A. Domokos-Cheng Ham, and G. K. Hong. (1993). *Transference and Empathy in Asian American Psychotherapy: Cultural Values and Treatment Needs.* New York: Praeger.

Chin, K. L. (1994). Out-of-town brides: International marriage and wife abuse among Chinese immigrants. *Journal of Comparative Family Studies,* 25 (1): 53–69.

Chin, K. L., J. Fagan, and R. J. Kelly. (1992). Patterns of Chinese gang extortion. *Justice Quarterly,* 9 (4): 625–646.

Chinn, D. H. (1997, October 3). Asian adoptees start an organization of peers. *Northwestern Asian Weekly*, 16 (41): 8.

Chiu, L. H. (1987). Child-rearing attitudes of Chinese, Chinese-American, and Anglo-American mothers. *International Journal of Psychology*, 22 (4): 409–419.

Choi, D. H. (1994). *The Passage*. http://hcs.harvard.edu/~yisei/backissues/fall_92/yf92_05.html.

Choi, K-H., S. Lew, E. Vittinghoff, J. A. Catania, D. C. Barrett, and T. J. Coates. (1996). The efficacy of brief group counseling on HIV risk reduction among homosexual Asian and Pacific Islanders. *AIDS*, 10 (1): 81–87.

Chow, C. (1998). *Leaving Deep Waters*. New York: Dutton.

Chow, E.N-L. (1987). Job decision, household work, and gender relations in the Asian American families. Paper presented at the annual meeting of the American Sociological Association, Chicago.

———. (1994). Asian American women at work: Survival, resistance, and coping. In M. B. Zinn and B. T. Dill (eds.), *Women of Color in U.S. Society*, 203–227. Philadelphia: Temple University Press.

———. (1995). From Pennsylvania Avenue to H Street, N.W.: The transformation of Chinatown in Washington, D.C. In F. Cary (ed.), *Urban Odyssey of Washington, D.C.: Many Voices on a Common Ground*. Washington, D.C.: Smithsonian Institution Press.

———. (1996). Family, economy, and the state: A legacy of struggle for Chinese American women. In S. Pedraza and R. G. Rumbaut (eds.), *Origins and Destinies: Immigration, Race, and Ethnicity in America*, 110–124. New York: Wadsworth.

Chow, S. (2000). The significance of race in the private sphere: Asian Americans and spousal preferences. *Sociological Inquiry*, 70 (1): 1–29.

Choy, B. Y. (1979). *Koreans in America*. Chicago: Nelson Hall.

Chun, C-A., E. Kana, and S. Sue. (1996). Health care issues among Asian Americans: Implications of somatization. In P. M. Kato and T. Mann (eds.), *Handbook of Diversity Issues in Health Psychology*. New York: Plenum.

Chun, K. M., K. L. Eastman, G. C. Wang, and S. S. Sue. (1998). Psychopathology. In L. C. Lee and N. W. S. Zane (eds.), *Handbook of Asian American Psychology*, 457–483. Thousand Oaks, Calif.: Sage.

Chung, D. K. (1992). Asian commonalities. In S. M. Furuto, R. Biswas, D. K. Chung, K. Murase, and F. Ross-Sheriff (eds.), *Social Work Practice with Asian Americans*, 27–44. Newbury Park, Calif.: Sage.

Chung, R.C-Y., and F. Bemak. (1996). The effects of welfare status on psychological distress among Southeast Asian refugees. *Journal of Nervous and Mental Disease*, 184 (6): 346–353.

Chung, Y. B., and M. Katayama. (1999). Ethnic and sexual identity development of Asian American lesbian and gay adolescents. In K. S. Ng (ed.), *Counseling Asian Families from a Systems Perspective*, 159–169. Alexandria, Va.: American Counseling Association.

Churgin, M. J. (1996). Mass exoduses: The response of the United States. *International Migration Review*, 30 (1): 310–324.

Clemetson, L. (2000a, May 8). Color my world: The promise and perils of life in the new multiracial mainstream. *Newsweek*, 70, 72, 74.

———. (2000b, November 6). The new victims of hate: Bias crimes hit America's fastest growing ethnic group. *Newsweek*, 61.

Clines, F. (1996, August 26). Clinton signs bill cutting welfare; states in new role. *New York Times*, A14.

Clinton, W. J. (1999, June 7). Remarks at the White House Conference on Mental Health, June 7, 1999. *Weekly Compilation of Presidential Documents*, 35 (23): 1052–1056.

Clinton, W. J. (2000, June 5). Statement on signing the Hmong Veterans Act of 2000. *Weekly Compilation of Presidential Documents*, 36 (22): 1242.

Cobb-Clark, D. A., and S. A. Kossoudji. (1994). Mobility in El Norte: Employment and occupational changes for undocumented Latina women. Illinois State University. Unpublished manuscript.

Cohen, D. K., and J. P. Spillane. (1992). Policy and practice: The relations between governance and instruction. *Review of Research in Education*, 18 (3): 3–49.

Cohen, P. (1978). Christian missions and their impact to 1900. In D. Twitchett and J. K. Fairbank (eds.), *The Cambridge History of China*, 543–590. Cambridge, U.K.: Cambridge University Press.

Cohen, R. (1994). *Frontiers of Identity: The British and the Others*. London: Longman.

———. (1995). Prologue to R. Cohen (ed.), *The Cambridge Survey of World Migration*. Cambridge, U.K.: Cambridge University Press, 1–9.

Coleman, J. (1966). *Equality of Educational Opportunity Report*. Washington, D.C.: U.S. Government Printing Office.

Collier, R. (2000, May 12). Shift toward Beijing in Bay area: Numerous Chinese Americans back trade, investment with homeland. *San Francisco Chronicle*, A14.

Combs-Orme, T. (1993). Should the federal government finance health care for all Americans?: Yes. In H. J. Karger and J. Midgley (eds.), *Controversial Issues in Social Policy*, 33–48. New York: Allyn and Bacon.

Committee on Government Operations. (1968). *Scientific Brain Drain from Developing Countries*. Washington, D.C.: U.S. Government Printing Office.

Connors, J. F. (1989). *Violence Against Women in the Family*. New York: United Nations.

Conroy, H. (1960). *The Japanese Seizure of Korea, 1868–1910*. Philadelphia: University of Pennsylvania Press.

Cooke, P. (1991, June 23). They cried until they could not see. *New York Times Magazine*, 8–9.

Copeland, V. (1988). *China 1977: End of the Revolutionary Mao Era*. http://www.workers.org/marcy/china/index.html.

Cordova, F. (1983). *Filipinos: Forgotten Asian Americans*. Dubuque, Iowa: Kendall/Hunt.

Corpuz, O. D. (1965). *The Philippines*. Englewood Cliffs, N.J.: Prentice-Hall.

Council on Medical Education. (1966). Medical education in the United States. *Journal of the American Medical Association*, 198 (8): 847–938.

Cowart, R., and M. F. Cowart. (1996). Communities held hostage: A profile of a Laotian street gang in Dallas. *Journal of Contemporary Criminal Justice*, 12 (4): 307–315.

Crystal, D. (1994). Concepts of deviance in children and adolescents: The case of Japan. *Deviant Behavior*, 15 (3): 241–266.

Cyphers, G. C. (1999). Out of the shadows: elder abuse and neglect. *Policy and Practice,* 57 (3): 25–30.

Dalaker, J., and M. Naifeh. (1998). Poverty in the United States: 1997. *Current Population Reports.* Ser. P-60, no. 201. Washington, D.C.: Government Printing Office.

Daly, G. (1996). Migrants and gatekeepers: The links between immigration and homelessness in Western Europe. *Cities,* 13 (1): 11–23.

Daniels, R. (1995). Changes in immigration law and nativism since 1924. In F. Ng (ed.), *The History and Immigration of Asian Americans,* 65–86. New York: Garland.

Dao, J. (1992, April 1). Asian street gangs emerging as a new underworld. *New York Times,* B2.

Das, P. (2000, January 14). It is a perfect chance to explore social issues. *India Abroad,* 25.

Dasgupta, S. (1998). Gender roles and cultural continuity in the Asian Indian immigrant community. *Sex Roles,* 38 (11/12): 953–974.

Dasgupta, S. C., and S Warrier. (1996). In the footsteps of "Arundhati": Asian Indian women's experience of domestic violence in the United States. *Violence Against Women,* 2: 238–259.

Day, C. L. (1990). Ethnocentrism, economic competition, and attitudes toward US immigration policy. Paper presented at the annual meeting of the Midwest Political Science Association, Chicago, April 5–7.

de Anda, D. (1997). *Controversial Issues in Multiculturalism.* Boston: Allyn and Bacon.

de Leon Siantz, M. L. (1997). Factors that impact development outcomes of immigrant children. In A. Booth and A. C. Crouter (eds.), *Immigration and the Family: Research and Policy on U.S. Immigrants,* 149–161. Mahwah, N.J.: Lawrence Erlbaum Associates.

Delevett, P. (1998, July 6). Mental health legislation upsets some. *Business Journal,* 16 (9): 1–2.

Delucchi, M., and H. D. Do. (1996). The model minority myth and perceptions of Asian-Americans as victims of racial harassment. *College Student Journal,* 30 (3): 411–414.

de Monchy, M. L. (1991). Recovery and rebuilding: The challenge for refugee children and service providers. In F. L. Ahern Jr. and J. I. Athey (eds.), *Refugee Children: Theory, Research, and Services,* 163–180. The Johns Hopkins Series in Contemporary Mental Health. Baltimore: Johns Hopkins University Press.

Denton, K., L. T. Love, and R. Slate. (1990). Eldercare in the '90s: Employee responsibility, employer challenge. *Families in Society,* 71 (6): 349–359.

Department of Health and Human Services. (1995). *Refugee Assistance Programs Should Be Limited to Newly-Arrived and Needy Refugees.* Washington, D.C.: HHS, A-04-93-00062.

Department of Justice. (1988). *Sourcebook of Criminal Justice Statistics—1987.* Washington, D.C.: Hindelang Criminal Justice Research Center.

———. (1990). *Sourcebook of Criminal Justice Statistics—1989.* Washington, D.C.: Hindelang Criminal Justice Research Center.

———. (1992). *Sourcebook of Criminal Justice Statistics—1991.* Washington, D.C.: Hindelang Criminal Justice Research Center.

———. (1996a). *Correctional Populations in the United States, 1996.* Washington, D.C.: U.S. Government Printing Office.

———. (1996b). *Sourcebook of Criminal Justice Statistics—1995.* Washington, D.C.: Hindelang Criminal Justice Research Center.

———. (2000). *Trends in Violent Crime, 1973–1998.* http://www.ojp.usdoj.gov/bjs/glance/viotrd.txt.

DeVos, G. (1978). Selective permeability and reference group sanctioning: Psychological continuities in role degradation. Paper presented at Comparative Studies on Ethnicity and Nationality seminar, University of Washington, Seattle.

DeWitt, H. A. (1996). The Watsonville Anti-Filipino Riot of 1930: A case study of the Great Depression and ethnic conflict in California. *Southern California Quarterly,* 61 (2): 291–302.

Didi, S. (2000, August 4). Opportunity denied to many professionals. *India Abroad,* 4.

DiNitto, D. M. (1995). *Social Welfare: Politics and Public Policy.* 4th ed. Needham Heights, Mass.: Allyn and Bacon.

Dobelstein, A. W. (1996). *Social Welfare: Policy and Analysis.* 2d ed. Chicago: Nelson Hall Publishers.

Dugger, C. W. (2000, February 29). Return passage to India: émigrés pay back. *New York Times.*

Dunphy, L. L., and L. Mera. (1991). A needs assessment of ethnic-language communities and child maltreatment prevention. Paper presented at the Ninth National Conference on Child Abuse and Neglect, Denver, September 14–17.

Dunn, C., and D. Woodward. (1991). *American Conservatism from Burke to Bush.* Lanham, Md.: Madison Books.

Dunn, T. (1996). *The Militarization of the U.S.-Mexico Border, 1978–1992.* Austin: Center for Mexican American Studies Press.

Durvasulas, R. S., and G. A. Mylvaganam. (1994). Mental health of Asian Indians: Relevant issues and community implications. *Journal of Community Psychology,* 22 (2): 97–108.

Dutt, E. (1999, November 5). Many Asian Indians in California lack health coverage. *India Abroad,* 52.

———. (2000, November 10). MO apartment owners charged with bias by U.S. housing authority. *India Abroad,* 44.

Easwaran, A. (1997, November 14). Discussion on education of Asian Pacific youth. *India Abroad,* 46.

Eckert, C. J., K-B. Lee, Y. I. Lew, M. Robinson, and E. W. Wagner. (1990). *Korea—Old and New: A History.* Seoul: Ilchokak Publishers.

Educational Testing Service. (1991). *ETS Policy Notes: Testing.* Princeton, N.J.: Educational Testing Service.

Elliott, D. (2000, February 5). Personal communication. Professor, School of Social Work, University of Texas-Arlington.

Embree, J. F. (1939). *Suye Mura: A Japanese Village.* Chicago: University of Chicago Press.

English, T. J. (1995). *Born to Kill.* New York: William Morrow.

Enrico, D. (1999, September 8). Connecting with our Korean heritage. *USA Today.*

Erickson D'Avanzo, C. (1997). Southeast Asians: Asian-Pacific Americans at risk for substance misuse. *Substance Use and Misuse,* 32 (7/8): 829–848.

Erikson, E. (1963). *Childhood and Society*. New York: Norton.

Ervin, N. (1994). Immigration and the environment. In N. Mills (ed.), *Arguing Immigration: Are New Immigrants a Wealth of Diversity . . . or a Crushing Burden?*, 90–94. New York: Simon and Schuster.

Espenshade, T. J. (1995). Unauthorized immigration to the United States. *Annual Review of Sociology*, 21: 195–216.

Espiritu, Y. L. (1996). Colonial oppression, labour importation, and group formation: Filipinos in the United States. *Ethnic and Racial Studies*, 19 (1): 29–48.

——. (1997). *Asian American Women and Men*. Thousand Oaks, Calif.: Sage.

Ethnic News Watch. (1996, December 19). Anti-Miscegenation in the '90s. *AsianWeek*, 18 (17): 11.

European Centre. (1999). *Follow-up to the World Summit for Social Development/ Dialogues in Social Theory and Policy Making*. http://www.euro.centre.org/ causa/ec/ec_pa1.htm.

Fairbank, J. K. (1992). *China: A New History*. Cambridge: Harvard University Press.

Falco, M. (1992). *The Making of a Drug-Free America*. New York: Times Books.

Faragallah, M. H., W. R. Schumm, and F. J. Webb. (1997). Acculturation of Arab-American immigrants: An exploratory study. *Journal of Comparative Family Studies*, 28 (3): 182–203.

Federal Bureau of Investigation. (1997). *Crime in the United States*. Washington, D.C.: Government Printing Office.

Feldman, S. S., and D. A. Rosenthal. (1990). The acculturation of autonomy expectations in Chinese high schoolers residing in two Western nations. *International Journal of Psychology*, 25 (3): 259–281.

Felsman, J. K., M. C. Johnson, F. T. L. Leong, and I. C. Felsman. (1989). *Vietnamese Amerasians: Practical Implications of Current Research*. Washington, D.C.: Office of Refugee Resettlement.

Flaskerud, J. H., and L. Hu. (1992). Relationship of ethnicity to psychiatric diagnosis. *Journal of Nervous and Mental Disease*, 180 (5): 296–303.

Flaskerud, J. H., and S. Kim. (1999). Health problems of Asian and Latino immigrants. *Nursing Clinics of North America*, 34 (2): 359–380.

Flowers, R. B. (1990). *Minorities and Criminality*. New York: Praeger.

Foner, N. E. (1978). *Jamaica Farewell: Jamaican Migrants in London*. Berkeley: University of California Press.

——. (1997). The immigrant family-cultural legacies and cultural changes. *International Migration Review*, 31 (4): 961–974.

Foulks, E. F., L. Merkel, and J. K. Boehnlein. (1992). Symptoms in non-patient Southeast Asian refugees. *Journal of Nervous and Mental Disease*, 180 (7): 466–468.

Freeley, M., and J. Simon. (1992). The new penology. *Criminology*, 30 (4): 451–458.

Freeman, J. M. (1989). *Hearts of Sorrow: Vietnamese-American Lives*. Stanford: Stanford University Press.

Freeman, R. J., and R. Roesch. (1989). Mental disorder and the criminal justice system: A review. *International Journal of Law and Psychiatry*, 12 (2/3): 105–115.

French, J. R. P., and B Raven. (1968). The bases of social power. In D. Cartwright and A. Zander (eds.), *Group Dynamics: Research and Theory*, 259–269. New York: Harper and Row.

Freundlich, M. (1999). Families without borders—I. *Un Chronicle*, 36 (2): 88–89.

Frolik, J. (2000, April 30). Bound by an enemy: In Little Havana and Little Saigon, freedom from communism comes first. *Los Angeles Times*, 1G.

Fugita, S., K. Ito, J. Abe, and D. Takeuchi. (1991). Japanese Americans. In N. Mokuau (ed.), *Handbook of Social Services for Asian and Pacific Islanders*, 61–77. New York: Greenwood Press.

Fujino, D. C. (1997). The rates, patterns, and reasons for forming heterosexual interracial dating relationships among Asian Americans. *Journal of Social and Personal Relationships*, 14 (6): 809–828.

Fukutaki, T. (1967). *Japanese Rural Society*. Ithaca: Cornell University Press.

Fukuyama, F. (1994). Immigrants and family values. In N. Mills (ed.), *Arguing Immigration: Are New Immigrants a Wealth of Diversity . . . or a Crushing Burden?*, 151–168. New York: Simon and Schuster.

Furuto, S. M., and K. Murase. (1992). Asian Americans in the future. In S. M. Furuto, R. Biswas, D. K. Chung, K. Murase, and F. Ross-Sheriff (eds.), *Social Work Practice with Asian Americans*, 240–253. Newbury Park, Calif.: Sage.

Gall, S. B., and T. L. Gall (eds.) (1993). *Statistical Record of Asian Americans*. Cleveland: Eastword Publications Development.

Ganesan, I. (1998). Food and the immigrant. In C. O'Hearn (ed.), *Half and Half: Writers on Growing Up Biracial and Bicultural*, 170–180. New York: Pantheon.

Ganesan, S., S. Fine, and T. Y. Yi Lin. (1989). Psychiatric symptoms in refugee families from South East Asia: Therapeutic challenges. *American Journal of Psychotherapy*, 43 (2): 218–228.

Garcia, M. C. (1996). *Havana USA: Cuban Exiles and Cuban Americans in South Florida, 1959–1994*. Los Angeles: University of California Press.

Gargan, E. A. (1981, April 3). House panel finds widespread and growing abuse of elderly. *New York Times Magazine*, 8–12.

Gelles, R. J. (1997). *Intimate Violence in Families*. Thousand Oaks, Calif.: Sage.

Gerber, L. (1996). We must hear each other's cry: Lessons from Pol Pot survivors. In C. B. Strozier and M. Flynn (eds.), *Genocide, War, and Human Survival*, 297–305. Lanham, Md.: Rowman and Littlefield.

Gersten, C. (1996, August 1). Committee on the Judiciary. Gersten statement regarding hearing on refugee resettlement by private organizations. http://www.house.gov/judiciary/632.htm.

Gibson, M. A. (1997). Complicating the immigrant involuntary minority typology-conclusion. *Anthropology and Education Quarterly*, 28 (3): 431–454.

Gil, D. (1973). *Violence Against Children*. Cambridge: Harvard University Press.

Gillmore, M. R., R. F. Catalano, D. M. Morrison, E. A. Wells, B. Iritani, and J. D. Hawkins. (1990). Racial differences in acceptability and availability of drugs and early initiation of substance use. *American Journal of Drug and Alcohol Abuse*, 16 (3/4): 185–206.

Glazer, N. (1954). Ethnic groups in America. In M. Berger, T. Abel, and C. Page (eds.), *Freedom and Control in Modern Society*. New York: Van Nostrand, 158–173.

——. (1994). The closing door. In N. Mills (ed.), *Arguing Immigration: Are New Immigrants a Wealth of Diversity . . . or a Crushing Burden?*, 37–47. New York: Simon and Schuster.

Gjerde, P. F., and H. Shimizu. (1995). Family relationships and adolescent development in Japan: A family systems perspective on the Japanese family. *Journal of Research on Adolescence*, 5 (3): 281–318.

Glenn, E. N. (1983). Split household, small producer, and dual wage earner: An analysis of Chinese-American families' strategies. *Journal of Marriage and the Family*, 45 (1): 35–46.

Glenn, E. N., and R. S. Parreñas. (1996). The other Issei: Japanese immigrant women in the pre–World War II period. In S. Pedraza and R. G. Rumbaut (eds.), *Origins and Destinies: Immigration, Race, and Ethnicity in America*, 125–140. New York: Wadsworth.

Goddard, R. (1998, June 11). Seen on the walls of NASA, Houston, Texas.

Gold, S. (2000, April 28). Aging immigrants try to keep cherished traditions alive in "Americanized" generation. *Los Angeles Times*, M3.

Gold, S., and M. Tran. (2000, April 28). From Vietnam to United States—and back again. *Los Angeles Times*, M8.

Goodno, J. B. (1991). *The Philippines: Land of Broken Promises*. Atlantic Highlands, N.J.: Zed Books.

Gordon, L. (1994). *Pitied But Not Entitled: Single Mothers and the History of Welfare, 1890–1935*. Ithaca: Cornell University Press.

Gordon, M. M. (1964). *Assimilation in American Life*. New York: Oxford University Press.

Government of India, Ministry of External Affairs. (2000). *The New State*. http://www.indiagov.org/culture/history/history9.htm.

Gray, E., and J. Cosgrove. (1985). Ethnocentric perception of childrearing practices in protective services. *Child Abuse and Neglect*, 9 (3): 389–396.

Green, D. A. (1999). Immigration occupational attainment: Assimilation and mobility. *Journal of Labor Economics*, 17 (1): 49–79.

Gupta, M. (1999). An alternative, combined approach to the treatment of premature ejaculation in Asian men. *Sexual and Marital Therapy*, 14 (1): 71–76.

Gurland, B. (1990). Symposium on role reversal: A discussant responds. *Journal of Gerontological Social Work*, 15 (1/2): 35–38.

Guthrie, H. A. (1968). Nutrition in a Philippine fishing community. In W. F. Bello and A. de Guzman II (eds.), *Modernization: Its Impact in the Philippines*, 3:129–148. Quezon City, Philippines. Ateneo de Manila University Press.

Hahn, E. (1963). *China Only Yesterday, 1850–1950*. Garden City, N.Y.: Doubleday.

Haines, D. W. (ed). (1989). *Refugees as Immigrants: Cambodians, Laotians, and Vietnamese in America*. Totowa, N.J.: Rowman and Littlefield.

Hall, R. E. (1997). Eurogamy among Asian-Americans: A note on Western assimilation. *Social Science Journal*, 34 (3): 403–308.

Handlin, O. (1973). *The Uprooted: The Epic Story of the Great Migrations That Made the American People*. Boston: Little, Brown.

Haniffa, A. (1999a, December 17). Being Indian is seen as a plus in Silicon Valley. *India Abroad*, 32, 34.

———. (1999b, September 17). New immigrants likely to be poor and stay poor, says study. *India Abroad*, 39.

———. (2000a, May 12). Clinton pays tribute to inventor of Pentium chip. *India Abroad*, 12.

———. (2000b, May 12). Need for community to influence public policy stressed. *India Abroad*, 14.

———. (2001, August 24). South Asian hand in smuggling racket exposed. *India Abroad*, 8.

Hartwell, R. (1982). Demographic, political, and social transformations of China, 750–1550. *Harvard Journal of Asiatic Studies*, 42 (2): 365–442.

Hays, C. L. (1990, July 31). Amid gang violence, Chinatown casts off quiet image. *New York Times*, B1.

Hebel, S., and P. Schmidt. (2000, March 17). Bob Jones U shifts its policies on interracial dating by students. *Chronicle of Higher Education*, A39.

Hechter, M. (1977). *Internal Colonialism: The Celtic Fringe in British National Development, 1536–1966*. Berkeley: University of California Press.

Heffernan, M. (1995). French colonial migration. In R. Cohen (ed.), *The Cambridge Survey of World Migration*, 33–38. Cambridge, U.K.: Cambridge University Press.

Hegde, R. S. (1998). Swinging the trapeze: The negotiation of the identity among Asian Indian immigrant women in the United States. In D. V. Tanno and A. Gonzalez (eds.), *Communication and Identity Across Cultures. International and Intercultural Communications Annual*, 21:34–55. Thousand Oaks, Calif.: Sage.

Heise, L., J. Pitanguy, and A. Germain. (1994). Violence against women: The hidden health burden. World Bank Discussion Paper 255. Washington, D.C.: World Bank.

Herrick, C., and H. N. Brown. (1998). Underutilization of mental health services by Asian-Americans residing in the United States. *Issues in Mental Health Nursing*, 19 (3): 225–240.

———. (1999). Mental disorders and syndromes found among Asians residing in the United States. *Issues in Mental Health Nursing*, 20 (3): 275–296.

Herrmann, K. J., Jr., and B. Kasper. (1992). International adoption: The exploitation of women and children. *Affilia—Journal of Women and Social Work*, 7 (1): 45–58.

2?Hess, G. R. (1998). The forgotten Asian Americans: The East Indian community in the United States. In F. Ng (ed), *The History and Immigration of Asian Americans*, 106–126. New York: Garland.

Hickman, M. J., and B. Walter. (1995). Deconstructing whiteness: Irish women in Britain. *Feminist Review*, 50 (Summer): 5–19.

Himmelstein, D. V., and S. Woolhandler. (1984). *The National Health Program Book: A Source Guide for Advocates*. Monroe, Me.: Common Courage Press.

Hing, B. O. (1995). *Making and Remaking Asian America Through Immigration Policy, 1850–1990*. Stanford: Stanford University Press.

Hirayama, K. K. (1982). Evaluating the effects of the employment of Vietnamese refugee wives on their family role and mental health. *California Sociologist*, 5 (1): 96–110.

Hirshberg, G. (2000, March 17). Gays and lesbians. Lecture presented by activist and clinical social worker to the Human Behavior and Social Environment class, Department of Social Work, University of Missouri–St. Louis.

Hjerm, M. (1998). National identities, national pride, and xenophobia: A comparison of four Western societies. *Acta Sociologica*, 41 (4): 335–347.

Ho, C. K. (1990). An analysis of domestic violence in Asian American communities: A multicultural approach to counseling. In L. Brown and M. P. P. Root (eds.), *Diversity and Complexity in Feminist Therapy*, 129–150. New York: Haworth.

Ho, M. K. (1987). *Family Therapy with Ethnic Minorities*. Newbury Park, Calif.: Sage.

————. (1992). Differential application of treatment modalities in working with Asian American youth. In L. A. Vargas and J. D. Koss-Chionino (eds.), *Working with Culture*, 182–203. San Francisco: Jossey-Bass.

Ho, T. (1998). Vice crimes and Asian Americans. In C. R. Mann and M. S. Zatz (eds.), *Images of Color, Images of Crime*, 188–194. Los Angeles: Roxbury.

Hoekstra, D. (2000, April 16). Hero's roost: Nisei Lounge started as a haven. *Chicago Sun-Times*, TRA, 5.

Hofstadter, R. (1989). *The American Political Tradition and the Men Who Made It*. New York: Vintage.

Hofstede, G. (1980). *Culture's Consequences*. Beverly Hills, Calif.: Sage.

Holmes, C. (1995). Jewish economic and refugee migrations, 1880–1950. In R. Cohen (ed.), *The Cambridge Survey of World Migration*, 148–153. Cambridge, U.K.: Cambridge University Press.

Hollinger, J. H. (1998). *Adoption Law and Practice*. Vol. 1, 1998 Supplement. New York: Matthew Bender.

Hong, G. K., and L. K. Hong. (1991). Comparative perspectives on child abuse and neglect: Chinese versus Hispanics and whites. *Child Welfare*, 70 (4): 463–475.

Hong, J., and M. Y. Yums. (2000). *Contemporary History of Korea*. http://socrates.berkeley.edu/~korea.

Hong, M. (1993). *Growing Up Asian American*. New York: Avon.

Hooper, L. M., and C. E. Bennett. (1997). The Asian and Pacific Islander population in the United States: March 1997 (update). *Current Population Reports*. http://www.census.gov.

Hostetter, M. K., S. Iverson, W. Thomas, D. McKenzie, K. Dole, and D. E. Johnson. (1991). Medical evaluation of internationally adopted children. *New England Journal of Medicine*, 325 (7): 479–485.

Houstoun, M. F., R. G. Kramer, and J. M. Barrett. (1984). Female predominance of immigration to the United States since 1930: A first look. *International Migration Review*, 18: 908–963.

Hu, W-Y. (1998). Elderly immigrants on welfare. *Journal of Human Resources*, 33 (3): 11–41.

Hudson, B. (1993). *Penal Policy and Social Justice*. Buffalo, N.Y.: University of Toronto Press.

Hudson, L. (1997, April 11). Diversity among Asian-American students stressed. *India Abroad*, 26 (11): 48.

Hudson, R. (2000, April 30). Orphans of Operation Babylift feel a kinship, share the desire to learn more. *St. Louis Post-Dispatch*, A5.

Hugman, R. (1995). The implications of the term "elder abuse" for problem definition and response in health and social welfare. *Journal of Social Policy*, 24 (4): 493–507.

Hugo, G. (1995). Illegal international migration in Asia. In R. Cohen (ed.), *The Cambridge Survey of World Migration*, 397–402. Cambridge, U.K.: Cambridge University Press.

Huisman, K. A. (1996). Wife battering in Asian American communities. *Violence Against Women*, 2 (3): 260–283.

Hummer, R. A., R. G. Rogers, C. B. Nam, and F. R. LeClere. (1999). Race/ethnicity, nativity, and U.S. adult mortality. *Social Science Quarterly*, 80 (1): 136–153.

Hurh, W. M., and K. C. Kim (1984). *Korean Immigrants in America*. Cranbury, N.J.: Associated University Press.

———. (1988). *Uprooting and Adjustment: A Sociological Study of Korean Immigrants' Mental Health*. Final report to the National Institute of Mental Health, Macomb, Ill.: Department of Sociology and Anthropology, Western Illinois University.

———. (1990). Correlates of Korean immigrants' mental health. *Journal of Nervous and Mental Disease*, 178 (11): 703–711.

Hwang, S-S., R. Saenz, and B. E. Aguirre. (1999). Structural and assimilationist explanations of Asian American intermarriage. *Journal of Marriage and the Family*, 59 (3): 758–773.

Hyung-chan, K. (1977). Korean community organizations in America: Their characteristics and problems. In K. Hyung-chan (ed.), *The Korean Diaspora*, 65–83. Santa Barbara, Calif.: Clio Press.

Ichihashi, Y. (1932). *Japanese in the United States*. Stanford: Stanford University Press.

Ichioka, Y. (1977). Ameyuki-san: Japanese prostitutes in Nineteenth Century America. *Amerasia*, 4 (1): 6–7.

———. (1988). *The Issei: The World of the First Generation Japanese Immigrants*. New York: Free Press.

Ima, K., and C. F. Hohm. (1991). Child maltreatment among Asian and Pacific Islander refugees and immigrants: The San Diego case. *Journal of Interpersonal Violence*, 6 (3): 267–285.

Ingrassia, M., P. King, A. Tizon, E. Scigliano, and P. Annin. (1994, April 4). America's new wave of runaways. *Newsweek*, 64–65.

Inouye, J. (1999). Asian American health and disease: An overview of the issues. In R. M. Huff and M. V. Kline (eds.), *Promoting Health in Multicultural Populations: A Handbook for Practitioners*, 337–356. Thousand Oaks, Calif.: Sage.

Insook, H. P., J. T. Fawcett, F. Arnold, and B. Gardnes. (1990). *Korean immigrants and U.S. Policy: A Predeparture Perspective*. Honolulu: East-West Population Institute.

International Crime Victim Survey. (2000). http://www.ifs.univie.ac.at/uncjin/mosaic/ccrimes.

International Organization for Migration. (1995). *Chinese migrants in Central and Eastern Europe: The Cases of the Czech Republic, Hungary, and Romania*. http://www.iom.int/IOM/Publications/books_studies_surveys/MIP_easterneurope_chinese_eng.htm.

Ishemo, S. L. (1995). Forced labour and migration in Portugal's African colonies. In R. Cohen (ed.), *The Cambridge Survey of World Migration*, 162–165. Cambridge, U.K.: Cambridge University Press.

Ishii-Kuntz, M. (1997). Intergenerational relationships among Chinese, Japanese, and Korean Americans. *Family Relations*, 46 (1): 23–33.

Ito, K. (1973). *Issei: A History of Japanese Immigrants in North America*. Translated by S. Nakamura and J. S. Gerard. Seattle: Japanese Community Service.

Iwamasa, G. Y., and K. M. Hilliard. (1999). Depression and anxiety among Asian American elders: A review of the literature. *Clinical Psychology Review*, 19 (3): 343–357.

Ja, D. Y., and B. Aoki. (1993). Substance abuse treatment: Cultural barriers in the Asian-American community. *Journal of Psychoactive Drugs*, 25 (1): 61–71.

Jain, M., and R. Menon. (1991, September 30). The greying of India. *India Today*, 24–33.

Jan, L. (1993). Asian gang problems and social policy solutions: A discussion and review. *Gang Journal*, 1 (4): 37–44.

Jansson, B. S. (1999). *Becoming an Effective Policy Advocate: From Policy Practice to Social Justice*. Pacific Grove, Calif.: Brooks/Cole.

Jenkins, J. H. (1996). Culture, emotion, and PTSD. In A. J. Marsella, M. J. Friedman, E. T. Gerrity, and R. M. Scurfield (eds.), *Ethnocultural Aspects of Posttraumatic Stress Disorder: Issues, Research, and Clinical Applications*, 165–182. Washington, D.C.: American Psychological Association.

Jensen, J. M. (1988). *Passage from India: Asian Indian Immigrants in North America*. New Haven: Yale University Press.

Jeong, S. (1999). The Asian upper eyelid: An anatomical study with comparison to the Caucasian eyelid. *JAMA, the Journal of the American Medical Association*, 282 (20): 1902.

Joint Commission on Mental Illness and Health. (1961). *Action for Mental Health*. New York: Basic Books.

Joyce, R., and C. Hunt. (1982). Philippine nursing and the brain drain. *Social Science Medicine*, 16 (4): 1223–1233.

Jung, M. (1998). *Chinese American Family Therapy*. San Francisco: Jossey-Bass.

Juthani, N. V. (1992). Immigrant mental health: Conflicts and concerns of Indian immigrants in the U.S.A. Special issue of *Psychology and Developing Societies*, 4 (2): 133–148.

Kang, K. C. (2000a, January 25). Rally decries China action on refugees. *Los Angeles Times*, B1.

——. (2000b, March 2). U.S. Asians seen as "alien," study finds. Ethnicity: American culture is not fully accepting, though bias has declined, report says. *Los Angeles Times*, A3.

Kanjanpan, W. (1995). The immigration of Asian professionals to the United States: 1980–1990. *International Migration Review*, 29 (1): 7–32.

Kantor, P. (1996). Domestic violence against women: A global issue. Unpublished manuscript. Department of City and Regional Planning, University of North Carolina at Chapel Hill.

Karger, H. J., and D. Stoesz. (1998). *American Social Welfare Policy: A Pluralist Approach*. 3d ed. New York: Longman.

Kelley, M. L., and H. Tseng. (1992). Cultural differences in child rearing: A comparison of immigrant Chinese and Caucasian American mothers. *Journal of Cross-Cultural Psychology*, 23 (4): 444–455.

Kent, D. R., and G. T. Felkenes. (1998). *Cultural Explanations for Vietnamese Youth Involvement in Street Gangs—Final Report*. Washington, D.C.: U.S. Department of Justice, Office of Juvenile Justice and Delinquency Prevention.

Keown, S. (1986). What Utah children believe. *Humanist*, 46 (4): 21–26.

Kessler, R. C., K. A. McGonagle, S. Zhao, C. B. Nelson, M. Hughes, S. Eshleman, H-V. Wittchen, and K. S. Kendler. (1994). Lifetime and 12-month prevalence of DSM-III-R psychiatric disorders in the United States: Results from the National Comorbidity Study. *Archives of General Psychiatry*, 51 (1): 8–19.

Kibria, N. (1993). *Family Tightrope: The Changing Lives of Vietnamese Americans.* Princeton: Princeton University Press.

Kiefer, C. W., S. Kim, K. Choi, L. Kim, B. L. Kim, S. Shon, and T. Kim. (1985). Adjustment problems of Korean American elderly. *The Gerontologist,* 25 (5): 477–482.

Kim, C. S. (1988). *Faithful Endurance.* Tucson: University of Arizona Press.

Kim, E. H. (1998). "At least you're not black": Asian Americans in U.S. race relations. *Social Justice,* 25 (3): 3–12.

———. (2000, March 19). In today's America, the choices belong to everyone. *San Francisco Chronicle,* 6.

Kim, H-C. (1994). *A Legal History of Asian Americans, 1790–1990.* Westport, Conn.: Greenwood Press.

Kim, K. C., W. M. Hurh, and M. Fernandez. (1989). Intra-group differences in business participation: Three Asian immigrant groups. *International Migration Review,* 23 (1): 73–95.

Kim, M. T. (1995). Cultural influences on depression in Korean Americans. *Journal of Psychosocial Nursing,* 33 (1): 13–17.

Kim, P. K., and J.-S. Kim. (1992). Korean elderly: Policy, program, and practice implications. In S. M. Furuto, R. Biswas, D. K. Chung, K. Murase, and F. Ross-Sheriff (eds.), *Social Work Practice with Asian Americans,* 227–240. Newbury Park, Calif.: Sage.

Kim, Y., and D. Grant. (1997). Immigration patterns, social support, and adaptation among Korean immigrant women and Korean American women. *Cultural Diversity and Mental Health,* 3 (4): 235–245.

Kingdon, J. W. (1999). *America the Unusual.* New York: Worth.

Kinzie, J. D., J. K. Boehnlein, P. K. Leung, L. J. Moore. (1990). The prevalence of post-traumatic stress disorder and its clinical significance among Southeast Asian refugees. *American Journal of Psychiatry,* 147 (7): 913–917.

Kitamura, T., N. Kijima, N. Iwata, Y. Senda, K. Takahashi, and I. Hayashi. (1999). Frequencies of child abuse in Japan: Hidden but prevalent crime. *International Journal of Offender Therapy and Comparative Criminology,* 43 (1): 21–33.

Kitano, H. L. (1960). Housing of Japanese-Americans in the San Francisco Bay Area. In N. Glazer and D. McEntire (eds.), *Studies in Housing and Minority Groups,* 178–197. Berkeley: University of California Press.

———. (1991). *Race Relations.* Englewood Cliffs, N.J.: Prentice-Hall.

Kitano, H. L., and R. Daniels. (1995). *Asian Americans: Emerging Minorities.* Englewood Cliffs, N.J.: Prentice-Hall.

Kitano, H. L., I. Chi, S. Rhee, C. K. Law, and J. E. Lubben. (1992). Norms and alcohol consumption: Japanese in Japan, Hawaii, and California. *Journal of Studies on Alcohol,* 53 (1): 33–39.

Kitano, H. L., D. C. Fujino, and J. T. Sato. (1998). Interracial marriages: Where are the Asian Americans and where are they going? In L. C. Lee and N. W. S. Zane (eds.), *Handbook of Asian American Psychology,* 233–260. Thousand Oaks, Calif.: Sage.

Kitano, K. J., and H. H. L. Kitano. (1998). The Japanese-American family. In C. H. Mindel, R. W. Habenstein, and R. Wright Jr. (eds.), *Ethnic Families in America,* 311–330. 4th ed. Upper Saddle River, N.J.: Prentice Hall.

Klatsky, A. L., A. B. Siegelaub, C. Landy, and G. D. Friedman. (1983). Racial patterns of alcoholic beverage use. *Alcoholism: Clinical and Experimental Research*, 7 (4): 372–377.

Kleiner, R. J., T. Sorensen, O. S. Dalgard, T. Moum, and D. Drews. (1986). International migration and internal migration: A comprehensive theoretical approach. In I. A. Glazier and L. De Rosa (eds.), *International Migration and Internal Migration: Migration Across Time and Nations*, 305–317. New York: Holmes and Meier.

Kline, M. V., and R. M. Huff. (1999). Tips for working with Asian American populations. In R. M. Huff and M. V. Kline (eds.), *Promoting Health in Multicultural Populations: A Handbook for Practitioners*, 383–394. Thousand Oaks, Calif.: Sage.

Knox, G. W., and T. F. McCurrie. (1997). Asian gangs: Recent research findings. *Journal of Contemporary Criminal Justice*, 13 (4): 301–308.

Korbin, J. (1991). Cross-cultural perspectives and research directions for the twenty-first century. *Child Abuse and Neglect*, 15, sup. 1: 67–77.

Kotkin, J. (1994, April 24). An emerging Asian tiger: The Vietnamese connection. *Los Angeles Times*, M1.

Koven, S. G., M. C. Shelley II, and B. E. Swanson. (1998). *American Public Policy*. Boston: Houghton Mifflin.

Kozu, J. (1999). Domestic violence in Japan. *American Psychologist*, 54 (1): 50–54.

Kposowa, A. J. (1995). The impact of immigration on unemployment and earnings among racial minorities in the United States. *Ethnic and Racial Studies*, 18 (3): 605–628.

Kumagai, F. (1983). Filial violence in Japan. *Victimology*, 8 (3/4): 173–194.

Kumagai, F., and M. Straus, M. (1983). Conflict resolution tactics in Japan, India, and the USA. *Journal of Comparative Family Studies*, 14 (2): 377–387.

Kuo, W. H., and Y. M. Tsai. (1986). Social networking, hardiness, and immigrants' mental health. *Journal of Health and Social Behavior*, 27: 133–149.

Kurian, G. T. (1994). *Datapedia of the United States, 1790–2000*. Lanham, Md.: Bernan Press.

LaBorde, P. (1996). Vietnamese cultural profile. http://www.hslib.washington.edu/clinical/ethnomed/vietnam.

La Brack, B. (1982). Immigration law and the revitalization process: The case of the California Sikhs. In S. Chandrashekhar (ed.), *From India to America: A Brief History of Immigration, Admission, and Assimilation*, 55–69. La Jolla: University of California Press.

La Brack, B., and K. Leonard. (1984). Conflict and compatibility in Punjabi-Mexican immigrant marriages in rural California, 1915–1965. *Journal of Marriage and the Family*, 46 (4): 527–537.

Lamb, D. (1997). Overseas Vietnamese are returning to help. *St. Louis Post-Dispatch*, A5.

Lambert, W. E., and D. M. Taylor. (1990). Language and culture in the lives of immigrants and refugees. In W. H. Holtzman and T. H. Bornemann (eds.), *Mental Health of Immigrants and Refugees*, 103–128. Austin: Hogg Foundation for Mental Health.

Lamm, R., and G. Imhoff. (1985). *The Immigration Time Bomb*. New York: Truman Tally Books.

Lang, A. A. (2000, March 8). When parents adopt a child and a whole other culture. *New York Times*, G9.

Lao Human Rights Council. (2000). Response to the Reports of the U.S. Department of State on Laos in 1999. http://home.earthlink.net/~laohumrights/response.html.

Laufman, D. H. (1986). Political bias in the United states Refugee Policy Since the Refugee Act of 1980. *Georgetown Immigration Law Journal*, 1 (3): 495–580.

Law, C. K., and L. Schneiderman. (1992). Policy implications of factors associated with economic self-sufficiency of Southeast Asian refugees. In S. M. Furuto, R. Biswas, D. K. Chung, K. Murase, and F. Ross-Sheriff (eds.), *Social Work Practice with Asian Americans*, 167–183. Newbury Park, Calif.: Sage.

Lazere, E. B., P. A. Leonard, C. N. Dolbeare, and B. Zigas. (1991). *A Place to Call Home: The Low Income Housing Crisis Continues*. Washington, D.C.: Center on Budget and Policy Priorities and Low-Income Housing Information Service, 45–47.

Le, Q. K. (1997). Mistreatment of Vietnamese elderly by their families in the United States. *Journal of Elder Abuse and Neglect*, 9 (2): 51–62.

Leclere, F. B., L. Jensen, and A. E. Biddlecom (1994). Health care utilization, family context, and adaptation among immigrants to the United States. *Journal of Health and Social Behavior*, 35 (4): 370–384.

Lee, B. W. K., L. N. Huang, and A. Lew. (1998). Families: Life-span socialization in a cultural context. In L. C. Lee and N. W. S. Zane (eds.), *Handbook of Asian American Psychology*, 83–136. Thousand Oaks, Calif.: Sage.

Lee, J. J. (1992). *Development, Delivery, and Utilization of Services Under the Older Americans Act: A Perspective of Asian American Elderly*. New York: Garland.

Lee, K. K. (1998). *Huddled Masses, Muddled Laws: Why Contemporary Immigration Policy Fails to Reflect Public Opinion*. Westport, Conn.: Praeger.

Lee, L. C. (1998). An overview. In L. C. Lee and N. W. S. Zane (eds.), *Handbook of Asian American Psychology*, 1–20. Thousand Oaks, Calif.: Sage.

Lee, L. C., and G. Zhan. (1998). Psychosocial status of children and youths. In L. C. Lee and N. W. S. Zane (eds.), *Handbook of Asian American Psychology*, 137–164. Thousand Oaks, Calif.: Sage.

Lee, M. P. (1990). *Quiet Odyssey*. Seattle: University of Washington Press.

Lee, P. H. (1993). *Sourcebook of Korean Civilization*. Vol. 1, *From Early Times to the Sixteenth Century*. New York: Columbia University Press.

Lee, R. A. (1998). *Philippine-American War, 1899–1902*. http://www.historyguy.com/ PhilipineAmericanwar.html.

Lee, R. H. (1956). The recent immigrant Chinese families of the San Francisco–Oakland area. *Marriage and the Family*, 18 (1): 14–24.

Lee, S. L. (1999). Are you Chinese or what? In R. S. Sheets and E. R. Hollins (eds.), *Racial and Ethnic Identity in School Practices: Aspects of Human Development*, 107–121. Mahwah, Japan: Lawrence Erlbaum Associates.

Lee, S. M., and M. Fernandez. (1998). Trends in Asian American racial/ethnic intermarriage: A comparison of 1980 and 1990 census data. *Sociological Perspectives*, 41 (2): 323–342.

Lee, S. M., and K. Yamanaka. (1990). Patterns of Asian American intermarriage and marital assimilation. *Journal of Marriage and Comparative Family Studies*, 21 (2): 287–305.

Lee, Y. H. (1998). Acculturation and delinquent behavior: The case of Korean American youths. *International Journal of Comparative and Applied Criminal Justice*, 22 (1/2): 273–292.

Lefferman, E. (1998, March 7). Another voice. *Los Angeles Times*, B7.

Lemarchand, L., L. R. Wilkens, L. N. Kolonel, J. H. Hankin, and L. C. Lyu. (197). Associations of sedentary lifestyle, obesity, smoking, alcohol use, and diabetes with the risk of colorectal cancer. *Cancer Research*, 57 (21): 4787–4794.

Leonard-Spark, P. J., and P. Saran. (1980). The Indian immigrant in America: A demographic profile. In E. Eames and P. Saran (eds.), *The New Ethnics*, 136–162. New York: Praeger.

Leung, P. (1990). Asian Americans and psychology: Unresolved issues. *Journal of Training and Practice in Professional Psychology*, 4 (1): 3–13.

Leveck, P. G. (1991). The role of culture in mental health and illness. In J. S. Cook and K. L. Fontaine (eds.), *Essentials of Mental Health Nursing*, 155–190. 2d ed. Reading, Mass.: Addison-Wesley.

LeVine, S., and R. LeVine. (1985). Age, gender, and the demographic transition: The life course in agrarian societies. In A. Rossi (ed.), *Gender and the Life Course*, 29–42. New York: Aldine.

Lieberman, R. C. (1995). Race, institutions, and the administration of social policy. *Social Science History*, 19 (4): 511–542.

Lightfoot, K. (1973). The Philippines. New York: Praeger.

Lin, C. Y. C., and V. R. Fu. (1990). A comparison of child-rearing practices among Chinese, immigrant Chinese, and Caucasian-American parents. *Child Development*, 61 (2): 429–433.

Lin, K., and W. W. Shen. (1991). Pharmacotherapy for Southeast Asian psychiatric patients. *Journal of Nervous and Mental Disease*, 179 (6): 346–350.

Lin, K-M., and F. Cheung. (1999). Mental health issues for Asian Americans. *Psychiatric Services*, 50 (6): 774–780.

Lindberg, K., J. Petrenko, J. Gladden, and W. A. Johnson. (1997). *New Faces of Organized Crime*. Technical assistance report. Chicago: Chicago Crime Commission.

Lindsay, J., M. Narayan, and K. Rea. (1998). The Vietnamese client. *Home Healthcare Nurse*, 16 (10): 693–700.

Lipat, C. T., T. A. Ordona, C. Pamintuan Stewart, and M. A. Ubaldo. (1997). Tomboy, dyke, lezzie, and bi: Filipina lesbian and bisexual women speak out. In P. P. Root (ed.), *Filipino Americans: Transformation and Identity*, 230–346. Thousand Oaks, Calif.: Sage.

Liu, J. M., P. M. Ong, and C. Rosenstein. (1995). Dual chain migration: Post-1965 Filipino immigration to the United States. In F. Ng (ed.), *The History and Immigration of Asian Americans*, 143–169. New York: Garland.

Liu, P., and C. Chan. (1996). Lesbian, gay, and bisexual Asian Americans and their families. In J. Laird and R-J. Green (eds.), *Ethnicity and Family Therapy*, 316–323. New York: Guilford Press.

Loiskandl, H. (1995). Illegal migrant workers in Japan. In R. Cohen (ed.), *The Cambridge Survey of World Migration*, 371–375. Cambridge, U.K.: Cambridge University Press.

Lone, S., and G. McCormack (1993). *Korea Since 1850*. New York: St. Martin's.

Loo, C., B. Tong, and R. True. (1989). A bitter bean: Mental health status and attitudes in Chinatown. *Journal of Community Psychology*, 17 (3): 283–296.

Look, K. M., and R. M. Look. (1997). Skin scraping, cupping, and moxibustion that may mimic physical abuse. *Journal of Forensic Sciences*, 42 (1): 103–105.

Loomis, A. W. (1869). Chinese women in California. *Overland Monthly*, 2 (2): 349–350.

Los Angles Times. (1997, June 6). Immigrant children said to prefer English. *St. Louis Post-Dispatch*.

Loue, S., S. D. Lane, L. S. Lloyd, and L. Loh. (1999). Integrating Buddhism and HIV prevention in U.S. Southeast Asian Communities. *Journal of Health for the Poor and Underserved*, 10 (1): 100–121.

Lum, D. (1992). *Social Work Practice with People of Color*. Pacific Grove, Calif.: Brooks/Cole.

Lum, J. (1998). Family violence. In L. C. Lee and N. W. S. Zane (eds.), *Handbook of Asian American Psychology*, 505–525. Thousand Oaks, Calif.: Sage.

Luu, V. (1989). The hardships of escape for Vietnamese women. In Asian Women United of California, (ed.), *Making Waves: An Anthology of Writings by and About Asian American Women*, 60–72. Boston: Beacon.

Lyman, S. M. (1968). Marriage and the family among Chinese immigrants to America, 1850–1960. *Phylon*, 29 (4): 321–330.

———. (1974). Chinese Americans. New York: Random House.

Lynch, J. (1995). Crime in international perspective. In J. Q. Wilson and J. Petersilia (eds.), *Crime and Public Policy*, 11–38. San Francisco: ICS Press.

Mackerras, C. (1989). *Western Images of China*. Hong Kong: Oxford University Press.

Mahat, G. (1998). Eastern Indians' childrearing practices and nursing implications. *Journal of Community Health Nursing*, 15 (3): 151–161.

Makimoto, K. (1998). Drinking patterns and drinking problems among Asian-Americans and Pacific Islanders. *Alcohol Health and Research World*, 22 (4): 270–275.

Manalansan, M. F. IV. (1997). At the frontiers of narrative: The mapping of Filipino gay men's lives in the U.S. In P. P. Root (ed.), *Filipino Americans: Transformation and Identity*, 247–256. Thousand Oaks, Calif.: Sage.

Manansala, P. K. (1999). Philippine prehistory. http://www.bibingka.com/dahon/misc/sites.htm.

Manisses Communications Group. (1999, August 2). Majority of states now have mental health parity laws. *Mental Health Weekly*, 9 (30): 6.

Mann, C. R. (1993). *Unequal Justice*. Bloomington: Indiana University Press.

Marchand, L. L., L. N. Kolonel, and C. N. Yoshizawa. (1989). Alcohol consumption patterns among the five major ethnic groups in Hawaii: Coreelations with incidence of esophageal and oropharyngeal cancer. In National Institute of Alcohol Abuse and Alcoholism (ed.), *Alcohol Use Among U.S. Ethnic Minorities*, 355–371. NIAAA Research Monograph 18, DHHS Publication No. [ADM] 89-1435, Rockville, Md.: NIAAA.

Marger, M. N. (2000). *Race and Ethnic Relations: American and Global Perspectives*. Belmont, Calif.: Wadsworth/Thomson Learning.

Marmor, T. R. (1973). *The Politics of Medicare*. Chicago: Aldine.

Marmor, T. R., and J. Godfrey. (1992, July 23). Canada's system works. *New York Times.*

Marsella, A. J. (1994). Ethnocultural diversity and international refugees: Challenges for the global economy. In A. J. Marsella, T. Bornemann, S. Ekblad, and J. Orley (eds.), *Amidst Peril and Pain: The Mental Health and Well-Being of the World's Refugees,* 341–364. Washington, D.C.: American Psychological Association.

Marsella, A. J., J. Kinzie, and P. Gordon. (1973). Ethnic variations in the expression of depression. *Journal of Cross-Cultural Psychology,* 4 (4): 435–458.

Marshall, I. H. (1997). Minorities, crime, and criminal justice in the United States. In I. H. Marshall (ed.), *Minorities, Migrants, and Crime,* 1–35. Thousand Oaks, Calif.: Sage.

Martin, S. F. (1994). A policy perspective on the mental health and psychosocial needs of refugees. In A. J. Marsella, T. Bornemann, S. Ekblad, and J. Orley (eds.), *Amidst Peril and Pain: The Mental Health and Well-being of the World's Refugees,* 69–80. Washington, D.C.: American Psychological Association.

Mass, A. I. (1992). Interracial Japanese Americans: The best of both worlds or the end of the Japanese American community? In M. P. P. Root (ed.), *Racially Mixed People in America,* 265–279. Newbury Park, Calif.: Sage.

Massey, D. S. (1988). International migration and economic development in comparative perspective. *Population Development Review,* 14 (3): 383–413.

———. (1990). Social structure, household strategies, and the cumulative causation of migration. *Population Index,* 56 (1): 3–26.

Massey, D. S., J. Arango, G. Hugo, A. Kouaouci, A. Pellerino, and J. E. Taylor. (1993). Theories of international migration: A review and appraisal. *Population Development Review,* 19 (3): 431–466.

Masuda, M., G. Matsumoto, and G. Meredith. (1970). Ethnic identity in three generations of Japanese-Americans. *Journal of Social Psychology,* 81: 199–207.

Mayadas, N. S., D. Elliott, and C. P. Ramanathan. (1998). A global model of ethnic diversity conflict: Implications for social work with populations at risk. In C. S. Ramanathan and R. Link (eds.), *All Our Futures,* 138–155. Boston: Brooks/Cole.

Mayadas, N. S., and U. A. Segal. (2000). Refugees in the United States. In P. Balgopal (ed.), *Immigration in the United States,* 198–227. New York: Columbia University Press.

Mayhew, P., and J. J. M. van Dijk. (1997). *Criminal Victimisation in Eleven Industrialised Countries. Key Findings from the 1996 International Crime Victims Survey.* The Hague: Ministry of Justice, Research and Document Centre.

Mazumdar, S. (1984). Punjabi agricultural people in California. In L. Cheng and E. Bonacich (eds.), *Labor Immigration Under Capitalism: Asian Workers in the United States Before World War II,* 549–578. Berkeley: University of California Press.

———. (1989). Racist response to racism: The Aryan myth and South Asians in the U.S. *South Asia Bulletin,* 9 (1): 47–55.

McCloskey, H., and J. Zaller, J. (1984). *The American Ethos: Public Attitudes Toward Capitalism and Democracy.* Cambridge: Harvard University Press.

McDonald, H. G., and P. R. Balgopal. (1998). Conflicts of American immigrants: Assimilate or retain ethnic identity. *Migration World Magazine,* 26 (4): 14–19.

McDowell, R. (1997). Anger voiced at Pol Pot. http://archive.abcnews.go.com/ sections/world/polpot1022/index.html.

McIntosh, J. L., and J. F. Santos. (1981). Suicide among minority elderly: A prelimi-
nary investigation. *Suicide—Life Threatening Behavior*, 11 (3): 151–166.

McKelvey, R. S., and J. A. Webb. (1995). A pilot study of abuse among Vietnamese
Amerasians. *Child Abuse and Neglect*, 19 (5): 545–553.

McKenna, M. A. J. (2000, February 11). International adoptees show high lead levels.
CDC: Chinese kids most likely exposed. *Atlanta Journal and Constitution*, IE.

McLaughlin, L. A., and K. L. Braun. (1998). Asian and Pacific Islander cultural values:
Considerations for health care decision making. *Health and Social Work*, 23 (2):
116–126.

McPhee, S. J., S. Stewart, K. C. Brock, J. A. Bird, C. N. H. Jenkins, and G. Q. Phan.
(1997). Factors associated with breast and cervical cancer screening practices among
Vietnamese American Women. *Cancer Detection and Prevention*, 21 (6): 510–521.

McRoy, R. G., and C. C. I. Hall. (1996). Transracial adoptions: In whose best interest?
In P. P. M. Root (ed.), *The Multiracial Experience: Racial Borders as the New
Frontier*, 63–78. Thousand Oaks, Calif.: Sage.

McRoy, R. G., L. Zurcher, M. Lauderdale, and R. Anderson. (1984). The identity of
transracial adoptees. *Social Casework*, 64 (1): 34–39.

McShane, M. D. (2000). Widening the workforce: Diversity in criminal justice employment. In Criminal Justice Collective of Northern Arizona University, (ed.),
Investigating Difference: Human and Cultural Relations in Criminal Justice,
207–218. Boston: Allyn and Bacon.

Mechanic, D. (1999). *Mental Health and Social Policy*. 4th ed. Needham Heights,
Mass.: Allyn and Bacon.

Medina, B. T. G., and J. N. Natividad. (1985). Filipino chain migration to the United
States. *Philippine Population Journal*, 1 (4): 67–94.

Mehrotra, M. (1999). The social construction of wife abuse: Experiences of Asian
Indian women in the United States. *Violence Against Women*, 5 (6): 619–640.

Mehta, S. (1998). Relationship between acculturation and mental health for Asian
Indian immigrants in the United States. *Genetic, Social, and General Psychology
Monographs*, 124 (1): 61–78.

Meinhardt, K., T. Soleng, T. Philip, and C. Y. Yu. (1985/1986). Southeast Asian
refugees in the "Silicon Valley": The Asian Health Assessment Project. *Amerasia*,
12 (1): 43–65.

Meissner, D. M., R. D. Hormats, A. G. Walker, and S. Ogata. S. (1993). *International
Migration Challenges in a New Era*. New York: Trilateral Commission.

Melendy, H. B. (1984). *Chinese and Japanese*. New York: Hippocrene.

Merriam, C. (1945). *Systematic Politics*. Chicago: University of Chicago Press.

Meston, C. M., J. R. Heiman, P. D. Trapnell, A. S. Carlin. (1999). Ethnicity, desirable
responding, and self-reports of abuse: A comparison of European- and Asian-ances-
try undergraduates. *Journal of Consulting and Clinical Psychology*, 67 (1): 139–144.

Meyer, M. W. (1993). *Japan: A Concise History*. Lanham, Md.: Rowman and Littlefield.

Miki, I. (1998). Assimilation and repatriation conflicts of the Hmong refugees in a
Wisconsin community: A qualitative study of five local groups. *Migration World
Magazine*, 26 (4): 26–28.

Miller, L. C. (1999). Caring for internationally adopted children. *New England Journal
of Medicine*, 341 (20): 1539–1540.

Miller, R., and B. Miller. (1990). Mothering the biracial child: Bridging the gaps between African American and white parenting styles. *Women and Therapy*, 10 (1/2): 169–179.

Miller, S. (1969). *The Unwelcome Immigrant: The American Image of the Chinese, 1785–1882*. Berkeley: University of California Press.

Mills, L. (1996). Empowering battered women transnational: The case for postmodern interventions. *Social Work*, 41, (3): 261–268.

Mills, N. (1994). Introduction: The era of the Golden Venture. In N. Mills (ed.), *Arguing Immigration: Are New Immigrants a Wealth of Diversity . . . or a Crushing Burden?*, 11–27. New York: Simon and Schuster.

Mills, P. K., and R. Yang. (1997). Cancer incidence in the Hmong of Central California, United States, 1987–94. *Cancer Causes and Control*, 8 (5): 705–712.

Min, P. G. (1995). *Asian Americans: Contemporary Issues and Trends*. Thousand Oaks, Calif.: Sage.

———. (1996). The entrepreneurial adaptation of Korean immigrants. In S. Pedraza and R. G. Rumbaut (eds.), *Origins and Destinies: Immigration, Race, and Ethnicity in America*, 302–314. New York: Wadsworth.

———. (1998). The Korean-American family. In C. H. Mindel, R. W. Habenstein, and R. Wright Jr. (eds.), *Ethnic Families in America*, 223–253. 4th ed. Upper Saddle River, N.J.: Prentice Hall.

Mink, G. (1995). *The Wages of Motherhood: Inequality in the Welfare State, 1917–1942*. Ithaca: Cornell University Press.

Mitra, N. (1995, May 26). Report warns of "Unheralded Crisis." *India Abroad*, 34.

Modell, J. (1971). Tradition and opportunity: The Japanese immigrant in America. *Pacific Historical Review*, 40 (2): 164–165.

Monbusho. (1997). Program for educational reform. http://www.monbu.go.jp/series-en/00000004.

Moon, A., and O. Williams. (1993). Perceptions of elder abuse and help-seeking patterns among African-American, Caucasian American, and Korean-American elderly women. *The Gerontologist*, 33 (3): 386–395.

Morales, R. (1974). *Makibaka: The Filipino-American Struggle*. Darby, Mont.: Mountain View.

Morgan, P., and B. Perry. (2000). Irreconcilable differences? Understanding the crime victim/criminal justice worker relationship. In Criminal Justice Collective of Northern Arizona University (ed.), *Investigating Difference: Human and Cultural Relations in Criminal Justice*, 253–268. Boston: Allyn and Bacon.

Moriyama, A. (1984). The causes of emigration: The background to Japanese emigration to Hawaii, 1885–1894. In L. Cheng and E. Bonacich (eds.), *Labor Immigration Under Capitalism: Asian Workers in the United States Before World War II*, 248–276. Berkeley: University of California Press.

Moorman, J. E., and D. J. Hernandez. (1989). Married-couple families with step, adopted, and biological children. *Demography*, 26 (2): 267–277.

Morrison, T. (1994). On the backs of Blacks. In N. Mills (ed.), *Arguing Immigration: Are New Immigrants a Wealth of Diversity . . . or a Crushing Burden?*, 97–100. New York: Simon and Schuster.

Morton, W. Scott. (1994). *Japan: Its History and Culture*. 3d ed. New York: McGraw Hill.

Mosher, W. D., and C. A. Bachrach. (1996). Understanding U.S. fertility: Continuity and change in the National Survey of Family Growth. *Family Planning Perspectives,* 28 (1): 4–12.

Muecke, M. A. (1992). New paradigms for refugee health problems. *Social Science and Medicine,* 35 (4): 515–523.

Mui, A. C., and R. J. Reid. (1999). HIV/AIDS knowledge, beliefs, and at-risk behaviors in the Chinese American community. *Journal of Social Service Research,* 25 (1): 61–75.

Muller, T., and T. Espenshade. (1985). *The Fourth Wave: California's Newest Immigrants.* Washington, D.C.: Urban Institute.

Mura, D. (1998). Reflections on my daughter. In C. O'Hearn (ed.), *Half and Half: Writers on Growing Up Biracial and Bicultural,* 80–98. New York: Pantheon.

Murnane, R. J., and F. Levy. (1992). Education and training. In H. J. Aaron and C. L. Schultze (eds.), *What Can Government Do?,* 191. Washington, D.C.: Brookings Institution.

Mydans, S. (1991, April 8). For Vietnamese, a wave of gang terror. *New York Times,* A11.

———. (1994, June 21). Laotian's arrest in killing bares a generation gap. *New York Times,* A8.

Myrdal, G. (1944). *An American Dilemma.* New York: Harper.

Nagpaul, K, (1997). Elder abuse among Asian Indians: Traditional versus modern perspectives. *Journal of Elder Abuse and Neglect,* 9 (2): 77–92.

National Asian Women's Health Organization. (1996). *A Health Needs Assessment of South Asian Women in Three California Counties: Alameda, Santa Clara, Sutter.* San Francisco: National Asian Women's Health Organization.

National Center for Health Statistics. (1997). *Fertility, Family Planning, and Women's Health: New Data from the 1995 National Survey of Family Growth.* Vital Health Statistics. Washington, D.C.: National Center for health Statistics.

National Commission on Excellence. (1983). *A Nation at Risk: The Imperative for Educational Reform.* Washington, D.C.: U.S. Government Printing Office.

National Geographic Society. (1998, October). Population: Millennium in maps. *National Geographic,* 194 (4): map insert.

National Immigration Forum. (1997). New poll shows Americans becoming more tolerant of immigrants, diversity. http://www.immigrationforum.org/currentissues.html.

———. (1999a). From newcomers to new Americans: The successful integration of immigrants. http://www.immigrationforum.org/fromnewcomers.htm.

———. (1999b). *Immigrants in the News.* Report prepared by the National Immigration Forum. February 1999. Washington, D.C.

National Research Council. (1995). Immigrant children and their families: Issues for research and policy. *Future of Children,* 5 (2): 72–89.

———. (1998). *The Immigration Debate: Studies on the Economic, Demographic, and Fiscal Effects of Immigration.* Washington, D.C.: National Academy Press.

National Public Radio. (2000, March 7). Asian Americans. Program: *Talk of the Nation,* 2:00 p.m.–3:00 p.m.

Nee, V., and H. Y. Wong. (1985). Asian American socioeconomic achievement: The strength of the family bond. *Sociological Perspectives,* 28 (3): 288–289.

Nehru, J. (1934). *Glimpses of World History*. Vol. 1. Allahabad, India: Kitabistan.
———. (1946). *The Discovery of India*. New York: John Day Company.
Nielsen, M. O. (2000). Talking through our differences: Intercultural and interpersonal communication. In Criminal Justice Collective of Northern Arizona University (ed.), *Investigating Difference: Human and Cultural Relations in Criminal Justice*, 235–252. Boston: Allyn and Bacon.
Nelson, R. (1968). *The Philippines*. New York: Walker.
Nemoto, T., B. Aoki, K. Huang, A. Morris, H. Nguyen, and W. Wong. (1999). Drug use behaviors among Asian drug users in San Francisco. *Addictive Behaviors*, 24 (6): 823–838.
Nerenberg, L., and P. Yap (eds.). *Elder Abuse in the Asian Community: A Conference Sponsored by Self-Help for the Elderly and the San Francisco Consortium for Elder Abuse Prevention*. San Francisco: U.S. Administration on Aging.
Netting, F. E., R. Huber, R. N. Paton, and J. R. Kautz III. (1995). Elder rights and the Long-Term Care Ombudsman Program. *Social Work*, 40 (3): 351–357.
Ng, F. (1995). The sojourner, return migration, and immigration history. In F. Ng (ed.), *The History and Immigration of Asian Americans*, 87–105. New York: Garland.
Nihai, G. (2000, April 14). Tallying the high cost of fitting in with American society. Review of Asian American dreams: The emergence of an American people, by Helen Zia. *Los Angeles Times*, E3.
Nishi, S. M. (1995). Japanese Americans. In P. G. Min (ed.), *Asian Americans: Contemporary Issues and Trends*, 95–133. Thousand Oaks, Calif.: Sage.
Ng, K. S. (1999). *Counseling Asian Families from a Systems Perspective*. Alexandria, Va.: American Counseling Association.
Nguyen, N. (1994). Life's biggest lemon. *Refugees*, 95: 25.
Nguyen, S. D. (1982). Psychiatric and psychosomatic problems among South East Asian refugees. *Psychiatric Journal of the University of Ottawa*, 7: 163–172.
Noonan, P. (1994). Why the world comes here. In N. Mills (ed.), *Arguing Immigration: Are New Immigrants a Wealth of Diversity . . . or a Crushing Burden?*, 176–180. New York: Simon and Schuster.
Noriyuki, D. (2000, May 1). Still searching for acceptance. *Los Angeles Times*, E1.
Norton, I. M., and S. M. Manson. (1992). An association between domestic violence and depression among Southeast Asian refugee women. *Journal of Nervous and Mental Disease*, 180 (1): 729–730.
Office of Refugee Resettlement. (1985). *Southeast Asian Refugee Self-sufficiency Study*. Washington, D.C.: U.S. Government Printing Office.
———. (1991). *Refugee Resettlement Program: Annual Report to Congress FY 1990*. Washington, D.C.: U.S. Government Printing Office.
O'Hare, T., and T. Van Tran. (1998). Substance abuse among Southeast Asians in the U.S.: Implications for practice and research. *Social Work in Health Care*, 26 (3): 69–80.
O'Hare, W. P., and J. C. Felt. (1992). *Asian Americans: America's Fastest-Growing Minority Group*. Washington, D.C.: Population Reference Bureau.
O'Hearn, C. (ed.) (1998). *Half and Half: Writers on Growing Up Biracial and Bicultural*. New York: Pantheon.
O'Kane, J. M. (1992). *Crooked Ladder: Gangsters, Ethnicity, and the American Dream*. Piscataway, N.Y.: Transaction Publishers.

Okihiro, G. Y. (1996). *Margins and Mainstreams*. Seattle: University of Washington Press.

Olasky, M. (1992). *The Tragedy of American Compassion*. Washington, D.C.: Regnery Gateway.

Omatsu, G. (1994). The "four prisons" and the movements of liberation: Asian American activism from the 1960s to the 1990s. In K. Aguilar-San Juan (ed.), *The State of Asian America: Activism and Resistance in the 1990s*, 19–70. Boston: South End Press.

Ong, P. M., L. Cheng, and L. Evans. (1992). Migration of highly education Asians and global dynamics. *Asian and Pacific Migration Journal*, 1 (3/4): 543–567.

Ordonez, R. Z. (1997). Mail-order brides: An emerging community. In M. P. P. Root (ed.), *Filipino Americans: Transformation and Identity*, 121–142. Thousand Oaks, Calif.: Sage.

Oyserman, D., and I. Sakamto. (1997). Being Asian American: Identity, cultural constructs, and stereotype perception. *Journal of Applied Behavioral Science*, 33 (4): 435–453.

Pablo, S., and K. L. Braun. (1997). Perceptions of elder abuse and neglect and help-seeking patterns among Filipino and Korean elderly women in Honolulu. *Journal of Elder Abuse and Neglect*, 9 (2): 63–76.

Palermo, G. B., E. J. Gumz, and F. J. Liska. (1992). Mental illness and criminal behavior revisited. *International Journal of Offender Theory and Comparative Criminology*, 36 (1): 53–61.

Pang, K. Y. (1990). Hwabyung: The construction of a popular illness among Korean elderly immigrant women in the United States. *Culture, Medicine, and Psychiatry*, 14 (4): 495–512.

Parfit, M. (1998, October). Human migration. *National Geographic* 194 (4): 6–35.

Parillo, V. (1985). *Strangers to These Shores: Race and Ethnic Relations in the U.S.* New York: John Wiley.

Park, R. E. (1926, 1950). *Race and Culture*. Glencoe, Ill.: Free Press.

———. (1928). Human migration and the marginal man. *American Journal of Sociology*, 33: 881–893.

Park, Y.-H. (1986). *Women of the Yi Dynasty*. Seoul: Research Center for Asian Women, Sookmyung Women's University.

Patterson, W. (1977). The first attempt to obtain Korean laborers for Hawaii. In H.-C. Kim (ed.), *The Korean Diaspora*, 9–32. Santa Barbara, Calif.: Clio Press.

———. (1988). *The Korean Frontier in America: Immigration to Hawaii, 1896–1910*. Honolulu: University of Hawaii Press.

Pedersen, P. (1991). Balance as a criterion for social services for Asian and Pacific Islander Americans. In N. Mokuau (ed.), *Handbook of Social Services for Asian and Pacific Islanders*, 37–57. New York: Greenwood Press.

Pedraza, S. (1991). Women and migration: The social consequences of gender. *Annual Review of Sociology*, 17: 303–325.

———. (1996). Origins and destinies: Immigration, race, and ethnicity in American history. In S. Pedraza and R. G. Rumbaut (eds.), *Origins and Destinies: Immigration, Race, and Ethnicity in America*, 1–20. New York: Wadsworth.

Peninsula Report. (1999, September 21). Open house to explore drug treatment choices. *San Francisco Chronicle*, A16.

Peralta, V., and H. Horikawa. (1978). *Needs and Potentialities Assessment of Asian American Elderly in Greater Philadelphia.* Report no. 3. Chicago: Pacific/Asian American Mental Health Research Center.

Perry, B. (2000a). Exclusion, inclusion, and violence: Immigrants and criminal justice. In Criminal Justice Collective of Northern Arizona University (ed.), *Investigating Difference: Human and Cultural Relations in Criminal Justice,* 59–70. Boston: Allyn and Bacon.

———. (2000b). Perpetual outsiders: Criminal justice and the Asian American experience. In Criminal Justice Collective of Northern Arizona University (ed.), *Investigating Difference: Human and Cultural Relations in Criminal Justice,* 99–110. Boston: Allyn and Bacon.

Perry, B., and M. O. Nielsen. (2000). Reinvestigating difference. In Criminal Justice Collective of Northern Arizona University (ed.), *Investigating Difference: Human and Cultural Relations in Criminal Justice,* 271–286. Boston: Allyn and Bacon.

Pertman, A. (1999, September 12). Korean adoptees gather to share history: Meeting blends history, research. *Boston Globe,* A14.

———. (2000, April 30). Vietnam adoptees revel in their common bond. *Boston Globe,* A24.

Peterson, W. (1971). *Japanese Americans: Oppression and Success.* New York: Random House.

Pham, A. X. (1996). Torn in two. Review of T. A. Bass, (1996), *Vietnamerica: The War Comes Home.* New York: Soho Press. http://www.metroactive.com/papers/metro/05.02.96/bass-9618.html.

Phinney, J. (1990). Ethnic identity in adolescents and adults: Review of research. *Psychological Bulletin,* 108: 499–514.

Phipps, E., M. H. Cohen, R. Sorn, and L. E. Braitman. (1999). A pilot study of cancer knowledge and screening behaviors of Vietnamese and Cambodian women. *Health Care for Women International,* 20 (2): 195–207.

Pido, L. L. L. (1986). *The Filipinos in America: Macro/Micro Dimensions of Immigration and Integration.* Staten Island, N.Y.: Center for Migration Studies.

Pillemer, K., and D. Finkelhor. (1988). The prevalence of elder abuse: A random survey. *The Gerontologist,* 28 (1): 51–57.

Pitts, L. (2000, July 4). What will Elian remember. *Milwaukee Journal Sentinel,* 15A.

Piven, F. F., and R. Coward. (1971). *Regulating the Poor.* New York: Vintage.

Pobzeb, V. (2001). Hmong population and education in the United States and the world. Lao Human Rights Council. Web site: http://home.earthlink.net/<tilde>laohumanrights/2001data.html.

Portes, A., and R. G. Rumbaut. (1990). *Immigrant America: A Portrait.* Berkeley: University of California Press.

Portes, A., and R. Schauffler. (1996). Language acquisition and loss among children of immigrants. In S. Pedraza and R. B. Rumbaut (eds.), *Origins and Destinies,* 432–443. New York: Wadsworth.

Portes, A., and M. Zhou. (1993). The new second generation: Segmented assimilation and its variants among post-1965 immgrant youth. *Annals of the American Academy of Political and Social Sciences,* 530 (November): 74–96.

Potocky, M. (1996). Toward a new definition of refugee economic integration. *International Social Welfare,* 39: 245–256.

Purcell, V. (1965). *The Chinese in Southeast Asia.* London: Oxford University Press.

Qian, Z. (1999). Who intermarries? Education, nativity, region, and interracial marriage. *Journal of Comparative Family Studies,* 30 (4): 579–598.

Quadagno, J. S. (1994). *The Color of Welfare: How Racism Undermined the War on Poverty.* New York: Oxford University Press.

Quarles, C. S., and J. H. Brodie. (1999). Primary care of international adoptees. *American Family Physician,* 58 (9): 2025–2032.

Radhakrishnan, S. (1940). *Indian Philosophy.* London: George Allen and Unrwin.

Rajaram, S. S., and A. Rashidi. (1999). Asian-Islamic women and breast cancer screening: A socio-cultural analysis. *Women and Health,* 28 (3): 45–58.

Ratner, M. S. (1996). Many routes to homeownership: A four-site ethnographic study of minority and immigrant experiences. *Housing Policy Debate,* 7 (1): 103–145.

Raven, B. H, and J. R. P. French Jr. (1958). Group support, legitimate power, and social influence. *Journal of Personality,* 26: 400–409.

——. (1959). Legitimate power, coercive power, and observability in social influence. *Sociometry,* 21: 83–97.

Ravina, M. (1999). *Land and Lordship in Early Modern Japan.* Stanford: Stanford University Press.

Reed, J. D., B. Kraft, and E. Rudulph. (1985, July 8). Now America is the thing to do. *Time,* 87.

Reiman, J. (1996). . . . *And the Poor Get Prison: Economic Bias in American Criminal Justice.* Boston: Allyn and Bacon.

Reitz, J. G., and S. M. Sklar. (1997). Race, culture, and the economic assimilation of immigrants. *Sociological Forum,* 12 (2): 233–277.

Reuters Press. (1999a, August 27). AIDS and women. *India Abroad,* 32.

——. (1999b, August 27). High incidence of TB. *India Abroad,* 32.

Reyes, E. A. (1993). How long a history do we have? *Health Alert.* http://tribung-pinoy.simplenet.com/kasaysayan/banana.html.

Reynolds, D. R. (1993). *China, 1898–1912: The Xinzheng Revolution and Japan.* Cambridge: Harvard University Press.

Rice, P. (1997, March 15). Speaking their language: Second-generation Korean American churchgoers seek inspiration—in English. *St. Louis Post-Dispatch,* 25.

Ridge, D., A. Hee, and V. Minichiello. (1999). "Asian" men on the scene: Challenges to "gay communities." *Journal of Homosexuality,* 36 (3/4): 43–68.

Riedel, R. L. (1998). Access to health care. In S. Loue (ed.), *Handbook of Immigrant Health,* 101–123. New York: Plenum.

Rimonte, N. (1989). Domestic violence among Pacific Asians. In Asian Women United of California (eds.). *Making Waves: An Anthology of Writings by and About Asian American Women,* 327–337. Boston: Beacon.

Rittman, M., L. B. Kuzmeskus, and M. A. Flum. 1999. A synthesis of current knowledge on minority elder abuse. In T. Tatara (ed.), *Understanding Elder Abuse in Minority Populations,* 221–238. Philadelphia: Brunner/Mazel.

Roberts, J. A. G. (1996). *A History of China: Prehistory to c. 1800.* New York: St. Martin's.

——. (1998). *Modern China: An Illustrated History.* Gloucestershire, Great Britain: Butler and Tanner, Frome, Somerset.

———. (1999). *A Concise History of China*. Cambridge: Harvard University Press.

Robertson, T. (2000, January 2). Changing the face of the racial divide: Mixed marriages alter longtime boundaries. *Boston Globe*, B1.

Robinson, M. E. (1988). *Cultural Nationalism in Colonial Korea, 1920–1925*. Seattle: University of Washington Press.

Rodriguez, C. (1999, November 1). No longer classified as minorities, Asians fear. *Boston Globe*, C6.

Rodriguez, R. (1994). Closed doors. In N. Mills (ed.), *Arguing Immigration: Are New Immigrants a Wealth of Diversity . . . or a Crushing Burden?*, 143–147. New York: Simon and Schuster.

Rohter, W. (1997, September 4). In the mirror, a ghostly replica of Pompeii. *New York Times*, E4.

Root, M. P. P. (1992). *Racially Mixed People in America*. Newbury Park, Calif.: Sage.

———. (1998a). Women. In L. C. Lee and N. W. S. Zane (eds.), *Handbook of Asian American Psychology*, 211–232. Thousand Oaks, Calif.: Sage.

———. (1998b). Multiracial Americans: Changing the face of Asian America. In L. C. Lee and N. W. S. Zane (eds.), *Handbook of Asian American Psychology*, pp. 261–288. Thousand Oaks, Calif.: Sage.

Ross-Sheriff, F. (1992). Adaptation and integration into American society: Major issues affecting Asian Americans. In S. M. Furuto, R. Biswas, D. K. Chung, K. Murase, and F. Ross-Sheriff (eds.), *Social Work Practice with Asian Americans*, 45–64. Newbury Park, Calif.: Sage.

Rothstein, R. (1994). Immigration dilemmas. In N. Mills (ed.), *Arguing Immigration: Are New Immigrants a Wealth of Diversity . . . or a Crushing Burden?*, 48–63. New York: Simon and Schuster.

Rozee, P. D., and G. van Boemel. (1989). The psychological effects of war trauma and abuse on older Cambodian refugee women. *Women and Therapy*, 8: 23–50.

Rumbaut, R. (1985). Mental health and the refugee experience: A comparative stud of Southeast Asian refugees. In T. C. Owan (ed.), *Southeast Asian Mental Health: Treatment, Prevention, Services, Training, and Research*, 433–486. Washington, D.C.: National Institute of Mental Health.

———. (1989). Portraits, patterns and predictors of the refugee adaptation process. In D. W. Haines (ed.), *Refugees as Immigrants: Cambodians, Laotians, and Vietnamese in America*, 138–182. Totowa, N.J.: Rowman and Littlefield.

———. (1991). The agony of exile: A study of the migration and adaptation of Indochinese refugee adults and children. In F. L. Ahearn and J. L. Athey (eds.), *Refugee Children: Theory, Research, and Services*. Baltimore: Johns Hopkins University Press.

———. (1995). Vietnamese, Laotian, and Cambodian Americans. In P. G. Min (ed.), *Asian Americans: Contemporary Issues and Trends*, 232–270. Thousand Oaks, Calif.: Sage.

———. (1996a). Origins and destinies: Immigration, race, and ethnicity in contemporary America. In S. Pedraza and R. G. Rumbaut (eds.), *Origins and Destinies: Immigration, Race, and Ethnicity in America*, 21–42. New York: Wadsworth.

———. (1996b). A legacy of war: Refugees from Vietnam, Laos, and Cambodia. In S. Pedraza and R. G. Rumbaut (eds.), *Origins and Destinies: Immigration, Race, and Ethnicity in America, 315–333*. New York: Wadsworth.

———. (1997a). Assimilation and its discontents: Between rhetoric and reality. *International Migration Review*, 31 (4): 923–960.

———. (1997b). Paradoxes (and orthodoxies) of assimilation. *Sociological Perspectives*, 40 (3): 483–511.

Ruthnaswamy, M. (1949). *India from the Dawn*. Milwaukee: Bruce Publishing.

Ryckman, L. L. (1998, March 22). Mixed messages: Multiethnic children have hard time deciding who they are in society that likes categories. *Denver Rocky Mountain News*, 16R.

Sachs, S. (1999, June 16). Tying drug and alcohol programs to immigrants' backgrounds. *New York Times*, B1.

Sack, W. H., R. H. Angell, J. D. Kinzie, and B. Rath. (1986). The psychiatric effects of massive trauma on Cambodian children: The family, the home, and the school. *Journal of the American Academy of Child Psychiatry*, 25: 3–377.

Sadler, G. R., F. Nguyen, Q. Doan, H. Au, and A. G. Thomas. (1998). Strategies for reaching Asian Americans with health information. *American Journal of Preventative Medicine*, 14 (3): 224–228.

Sailer, S. (1997, July 14). Is love colorblind? *National Review*, 49 (13): 30–33.

Samuda, G. M. (1988). Child discipline and abuse in Hong Kong. *Child Abuse and Neglect*, 12 (2): 283–287.

Sanchez, L. (2000, March 29). Human rights development in Vietnam. http://www.vpac-usa.org/humanrights/chrc_briefing_2000/statement_sanchez.htm.

Sanitioso, R. (1999). A social psychological perspective on HIV/AIDS and gay or homosexually active Asian men. *Journal of Homosexuality*, 36 (3/4): 69–85.

Saran, P. (1985). *The Asian Indian experience in the United States*. New Delhi: Vikas Publishing House, PVT, Ltd.

Saslow, L. (2000, March 26). Korea to Syosset: A two-generation bridge. *New York Times*.

Sastry, J., and C. E. Ross. (1998). Asian ethnicity and the sense of personal control. *Social Psychology Quarterly*, 61 (2): 101–120.

Sauerwein, K. (1996, January 22). Immigrant children help parents get their word's worth. *St. Louis Post-Dispatch*, B1.

Savada, A. M. (ed.). (1995). *Laos: A Country Study*. Washington, D.C.: U.S. Library of Congress.

Scally, R. (1995). The Irish and the "Famine Exodus" of 1847. In Cohen, R. (ed.), *The Cambridge Survey of World Migration*, 80–84. Cambridge, U.K.: Cambridge University Press.

Schaefer, R. (1991). *Racial and Ethnic Groups*. Boston: Little, Brown.

Schmallerger, R. (1995). *Criminal Justice Today*. 3d ed. Englewood Cliffs, N.J.: Prentice-Hall.

Schneider, H. (1998, February). The new pool of homebuyers. *Mortgage Banking*, 58 (5): 64–70.

Scrivo, K. L. (2000, March 4). The parent trap: Overseas adoptions pose diplomatic and personal dilemmas for parents and for Congress. *National Journal*, 32 (10): 695.

See, L. (1998). The funeral banquet. In C. C. O'Hearn (ed.), *Half and Half: Writers on Growing Up Biracial and Bicultural*, 125–138. New York: Pantheon.

Segal, M. N., U. A. Segal, and M. A. P. Niemczycki. (1993). Value network for cross-national marketing management: A framework for analysis and application. *Journal of Business Research*, 27 (1): 65–83.

Segal, U. A. (1995). Child abuse by the middle class? A study of professionals in India. *Child Abuse and Neglect*, 19 (2): 213–227.

——. (1998). The Asian Indian–American family. In C. H. Mindel, R. W. Habenstein, and R. Wright Jr. (eds.), *Ethnic Families in America*, 331–360. 4th ed. Upper Saddle River, N.J.: Prentice Hall.

——. (1999). Family violence: A focus on India. *Review of Aggression and Violent Behavior*, 4 (2): 213–231.

——. (2000a). Exploring child abuse among Vietnamese refugees. In D. de Anda and R. M. Becerra (eds.), *Violence: Diverse Populations and Communities*, 159–191. Binghamton, N.Y.: Haworth Press.

——. (2000b). A pilot exploration of family violence among a non-clinical Vietnamese sample. *Journal of Interpersonal Violence*, 15 (5): 523–533.

Seith, P. A. (1997). Escaping domestic violence: Asylum as a means of protection for battered women. *Columbia Law Review*, 97 (6): 1804–1843.

Serafica, F. C. (1997). Psychopathology and resilience in Asian American children and adolescents. *Applied Developmental Science*, 1 (3): 15–155.

Sevrens, D. (2000, April 30). The melting pot is seasoned anew. *San Diego Union-Tribune*, G1.

Shah, G., and R. Veedon. (1995). Elder abuse in India. *Journal of Elder Abuse and Neglect*, 5 (1): 101–118.

Shah, R. (1997). Improving services to Asian families and children with disabilities. *Child: Care, Health Development*, 23 (1): 41–46.

Sharry, F. (1999, July 3). Immigrants assimilating in U.S., report concludes. *Fort Worth Star-Telegram*, 2.

Shepherd, J. (1992). Vietnamese women immigrants and refugees in the United States: Historical perspectives on casework. In S. M. Furuto, R, Biswas, D. K. Chung, K. Murase, and F. Ross-Sheriff (eds.), *Social Work Practice with Asian Americans*, 85–100. Newbury Park, Calif.: Sage.

Sheth, M. (1995). Asian Indian Americans. In P. G. Min (ed.), *Asian Americans: Contemporary Issues and Trends*, 169–198. Thousand Oaks, Calif.: Sage.

Shin, E. H. (1987). Interracially married Korean women in the United States: An analysis based on hypergamy-exchange theory. In E. Y. Yu, and E. Phillips (eds.), *Korean Women in Transition: At Home and Abroad*, 249–276. Los Angeles: Center for Korean-American and Korean Studies, California State University.

Shin, H., and N. Abell. (1999). The Homesickness and Contentment Scale: Developing a culturally sensitive measure of adjustment for Asians. *Research on Social Work Practice*, 9 (1): 45–60.

Shin, S. H. (1972). *History in Korea: Past and Present*. Seoul, Korea: Kwangmyong Publishing, 42–84.

Shinn, R.-S., and R. L. Worden. (1994). *History of China*. Army Area Handbook. http://lcweb2.loc.gov/frd/cs/cntoc.html.

Shuval, J. T. (1998). Migration to Israel: The mythology of uniqueness. *International Migration*, 36 (1): 3–26.

Simon, J. L. (1989). *The Economic Consequences of Immigration*. Lexington, Mass.: Lexington Books.

———. (1996). Public expenditures on immigrants to the United States, past and present. *Population and Development Review*, 22 (1): 99–109.

Simon, R. J., and S. H. Alexander. (1993). *The Ambivalent Welcome: Print Media, Public Opinion, and Immigration*. Westport, Conn.: Praeger.

Singh, R. N., and N. P. Unnithan. (1999). Wife burning: Cultural cues for lethal violence against women among Asian Indians in the United States. *Violence Against Women*, 5 (6): 641–653.

Siu, P. C. T. (1952). The sojourners. *American Journal of Sociology*, 8 (1): 32–44.

Skeldon, R. (1996). Migration from China. *Journal of International Affairs*. http;//www.columbia.edu/cu/sipa/PUBS/JOURNAL/china.html.

Skinner, K., and G. Hendrick. (1977). The shaping of ethnic self-identity among Indochinese refugees. *Journal of Ethnic Studies*, 7 (3): 25–41.

Skocpol, T. (1992). *Protecting Soldiers and Mothers: The Political Origins of Social Policy in the United States*. Cambridge: Harvard University Press.

SLIK Designs. (1996). What is elder abuse? http://www.interinc.co/ncea/elder-abuse/main.html.

Smith, C. E. (1993). *Courts and Public Policy*. Chicago: Nelson-Hall.

Smith, D. G. (1994). *Transracial and Transcultural Adoption*. Rockville, Md.: National Adoption Clearinghouse.

Smith, P. (1997). *Japan: A Reinterpretation*. New York: Pantheon.

Smith, T. W. (1991). *What Americans Think About Jews*. New York: American Jewish Committee.

Soh, J. (2000a, July 3). Illegal overseas study rampant: Fever high among primary school students. *Korea Times*, 4.

———. (2000b, July 6). Major economic bodies oppose work permit for foreigners. *Korea Times*, 5.

Song, Y. (1996). *Battered Women in Korean Immigrant Families*. New York: Garland.

Special Services for Groups. (1978). *Pacific/Asian Elderly Research Project: Final Report*. Los Angeles: Special Services for Groups.

Spencer, M., and C. Markstrom-Adams. (1990). Identity processes among racial and ethnic minority children in America. *Child Development*, 61 (2): 290–310.

Steinmetz, S. (1981). A cross-cultural comparison of sibling violence. *International Journal of Family Psychiatry*, 2 (3/4): 337–351.

Steinmo, S. (1993). *Taxation and Democracy: Swedish, British, and American Approaches to Financing the Modern State*. New Haven: Yale University Press.

Sterba, J. (1987, January 27). Immigrant saga. *Wall Street Journal*, 2.

Steven, L. D. (1990). Refugee services of San Antonio: The Fresh Air Program. In W. H. Holtzman and T. Bornemann (eds.), *Mental Health of Immigrants and Refugees*, 290–296. Austin: Hogg Foundation for Mental Health.

Stevens, R., and J. Vermeulen. (1972). *Foreign Trained Physicians and American Medicine*. Washington, D.C.: Government Printing Office.

Stewart, J. Y. (2000, April 2). Few plan for the hard realities of infirm parents' care. Aging: Most families haven't even discussed the issue, Times poll finds. Limited availability of aid can be a shock. *Los Angeles Times*, A1.

Stokes, L., and J. Scott. (1996). Affirmative action and selected minority groups in law enforcement. *Journal of Criminal Justice*, 24 (1): 29–38.

Stolzenberg, R. M., and M. Tienda. (1997). English proficiency, education, and the conditional economic assimilation of Hispanic and Asian men. *Social Science Research*, 26 (1): 25–51.

Stone, R. L., and J. Marsella. (1968). Mahirap: A squatter community in a Manila suburb. In W. F. Bello and A. de Guzman II (eds.), *Modernization: Its Impact in the Philippines*, 3:64–91. Quezon City, Philippines: Ateneo de Manila University Press.

Strand, P. J., and W. Jones Jr. (1985). *Indochinese Refugees in America: Problems of Adaptation and Assimilation*. Durham: Duke University Press.

Straus, M. A., R. Gelles, and S. Steinmetz. (1980). *Behind Closed Doors: Violence in the American Family*. New York: Doubleday.

Strong, E. K. Jr. (1933). *Japanese in California*. Stanford: Stanford University Press.

Strozier, M. (1997, November 21). A new report on Asian Americans. *India Abroad*, 41.

Struwe, G. (1994). Training health and medical professionals to care for refugees: Issues and methods. In A. J. Marsella, T. Bornemann, S. Ekblad, and J. Orley (eds.), *Amidst Peril and Pain: The Mental Health and Well-being of the World's Refugees*, 311–324. Washington, D.C.: American Psychological Association.

Sue, David, W. S. Mak, and Derald W. Sue. (1998). Ethnic identity. In L. C. Lee and N. W. S. Zane (eds.), *Handbook of Asian American Psychology*, 289–324. Thousand Oaks, Calif.: Sage.

Sue, D., and S. Sue. (1987). Cultural factors in the clinical assessment of Asian Americans. *Journal of Consulting and Clinical Psychology*, 55: 479–487.

Sue, S., and H. McKinney. (1975). Asian-Americans in the community mental health care system. *American Journal of Orthopsychiatry*, 45: 111–118.

Sue, S., and J. K. Morishima. (1982). *The Mental Health of Asian Americans*. San Francisco: Jossey-Bass.

Sue, S., D. W. Sue, L. Sue, and D. T. Takeuchi. (1995). Psychopathology among Asian Americans: A model minority? *Cultural Diversity and Mental Health*, 1 (1): 39–51.

Sung, B. (1990). Chinese American intermarriage. *Journal of Comparative American Studies*, 21 (3): 337–352.

Suro, R. (1999, November). Mixed doubles. *American Demographics*, cover story.

Takenaka, A. (1999). Transnational community and its ethnic consequences: The return migration and the transformation of ethnicity of Japanese Peruvians. *American Behavioral Scientist*, 42 (9): 1459–1463.

Tanjasiri, S. P., S. P. Wallace, and K. Shibata. (1995). Picture perfect: Hidden problems among Asian Pacific Islander elderly. *The Gerontologist*, 35 (6): 753–760.

Tanwar, T. (1988). Media and child abuse. In National Institute of Public Cooperation and Child Development (ed.), *National Seminar on Child Abuse in India, 22–24 June 1988*, 120–136. New Delhi: NIPCCD.

TaKaki, R. (1989). *Strangers from a Different Shore: A History of Asian Americans*. Boston: Little, Brown.

Tatara, T. (ed). (1999). *Understanding Elder Abuse in Minority Populations*. Philadelphia: Brunner/Mazel.

Tawa, R. (1999, December 19). Asian-themed toys give children cultural identity. *Fort Worth Star-Telegram*, 5G.

Teicher, S. A. (1999, September 16). Tearful reunion of a war's "lost" children. *Christian Science Monitor*, 3.

Tennant, R. (1996). *A History of Korea*. New York: Kegan Paul International.

Thapar, R. (1982). *A History of India*. Vol. 1. Middlesex, U.K.: Penguin.

Thomas, K. (1999, August 9). Good and bad HMDA news. *National Mortgage News*.

Thompson, B. (1998, November). X marks the spot. *Builder*, 21 (14): 19.

Thompson, J. (2000, May 1). Vietnamese adoptees reunited: 100 of those brought to the United States in a 1975 airlift trade stories of their lives. *Omaha World-Herald*, 1.

Tien, L. (1994). Southeast Asian women. In L. Comas Diaz and B. Greene (eds.), *Women of Color: Integrating Ethnic and Gender Identities in Psychotherapy*, 479–503. New York: Guilford.

Tienda, M., and A. Singer. (1995). Wage mobility of undocumented workers in the United States. *International Migration Review*, 29 (1): 112–138.

Tienda, M., and H. Stier. (1996). The wages of race: Color and employment opportunity in Chicago's inner city. In S. Pedraza and R. G. Rumbaut (eds.), *Origins and Destinies: Immigration, Race, and Ethnicity in America*, 417–431. New York: Wadsworth.

Tinker, H. (1977). *The Banyan Tree*. New York: Oxford University Press.

———. (1995). The British colonies of settlement. In R. Cohen (ed.), *The Cambridge Survey of World Migration*, 14–20. Cambridge, U.K.: Cambridge University Press.

Tjaden, P., and M. Thoennes. (1998). *Prevalence, Incidence, and Consequences of Violence Against Women: Findings from the National Violence Against Women Survey*. Washington, D.C.: U.S. Department of Justice.

Tomita, S. K. (1998). The consequences of belonging: Conflict management techniques among Japanese Americans. *Journal of Elder Abuse and Neglect*, 9 (3): 41–68.

Tong, B. (1994). *Unsubmissive Women: Chinese Prostitutes in Nineteenth-Century San Francisco*. Norman: University of Oklahoma Press.

Torres-Gil, F. M., and M. A. Puccinelli. (1994). Mainstreaming gerontology in the policy arena. *The Gerontologist*, 34 (6): 749–752.

Tran, T. V. (1998). The Vietnamese-American family. In C. H. Mindel, R. W. Habenstein, and R. Wright Jr. (eds.), *Ethnic Families in America*, 254–282. 4th ed. Upper Saddle River, N.J.: Prentice Hall.

Tran, T. V., and D. L. Ferullo. (1997). Indochinese mental health in North America: Measures, status, and treatments. *Journal of Sociology and Social Welfare*, 24 (2): 3–20.

Tranton, J., and W. Lutton. (1993). Immigration and criminality in the USA. *Journal of Social, Political, and Economic Studies*, 18 (2): 217–234.

Trattner, W. (1974). *From Poor Law to Welfare State*. New York: Free Press.

Triandis, H. C. (1989). The self and social behavior in differing cultural contexts. *Psychological Review*, 96 (3): 506–520.

Triandis, H. C., R. Bontempo, M. Villareal, M. Asai, and N. Lucca. (1988). Individualism and collectivism: Cross-cultural perspective on self-group relationships. *Journal of Personality and Social Psychology*, 54 (2): 323–338.

Trolley, B. C. (1994). Grief issues and positive aspects associated with international adoption. *Omega*, 30 (4): 257–268.

Tsai, M., L. N. Teng, and S. Sue. (1975). Mental status of Chinese in the United States. *American Journal of Orthopsychiatry*, 45 (1): 111–118.

Tsuda, T. (1999). The motivation to migrate: The ethnic and sociocultural constitution of the Japanese-Brazilian return-migration system. *Economic Development and Cultural Change*, 48 (1): 1–32.

Tu, S-P., S. H. Taplin, W. E. Barlow, and E. J. Boyko. (1999). Breast cancer screening by Asian-American women in a managed care environment. *American Journal of Preventative Medicine*, 17 (1): 55–61.

Uba, L. (1994). *Asian Americans*. New York: Guilford Press.

United Nations Conference on Trade and Development. (1975). *The Reverse Transfer of Technology: Its Dimensions, Economic Effects, and Policy Implications*. New York: UNCTAD Secretariat.

Ungar, S. J. (1995). *Fresh Blood: The New American Immigrants*. New York: Simon and Schuster.

UNHCR. (1996, May). *Community Services Manual*. Rev. ed. Geneva, Switzerland: United Nations High Commission for Refugees.

U.S. Bureau of the Census. (1991). *Statistical Abstract of the United States, 1991*. Washington, D.C.: Government Printing Office.

——. (1993). *1990 Census of Population, Asians and Pacific Islanders in the United States*. Series PC3–5. Washington, D.C.: U.S. Government Printing Office.

——. (1995). *Statistical Abstract of the United States: The National Data Book*. 112th ed. Washington, D.C.: U.S. Government Printing Office.

——. (1998a). *Current Population Reports*. Series P23-194. Population Profile of the United States: 1997. Washington, D.C.: U.S. Government Printing Office.

——. (1998b). *Money Income in the United States, 1997*. CPR P60-200. Washington, D.C.: U.S. Government Printing Office.

——. (1998c). *The Asian and Pacific Islander Population in the United States: March 1997 (Update)*. Current Population Reports, P70-63. Washington, D.C.: U.S. Government Printing Office.

——. (1999, December 23). *Resident Population Estimates of the United States by Sex, Race, and Hispanic Origin: April 1, 1990, to November 1, 1999*. Population Estimates Program, Population Division. Washington, D.C.: U.S. Government Printing Office.

——. (2000a, February 11). *Home Ownership Rates by Race and Ethnicity of Householder*. Housing Vacancies and Home Ownership Annual Statistics: 1999. Washington, D.C.: U.S. Government Printing Office. http://www.census.gov/hhes/www/housing/hvs/annual99/ann99t20.html.

——. (2000b, January 2). Census on Centenarians. Report for the National Institute on Aging. *Chicago Sun-Times*, Sunday News, 23.

——. (2001). *Income 1999*. http://www.census.gov/hhes/income/income99/99tableb.html.

U.S. Commission on Civil Rights. (1992). *Civil Rights Issues Facing Asian Americans in the 1990s*. Washington, D.C.: U.S. Government Printing Office.

U.S. Committee for Refugees. (2000, September 14). News and resources. http://www.refugees.org/news/newsmain.htm.

U.S. Department of the Army. (1993). *The Korean War, 1950–1953*. Army Area Handbook. gopher://gopher.umsl.edu/00/library/govdocs/armyahbs/aahb1/aahb0087.

U.S. Department of Commerce. (1993). *We the Americans: Asians.* Washington, D.C.: U.S. Government Printing Office.

U.S. Department of Justice. (1999a). *Refugees, Fiscal Year 1997.* No. 4. Washington, D.C.: U.S. Government Printing Office.

———. (1999b). *Crimes Against Property, 1998. Hate Crime Statistics, 1998.* Uniform Crime Reports, Federal Bureau of Investigation, Criminal Justice Information Services Division. Washington, D.C.: Government Printing Office.

U.S. Department of State. (1969). *Korea: 1945–1948.* New York: Greenwood Press.

U.S. Immigration and Naturalization Service. (1995). *Korean Immigration to the United States, 1903–1994.* Annual Report. Washington, D.C.: U.S. Government Printing Office.

U.S. Immigration and Naturalization Service (INS). (1999a). Illegal alien resident population. http://www.ins.usdoj.gov/graphics/aboutins/statistics/illegalalien/index.htm.

———. (1999b). Foreign-born population. http://www.ins.usdoj.gov/graphics/aboutins/statistics/299.htm.

———. (2000, July 7). Applications for immigration benefits. http://www.ins.usdoj.gov/graphics/aboutins/statistics

U.S. Immigration Commission. (1911). *Japanese and Other Immigrant Races in the Pacific Coast and Rocky Mountain States.* Washington, D.C.: Government Printing Office.

U.S. Library of Congress. (1990). *South Korea: A Country Study.* http://www.lcweb2.loc.gov/frd/cs/krtoc.html.

Van Oudenhoven, J. P., K. S. Prins, and P. B. Buunk. (1998). Attitudes of minority and majority members towards adaptation of immigrants. *European Journal of Social Psychology,* 28 (6): 995–1013.

van Wormer, K. (1997). *Social Welfare: A World View.* Chicaco: Nelson-Hall.

Vanselm, K., D. L. Sam, and J. P. Van Oudenhoven. (1997). Life satisfaction and competence of Bosnian refugees in Norway. *Scandinavian Journal of Psychology,* 38 (2): 143–149.

Varadarajan, T. (1999, July 4). A Patel motel cartel? *New York Times Magazine,* 36–39.

Varma, S. C., and S. G. Siris. (1996). Alcohol abuse in Asian Americans: Epidemiological and treatment issues. *American Journal on Addictions,* 5 (2): 136–143.

Varner, L. K. (1999, September 20). Gateses' grants: Asians feel snubbed. *Seattle Times,* B1.

Vatz, R. E., and L. S. Weinberg. (1997). Parity: The new buzzward in mental health. *USA Today* magazine, 125 (2624): 61–62.

Vega, W. A., and R. G. Rumbaut. (1991). Ethnic minorities and mental health. *Annual Review of Sociology,* 17:351–383.

Vigoda, A. (2000, April 11). Lisa Ling defends Old Navy ads as "sassy," not stereotypical. *USA Today,* 2D.

Vonk, M. E., P. J. Simms, and L. Nackerud. (1999). Political and personal aspects of intercountry adoption of Chinese children in the United States. *Families in Society,* 80 (5): 496–518.

Vu, T. Q. (1990). Refugee welfare dependency: The trauma of resettlement. In W. H. Holtzman and T. H. Bornemann (eds.), *Mental Health of Immigrants and Refugees,* 234–244. Austin: Hogg Foundation for Mental Health.

Walker, S. (1998). *Sense and Nonsense About Crime and Drugs.* Belmont, Calif.: West/Wadsworth.

Walker, S., C. Spohn, and M. Delone. (1999). *The Color of Justice: Race, Ethnicity, and Crime in America.* Belmont, Calif.: Wadsworth/Thomson Learning.

Wallace, H. (1999). *Family Violence: Legal, Medical, and Social Perspectives.* 2d ed. Boston: Allyn and Bacon.

Wallace, S. P., V. M. Villa, C. L. Estes, and M. Minkler. (1998). Caught in hostile cross-fire: Public policy and minority elderly in the United States. In C. L. Estes and M. Minkler (eds.), *Critical Gerontology: Perspectives from Political and Moral Economy,* 237–255. Amityville, N.Y.: Baywood.

Wang, M. (1999, July 22). Teens explore what it means to be biracial. *Houston Chronicle,* 5.

Warner, W. L., and L. Srole (1945). *The Social Systems of American Ethnic Groups.* New Haven: Yale University Press.

Warshaw, S. (1987). *China Emerges.* Berkeley: Diablo Press.

Waswo, A. (1996). *Modern Japanese Society, 1868–1994.* New York: Oxford University Press.

Waters, M. C., and K. Eschbach. (1995). Immigration and ethnic and racial inequality in the United States. *Annual Review of Sociology,* 21:419–446.

Weinberg, D. (1996, September 26). Press briefing on 1995 income, poverty, and health insurance estimates. Washington, D.C.: U.S. Bureau of the Census, Household Economic Statistics Division.

Weir, F. (2000). *A Centennial of History of Philippine independence, 1898–1998.* http://www.ualberta.ca/~vmitchel/.

Weitzman, M., H. M. Duplessis, S. I. Fixch, R. E. Holmberg, A. Lavin, C. J. Mckay, P. Melinkovick, R. L. Meuli, Y. L. Piovanetti, D. A. Varrasso, W. Bithoney, A. E. Dyson, L. K. Grossman, C. Jones, J. A. McLaurin, C. Poland, D. Ohare, and H. Wilson. (1997). Health care for children of immigrant families. *Pediatrics,* 100 (1): 153–156.

Weller, R. P. (1994). *Resistance, Chaos, and Control in China.* Seattle: University of Washington Press.

Westermeyer, J., and P. Chitasombat. (1996). Ethnicity and the course of opiate addiction: Native-born Americans vs. Hmong in Minnesota. *American Journal on Addictions,* 5 (3): 231–240.

Westermeyer, J., T. Lyfoung, M. Westermeyer, and J. Neider. (1991). Opium addiction among Indochinese refugees in the United States: Characteristics of addicts and their opium use. *American Journal of Drug and Alcohol Use,* 17 (3): 267–277.

Wilensky, H. L. (1965). Introduction to H. L. Wilensky and C. M. Lebeaux, *Industrial Society and Social Welfare.* New York: Free Press, xvi–xvii.

Williamson, C. Jr. (1996). *The Immigration Mystique.* New York: Basic Books.

Wilson, C. (1997). Home buyers of the future. *America's Community Banker,* 6 (10): 33–35.

Wise, C. (1997, December). Pulling in new borrowers. *Mortgage Banking,* 58 (3): 24–29.

Wolf, D. L. (1997). Family secrets: Transnational struggles among children of Filipino immigrants. *Sociological Perspectives,* 40 (3): 457–483.

Wong, B. K. (1998). Raising Asian children in America: Who am I? *Family/Culture Newsletter*, 4, 8.

——. (1999). The invisible crisis: Asian teens in America. http://www.familyculture.com/feature_articles.htm.

Wong, M. G. (1980). Changes in socioeconomic status of the Chinese male population in the United States from 1960 to 1970. *International Migration Review*, 14 (4): 511–524.

——. (1995a). Chinese Americans. In P. G. Min (ed.), *Asian Americans: Contemporary Issues and Trends*, 58–94. Thousand Oaks, Calif.: Sage.

——. (1995b). Post-1965 Asian immigrations: Where do they come from, where are they now, and where are they going? In F. Ng, *The History and Immigration of Asian Americans*, 150–167. New York: Garland.

Wong, P. T. P., and K. V. Ujimoto. (1998). The elderly: Their stress, coping, and mental health. In L. C. Lee and N. W. S. Zane (eds.), *Handbook of Asian American Psychology*, 165–210. Thousand Oaks, Calif.: Sage.

Wood, E. (1998). More foreign adoptees return to homelands to adopt children. *Houston Chronicle*, 7.

Wood, G. S. (1969). *The Creation of the American Republic: 1776–1787*. Chapel Hill: University of North Carolina Press.

Wu, A. (2000, March 29). What kind of Chinese am I? *Christian Science Monitor*, 9.

Xie, Y., and K. Goyette. (1998). The racial identification of biracial children with one Asian parent: Evidence from the 1990 census. *Social Forces*, 76 (2): 547–570.

Yamamoto, J., J. A. Silva, and C. Y. Chang. (1998). Transitions in Asian-American elderly. In G. H. Pollock and S. I. Greenspan (eds.), *The Course of Life*. Vol. 7, Completing the Journey, 135–159. Madison, Conn.: International Universities Press.

Yanagisako, S. J. (1975). Two processes of change in Japanese-American kinship. *Journal of Anthropological Research*, 31 (3): 196–224.

Yee, B. W., and N. D. Thu. (1987). Correlates of drug use and abuse among Indochinese refugees: Mental health implications. *Journal of Psychoactive Drugs*, 19 (1): 77–83.

Yee, B. W. K., L. N. Huang, and A. Lew. (1998). Families: Life-span socialization in cultural context. In L. C. Lee and N. W. S. Zane (eds.), *Handbook of Asian American Psychology*, 83–136. Thousand Oaks, Calif.: Sage.

Yee, D. L. (1992). Health care access and advocacy for immigrant and other underserved elders. *Journal of Health Care for the Poor and Underserved*, 2 (4): 448–464.

Yi, J. K. (1996). Factors affecting cervical cancer screening behavior among Cambodian women in Houston, Texas. *Family and Community Health*, 18 (4): 49–57.

Ying, Y. (1988). Depressive symptomatology among Chinese-Americans measured by the CES-D. *Journal of Clinical Psychology*, 44 (5): 739–746.

Ying, Y.-W., P. D. Akutsu, X. Zhang, L. N. Huang. (1997). Psychological dysfunction in Southeast Asian refugees as mediated by sense of coherence. *American Journal of Community Psychology*, 25 (6): 839–859.

Yinger, J. (1988). Examining racial discrimination with fair housing audits. In H. S. Bloom, D. S. Conray, and R. J. Light (eds.), *Lessons from Selected Program and Policy Areas*, 47–62. San Francisco: Jossey-Bass.

Yochum, F., and V. Agarwal. (1988). Permanent labor certifications for alien professionals. *International Migration Review*, 22 (2): 265–281.

Yoder-Wise, P. S. (1999). *Leading and Managing in Nursing*. 2d ed. St. Louis: Mosby.

Yoshihama, M. (1999). Domestic violence against women of Japanese descent in Los Angeles: Two methods of estimating prevalence. *Violence Against Women*, 5 (8): 869–897.

Yoshihama, M., and S. B. Sorenson. (1994). Physical, sexual, and emotional abuse by male intimates: Experiences of women in Japan. *Violence and Victims*, 9 (1): 63–77.

Young, K., and D. T. Takeuchi. (1998). Racism. In L. C. Lee and N. W. S. Zane (eds.), *Handbook of Asian American Psychology*, 401–432. Thousand Oaks, Calif.: Sage.

Yu, E. S. (1991). The health risks of Asian Americans. *American Journal of Public Health*, 81 (1): 1391–1393.

Yung, J. (1986). *Chinese Women in America: A Pictorial History*. Seattle: University of Washington Press.

Ywan, A. Y. (1995). Elderly abuse in Hong Kong: A new family problem in the old East? *Journal of Elder Abuse and Neglect*, 6 (3–4): 65–80.

Zaide, G. F. (1970). *The Republic of the Philippines*. Manila: Rex Book Store.

Zane, N., and J. Huh-Kim. (1998). Addictive behaviors. In L. C. Lee and N. W. S. Zane (eds.), *Handbook of Asian American Psychology*, 527–554. Thousand Oaks, Calif.: Sage.

Zane, N., and J. Kim. (1994). Substance use and abuse Among Asian Americans. In D. Zane, D. Takeuchi, and K. Young (eds.), *Confronting Critical Health Issues of Asian and Pacific Islander Americans*. Thousand Oaks, Calif.: Sage.

Zane, N., and S. Toshiaki. (1992). Research on drug abuse among Asian Pacific Americans. *Drugs and Society*, 6 (3/4): 181–209.

Zarembka, A. (1990). *The Urban Housing Crisis: Social, Economic, and Legal Issues and Proposals*. Westport, Conn.: Greenwood Press.

Zegeye, A. (1995). Hunger, war and flight: The Horn of Africa. In R. Cohen (ed.), *The Cambridge Survey of World Migration*. Cambridge, U.K.: Cambridge University Press.

Zhou, M. (1997). Segmented assimilation-issues, controversies, and recent research on the new second generation. *International Migration Review*, 31 (4): 975–1008.

Zhou, M., and C. L. Bankston III. (2000). *Straddling Two Social Worlds: The Experience of Vietnamese Refugee Children in the United States*. Washington, D.C.: ERIC Clearinghouse of Urban Education. http://eric-web.tc.columbia.edu/monographs/uds111/index.html.

Zia, H. (2000). *Asian American Dreams: The Emergence of an American People*. New York: Farrar, Straus, and Giroux.

Zuckoff, M. (2000, April 30). Assimilation: A new life in a new land. *Boston Globe*, M16.

INDEX

Assimilation (*continued*)
of Korean immigrants, 70; and mental health care, 299; and phenotype, 30, 309, 316; and political participation, 313; segmented, 29, 30–31, 323, 324, 380, 381; structural, 312; into underclass, 30; and underutilization of services, 363; and upward mobility, 323–24; of USAsians, 310, 324; and youth gangs, 264
Association of Southeast Asian Nations (ASEAN), 125
Asylum, 13, 20, 24, 27; for Chinese refugees, 88; for Indian refugees, 57, 95; seekers of, 3, 80, 137, 356; for Vietnam War refugees, 76–77; for women, 7, 9
Au Lac (Vietnam), 113
Australia, 42, 108, 121, 125, 126, 202
Authority: American distrust of, 192, 307; Asian respect for, 165, 186, 187–88; of elderly, 203, 241; within family, 190, 197, 198, 214; fear of, 250, 266; and health care, 282, 370; and human services, 376, 377, 378; and mental health care, 295, 296, 372; patriarchal, 199, 215, 220; and social roles, 188, 317; and welfare, 243
Ayers, S. M., 270

Balkans, 164
Bangladesh, 58, 91, 206; immigrants from, 128, 154, 155
Barred Zone Act (Immigration Act of 1917), 134
Bataan (Philippines), 108; death march in, 60–61
Batavia (Indonesia), 108
Behavior: and adjustment, 170, 264, 265; American, of Asian Americans, 186, 189, 192–93; in American culture, 191–92, 357; antisocial, 156, 170, 213–14, 264, 265; Asian vs. Euro-American, 193–97; cultural norms of, 316; emotionally restrained, 185, 186, 187, 189; and family, 197, 244; and generational status, 321, 324; high-risk, 208; homosexual, 202; human, 362; and identity, 321; and intermarriage, 335; and perceptions of

Asian Americans, 355; problematic, 212–20; and segmented assimilation, 323; shame as influence on, 186, 188; situation-specific, 189, 204, 205; and welfare, 231–32
Bhatia, Sabeer, 158
Biculturalism: and adjustment, 381; and generational status, 379; and globalization, 326–27; in human services, 382; and identity, 310, 359–62; of immigrants, 322–23; of USAsians, 321, 322–24, 389; of women, 326; *see also* Multiculturalism
Bimodal distribution, 356, 364, 384; of academic performance, 253–55, 256, 258, 367; of adjustment, 247; by class, 207; of health care, 276; of housing, 249, 365; of knowledge of U.S., 279; and mental health, 295; of occupation, 176, 179, 180, 181; of resources, 281
Boat people, 263; Chinese, 87–88; Vietnamese, 115–16
Bob Jones University (South Carolina), 332
Bonifacio, Andres, 60
Bosnia-Herzegovina, 6, 12
Bosnian Muslims, 9
Boston (Massachusetts), 138
Boxer Uprising (China; 1900), 42, 57
Brain drain, 8, 78, 176; from China, 86; from India, 93; from Philippines, 62, 99; *see also* Professionals
Braun, K. L., 218
Brazil, 47, 71, 111, 353
Britain, 108, 126, 387, 389; and China, 40, 107; health care insurance in, 272, 273–74, 280; immigration from, 131; and India, 54–56, 90, 145, 173; Indian immigrants in, 93, 95; and Japan, 49, 107
British Commonwealth of Nations, 90
Brown, H. N., 296
Buddhism, 54, 193, 197, 243, 296; in Japan, 46; in Korea, 64, 65; in Laos, 124
Burma, *see* Myanmar
Bush, George H. W., 228
Bush, George W., 228, 314
Business, 63, 71, 110, 162, 188, 325; and acceptance of immigrants, 27; and

Education (*continued*)
and crime, 260; in criminal justice system, 267; and culture, 175, 251, 256; discrimination in, 156, 252, 256–58, 368; and economics, 78, 252–53; and elderly, 202, 204; and family, 78–79, 82, 368; and family violence, 244, 253, 365, 374; and Filipino immigrants, 61, 62, 63, 101–2, 147; and globalization, 177, 252; government subsidies for, 306; and health care, 35, 207, 208, 275, 279, 280, 281, 282, 369; higher, 79, 84, 92, 93, 174, 257, 258, 368; and housing, 247, 249, 366; and immigration, 4, 26, 74, 100; and immigration policy, 76, 77–80, 136, 157, 251; of Indian immigrants, 56, 92, 93, 94, 95; and intermarriage, 336–37; in Japan, 47, 48, 50, 110–11, 142; and Japanese immigrants, 112, 151; in Korea, 66, 104; and Korean immigrants, 71, 105–6, 150; and language, 34, 223, 251, 282; in Laos, 125; and Laotian refugees, 127; and mainstreaming, 312; and marriage, 327, 333; and mental health, 297, 298, 299; and occupational distribution, 178; and opportunity, 10, 25; in Philippines, 61, 78, 79, 174; public, 255; public policy on, 33, 34, 226, 250–58, 308, 363, 367–69; as push or pull factor, 14, 15, 53; quotas in, 257, 368; and refugees, 80–81, 121, 160; and response to immigration, 21, 22; as right, 270; and social mobility, 174–75; and Southeast-Asian immigrants, 160, 173, 178; and status, 8–9, 382; and substance abuse, 303, 305; and technology, 252, 257; in U.S., 317, 358; and USAsians, 318; vocational, 34, 36; and welfare, 163, 242; for women, 36, 52; *see also* Academic performance
Educational Testing Service (ETS), 253, 256, 367
Elder Abuse Incidence Study, National, 242
Elderly: abuse of, 218–19, 241–42, 292, 364–65, 373; and acculturation, 204, 218, 241, 292; in American culture, 191, 192, 196; in Asian culture, 186–87, 190, 196, 197, 203, 204, 241; and bicultural identity, 360; changing status of, 198, 202–5; dependency of, 241, 242; and English-language acquisition, 223; health care for, 207, 276, 277, 278, 280; and home country, 325, 353; homeless, 246; and housing programs, 249; income of, 233, 364; mental health of, 286, 290–92, 295–96; among nonwhite minorites, 361; poverty of, 236; and substance abuse, 303; U.S.-born, 292; and welfare, 235–36, 240–42, 364

Elite, 45, 125, 145, 146, 261; Chinese, 39, 40, 42; and phases of emigration, 126–27; as refugees, 18, 115, 121, 127, 160

Emigration: Chinese, 39–45; defined, 16; experience of, 16–19; Filipino, 59–64; forced, 17; government control of, 17, 50–51, 118–19; Indian, 54–58; and intermediate countries, 21; Japanese, 45–53, 111; Korean, 64–73, 102–7; legal, 16, 17, 18; motivations for, 3–7, 38–39; occupational, 99; phases of, 126–27; planned, 16, 17, 18; post-1965, 75–128; pre-1965, 38–73; Southeast-Asian, 112–27; temporary, 73, 105; unplanned, 18, 19; Vietnamese, 118–19; voluntary, 16, 17, 18, 21; of women, 13, 18, 45, 51–53, 105; *see also* Push-pull theory

Employment: and adjustment, 169, 170; of Asian Americans, vii, 177–81; of Asian immigrants, 73, 171, 173, 176–81; bimodal distribution of, 176, 179, 180, 181; in criminal justice system, 267–68; and the Depression, 230–31; discrimination in, 26, 158, 163; of Filipino immigrants, 102, 147, 148; glass ceiling in, 159, 181; in government, 48; and health care, 283; and health care insurance, 272, 273, 275, 277, 278; in home country, 4; and homelessness, 246; immigrants as threat to, 25, 141–42, 144, 146, 147; immigration based on, 153, 162, 178; and Indian migration, 92, 93; in Indonesia, 6;

Employment: and adjustment (*continued*) in Japan, 47–48, 48, 110; in Korea, 102; and Korean emigration, 106; and language skills, 22; and mental health, 289, 290; and modernization, 47–48; opportunities for, 15, 25, 26; of post-1965 immigrants, 77, 163; as pull factor, 15, 16; of refugees, 162, 235, 289; self-, 275; and self-sufficiency, 234–35; services for, 4, 362; and Social Security Act, 231, 233; and status, 382; of undocumented immigrants, 20, 83, 102, 162; and USAsians, 320; and wages, 6, 8–9, 42, 48, 61, 158; of women, 48, 199, 215; see also Business

English as a Second Language (ESL), 257, 282

English language: and academic achievement, 255; acquisition of, 222–23; children's acquisition of, 197, 223, 317, 318; and commitment, 221, 222–23; competence in, 173, 174, 178, 234, 235, 334; and educational policy, 368; and housing, 249; lack of, 74; and public policy, 257

Erikson, Erik, 184

Estrada, Joseph, 99

Ethnic cleansing, 164

Ethnic enclaves: Chinese, 16; crime in, 263, 264, 371; and English-language acquisition, 223; functioning in, 381; and generational status, 168, 318, 319; housing in, 365; human services in, 279, 362, 363; and identity, 183, 323; Indian, 16, 145; Japanese, 144, 151, 152, 182; as pull factor, 16; and response to immigration, 23; segregation in, 29, 32, 157, 246–47; undocumented immigrants in, 83

Ethnicity: and adjustment, 170; adoption of, 183; and assimilation, 31, 165; awareness of, 183; and crime, 130, 264, 265, 266; discrimination by, 164; diversity of, 144, 156, 165–66; and employment, 158; and family, 183, 185, 225; and family violence, 214, 216, 240; and generational status, 168, 183, 185, 321; and health care, 276, 369; and homosexuality, 200; and housing, 246–47,

249; and human services, 375–76; hypenated, 361; and identity, 168, 183, 185, 320–21, 326, 345, 360–62; and intermarriage, 224, 225; in Laos, 122–23; and marginalization, 32; and marriage, 327; measurement of, 182–83; and mental health, 291, 295; multiracial, 338–45; and race, 181–85; and rivalry, 147; and role of women, 200; situational, 343; and substance abuse, 301, 304

Ethnocentrism, 130

Eugenics movement, 284

Euro-Americans: adoptions by, 345, 346, 348; Asian-American preference for, 336, 344; and Asian culture, 354; and crime, 213, 263; culture of, 193–97; homeless, 248; and home ownership, 247; and intermarriage, 224, 225, 333, 337; locus of control among, 195, 196; marriage among, 327; mental health of, 210–11; and minorities, 310–11; and multiculturalism, 225; and multiracial individuals, 343; phenotypes of, 184–85, 360; and substance abuse, 302; and USAsians, 318

Eurogamy, 336, 344

Europe, 60, 105, 233; Eastern, 67, 87, 129; immigrants from, 50, 131, 132, 135, 140–41

Evans, L., 176

Fair Housing Act (1968), 247, 249

Falun Gong movement, 6

Family: and acculturation, 30, 197–98; and adjustment, 170; and adolescence, 319; of Amerasian children, 118; in American culture, 191, 192, 194, 196, 317, 357; in Asian culture, 82, 136, 190, 193, 194, 196, 225, 239, 363; and assimilation, 31; authority in, 190, 197, 198, 214; businesses run by, 180, 187, 199, 319; children in, 187, 329; Chinese, 43–44, 83, 84, 87, 141, 142; conflict avoidance in, 185; and contributions of Asian Americans, 383–84, 385; and crime, 213, 260, 264; daughters-in-law in, 219–20; and education, 78–79, 368;

Migration (*continued*)
duration of, 8; economic, 121, 126; in film, 14; forced, 7, 17; internal, 45, 47, 126; international, 11, 27; in literature, 14; mass, 6; occupational-selective, 101; planned, 24; return, 353–54; temporary vs. permanent, 11–12; voluntary, 7–9, 24, 139

Military, 48–49, 84, 106, 201

Mineta, Norman, 314

Mink, Patsy, 313

Minorities: Asian Americans as, 287, 360–62; and cultural compentence, 294; and education, 175, 253, 256–58, 367–68; and health care, 274; and home ownership, 222, 250; homosexuals as, 201; and human services, 375–76; and identity, 181, 320–21; and inter-group violence, 163; and majority culture, 310; mental health of, 286, 289, 291, 298, 299; and perceptions of Asian Americans, 358; and public policy, 228, 229; as refugees, 9; and role of government, 308; and substance abuse, 302

Mirikitani, Janet, 315

Miscegenation, *see* Antimiscegenation laws

Mississippi Masala (film), 336

Model-minority stereotype, 130, 157–59, 382; and academic achievement, 255, 367, 368, 369; and crime, 213, 262, 267, 373; disadvantages of, 166; and education, 174; and elderly, 202; exceptions to, 179; and family violence, 265; and health care, 207–8, 274; and identity, 165; and mental health, 290, 291, 295, 371; and public policy, 308; and substance abuse, 304; and violence, 163

Modernization: in China, 42, 84, 85; in India, 92; in Japan, 46–49, 142; in Korea, 66, 68, 104; in Philippines, 63; and prostitution, 52

Moghul Empire (India), 54

Mohenjodaro (India), 54

Monbusho (Japanese Ministry of Education), 34

Mongols, 122, 123

Moscow Agreement (1945), 67

Multiculturalism, 328–29, 351–52, 354, 362, 375; and acceptance of immigrants, 27, 385; of U.S., 310–11, 356; *see also* Biculturalism

The Multiracial Experience (Root), 345

Multiracial population, 118, 133, 150, 225, 315, 338–45; statistics on, 155, 338–39, 341

Mura, D., 340

Muslims, 280; Bosnian, 9; Indian, 54, 55, 56, 145; rebellions of, 41

Myanmar (Burma), 12–13, 108, 122, 123; immigrants from, 128, 155

Nagasaki (Japan), 108–9, 151

Napoleon III, 113

National Geographic Society, 11

National Immigration Forum, 169, 170, 176, 205, 221, 223

Nationalism, 42, 60, 66

Nationality Act (1790), 142

Nationality Origins Act (Immigration Act of 1924), 75–76, 134

National Opinion Research Center (University of Chicago), 333

Native Americans, 3, 142, 170, 181, 256, 265, 301, 315

Natural disasters, 6, 13, 83; as push factor, 4, 12, 57, 73; and unplanned emigration, 18, 19

Naturalization, 76, 116, 122, 128, 129, 359, 392n5b; rates of, 221; restrictions on, 132, 142; *see also* Citizenship

Nav Nirmaan (drug and alcohol treatment program), 303–4

Nehru, Jawarharlal, 89

Nepal, 128

Netherlands, 108

New Deal, 231

New York, 249, 264, 375

Nian Rebellion (China), 41

Nihai, G., 316

Nisei (second generation of Japanese immigrants), 182, 183, 184, 316, 322, 379

Nisei Lounge (Chicago), 310

Nishi, S. M., 175

Nixon, Richard, 83, 84, 114–15, 228, 232, 261

Stevens, R., 93
Stoesz, D., 258, 274, 299
Straus, M., 216
Students, 78, 79, 136, 139, 162, 171;
Asian, 128; Cambodian, 122; Chinese,
84, 85, 86–87; and family reunification,
88; Filipino, 61, 62, 99–100, 133, 148;
Indian, 92–94, 145; Japanese, 112, 139;
Korean, 69, 70, 71, 73, 102, 105–6,
149, 150; *see also* Education
Substance abuse: among adolescents, 264,
300–301, 302, 305; among Asian
Americans, 212, 294, 295, 301–4; and
child abuse, 217; and cigarettes, 300;
costs of, 300, 305; and crime, 259; and
health care insurance, 286, 305–6; pub-
lic policy on, 299–306, 363; residual
approach to, 233; services for, 371–73;
see also Drugs, illegal
Sue, David, 183
Sue, Derald W., 183
Sue, S., 298
Suicide, 210, 211, 218, 294, 295, 311
Sumatra, 59
Sun, David, 177
Sunshine policy (Korea), 103
Supplemental Security Income (SSI),
232–35, 287, 364; restrictions on, 236,
392*n*6
Supreme Court, U.S., 228, 339; on
antimiscegenation laws, 330, 331, 332
Swanson, B. E., 227, 229
Sweden, 125

Tabuchi, Shoji, 177
Taiping Rebellion (China), 41
Taisho Period (Japan), 48–49
Taiwan, 78, 85, 128, 177
Takaki, R., 38
Tangshan earthquake (China; 1976), 83
Tanzania, 85
Taoism, 243
taxes, 170–71, 245, 252, 306, 356
Taylor, D. M., 299
Taylor, Laura, 352
Technology, 10, 325; Asian-American con-
tributions to, 176–77, 356; in Asian vs.
Euro-American cultures, 195; in China,

40, 84; computer, 79–80, 93–94, 100,
158, 176–77; and education, 252, 257;
and health care, 271, 274; Indian, 90,
91, 92; Korean, 65
Temporary Assistance to Needy Families
(TANF), 233, 236, 237
Tet Offensive (Vietnam), 114
Texas, 264
Thai Americans, 203, 315
Thai immigrants, 128, 136, 155
Thailand: and Khmer Empire, 119; and
Laos, 122, 123, 125; persecution in,
12–13; refugees in, 116, 121–22, 126,
127, 288; Tiger Woods in, 315
Three Kingdoms (Korea), 64
Tiananmen Square Massacre (1989), 85, 86
Tien, Chang-Lin, 177
Tokugawa Period (Japan), 46
Torture, 6, 12
Trade: agreements on, 62; Chinese, 40, 41,
84; Filipino, 59, 60; Indian, 55–56, 90;
Japanese, 46, 47, 48; Korean, 65, 69;
Most Favored Nation status in, 85
Tradition: and acculturation, 31; and adolescence, 319; Asian, 185–97; and
assimilation, 31, 320; and authority,
317; changes in, 16, 194; and counter-
culture, 321; and family violence, 217,
220; freedom from, 14, 15, 357; and
generational status, 321–22; and
human services, 36, 242; and identity,
360; of immigrants, 225; and intermarriage, 335, 344; Japanese, 47, 110, 111;
Korean, 69; loss of, 17, 323; and marriage, 327; and mental health, 290, 298;
and multiracial heritage, 342; and
return to home country, 326; and social
status, 11; and women, 7, 13, 196
Tran, Pascal, 324
Transportation, 20, 21, 33, 37, 45
Trauma, 4, 20–22, 34; and PTSD, 23, 35,
210, 211, 279, 289, 303, 393*n*3a
Truman, Harry, 67, 148
Tu, John, 177
Turkey, 134
Tutsis (Rwanda), 9
Tydings-McDuffie Act (1934), 62, 134,
148

WITHDRAWN